ALCOHOLICS ANONYMOUS

OTHER BOOKS

TWELVE STEPS AND TWELVE TRADITIONS
*An interpretive commentary on the A.A. program
by a co-founder*

ALCOHOLICS ANONYMOUS COMES OF AGE
A brief history of A.A.'s first two decades

AS BILL SEES IT
(formerly THE A.A. WAY OF LIFE)
Selected writings of A.A.'s co-founder

DR. BOB AND THE GOOD OLDTIMERS
A biography, with recollections of early A.A. in the Midwest

PASS IT ON
Bill W.'s life story; how the A.A. message reached the world

DAILY REFLECTIONS
A book of reflections by A.A. members for A.A. members

BOOKLETS
CAME TO BELIEVE . . .
Spiritual experiences of 75 A.A.'s

LIVING SOBER
Practical suggestions heard at meetings

A.A. IN PRISON: INMATE TO INMATE
Former Grapevine articles by people who found A.A. in prison

ALCOHOLICS ANONYMOUS

The Story of
How Many Thousands of Men and Women
Have Recovered from Alcoholism

FOURTH EDITION

ALCOHOLICS ANONYMOUS WORLD SERVICES, INC.

NEW YORK CITY

2001

Library of Congress Control Number: 2001094693
ISBN 978-1-893007-17-8
Printed in the United States of America

220M - 12/12 (BVG)

CONTENTS

PERSONAL STORIES

PART I
Pioneers of A.A.

> A co-founder of Alcoholics Anonymous. The
> birth of our Society dates from his first day of
> permanent sobriety, June 10, 1935.

Page

CONTENTS

PART II
They Stopped in Time

1 THE MISSING LINK   281
He looked at everything as the cause of his unhappiness—except alcohol.

2 FEAR OF FEAR   289
This lady was cautious. She decided she wouldn't let herself go in her drinking. And she would never, never take that morning drink!

3 THE HOUSEWIFE WHO DRANK AT HOME   295
She hid her bottles in clothes hampers and dresser drawers. In A.A., she discovered she had lost nothing and had found everything.

4 PHYSICIAN, HEAL THYSELF!   301
Psychiatrist and surgeon, he had lost his way until he realized that God, not he, was the Great Healer.

5 MY CHANCE TO LIVE   309
A.A. gave this teenager the tools to climb out of her dark abyss of despair.

6 STUDENT OF LIFE   319
Living at home with her parents, she tried using willpower to beat the obsession to drink. But it wasn't until she met another alcoholic and went to an A.A. meeting that sobriety took hold.

7 CROSSING THE RIVER OF DENIAL   328
She finally realized that when she enjoyed her drinking, she couldn't control it, and when she controlled it, she couldn't enjoy it.

8 BECAUSE I'M AN ALCOHOLIC   338
This drinker finally found the answer to her nagging question, "Why?"

Page

PART III
They Lost Nearly All

Page

PREFACE

THIS IS the fourth edition of the book "Alcoholics Anonymous." The first edition appeared in April 1939, and in the following sixteen years, more than 300,000 copies went into circulation. The second edition, published in 1955, reached a total of more than 1,150,500 copies. The third edition, which came off press in 1976, achieved a circulation of approximately 19,550,000 in all formats.

Because this book has become the basic text for our Society and has helped such large numbers of alcoholic men and women to recovery, there exists strong sentiment against any radical changes being made in it. Therefore, the first portion of this volume, describing the A.A. recovery program, has been left largely untouched in the course of revisions made for the second, third, and fourth editions. The section called "The Doctor's Opinion" has been kept intact, just as it was originally written in 1939 by the late Dr. William D. Silkworth, our Society's great medical benefactor.

The second edition added the appendices, the Twelve Traditions, and the directions for getting in touch with A.A. But the chief change was in the section of personal stories, which was expanded to reflect the Fellowship's growth. "Bill's Story," "Doctor Bob's Nightmare," and one other personal history from the first edition were retained intact; three were edited and one of these was retitled; new versions of two stories were written, with new titles; thirty completely new stories were added; and the story section was divided into three parts, under the same headings that are used now.

In the third edition, Part I ("Pioneers of A.A.") was left unchanged. Nine of the stories in Part II ("They Stopped in Time") were carried over from the second edition; eight new stories were added. In Part III ("They Lost Nearly All"), eight stories were retained; five new ones were added.

This fourth edition includes the Twelve Concepts for World Service and revises the three sections of personal stories as follows. One new story has been added to Part I, and two that originally appeared in Part III have been repositioned there; six stories have been deleted. Six of the stories in Part II have been carried over, eleven new ones have been added, and eleven taken out. Part III now includes twelve new stories; eight were removed (in addition to the two that were transferred to Part I).

All changes made over the years in the Big Book (A.A. members' fond nickname for this volume) have had the same purpose: to represent the current membership of Alcoholics Anonymous more accurately, and thereby to reach more alcoholics. If you have a drinking problem, we hope that you may pause in reading one of the forty-two personal stories and think: "Yes, that happened to me"; or, more important, "Yes, I've felt like that"; or, most important, "Yes, I believe this program can work for me too."

FOREWORD TO FIRST EDITION

*This is the Foreword as it appeared in the first
printing of the first edition in 1939.*

WE, OF Alcoholics Anonymous, are more than
one hundred men and women who have recovered from a seemingly hopeless state of mind and
body. To show other alcoholics *precisely how we
have recovered* is the main purpose of this book. For
them, we hope these pages will prove so convincing
that no further authentication will be necessary. We
think this account of our experiences will help everyone to better understand the alcoholic. Many do not
comprehend that the alcoholic is a very sick person.
And besides, we are sure that our way of living has
its advantages for all.

It is important that we remain anonymous because
we are too few, at present to handle the overwhelming number of personal appeals which may result
from this publication. Being mostly business or professional folk, we could not well carry on our occupations in such an event. We would like it understood
that our alcoholic work is an avocation.

When writing or speaking publicly about alcoholism, we urge each of our Fellowship to omit his
personal name, designating himself instead as "a
member of Alcoholics Anonymous."

Very earnestly we ask the press also, to observe this
request, for otherwise we shall be greatly handicapped.

We are not an organization in the conventional

sense of the word. There are no fees or dues whatsoever. The only requirement for membership is an honest desire to stop drinking. We are not allied with any particular faith, sect or denomination, nor do we oppose anyone. We simply wish to be helpful to those who are afflicted.

We shall be interested to hear from those who are getting results from this book, particularly from those who have commenced work with other alcoholics. We should like to be helpful to such cases.

Inquiry by scientific, medical, and religious societies will be welcomed.

ALCOHOLICS ANONYMOUS.

FOREWORD TO SECOND EDITION

*Figures given in this foreword describe the
Fellowship as it was in 1955.*

SINCE the original Foreword to this book was
written in 1939, a wholesale miracle has taken
place. Our earliest printing voiced the hope "that
every alcoholic who journeys will find the Fellowship
of Alcoholics Anonymous at his destination. Already,"
continues the early text "twos and threes and fives of
us have sprung up in other communities."

Sixteen years have elapsed between our first printing
of this book and the presentation in 1955 of our second
edition. In that brief space, Alcoholics Anonymous
has mushroomed into nearly 6,000 groups whose membership is far above 150,000 recovered alcoholics.
Groups are to be found in each of the United States
and all of the provinces of Canada. A.A. has flourish-
ing communities in the British Isles, the Scandinavian
countries, South Africa, South America, Mexico,
Alaska, Australia and Hawaii. All told, promising
beginnings have been made in some 50 foreign countries and U. S. possessions. Some are just now taking
shape in Asia. Many of our friends encourage us by
saying that this is but a beginning, only the augury of
a much larger future ahead.

The spark that was to flare into the first A.A. group
was struck at Akron, Ohio, in June 1935, during a talk
between a New York stockbroker and an Akron
physician. Six months earlier, the broker had been
relieved of his drink obsession by a sudden spiritual

experience, following a meeting with an alcoholic friend who had been in contact with the Oxford Groups of that day. He had also been greatly helped by the late Dr. William D. Silkworth, a New York specialist in alcoholism who is now accounted no less than a medical saint by A.A. members, and whose story of the early days of our Society appears in the next pages. From this doctor, the broker had learned the grave nature of alcoholism. Though he could not accept all the tenets of the Oxford Groups, he was convinced of the need for moral inventory, confession of personality defects, restitution to those harmed, helpfulness to others, and the necessity of belief in and dependence upon God.

Prior to his journey to Akron, the broker had worked hard with many alcoholics on the theory that only an alcoholic could help an alcoholic, but he had succeeded only in keeping sober himself. The broker had gone to Akron on a business venture which had collapsed, leaving him greatly in fear that he might start drinking again. He suddenly realized that in order to save himself he must carry his message to another alcoholic. That alcoholic turned out to be the Akron physician.

This physician had repeatedly tried spiritual means to resolve his alcoholic dilemma but had failed. But when the broker gave him Dr. Silkworth's description of alcoholism and its hopelessness, the physician began to pursue the spiritual remedy for his malady with a willingness he had never before been able to muster. He sobered, never to drink again up to the moment of his death in 1950. This seemed to prove that one alcoholic could affect another as no nonalcoholic could. It also indicated that strenuous work, one alcoholic with another, was vital to permanent recovery.

Hence the two men set to work almost frantically upon alcoholics arriving in the ward of the Akron City Hospital. Their very first case, a desperate one, recovered immediately and became A.A. number three. He never had another drink. This work at Akron continued through the summer of 1935. There were many failures, but there was an occasional heartening success. When the broker returned to New York in the fall of 1935, the first A.A. group had actually been formed, though no one realized it at the time.

A second small group promptly took shape at New York, to be followed in 1937 with the start of a third at Cleveland. Besides these, there were scattered alcoholics who had picked up the basic ideas in Akron or New York who were trying to form groups in other cities. By late 1937, the number of members having substantial sobriety time behind them was sufficient to convince the membership that a new light had entered the dark world of the alcoholic.

It was now time, the struggling groups thought, to place their message and unique experience before the world. This determination bore fruit in the spring of 1939 by the publication of this volume. The membership had then reached about 100 men and women. The fledgling society, which had been nameless, now began to be called Alcoholics Anonymous, from the title of its own book. The flying-blind period ended and A.A. entered a new phase of its pioneering time.

With the appearance of the new book a great deal began to happen. Dr. Harry Emerson Fosdick, the noted clergyman, reviewed it with approval. In the fall of 1939 Fulton Oursler, then editor of *Liberty*, printed a piece in his magazine, called "Alcoholics and God." This brought a rush of 800 frantic inquiries into the little New York office which meanwhile had been established. Each inquiry was painstakingly answered; pamphlets and books were sent out. Businessmen, traveling out of existing groups, were referred to these prospective newcomers. New groups started up and it was found, to the astonishment of everyone, that A.A.'s message could be transmitted in the mail as well as by word of mouth. By the end of 1939 it was estimated that 800 alcoholics were on their way to recovery.

In the spring of 1940, John D. Rockefeller, Jr. gave a dinner for many of his friends to which he invited A.A. members to tell their stories. News of this got on the world wires; inquiries poured in again and many people went to the bookstores to get the book "Alcoholics Anonymous." By March 1941 the membership had shot up to 2,000. Then Jack Alexander wrote a feature article in the *Saturday Evening Post* and placed such a compelling picture of A.A. before the general public that alcoholics in need of help really deluged us. By the close of 1941, A.A. numbered 8,000 members. The mushrooming process was in full swing. A.A. had become a national institution.

Our Society then entered a fearsome and exciting adolescent period. The test that it faced was this: Could these large numbers of erstwhile erratic alcoholics successfully meet and work together? Would there be quarrels over membership, leadership, and money? Would there be strivings for power and prestige? Would there be schisms which would split A.A. apart? Soon A.A. was beset by these very problems on every side and in every group. But out of this frightening and at first disrupting experience the conviction grew that A.A.'s had to hang together or die separately. We had to unify our Fellowship or pass off the scene.

As we discovered the principles by which the individual alcoholic could live, so we had to evolve principles by which the A.A. groups and A.A. as a whole could survive and function effectively. It was thought that no alcoholic man or woman could be excluded from our Society; that our leaders might serve but never govern; that each group was to be autonomous and there was to be no professional class of therapy. There were to be no fees or dues; our expenses were to be met by our own voluntary contributions. There was to be the least possible organization, even in our service centers. Our public relations were to be based upon attraction rather than promotion. It was decided that all members ought to be anonymous at the level of press, radio, TV and films. And in no circumstances should we give endorsements, make alliances, or enter public controversies.

This was the substance of A.A.'s Twelve Traditions, which are stated in full on page 561 of this book. Though none of these principles had the force of rules or laws, they had become so widely accepted by 1950 that they were confirmed by our first International Conference held at Cleveland. Today the remarkable unity of A.A. is one of the greatest assets that our Society has.

While the internal difficulties of our adolescent

period were being ironed out, public acceptance of
A.A. grew by leaps and bounds. For this there were two
principal reasons: the large numbers of recoveries, and
reunited homes. These made their impressions everywhere. Of alcoholics who came to A.A. and really tried,
50% got sober at once and remained that way; 25%
sobered up after some relapses, and among the remainder,
those who stayed on with A.A. showed improvement.
Other thousands came to a few A.A. meetings and at
first decided they didn't want the program. But great
numbers of these—about two out of three—began to
return as time passed.

Another reason for the wide acceptance of A.A. was
the ministration of friends—friends in medicine, religion, and the press, together with innumerable others
who became our able and persistent advocates. Without such support, A.A. could have made only the
slowest progress. Some of the recommendations of
A.A.'s early medical and religious friends will be found
further on in this book.

Alcoholics Anonymous is not a religious organization. Neither does A.A. take any particular medical
point of view, though we cooperate widely with the
men of medicine as well as with the men of religion.

Alcohol being no respecter of persons, we are an
accurate cross section of America, and in distant lands,
the same democratic evening-up process is now going
on. By personal religious affiliation, we include Catholics, Protestants, Jews, Hindus, and a sprinkling of
Moslems and Buddhists. More than 15% of us are
women.

At present, our membership is pyramiding at the
rate of about twenty per cent a year. So far, upon the

total problem of several million actual and potential alcoholics in the world, we have made only a scratch. In all probability, we shall never be able to touch more than a fair fraction of the alcohol problem in all its ramifications. Upon therapy for the alcoholic himself, we surely have no monopoly. Yet it is our great hope that all those who have as yet found no answer may begin to find one in the pages of this book and will presently join us on the high road to a new freedom.

FOREWORD TO THIRD EDITION

*B*Y March 1976, when this edition went to the printer, the total worldwide membership of Alcoholics Anonymous was conservatively estimated at more than 1,000,000, with almost 28,000 groups meeting in over 90 countries.

Surveys of groups in the United States and Canada indicate that A.A. is reaching out, not only to more and more people, but to a wider and wider range. Women now make up more than one-fourth of the membership; among newer members, the proportion is nearly one-third. Seven percent of the A.A.'s surveyed are less than 30 years of age—among them, many in their teens.

The basic principles of the A.A. program, it appears, hold good for individuals with many different lifestyles, just as the program has brought recovery to those of many different nationalities. The Twelve Steps that summarize the program may be called *los Doce Pasos* in one country, *les Douze Etapes* in another, but they trace exactly the same path to recovery that was blazed by the earliest members of Alcoholics Anonymous.

In spite of the great increase in the size and the span of this Fellowship, at its core it remains simple and personal. Each day, somewhere in the world, recovery begins when one alcoholic talks with another alcoholic, sharing experience, strength, and hope.

FOREWORD TO FOURTH EDITION

THIS fourth edition of "Alcoholics Anonymous" came off press in November 2001, at the start of a new millennium. Since the third edition was published in 1976, worldwide membership of A.A. has just about doubled, to an estimated two million or more, with nearly 100,800 groups meeting in approximately 150 countries around the world.

Literature has played a major role in A.A.'s growth, and a striking phenomenon of the past quarter-century has been the explosion of translations of our basic literature into many languages and dialects. In country after country where the A.A. seed was planted, it has taken root, slowly at first, then growing by leaps and bounds when literature has become available. Currently, "Alcoholics Anonymous" has been translated into forty-three* languages.

As the message of recovery has reached larger numbers of people, it has also touched the lives of a vastly greater variety of suffering alcoholics. When the phrase "We are people who normally would not mix" (page 17 of this book) was written in 1939, it referred to a Fellowship composed largely of men (and a few women) with quite similar social, ethnic, and economic backgrounds. Like so much of A.A.'s basic text, those words have proved to be far more visionary than the founding members could ever have imagined. The stories added to this edition represent a membership whose characteristics—of age, gender, race, and culture—have widened and have deepened to encompass

*In 2012, *Alcoholics Anonymous* is in sixty-seven languages.

virtually everyone the first 100 members could have hoped to reach.

While our literature has preserved the integrity of the A.A. message, sweeping changes in society as a whole are reflected in new customs and practices within the Fellowship. Taking advantage of technological advances, for example, A.A. members with computers can participate in meetings online, sharing with fellow alcoholics across the country or around the world. In any meeting, anywhere, A.A.'s share experience, strength, and hope with each other, in order to stay sober and help other alcoholics. Modem-to-modem or face-to-face, A.A.'s speak the language of the heart in all its power and simplicity.

THE DOCTOR'S OPINION

*W*E OF Alcoholics Anonymous believe that the reader will be interested in the medical estimate of the plan of recovery described in this book. Convincing testimony must surely come from medical men who have had experience with the sufferings of our members and have witnessed our return to health. A well-known doctor, chief physician at a nationally prominent hospital specializing in alcoholic and drug addiction, gave Alcoholics Anonymous this letter:

To Whom It May Concern:

I have specialized in the treatment of alcoholism for many years.

In late 1934 I attended a patient who, though he had been a competent businessman of good earning capacity, was an alcoholic of a type I had come to regard as hopeless.

In the course of his third treatment he acquired certain ideas concerning a possible means of recovery. As part of his rehabilitation he commenced to present his conceptions to other alcoholics, impressing upon them that they must do likewise with still others. This has become the basis of a rapidly growing fellowship of these men and their families. This man and over one hundred others appear to have recovered.

I personally know scores of cases who were of the type with whom other methods had failed completely.

These facts appear to be of extreme medical importance; because of the extraordinary possibilities of rapid growth inherent in this group they may mark a new epoch in the annals of alcoholism. These men may well have a remedy for thousands of such situations.

You may rely absolutely on anything they say about themselves.

Very truly yours,
William D. Silkworth, M.D.

The physician who, at our request, gave us this letter, has been kind enough to enlarge upon his views in another statement which follows. In this statement he confirms what we who have suffered alcoholic torture must believe—that the body of the alcoholic is quite as abnormal as his mind. It did not satisfy us to be told that we could not control our drinking just because we were maladjusted to life, that we were in full flight from reality, or were outright mental defectives. These things were true to some extent, in fact, to a considerable extent with some of us. But we are sure that our bodies were sickened as well. In our belief, any picture of the alcoholic which leaves out this physical factor is incomplete.

The doctor's theory that we have an allergy to alcohol interests us. As laymen, our opinion as to its soundness may, of course, mean little. But as ex-problem drinkers, we can say that his explanation makes good sense. It explains many things for which we cannot otherwise account.

Though we work out our solution on the spiritual as well as an altruistic plane, we favor hospitalization for the alcoholic who is very jittery or befogged. More often than not, it is imperative that a man's brain be cleared before he is approached, as he has then a better chance of understanding and accepting what we have to offer.

The doctor writes:

The subject presented in this book seems to me to be of paramount importance to those afflicted with alcoholic addiction.

I say this after many years' experience as Medical Director of one of the oldest hospitals in the country treating alcoholic and drug addiction.

There was, therefore, a sense of real satisfaction when I was asked to contribute a few words on a subject which is covered in such masterly detail in these pages.

We doctors have realized for a long time that some form of moral psychology was of urgent importance to alcoholics, but its application presented difficulties beyond our conception. What with our ultra-modern standards, our scientific approach to everything, we are perhaps not well equipped to apply the powers of good that lie outside our synthetic knowledge.

Many years ago one of the leading contributors to this book came under our care in this hospital and while here he acquired some ideas which he put into practical application at once.

Later, he requested the privilege of being allowed to tell his story to other patients here and with some misgiving, we consented. The cases we have followed through have been most interesting; in fact, many of them are amazing. The unselfishness of these men as we have come to know them, the entire absence of profit motive, and their community spirit, is indeed inspiring to one who has labored long and wearily in this alcoholic field. They believe in themselves, and still more in the Power which pulls chronic alcoholics back from the gates of death.

Of course an alcoholic ought to be freed from his physical

craving for liquor, and this often requires a definite hospital procedure, before psychological measures can be of maximum benefit.

We believe, and so suggested a few years ago, that the action of alcohol on these chronic alcoholics is a manifestation of an allergy; that the phenomenon of craving is limited to this class and never occurs in the average temperate drinker. These allergic types can never safely use alcohol in any form at all; and once having formed the habit and found they cannot break it, once having lost their self-confidence, their reliance upon things human, their problems pile up on them and become astonishingly difficult to solve.

Frothy emotional appeal seldom suffices. The message which can interest and hold these alcoholic people must have depth and weight. In nearly all cases, their ideals must be grounded in a power greater than themselves, if they are to re-create their lives.

If any feel that as psychiatrists directing a hospital for alcoholics we appear somewhat sentimental, let them stand with us a while on the firing line, see the tragedies, the despairing wives, the little children; let the solving of these problems become a part of their daily work, and even of their sleeping moments, and the most cynical will not wonder that we have accepted and encouraged this movement. We feel, after many years of experience, that we have found nothing which has contributed more to the rehabilitation of these men than the altruistic movement now growing up among them.

Men and women drink essentially because they like the effect produced by alcohol. The sensation is so elusive that, while they admit it is injurious, they cannot after a time differentiate the true from the false. To them, their alcoholic life seems the only normal one. They are restless, irritable and discontented, unless they can again experience the sense of ease and comfort which comes at once by taking a few drinks—drinks which they see others taking with impunity. After they have succumbed to the desire again, as so many do, and the phenomenon of craving develops, they pass through the well-known stages of a spree, emerging remorseful, with a firm resolution not to drink again. This is repeated over and over, and unless this person can experience an entire psychic change there is very little hope of his recovery.

On the other hand—and strange as this may seem to those who do not understand—once a psychic change has occurred, the very same person who seemed doomed, who had so many problems he despaired of ever solving them, suddenly finds himself easily able to control his desire for alcohol, the only effort necessary being that required to follow a few simple rules.

Men have cried out to me in sincere and despairing appeal: "Doctor, I cannot go on like this! I have everything to live for! I must stop, but I cannot! You must help me!"

Faced with this problem, if a doctor is honest with himself, he must sometimes feel his own inadequacy. Although he gives all that is in him, it often is not enough. One feels that something more than human power is needed to produce the essential psychic change. Though the aggregate of recoveries resulting from psychiatric effort is considerable, we physicians must admit we have made little impression upon the problem as a whole. Many types do not respond to the ordinary psychological approach.

I do not hold with those who believe that alcoholism is entirely a problem of mental control. I have had many men who had, for example, worked a period of months on some problem or business deal which was to be settled on a certain date, favorably to them. They took a drink a day or so prior to the date, and then the phenomenon of craving at once became paramount to all other interests so that the important appointment was not met. These men were not drinking to escape; they were drinking to overcome a craving beyond their mental control.

There are many situations which arise out of the phenomenon of craving which cause men to make the supreme sacrifice rather than continue to fight.

The classification of alcoholics seems most difficult, and in much detail is outside the scope of this book. There are, of course, the psychopaths who are emotionally unstable. We are all familiar with this type. They are always "going on the wagon for keeps." They are over-remorseful and make many resolutions, but never a decision.

There is the type of man who is unwilling to admit that he cannot take a drink. He plans various ways of drinking. He changes his brand or his environment. There is the type who always believes that after being entirely free from alcohol for a period of time he can take a drink without danger. There is the manic-depressive type, who is, perhaps, the least understood by his friends, and about whom a whole chapter could be written.

Then there are types entirely normal in every respect except in the effect alcohol has upon them. They are often able, intelligent, friendly people.

All these, and many others, have one symptom in common: they cannot start drinking without developing the phenomenon of craving. This phenomenon, as we have suggested, may be the manifestation of an allergy which differentiates these people, and sets them apart as a distinct entity. It has never been, by any treatment with which we are familiar, permanently eradicated. The only relief we have to suggest is entire abstinence.

This immediately precipitates us into a seething caldron of debate. Much has been written pro and con, but among physicians, the general opinion seems to be that most chronic alcoholics are doomed.

What is the solution? Perhaps I can best answer this by relating one of my experiences.

About one year prior to this experience a man was brought in to be treated for chronic alcoholism. He had but partially recovered from a gastric hemorrhage and seemed to be a case of pathological mental deterioration. He had lost everything worthwhile in life and was only living, one might say, to drink. He frankly admitted and believed that for him there was no hope. Following the elimination of alcohol, there was found to be no permanent brain injury. He accepted the plan outlined in this book. One year later he called to see me, and I experienced a very strange sensation. I knew the man by name, and partly recognized his features, but there all resemblance ended. From a trembling, despairing, nervous wreck, had emerged a man brimming over with self-reliance and contentment. I talked with him for some time, but was not able to bring myself to feel that I had known him before. To me he was a stranger, and so he left me. A long time has passed with no return to alcohol.

When I need a mental uplift, I often think of another case brought in by a physician prominent in New York. The patient had made his own diagnosis, and deciding his situation hopeless, had hidden in a deserted barn determined to die. He was rescued by a searching party, and, in desperate condition, brought to me. Following his physical rehabilitation, he had a talk with me in which he frankly stated he thought the treatment a waste of effort, unless I could assure him, which no one ever had, that in the future he would have the "will power" to resist the impulse to drink.

His alcoholic problem was so complex, and his depression so great, that we felt his only hope would be through what we then called "moral psychology," and we doubted if even that would have any effect.

However, he did become "sold" on the ideas contained in this book. He has not had a drink for a great many years. I see him now and then and he is as fine a specimen of manhood as one could wish to meet.

I earnestly advise every alcoholic to read this book through, and though perhaps he came to scoff, he may remain to pray.

William D. Silkworth, M.D.

Chapter 1

BILL'S STORY

*W*AR FEVER ran high in the New England town to which we new, young officers from Plattsburg were assigned, and we were flattered when the first citizens took us to their homes, making us feel heroic. Here was love, applause, war; moments sublime with intervals hilarious. I was part of life at last, and in the midst of the excitement I discovered liquor. I forgot the strong warnings and the prejudices of my people concerning drink. In time we sailed for "Over There." I was very lonely and again turned to alcohol.

We landed in England. I visited Winchester Cathedral. Much moved, I wandered outside. My attention was caught by a doggerel on an old tombstone:

> "Here lies a Hampshire Grenadier
> Who caught his death
> Drinking cold small beer.
> A good soldier is ne'er forgot
> Whether he dieth by musket
> Or by pot."

Ominous warning—which I failed to heed.

Twenty-two, and a veteran of foreign wars, I went home at last. I fancied myself a leader, for had not the men of my battery given me a special token of appreciation? My talent for leadership, I imagined, would place me at the head of vast enterprises which I would manage with the utmost assurance.

1

I took a night law course, and obtained employment as investigator for a surety company. The drive for success was on. I'd prove to the world I was important. My work took me about Wall Street and little by little I became interested in the market. Many people lost money—but some became very rich. Why not I? I studied economics and business as well as law. Potential alcoholic that I was, I nearly failed my law course. At one of the finals I was too drunk to think or write. Though my drinking was not yet continuous, it disturbed my wife. We had long talks when I would still her forebodings by telling her that men of genius conceived their best projects when drunk; that the most majestic constructions of philosophic thought were so derived.

By the time I had completed the course, I knew the law was not for me. The inviting maelstrom of Wall Street had me in its grip. Business and financial leaders were my heroes. Out of this alloy of drink and speculation, I commenced to forge the weapon that one day would turn in its flight like a boomerang and all but cut me to ribbons. Living modestly, my wife and I saved $1,000. It went into certain securities, then cheap and rather unpopular. I rightly imagined that they would some day have a great rise. I failed to persuade my broker friends to send me out looking over factories and managements, but my wife and I decided to go anyway. I had developed a theory that most people lost money in stocks through ignorance of markets. I discovered many more reasons later on.

We gave up our positions and off we roared on a motorcycle, the sidecar stuffed with tent, blankets, a change of clothes, and three huge volumes of a financial reference service. Our friends thought a lunacy commission should be appointed. Perhaps they were right. I had had some success at speculation, so we had a little money, but we once worked on a farm for a month to avoid drawing on our small capital. That was the last honest manual labor on my part for many a day. We covered the whole eastern United States in a year. At the end of it, my reports to Wall Street procured me a position there and the use of a large expense account. The exercise of an option brought in more money, leaving us with a profit of several thousand dollars for that year.

For the next few years fortune threw money and applause my way. I had arrived. My judgment and ideas were followed by many to the tune of paper millions. The great boom of the late twenties was seething and swelling. Drink was taking an important and exhilarating part in my life. There was loud talk in the jazz places uptown. Everyone spent in thousands and chattered in millions. Scoffers could scoff and be damned. I made a host of fair-weather friends.

My drinking assumed more serious proportions, continuing all day and almost every night. The remonstrances of my friends terminated in a row and I became a lone wolf. There were many unhappy scenes in our sumptuous apartment. There had been no real infidelity, for loyalty to my wife, helped at times by extreme drunkenness, kept me out of those scrapes.

In 1929 I contracted golf fever. We went at once to the country, my wife to applaud while I started out to overtake Walter Hagen. Liquor caught up with me much faster than I came up behind Walter. I began to be jittery in the morning. Golf permitted drinking every day and every night. It was fun to carom around the exclusive course which had inspired such awe in me as a lad. I acquired the impeccable coat of tan one sees upon the well-to-do. The local banker watched me whirl fat checks in and out of his till with amused skepticism.

Abruptly in October 1929 hell broke loose on the New York stock exchange. After one of those days of inferno, I wobbled from a hotel bar to a brokerage office. It was eight o'clock—five hours after the market closed. The ticker still clattered. I was staring at an inch of the tape which bore the inscription XYZ-32. It had been 52 that morning. I was finished and so were many friends. The papers reported men jumping to death from the towers of High Finance. That disgusted me. I would not jump. I went back to the bar. My friends had dropped several million since ten o'clock—so what? Tomorrow was another day. As I drank, the old fierce determination to win came back.

Next morning I telephoned a friend in Montreal. He had plenty of money left and thought I had better go to Canada. By the following spring we were living in our accustomed style. I felt like Napoleon returning from Elba. No St. Helena for me! But drinking caught up with me again and my generous friend had to let me go. This time we stayed broke.

We went to live with my wife's parents. I found a job; then lost it as the result of a brawl with a taxi driver. Mercifully, no one could guess that I was to have no real employment for five years, or hardly draw a sober breath. My wife began to work in a department store, coming home exhausted to find me drunk.

I became an unwelcome hanger-on at brokerage places.

Liquor ceased to be a luxury; it became a necessity. "Bathtub" gin, two bottles a day, and often three, got to be routine. Sometimes a small deal would net a few hundred dollars, and I would pay my bills at the bars and delicatessens. This went on endlessly, and I began to waken very early in the morning shaking violently. A tumbler full of gin followed by half a dozen bottles of beer would be required if I were to eat any breakfast. Nevertheless, I still thought I could control the situation, and there were periods of sobriety which renewed my wife's hope.

Gradually things got worse. The house was taken over by the mortgage holder, my mother-in-law died, my wife and father-in-law became ill.

Then I got a promising business opportunity. Stocks were at the low point of 1932, and I had somehow formed a group to buy. I was to share generously in the profits. Then I went on a prodigious bender, and the chance vanished.

I woke up. This had to be stopped. I saw I could not take so much as one drink. I was through forever. Before then, I had written lots of sweet promises, but my wife happily observed that this time I meant business. And so I did.

Shortly afterward I came home drunk. There had been no fight. Where had been my high resolve? I simply didn't know. It hadn't even come to mind. Someone had pushed a drink my way, and I had taken it. Was I crazy? I began to wonder, for such an appalling lack of perspective seemed near being just that.

Renewing my resolve, I tried again. Some time

passed, and confidence began to be replaced by cock-sureness. I could laugh at the gin mills. Now I had what it takes! One day I walked into a cafe to telephone. In no time I was beating on the bar asking myself how it happened. As the whisky rose to my head I told myself I would manage better next time, but I might as well get good and drunk then. And I did.

The remorse, horror and hopelessness of the next morning are unforgettable. The courage to do battle was not there. My brain raced uncontrollably and there was a terrible sense of impending calamity. I hardly dared cross the street, lest I collapse and be run down by an early morning truck, for it was scarcely daylight. An all night place supplied me with a dozen glasses of ale. My writhing nerves were stilled at last. A morning paper told me the market had gone to hell again. Well, so had I. The market would recover, but I wouldn't. That was a hard thought. Should I kill myself? No—not now. Then a mental fog settled down. Gin would fix that. So two bottles, and—oblivion.

The mind and body are marvelous mechanisms, for mine endured this agony two more years. Sometimes I stole from my wife's slender purse when the morning terror and madness were on me. Again I swayed dizzily before an open window, or the medicine cabinet where there was poison, cursing myself for a weakling. There were flights from city to country and back, as my wife and I sought escape. Then came the night when the physical and mental torture was so hellish I feared I would burst through my window, sash and all. Somehow I managed to drag my mattress to a lower floor, lest I suddenly leap. A doctor came with a heavy sedative. Next day found me drinking both gin and sedative. This combination soon landed me on the rocks. People feared for my sanity. So did I. I could eat little or nothing when drinking, and I was forty pounds under weight.

My brother-in-law is a physician, and through his kindness and that of my mother I was placed in a nationally-known hospital for the mental and physical rehabilitation of alcoholics. Under the so-called belladonna treatment my brain cleared. Hydrotherapy and mild exercise helped much. Best of all, I met a kind doctor who explained that though certainly selfish and foolish, I had been seriously ill, bodily and mentally.

It relieved me somewhat to learn that in alcoholics the will is amazingly weakened when it comes to combating liquor, though it often remains strong in other respects. My incredible behavior in the face of a desperate desire to stop was explained. Understanding myself now, I fared forth in high hope. For three or four months the goose hung high. I went to town regularly and even made a little money. Surely this was the answer—self-knowledge.

But it was not, for the frightful day came when I drank once more. The curve of my declining moral and bodily health fell off like a ski-jump. After a time I returned to the hospital. This was the finish, the curtain, it seemed to me. My weary and despairing wife was informed that it would all end with heart failure during delirium tremens, or I would develop a wet brain, perhaps within a year. She would soon have to give me over to the undertaker or the asylum.

They did not need to tell me. I knew, and almost welcomed the idea. It was a devastating blow to my pride. I, who had thought so well of myself and my abilities, of my capacity to surmount obstacles, was cornered at last. Now I was to plunge into the dark, joining that endless procession of sots who had gone on before. I thought of my poor wife. There had been much happiness after all. What would I not give to make amends. But that was over now.

No words can tell of the loneliness and despair I found in that bitter morass of self-pity. Quicksand stretched around me in all directions. I had met my match. I had been overwhelmed. Alcohol was my master.

Trembling, I stepped from the hospital a broken man. Fear sobered me for a bit. Then came the insidious insanity of that first drink, and on Armistice Day 1934, I was off again. Everyone became resigned to the certainty that I would have to be shut up somewhere, or would stumble along to a miserable end. How dark it is before the dawn! In reality that was the beginning of my last debauch. I was soon to be catapulted into what I like to call the fourth dimension of existence. I was to know happiness, peace, and usefulness, in a way of life that is incredibly more wonderful as time passes.

Near the end of that bleak November, I sat drinking in my kitchen. With a certain satisfaction I reflected there was enough gin concealed about the house to carry me through that night and the next day. My wife was at work. I wondered whether I dared hide a full bottle of gin near the head of our bed. I would need it before daylight.

My musing was interrupted by the telephone. The cheery voice of an old school friend asked if he might come over. *He was sober.* It was years since I could remember his coming to New York in that condition. I was amazed. Rumor had it that he had been committed for alcoholic insanity. I wondered how he had escaped. Of course he would have dinner, and then I could drink openly with him. Unmindful of his welfare, I thought only of recapturing the spirit of other days. There was that time we had chartered an airplane to complete a jag! His coming was an oasis in this dreary desert of futility. The very thing—an oasis! Drinkers are like that.

The door opened and he stood there, fresh-skinned and glowing. There was something about his eyes. He was inexplicably different. What had happened?

I pushed a drink across the table. He refused it. Disappointed but curious, I wondered what had got into the fellow. He wasn't himself.

"Come, what's all this about?" I queried.

He looked straight at me. Simply, but smilingly, he said, "I've got religion."

I was aghast. So that was it—last summer an alcoholic crackpot; now, I suspected, a little cracked about religion. He had that starry-eyed look. Yes, the old boy was on fire all right. But bless his heart, let him rant! Besides, my gin would last longer than his preaching.

But he did no ranting. In a matter of fact way he told how two men had appeared in court, persuading the judge to suspend his commitment. They had told of a simple religious idea and a practical program of action. That was two months ago and the result was self-evident. It worked!

He had come to pass his experience along to me—if

I cared to have it. I was shocked, but interested. Certainly I was interested. I had to be, for I was hopeless.

He talked for hours. Childhood memories rose before me. I could almost hear the sound of the preacher's voice as I sat, on still Sundays, way over there on the hillside; there was that proffered temperance pledge I never signed; my grandfather's good natured contempt of some church folk and their doings; his insistence that the spheres really had their music; but his denial of the preacher's right to tell him how he must listen; his fearlessness as he spoke of these things just before he died; these recollections welled up from the past. They made me swallow hard.

That war-time day in old Winchester Cathedral came back again.

I had always believed in a Power greater than myself. I had often pondered these things. I was not an atheist. Few people really are, for that means blind faith in the strange proposition that this universe originated in a cipher and aimlessly rushes nowhere. My intellectual heroes, the chemists, the astronomers, even the evolutionists, suggested vast laws and forces at work. Despite contrary indications, I had little doubt that a mighty purpose and rhythm underlay all. How could there be so much of precise and immutable law, and no intelligence? I simply had to believe in a Spirit of the Universe, who knew neither time nor limitation. But that was as far as I had gone.

With ministers, and the world's religions, I parted right there. When they talked of a God personal to me, who was love, superhuman strength and direction, I became irritated and my mind snapped shut against such a theory.

To Christ I conceded the certainty of a great man, not too closely followed by those who claimed Him. His moral teaching—most excellent. For myself, I had adopted those parts which seemed convenient and not too difficult; the rest I disregarded.

The wars which had been fought, the burnings and chicanery that religious dispute had facilitated, made me sick. I honestly doubted whether, on balance, the religions of mankind had done any good. Judging from what I had seen in Europe and since, the power of God in human affairs was negligible, the Brotherhood of Man a grim jest. If there was a Devil, he seemed the Boss Universal, and he certainly had me.

But my friend sat before me, and he made the point-blank declaration that God had done for him what he could not do for himself. His human will had failed. Doctors had pronounced him incurable. Society was about to lock him up. Like myself, he had admitted complete defeat. Then he had, in effect, been raised from the dead, suddenly taken from the scrap heap to a level of life better than the best he had ever known!

Had this power originated in him? Obviously it had not. There had been no more power in him than there was in me at that minute; and this was none at all.

That floored me. It began to look as though religious people were right after all. Here was something at work in a human heart which had done the impossible. My ideas about miracles were drastically revised right then. Never mind the musty past; here sat a miracle directly across the kitchen table. He shouted great tidings.

I saw that my friend was much more than inwardly

reorganized. He was on a different footing. His roots grasped a new soil.

Despite the living example of my friend there remained in me the vestiges of my old prejudice. The word God still aroused a certain antipathy. When the thought was expressed that there might be a God personal to me this feeling was intensified. I didn't like the idea. I could go for such conceptions as Creative Intelligence, Universal Mind or Spirit of Nature but I resisted the thought of a Czar of the Heavens, however loving His sway might be. I have since talked with scores of men who felt the same way.

My friend suggested what then seemed a novel idea. He said, *"Why don't you choose your own conception of God?"*

That statement hit me hard. It melted the icy intellectual mountain in whose shadow I had lived and shivered many years. I stood in the sunlight at last.

It was only a matter of being willing to believe in a Power greater than myself. Nothing more was required of me to make my beginning. I saw that growth could start from that point. Upon a foundation of complete willingness I might build what I saw in my friend. Would I have it? Of course I would!

Thus was I convinced that God is concerned with us humans when we want Him enough. At long last I saw, I felt, I believed. Scales of pride and prejudice fell from my eyes. A new world came into view.

The real significance of my experience in the Cathedral burst upon me. For a brief moment, I had needed and wanted God. There had been a humble willingness to have Him with me—and He came. But soon the sense of His presence had been blotted out by worldly clamors, mostly those within myself. And so it had been ever since. How blind I had been.

At the hospital I was separated from alcohol for the last time. Treatment seemed wise, for I showed signs of delirium tremens.

There I humbly offered myself to God, as I then understood Him, to do with me as He would. I placed myself unreservedly under His care and direction. I admitted for the first time that of myself I was nothing; that without Him I was lost. I ruthlessly faced my sins and became willing to have my new-found Friend take them away, root and branch. I have not had a drink since.

My schoolmate visited me, and I fully acquainted him with my problems and deficiencies. We made a list of people I had hurt or toward whom I felt resentment. I expressed my entire willingness to approach these individuals, admitting my wrong. Never was I to be critical of them. I was to right all such matters to the utmost of my ability.

I was to test my thinking by the new God-consciousness within. Common sense would thus become uncommon sense. I was to sit quietly when in doubt, asking only for direction and strength to meet my problems as He would have me. Never was I to pray for myself, except as my requests bore on my usefulness to others. Then only might I expect to receive. But that would be in great measure.

My friend promised when these things were done I would enter upon a new relationship with my Creator; that I would have the elements of a way of living which answered all my problems. Belief in the power of God, plus enough willingness, honesty and humility to establish and maintain the new order of things, were the essential requirements.

Simple, but not easy; a price had to be paid. It meant destruction of self-centeredness. I must turn in all things to the Father of Light who presides over us all.

These were revolutionary and drastic proposals, but the moment I fully accepted them, the effect was electric. There was a sense of victory, followed by such a peace and serenity as I had never known. There was utter confidence. I felt lifted up, as though the great clean wind of a mountain top blew through and through. God comes to most men gradually, but His impact on me was sudden and profound.

For a moment I was alarmed, and called my friend, the doctor, to ask if I were still sane. He listened in wonder as I talked.

Finally he shook his head saying, "Something has happened to you I don't understand. But you had better hang on to it. Anything is better than the way you were." The good doctor now sees many men who have such experiences. He knows that they are real.

While I lay in the hospital the thought came that there were thousands of hopeless alcoholics who might be glad to have what had been so freely given me. Perhaps I could help some of them. They in turn might work with others.

My friend had emphasized the absolute necessity of demonstrating these principles in all my affairs. Particularly was it imperative to work with others as he had worked with me. Faith without works was dead, he said. And how appallingly true for the alcoholic! For if an alcoholic failed to perfect and enlarge his spiritual life through work and self-sacrifice for others, he could not survive the certain trials and low spots ahead. If he did not work, he would surely drink again, and if he drank, he would surely die. Then faith would be dead indeed. With us it is just like that.

My wife and I abandoned ourselves with enthusiasm to the idea of helping other alcoholics to a solution of their problems. It was fortunate, for my old business associates remained skeptical for a year and a half, during which I found little work. I was not too well at the time, and was plagued by waves of self-pity and resentment. This sometimes nearly drove me back to drink, but I soon found that when all other measures failed, work with another alcoholic would save the day. Many times I have gone to my old hospital in despair. On talking to a man there, I would be amazingly lifted up and set on my feet. It is a design for living that works in rough going.

We commenced to make many fast friends and a fellowship has grown up among us of which it is a wonderful thing to feel a part. The joy of living we really have, even under pressure and difficulty. I have seen hundreds of families set their feet in the path that really goes somewhere; have seen the most impossible domestic situations righted; feuds and bitterness of all sorts wiped out. I have seen men come out of asylums and resume a vital place in the lives of their families and communities. Business and professional men have regained their standing. There is scarcely any form of trouble and misery which has not been overcome among us. In one western city and its environs there are one thousand of us and our families. We meet frequently so that newcomers may find the fellowship they seek. At these informal gatherings one may often see from 50 to 200 persons. We are growing in numbers and power.*

An alcoholic in his cups is an unlovely creature. Our struggles with them are variously strenuous, comic, and tragic. One poor chap committed suicide in my home. He could not, or would not, see our way of life.

There is, however, a vast amount of fun about it all. I suppose some would be shocked at our seeming worldliness and levity. But just underneath there is deadly earnestness. Faith has to work twenty-four hours a day in and through us, or we perish.

Most of us feel we need look no further for Utopia. We have it with us right here and now. Each day my friend's simple talk in our kitchen multiplies itself in a widening circle of peace on earth and good will to men.

Bill W., co-founder of A.A.,
died January 24, 1971.

---

*In 2012, A.A. is composed of approximately 114,000 groups.

Chapter 2

THERE IS A SOLUTION

*W*E, OF ALCOHOLICS ANONYMOUS, know thousands of men and women who were once just as hopeless as Bill. Nearly all have recovered. They have solved the drink problem.

We are average Americans. All sections of this country and many of its occupations are represented, as well as many political, economic, social, and religious backgrounds. We are people who normally would not mix. But there exists among us a fellowship, a friendliness, and an understanding which is indescribably wonderful. We are like the passengers of a great liner the moment after rescue from shipwreck when camaraderie, joyousness and democracy pervade the vessel from steerage to Captain's table. Unlike the feelings of the ship's passengers, however, our joy in escape from disaster does not subside as we go our individual ways. The feeling of having shared in a common peril is one element in the powerful cement which binds us. But that in itself would never have held us together as we are now joined.

The tremendous fact for every one of us is that we have discovered a common solution. We have a way out on which we can absolutely agree, and upon which we can join in brotherly and harmonious action. This is the great news this book carries to those who suffer from alcoholism.

An illness of this sort—and we have come to believe it an illness—involves those about us in a way no other human sickness can. If a person has cancer all are sorry for him and no one is angry or hurt. But not so with the alcoholic illness, for with it there goes annihilation of all the things worth while in life. It engulfs all whose lives touch the sufferer's. It brings misunderstanding, fierce resentment, financial insecurity, disgusted friends and employers, warped lives of blameless children, sad wives and parents—anyone can increase the list.

We hope this volume will inform and comfort those who are, or who may be affected. There are many.

Highly competent psychiatrists who have dealt with us have found it sometimes impossible to persuade an alcoholic to discuss his situation without reserve. Strangely enough, wives, parents and intimate friends usually find us even more unapproachable than do the psychiatrist and the doctor.

But the ex-problem drinker who has found this solution, who is properly armed with facts about himself, can generally win the entire confidence of another alcoholic in a few hours. Until such an understanding is reached, little or nothing can be accomplished.

That the man who is making the approach has had the same difficulty, that he obviously knows what he is talking about, that his whole deportment shouts at the new prospect that he is a man with a real answer, that he has no attitude of Holier Than Thou, nothing whatever except the sincere desire to be helpful; that there are no fees to pay, no axes to grind, no people to please, no lectures to be endured—these are the conditions we have found most effective. After such an approach many take up their beds and walk again.

None of us makes a sole vocation of this work, nor do we think its effectiveness would be increased if we did. We feel that elimination of our drinking is but a beginning. A much more important demonstration of our principles lies before us in our respective homes, occupations and affairs. All of us spend much of our spare time in the sort of effort which we are going to describe. A few are fortunate enough to be so situated that they can give nearly all their time to the work.

If we keep on the way we are going there is little doubt that much good will result, but the surface of the problem would hardly be scratched. Those of us who live in large cities are overcome by the reflection that close by hundreds are dropping into oblivion every day. Many could recover if they had the opportunity we have enjoyed. How then shall we present that which has been so freely given us?

We have concluded to publish an anonymous volume setting forth the problem as we see it. We shall bring to the task our combined experience and knowledge. This should suggest a useful program for anyone concerned with a drinking problem.

Of necessity there will have to be discussion of matters medical, psychiatric, social, and religious. We are aware that these matters are, from their very nature, controversial. Nothing would please us so much as to write a book which would contain no basis for contention or argument. We shall do our utmost to achieve that ideal. Most of us sense that real tolerance of other people's shortcomings and viewpoints and a respect for their opinions are attitudes which make us more useful to others. Our very lives, as ex-problem drinkers, depend upon our constant thought of others and how we may help meet their needs.

You may already have asked yourself why it is that all of us became so very ill from drinking. Doubtless you are curious to discover how and why, in the face of expert opinion to the contrary, we have recovered from a hopeless condition of mind and body. If you are an alcoholic who wants to get over it, you may already be asking—"What do I have to do?"

It is the purpose of this book to answer such questions specifically. We shall tell you what we have done. Before going into a detailed discussion, it may be well to summarize some points as we see them.

How many times people have said to us: "I can take it or leave it alone. Why can't he?" "Why don't you drink like a gentleman or quit?" "That fellow can't handle his liquor." "Why don't you try beer and wine?" "Lay off the hard stuff." "His will power must be weak." "He could stop if he wanted to." "She's such a sweet girl, I should think he'd stop for her sake." "The doctor told him that if he ever drank again it would kill him, but there he is all lit up again."

Now these are commonplace observations on drinkers which we hear all the time. Back of them is a world of ignorance and misunderstanding. We see that these expressions refer to people whose reactions are very different from ours.

Moderate drinkers have little trouble in giving up liquor entirely if they have good reason for it. They can take it or leave it alone.

Then we have a certain type of hard drinker. He may have the habit badly enough to gradually impair him physically and mentally. It may cause him to die a few years before his time. If a sufficiently strong reason—ill health, falling in love, change of environment, or the warning of a doctor—becomes operative, this man can also stop or moderate, although he may find it difficult and troublesome and may even need medical attention.

But what about the real alcoholic? He may start off as a moderate drinker; he may or may not become a continuous hard drinker; but at some stage of his drinking career he begins to lose all control of his liquor consumption, once he starts to drink.

Here is the fellow who has been puzzling you, especially in his lack of control. He does absurd, incredible, tragic things while drinking. He is a real Dr. Jekyll and Mr. Hyde. He is seldom mildly intoxicated. He is always more or less insanely drunk. His disposition while drinking resembles his normal nature but little. He may be one of the finest fellows in the world. Yet let him drink for a day, and he frequently becomes disgustingly, and even dangerously anti-social. He has a positive genius for getting tight at exactly the wrong moment, particularly when some important decision must be made or engagement kept. He is often perfectly sensible and well balanced concerning everything except liquor, but in that respect he is incredibly dishonest and selfish. He often possesses special abilities, skills, and aptitudes, and has a promising career ahead of him. He uses his gifts to build up a bright outlook for his family and himself, and then pulls the structure down on his head by a senseless series of sprees. He is the fellow who goes to bed so intoxicated he ought to sleep the clock around. Yet early next morning he searches madly for the bottle he misplaced the night before. If he can afford it, he may have liquor concealed all over his house to be certain no one gets his entire supply away from him to throw down the wastepipe. As matters grow worse, he begins to use a combination of high-powered sedative and liquor to quiet his nerves so he can go to work. Then comes the day when he simply cannot make it and gets drunk all over again. Perhaps he goes to a doctor who gives him morphine or some sedative with which to taper off. Then he begins to appear at hospitals and sanitariums.

This is by no means a comprehensive picture of the true alcoholic, as our behavior patterns vary. But this description should identify him roughly.

Why does he behave like this? If hundreds of experiences have shown him that one drink means another debacle with all its attendant suffering and humiliation, why is it he takes that one drink? Why can't he stay on the water wagon? What has become of the common sense and will power that he still sometimes displays with respect to other matters?

Perhaps there never will be a full answer to these questions. Opinions vary considerably as to why the alcoholic reacts differently from normal people. We are not sure why, once a certain point is reached, little can be done for him. We cannot answer the riddle.

We know that while the alcoholic keeps away from drink, as he may do for months or years, he reacts much like other men. We are equally positive that once he takes any alcohol whatever into his system, something happens, both in the bodily and mental sense, which makes it virtually impossible for him to stop. The experience of any alcoholic will abundantly confirm this.

These observations would be academic and pointless if our friend never took the first drink, thereby setting the terrible cycle in motion. Therefore, the main problem of the alcoholic centers in his mind, rather than in his body. If you ask him why he started on that last bender, the chances are he will offer you any one of a hundred alibis. Sometimes these excuses have a certain plausibility, but none of them really makes sense in the light of the havoc an alcoholic's drinking bout creates. They sound like the philosophy of the man who, having a headache, beats himself on the head with a hammer so that he can't feel the ache. If you draw this fallacious reasoning to the attention of an alcoholic, he will laugh it off, or become irritated and refuse to talk.

Once in a while he may tell the truth. And the truth, strange to say, is usually that he has no more idea why he took that first drink than you have. Some drinkers have excuses with which they are satisfied part of the time. But in their hearts they really do not know why they do it. Once this malady has a real hold, they are a baffled lot. There is the obsession that somehow, someday, they will beat the game. But they often suspect they are down for the count.

How true this is, few realize. In a vague way their families and friends sense that these drinkers are abnormal, but everybody hopefully awaits the day when the sufferer will rouse himself from his lethargy and assert his power of will.

The tragic truth is that if the man be a real alcoholic, the happy day may not arrive. He has lost control. At a certain point in the drinking of every alcoholic, he passes into a state where the most powerful desire to stop drinking is of absolutely no avail. This tragic situation has already arrived in practically every case long before it is suspected.

The fact is that most alcoholics, for reasons yet obscure, have lost the power of choice in drink. Our so-called will power becomes practically nonexistent. We are unable, at certain times, to bring into our consciousness with sufficient force the memory of the suffering and humiliation of even a week or a month ago. We are without defense against the first drink.

The almost certain consequences that follow taking even a glass of beer do not crowd into the mind to deter us. If these thoughts occur, they are hazy and readily supplanted with the old threadbare idea that this time we shall handle ourselves like other people. There is a complete failure of the kind of defense that keeps one from putting his hand on a hot stove.

The alcoholic may say to himself in the most casual way, "It won't burn me this time, so here's how!" Or perhaps he doesn't think at all. How often have some of us begun to drink in this nonchalant way, and after the third or fourth, pounded on the bar and said to ourselves, "For God's sake, how did I ever get started again?" Only to have that thought supplanted by "Well, I'll stop with the sixth drink." Or "What's the use anyhow?"

When this sort of thinking is fully established in an individual with alcoholic tendencies, he has probably placed himself beyond human aid, and unless locked up, may die or go permanently insane. These stark and ugly facts have been confirmed by legions of alcoholics throughout history. But for the grace of God, there would have been thousands more convincing demonstrations. So many want to stop but cannot.

There is a solution. Almost none of us liked the self-searching, the leveling of our pride, the confession of shortcomings which the process requires for its successful consummation. But we saw that it really worked in others, and we had come to believe in the hopelessness and futility of life as we had been living it. When, therefore, we were approached by those in whom the problem had been solved, there was nothing left for us but to pick up the simple kit of spiritual tools laid at our feet. We have found much of heaven and we have been rocketed into a fourth dimension of existence of which we had not even dreamed.

The great fact is just this, and nothing less: That we have had deep and effective spiritual experiences* which have revolutionized our whole attitude toward life, toward our fellows and toward God's universe. The central fact of our lives today is the absolute certainty that our Creator has entered into our hearts and lives in a way which is indeed miraculous. He has commenced to accomplish those things for us which we could never do by ourselves.

If you are as seriously alcoholic as we were, we believe there is no middle-of-the-road solution. We were in a position where life was becoming impossible, and if we had passed into the region from which there is no return through human aid, we had but two alternatives: One was to go on to the bitter end, blotting out the consciousness of our intolerable situation as best we could; and the other, to accept spiritual help. This

*Fully explained—Appendix II.

we did because we honestly wanted to, and were willing to make the effort.

A certain American business man had ability, good sense, and high character. For years he had floundered from one sanitarium to another. He had consulted the best known American psychiatrists. Then he had gone to Europe, placing himself in the care of a celebrated physician (the psychiatrist, Dr. Jung) who prescribed for him. Though experience had made him skeptical, he finished his treatment with unusual confidence. His physical and mental condition were unusually good. Above all, he believed he had acquired such a profound knowledge of the inner workings of his mind and its hidden springs that relapse was unthinkable. Nevertheless, he was drunk in a short time. More baffling still, he could give himself no satisfactory explanation for his fall.

So he returned to this doctor, whom he admired, and asked him point-blank why he could not recover. He wished above all things to regain self-control. He seemed quite rational and well-balanced with respect to other problems. Yet he had no control whatever over alcohol. Why was this?

He begged the doctor to tell him the whole truth, and he got it. In the doctor's judgment he was utterly hopeless; he could never regain his position in society and he would have to place himself under lock and key or hire a bodyguard if he expected to live long. That was a great physician's opinion.

But this man still lives, and is a free man. He does not need a bodyguard nor is he confined. He can go anywhere on this earth where other free men may go without disaster, provided he remains willing to maintain a certain simple attitude.

Some of our alcoholic readers may think they can do without spiritual help. Let us tell you the rest of the conversation our friend had with his doctor.

The doctor said: "You have the mind of a chronic alcoholic. I have never seen one single case recover, where that state of mind existed to the extent that it does in you." Our friend felt as though the gates of hell had closed on him with a clang.

He said to the doctor, "Is there no exception?"

"Yes," replied the doctor, "there is. Exceptions to cases such as yours have been occurring since early times. Here and there, once in a while, alcoholics have had what are called vital spiritual experiences. To me these occurrences are phenomena. They appear to be in the nature of huge emotional displacements and rearrangements. Ideas, emotions, and attitudes which were once the guiding forces of the lives of these men are suddenly cast to one side, and a completely new set of conceptions and motives begin to dominate them. In fact, I have been trying to produce some such emotional rearrangement within you. With many individuals the methods which I employed are successful, but I have never been successful with an alcoholic of your description."*

Upon hearing this, our friend was somewhat relieved, for he reflected that, after all, he was a good church member. This hope, however, was destroyed by the doctor's telling him that while his religious convictions were very good, in his case they did not spell the necessary vital spiritual experience.

*For amplification—see Appendix II.

Here was the terrible dilemma in which our friend found himself when he had the extraordinary experience, which as we have already told you, made him a free man.

We, in our turn, sought the same escape with all the desperation of drowning men. What seemed at first a flimsy reed, has proved to be the loving and powerful hand of God. A new life has been given us or, if you prefer, "a design for living" that really works.

The distinguished American psychologist, William James, in his book "Varieties of Religious Experience," indicates a multitude of ways in which men have discovered God. We have no desire to convince anyone that there is only one way by which faith can be acquired. If what we have learned and felt and seen means anything at all, it means that all of us, whatever our race, creed, or color are the children of a living Creator with whom we may form a relationship upon simple and understandable terms as soon as we are willing and honest enough to try. Those having religious affiliations will find here nothing disturbing to their beliefs or ceremonies. There is no friction among us over such matters.

We think it no concern of ours what religious bodies our members identify themselves with as individuals. This should be an entirely personal affair which each one decides for himself in the light of past associations, or his present choice. Not all of us join religious bodies, but most of us favor such memberships.

In the following chapter, there appears an explanation of alcoholism, as we understand it, then a chapter addressed to the agnostic. Many who once were in this class are now among our members. Surprisingly enough, we find such convictions no great obstacle to a spiritual experience.

Further on, clear-cut directions are given showing how we recovered. These are followed by forty-two personal experiences.

Each individual, in the personal stories, describes in his own language and from his own point of view the way he established his relationship with God. These give a fair cross section of our membership and a clear-cut idea of what has actually happened in their lives.

We hope no one will consider these self-revealing accounts in bad taste. Our hope is that many alcoholic men and women, desperately in need, will see these pages, and we believe that it is only by fully disclosing ourselves and our problems that they will be persuaded to say, "Yes, I am one of them too; I must have this thing."

Chapter 3

MORE ABOUT ALCOHOLISM

*M*OST OF US have been unwilling to admit we were real alcoholics. No person likes to think he is bodily and mentally different from his fellows. Therefore, it is not surprising that our drinking careers have been characterized by countless vain attempts to prove we could drink like other people. The idea that somehow, someday he will control and enjoy his drinking is the great obsession of every abnormal drinker. The persistence of this illusion is astonishing. Many pursue it into the gates of insanity or death.

We learned that we had to fully concede to our innermost selves that we were alcoholics. This is the first step in recovery. The delusion that we are like other people, or presently may be, has to be smashed.

We alcoholics are men and women who have lost the ability to control our drinking. We know that no real alcoholic *ever* recovers control. All of us felt at times that we were regaining control, but such intervals—usually brief—were inevitably followed by still less control, which led in time to pitiful and incomprehensible demoralization. We are convinced to a man that alcoholics of our type are in the grip of a progressive illness. Over any considerable period we get worse, never better.

We are like men who have lost their legs; they never grow new ones. Neither does there appear to be any kind of treatment which will make alcoholics of our kind like other men. We have tried every imaginable remedy. In some instances there has been brief recovery, followed always by a still worse relapse. Physicians who are familiar with alcoholism agree there is no such thing as making a normal drinker out of an alcoholic. Science may one day accomplish this, but it hasn't done so yet.

Despite all we can say, many who are real alcoholics are not going to believe they are in that class. By every form of self-deception and experimentation, they will try to prove themselves exceptions to the rule, therefore nonalcoholic. If anyone who is showing inability to control his drinking can do the right-about-face and drink like a gentleman, our hats are off to him. Heaven knows, we have tried hard enough and long enough to drink like other people!

Here are some of the methods we have tried: Drinking beer only, limiting the number of drinks, never drinking alone, never drinking in the morning, drinking only at home, never having it in the house, never drinking during business hours, drinking only at parties, switching from scotch to brandy, drinking only natural wines, agreeing to resign if ever drunk on the job, taking a trip, not taking a trip, swearing off forever (with and without a solemn oath), taking more physical exercise, reading inspirational books, going to health farms and sanitariums, accepting voluntary commitment to asylums—we could increase the list ad infinitum.

We do not like to pronounce any individual as alcoholic, but you can quickly diagnose yourself. Step over to the nearest barroom and try some controlled drinking. Try to drink and stop abruptly. Try it more than once. It will not take long for you to decide, if you are honest with yourself about it. It may be worth a bad case of jitters if you get a full knowledge of your condition.

Though there is no way of proving it, we believe that early in our drinking careers most of us could have stopped drinking. But the difficulty is that few alcoholics have enough desire to stop while there is yet time. We have heard of a few instances where people, who showed definite signs of alcoholism, were able to stop for a long period because of an overpowering desire to do so. Here is one.

A man of thirty was doing a great deal of spree drinking. He was very nervous in the morning after these bouts and quieted himself with more liquor. He was ambitious to succeed in business, but saw that he would get nowhere if he drank at all. Once he started, he had no control whatever. He made up his mind that until he had been successful in business and had retired, he would not touch another drop. An exceptional man, he remained bone dry for twenty-five years and retired at the age of fifty-five, after a successful and happy business career. Then he fell victim to a belief which practically every alcoholic has —that his long period of sobriety and self-discipline had qualified him to drink as other men. Out came his carpet slippers and a bottle. In two months he was in a hospital, puzzled and humiliated. He tried to regulate his drinking for a while, making several trips to the hospital meantime. Then, gathering all his forces, he attempted to stop altogether and found he could not. Every means of solving his problem which money could buy was at his disposal. Every attempt failed. Though a robust man at retirement, he went to pieces quickly and was dead within four years.

This case contains a powerful lesson. Most of us have believed that if we remained sober for a long stretch, we could thereafter drink normally. But here is a man who at fifty-five years found he was just where he had left off at thirty. We have seen the truth demonstrated again and again: "Once an alcoholic, always an alcoholic." Commencing to drink after a period of sobriety, we are in a short time as bad as ever. If we are planning to stop drinking, there must be no reservation of any kind, nor any lurking notion that someday we will be immune to alcohol.

Young people may be encouraged by this man's experience to think that they can stop, as he did, on their own will power. We doubt if many of them can do it, because none will really want to stop, and hardly one of them, because of the peculiar mental twist already acquired, will find he can win out. Several of our crowd, men of thirty or less, had been drinking only a few years, but they found themselves as helpless as those who had been drinking twenty years.

To be gravely affected, one does not necessarily have to drink a long time nor take the quantities some of us have. This is particularly true of women. Potential female alcoholics often turn into the real thing and are gone beyond recall in a few years. Certain drinkers, who would be greatly insulted if called alcoholics, are astonished at their inability to stop. We, who are familiar with the symptoms, see large numbers of potential alcoholics among young people everywhere. But try and get them to see it!*

As we look back, we feel we had gone on drinking many years beyond the point where we could quit on our will power. If anyone questions whether he has entered this dangerous area, let him try leaving liquor alone for one year. If he is a real alcoholic and very far advanced, there is scant chance of success. In the early days of our drinking we occasionally remained sober for a year or more, becoming serious drinkers again later. Though you may be able to stop for a considerable period, you may yet be a potential alcoholic. We think few, to whom this book will appeal, can stay dry anything like a year. Some will be drunk the day after making their resolutions; most of them within a few weeks.

For those who are unable to drink moderately the question is how to stop altogether. We are assuming, of course, that the reader desires to stop. Whether such a person can quit upon a nonspiritual basis depends upon the extent to which he has already lost the power to choose whether he will drink or not. Many of us felt that we had plenty of character. There was a tremendous urge to cease forever. Yet we found it impossible. This is the baffling feature of alcoholism as we know it—this utter inability to leave it alone, no matter how great the necessity or the wish.

How then shall we help our readers determine, to their own satisfaction, whether they are one of us? The experiment of quitting for a period of time will be helpful, but we think we can render an even greater service to alcoholic sufferers and perhaps to the medi-

* True when this book was first published. But a 2011 U.S./Canada membership survey showed about one-twelfth of A.A.'s were thirty and under.

cal fraternity. So we shall describe some of the mental states that precede a relapse into drinking, for obviously this is the crux of the problem.

What sort of thinking dominates an alcoholic who repeats time after time the desperate experiment of the first drink? Friends who have reasoned with him after a spree which has brought him to the point of divorce or bankruptcy are mystified when he walks directly into a saloon. Why does he? Of what is he thinking?

Our first example is a friend we shall call Jim. This man has a charming wife and family. He inherited a lucrative automobile agency. He had a commendable World War record. He is a good salesman. Everybody likes him. He is an intelligent man, normal so far as we can see, except for a nervous disposition. He did no drinking until he was thirty-five. In a few years he became so violent when intoxicated that he had to be committed. On leaving the asylum he came into contact with us.

We told him what we knew of alcoholism and the answer we had found. He made a beginning. His family was re-assembled, and he began to work as a salesman for the business he had lost through drinking. All went well for a time, but he failed to enlarge his spiritual life. To his consternation, he found himself drunk half a dozen times in rapid succession. On each of these occasions we worked with him, reviewing carefully what had happened. He agreed he was a real alcoholic and in a serious condition. He knew he faced another trip to the asylum if he kept on. Moreover, he would lose his family for whom he had a deep affection.

Yet he got drunk again. We asked him to tell us exactly how it happened. This is his story: "I came to work on Tuesday morning. I remember I felt irritated that I had to be a salesman for a concern I once owned. I had a few words with the boss, but nothing serious. Then I decided to drive into the country and see one of my prospects for a car. On the way I felt hungry so I stopped at a roadside place where they have a bar. I had no intention of drinking. I just thought I would get a sandwich. I also had the notion that I might find a customer for a car at this place, which was familiar for I had been going to it for years. I had eaten there many times during the months I was sober. I sat down at a table and ordered a sandwich and a glass of milk. Still no thought of drinking. I ordered another sandwich and decided to have another glass of milk.

"*Suddenly the thought crossed my mind that if I were to put an ounce of whiskey in my milk it couldn't hurt me on a full stomach. I ordered a whiskey and poured it into the milk. I vaguely sensed I was not being any too smart, but felt reassured as I was taking the whiskey on a full stomach.* The experiment went so well that I ordered another whiskey and poured it into more milk. That didn't seem to bother me so I tried another."

Thus started one more journey to the asylum for Jim. Here was the threat of commitment, the loss of family and position, to say nothing of that intense mental and physical suffering which drinking always caused him. *He had much knowledge about himself as an alcoholic. Yet all reasons for not drinking were*

easily pushed aside in favor of the foolish idea that he
could take whiskey if only he mixed it with milk!

Whatever the precise definition of the word may be,
we call this plain insanity. How can such a lack of
proportion, of the ability to think straight, be called
anything else?

You may think this an extreme case. To us it is not
far-fetched, for this kind of thinking has been charac-
teristic of every single one of us. We have sometimes
reflected more than Jim did upon the consequences.
But there was always the curious mental phenomenon
that parallel with our sound reasoning there inevitably
ran some insanely trivial excuse for taking the first
drink. Our sound reasoning failed to hold us in check.
The insane idea won out. Next day we would ask ourselves, in all earnestness and sincerity, how it could
have happened.

In some circumstances we have gone out deliberately to get drunk, feeling ourselves justified by
nervousness, anger, worry, depression, jealousy or the
like. But even in this type of beginning we are obliged
to admit that our justification for a spree was insanely
insufficient in the light of what always happened. We
now see that when we began to drink deliberately,
instead of casually, there was little serious or effective
thought during the period of premeditation of what
the terrific consequences might be.

Our behavior is as absurd and incomprehensible
with respect to the first drink as that of an individual
with a passion, say, for jay-walking. He gets a thrill
out of skipping in front of fast-moving vehicles. He
enjoys himself for a few years in spite of friendly warnings. Up to this point you would label him as a foolish

chap having queer ideas of fun. Luck then deserts him and he is slightly injured several times in succession. You would expect him, if he were normal, to cut it out. Presently he is hit again and this time has a fractured skull. Within a week after leaving the hospital a fast-moving trolley car breaks his arm. He tells you he has decided to stop jay-walking for good, but in a few weeks he breaks both legs.

On through the years this conduct continues, accompanied by his continual promises to be careful or to keep off the streets altogether. Finally, he can no longer work, his wife gets a divorce and he is held up to ridicule. He tries every known means to get the jay-walking idea out of his head. He shuts himself up in an asylum, hoping to mend his ways. But the day he comes out he races in front of a fire engine, which breaks his back. Such a man would be crazy, wouldn't he?

You may think our illustration is too ridiculous. But is it? We, who have been through the wringer, have to admit if we substituted alcoholism for jay-walking, the illustration would fit us exactly. However intelligent we may have been in other respects, where alcohol has been involved, we have been strangely insane. It's strong language—but isn't it true?

Some of you are thinking: "Yes, what you tell us is true, but it doesn't fully apply. We admit we have some of these symptoms, but we have not gone to the extremes you fellows did, nor are we likely to, for we understand ourselves so well after what you have told us that such things cannot happen again. We have not lost everything in life through drinking and we certainly do not intend to. Thanks for the information."

That may be true of certain nonalcoholic people who, though drinking foolishly and heavily at the present time, are able to stop or moderate, because their brains and bodies have not been damaged as ours were. But the actual or potential alcoholic, with hardly an exception, will be *absolutely unable to stop drinking on the basis of self-knowledge.* This is a point we wish to emphasize and re-emphasize, to smash home upon our alcoholic readers as it has been revealed to us out of bitter experience. Let us take another illustration.

Fred is partner in a well known accounting firm. His income is good, he has a fine home, is happily married and the father of promising children of college age. He has so attractive a personality that he makes friends with everyone. If ever there was a successful business man, it is Fred. To all appearance he is a stable, well balanced individual. Yet, he is alcoholic. We first saw Fred about a year ago in a hospital where he had gone to recover from a bad case of jitters. It was his first experience of this kind, and he was much ashamed of it. Far from admitting he was an alcoholic, he told himself he came to the hospital to rest his nerves. The doctor intimated strongly that he might be worse than he realized. For a few days he was depressed about his condition. He made up his mind to quit drinking altogether. It never occurred to him that perhaps he could not do so, in spite of his character and standing. Fred would not believe himself an alcoholic, much less accept a spiritual remedy for his problem. We told him what we knew about alcoholism. He was interested and conceded that he had some of the symptoms, but he was a long way from admitting that he could do nothing about it himself. He was positive that this humiliating experience, plus the knowledge he had acquired, would keep him sober the rest of his life. Self-knowledge would fix it.

We heard no more of Fred for a while. One day we were told that he was back in the hospital. This time he was quite shaky. He soon indicated he was anxious to see us. The story he told is most instructive, for here was a chap absolutely convinced he had to stop drinking, who had no excuse for drinking, who exhibited splendid judgment and determination in all his other concerns, yet was flat on his back nevertheless.

Let him tell you about it: "I was much impressed with what you fellows said about alcoholism, and I frankly did not believe it would be possible for me to drink again. I rather appreciated your ideas about the subtle insanity which precedes the first drink, but I was confident it could not happen to me after what I had learned. I reasoned I was not so far advanced as most of you fellows, that I had been usually successful in licking my other personal problems, and that I would therefore be successful where you men failed. I felt I had every right to be self-confident, that it would be only a matter of exercising my will power and keeping on guard.

"In this frame of mind, I went about my business and for a time all was well. I had no trouble refusing drinks, and began to wonder if I had not been making too hard work of a simple matter. One day I went to Washington to present some accounting evidence to a government bureau. I had been out of town before during this particular dry spell, so there was nothing new about that. Physically, I felt fine. Neither did I have any pressing problems or worries. My business came off well, I was pleased and knew my partners would be too. It was the end of a perfect day, not a cloud on the horizon.

"I went to my hotel and leisurely dressed for dinner. *As I crossed the threshold of the dining room, the thought came to mind that it would be nice to have a couple of cocktails with dinner. That was all. Nothing more.* I ordered a cocktail and my meal. Then I ordered another cocktail. After dinner I decided to take a walk. When I returned to the hotel it struck me a highball would be fine before going to bed, so I stepped into the bar and had one. I remember having several more that night and plenty next morning. I have a shadowy recollection of being in an airplane bound for New York, and of finding a friendly taxicab driver at the landing field instead of my wife. The driver escorted me about for several days. I know little of where I went or what I said and did. Then came the hospital with unbearable mental and physical suffering.

"As soon as I regained my ability to think, I went carefully over that evening in Washington. *Not only had I been off guard, I had made no fight whatever against the first drink. This time I had not thought of the consequences at all.* I had commenced to drink as carelessly as though the cocktails were ginger ale. I now remembered what my alcoholic friends had told me, how they prophesied that if I had an alcoholic mind, the time and place would come—I would drink again. They had said that though I did raise a defense, it would one day give way before some trivial reason for having a drink. Well, just that did happen and more, for what I had learned of alcoholism did not occur to me at all. I knew from that moment that I had an alcoholic mind. I saw that will power and self-knowledge would not help in those strange mental blank spots. I had never been able to understand people who said that a problem had them hopelessly defeated. I knew then. It was a crushing blow.

"Two of the members of Alcoholics Anonymous came to see me. They grinned, which I didn't like so much, and then asked me if I thought myself alcoholic and if I were really licked this time. I had to concede both propositions. They piled on me heaps of evidence to the effect that an alcoholic mentality, such as I had exhibited in Washington, was a hopeless condition. They cited cases out of their own experience by the dozen. This process snuffed out the last flicker of conviction that I could do the job myself.

"Then they outlined the spiritual answer and program of action which a hundred of them had followed successfully. Though I had been only a nominal churchman, their proposals were not, intellectually, hard to swallow. But the program of action, though entirely sensible, was pretty drastic. It meant I would have to throw several lifelong conceptions out of the window. That was not easy. But the moment I made up my mind to go through with the process, I had the curious feeling that my alcoholic condition was relieved, as in fact it proved to be.

"Quite as important was the discovery that spiritual principles would solve all my problems. I have since

been brought into a way of living infinitely more satisfying and, I hope, more useful than the life I lived
before. My old manner of life was by no means a bad
one, but I would not exchange its best moments for
the worst I have now. I would not go back to it even
if I could."

Fred's story speaks for itself. We hope it strikes
home to thousands like him. He had felt only the first
nip of the wringer. Most alcoholics have to be pretty
badly mangled before they really commence to solve
their problems.

Many doctors and psychiatrists agree with our conclusions. One of these men, staff member of a world-
renowned hospital, recently made this statement to
some of us: "What you say about the general hopelessness of the average alcoholic's plight is, in my opinion,
correct. As to two of you men, whose stories I have
heard, there is no doubt in my mind that you were
100% hopeless, apart from divine help. Had you offered yourselves as patients at this hospital, I would
not have taken you, if I had been able to avoid it.
People like you are too heartbreaking. Though not a
religious person, I have profound respect for the
spiritual approach in such cases as yours. For most
cases, there is virtually no other solution."

Once more: The alcoholic at certain times has no
effective mental defense against the first drink. Except in a few rare cases, neither he nor any other
human being can provide such a defense. His defense
must come from a Higher Power.

Chapter 4

WE AGNOSTICS

*I*N THE PRECEDING chapters you have learned something of alcoholism. We hope we have made clear the distinction between the alcoholic and the non-alcoholic. If, when you honestly want to, you find you cannot quit entirely, or if when drinking, you have little control over the amount you take, you are probably alcoholic. If that be the case, you may be suffering from an illness which only a spiritual experience will conquer.

To one who feels he is an atheist or agnostic such an experience seems impossible, but to continue as he is means disaster, especially if he is an alcoholic of the hopeless variety. To be doomed to an alcoholic death or to live on a spiritual basis are not always easy alternatives to face.

But it isn't so difficult. About half our original fellowship were of exactly that type. At first some of us tried to avoid the issue, hoping against hope we were not true alcoholics. But after a while we had to face the fact that we must find a spiritual basis of life —or else. Perhaps it is going to be that way with you. But cheer up, something like half of us thought we were atheists or agnostics. Our experience shows that you need not be disconcerted.

If a mere code of morals or a better philosophy of life were sufficient to overcome alcoholism, many of us would have recovered long ago. But we found that such codes and philosophies did not save us, no matter how much we tried. We could wish to be moral, we could wish to be philosophically comforted, in fact, we could will these things with all our might, but the needed power wasn't there. Our human resources, as marshalled by the will, were not sufficient; they failed utterly.

Lack of power, that was our dilemma. We had to find a power by which we could live, and it had to be a *Power greater than ourselves.* Obviously. But where and how were we to find this Power?

Well, that's exactly what this book is about. Its main object is to enable you to find a Power greater than yourself which will solve your problem. That means we have written a book which we believe to be spiritual as well as moral. And it means, of course, that we are going to talk about God. Here difficulty arises with agnostics. Many times we talk to a new man and watch his hope rise as we discuss his alcoholic problems and explain our fellowship. But his face falls when we speak of spiritual matters, especially when we mention God, for we have re-opened a subject which our man thought he had neatly evaded or entirely ignored.

We know how he feels. We have shared his honest doubt and prejudice. Some of us have been violently anti-religious. To others, the word "God" brought up a particular idea of Him with which someone had tried to impress them during childhood. Perhaps we rejected this particular conception because it seemed inadequate. With that rejection we imagined we had abandoned the God idea entirely. We were bothered with the thought that faith and dependence upon a Power beyond ourselves was somewhat weak, even cowardly. We look upon this world of warring individuals, warring theological systems, and inexplicable calamity, with deep skepticism. We looked askance at many individuals who claimed to be godly. How could a Supreme Being have anything to do with it all? And who could comprehend a Supreme Being anyhow? Yet, in other moments, we found ourselves thinking, when enchanted by a starlit night, "Who, then, made all this?" There was a feeling of awe and wonder, but it was fleeting and soon lost.

Yes, we of agnostic temperament have had these thoughts and experiences. Let us make haste to reassure you. We found that as soon as we were able to lay aside prejudice and express even a willingness to believe in a Power greater than ourselves, we commenced to get results, even though it was impossible for any of us to fully define or comprehend that Power, which is God.

Much to our relief, we discovered we did not need to consider another's conception of God. Our own conception, however inadequate, was sufficient to make the approach and to effect a contact with Him. As soon as we admitted the possible existence of a Creative Intelligence, a Spirit of the Universe underlying the totality of things, we began to be possessed of a new sense of power and direction, provided we took other simple steps. We found that God does not make too hard terms with those who seek Him. To us, the Realm of Spirit is broad, roomy, all inclusive; never exclusive or forbidding to those who earnestly seek. It is open, we believe, to all men.

When, therefore, we speak to you of God, we mean your own conception of God. This applies, too, to other spiritual expressions which you find in this book. Do not let any prejudice you may have against spiritual terms deter you from honestly asking yourself what they mean to you. At the start, this was all we needed to commence spiritual growth, to effect our first conscious relation with God as we understood Him. Afterward, we found ourselves accepting many things which then seemed entirely out of reach. That was growth, but if we wished to grow we had to begin somewhere. So we used our own conception, however limited it was.

We needed to ask ourselves but one short question. "Do I now believe, or am I even willing to believe, that there is a Power greater than myself?" As soon as a man can say that he does believe, or is willing to believe, we emphatically assure him that he is on his way. It has been repeatedly proven among us that upon this simple cornerstone a wonderfully effective spiritual structure can be built.*

That was great news to us, for we had assumed we could not make use of spiritual principles unless we accepted many things on faith which seemed difficult to believe. When people presented us with spiritual approaches, how frequently did we all say, "I wish I had what that man has. I'm sure it would work if I could only believe as he believes. But I cannot accept as surely true the many articles of faith which are so plain to him." So it was comforting to learn that we could commence at a simpler level.

Besides a seeming inability to accept much on faith,

* Please be sure to read Appendix II on "Spiritual Experience."

we often found ourselves handicapped by obstinacy, sensitiveness, and unreasoning prejudice. Many of us have been so touchy that even casual reference to spiritual things made us bristle with antagonism. This sort of thinking had to be abandoned. Though some of us resisted, we found no great difficulty in casting aside such feelings. Faced with alcoholic destruction, we soon became as open minded on spiritual matters as we had tried to be on other questions. In this respect alcohol was a great persuader. It finally beat us into a state of reasonableness. Sometimes this was a tedious process; we hope no one else will be prejudiced for as long as some of us were.

The reader may still ask why he should believe in a Power greater than himself. We think there are good reasons. Let us have a look at some of them.

The practical individual of today is a stickler for facts and results. Nevertheless, the twentieth century readily accepts theories of all kinds, provided they are firmly grounded in fact. We have numerous theories, for example, about electricity. Everybody believes them without a murmur of doubt. Why this ready acceptance? Simply because it is impossible to explain what we see, feel, direct, and use, without a reasonable assumption as a starting point.

Everybody nowadays, believes in scores of assumptions for which there is good evidence, but no perfect visual proof. And does not science demonstrate that visual proof is the weakest proof? It is being constantly revealed, as mankind studies the material world, that outward appearances are not inward reality at all. To illustrate:

The prosaic steel girder is a mass of electrons whirling around each other at incredible speed. These tiny bodies are governed by precise laws, and these laws hold true throughout the material world. Science tells us so. We have no reason to doubt it. When, however, the perfectly logical assumption is suggested that underneath the material world and life as we see it, there is an All Powerful, Guiding, Creative Intelligence, right there our perverse streak comes to the surface and we laboriously set out to convince ourselves it isn't so. We read wordy books and indulge in windy arguments, thinking we believe this universe needs no God to explain it. Were our contentions true, it would follow that life originated out of nothing, means nothing, and proceeds nowhere.

Instead of regarding ourselves as intelligent agents, spearheads of God's ever advancing Creation, we agnostics and atheists chose to believe that our human intelligence was the last word, the alpha and the omega, the beginning and end of all. Rather vain of us, wasn't it?

We, who have traveled this dubious path, beg you to lay aside prejudice, even against organized religion. We have learned that whatever the human frailties of various faiths may be, those faiths have given purpose and direction to millions. People of faith have a logical idea of what life is all about. Actually, we used to have no reasonable conception whatever. We used to amuse ourselves by cynically dissecting spiritual beliefs and practices when we might have observed that many spiritually-minded persons of all races, colors, and creeds were demonstrating a degree of stability, happiness and usefulness which we should have sought ourselves.

Instead, we looked at the human defects of these people, and sometimes used their shortcomings as a basis of wholesale condemnation. We talked of intolerance, while we were intolerant ourselves. We missed the reality and the beauty of the forest because we were diverted by the ugliness of some of its trees. We never gave the spiritual side of life a fair hearing.

In our personal stories you will find a wide variation in the way each teller approaches and conceives of the Power which is greater than himself. Whether we agree with a particular approach or conception seems to make little difference. Experience has taught us that these are matters about which, for our purpose, we need not be worried. They are questions for each individual to settle for himself.

On one proposition, however, these men and women are strikingly agreed. Every one of them has gained access to, and believes in, a Power greater than himself. This Power has in each case accomplished the miraculous, the humanly impossible. As a celebrated American statesman put it, "Let's look at the record."

Here are thousands of men and women, worldly indeed. They flatly declare that since they have come to believe in a Power greater than themselves, to take a certain attitude toward that Power, and to do certain simple things, there has been a revolutionary change in their way of living and thinking. In the face of collapse and despair, in the face of the total failure of their human resources, they found that a new power, peace, happiness, and sense of direction flowed into them. This happened soon after they wholeheartedly met a few simple requirements. Once confused and baffled by the seeming futility of existence, they show the underlying reasons why they were making heavy going of life. Leaving aside the drink question, they tell why living was so unsatisfactory. They show how the change came over them. When many hundreds of people are able to say that the consciousness of the Presence of God is today the most important fact of their lives, they present a powerful reason why one should have faith.

This world of ours has made more material progress in the last century than in all the millenniums which went before. Almost everyone knows the reason. Students of ancient history tell us that the intellect of men in those days was equal to the best of today. Yet in ancient times material progress was painfully slow. The spirit of modern scientific inquiry, research and invention was almost unknown. In the realm of the material, men's minds were fettered by superstition, tradition, and all sorts of fixed ideas. Some of the contemporaries of Columbus thought a round earth preposterous. Others came near putting Galileo to death for his astronomical heresies.

We asked ourselves this: Are not some of us just as biased and unreasonable about the realm of the spirit as were the ancients about the realm of the material? Even in the present century, American newspapers were afraid to print an account of the Wright brothers' first successful flight at Kitty Hawk. Had not all efforts at flight failed before? Did not Professor Langley's flying machine go to the bottom of the Potomac River? Was it not true that the best mathematical minds had proved man could never fly? Had not people said God had reserved this privilege to the birds? Only thirty years later the conquest of the air was almost an old story and airplane travel was in full swing.

But in most fields our generation has witnessed complete liberation of our thinking. Show any longshoreman a Sunday supplement describing a proposal to explore the moon by means of a rocket and he will say, "I bet they do it—maybe not so long either." Is not our age characterized by the ease with which we discard old ideas for new, by the complete readiness with which we throw away the theory or gadget which does not work for something new which does?

We had to ask ourselves why we shouldn't apply to our human problems this same readiness to change our point of view. We were having trouble with personal relationships, we couldn't control our emotional natures, we were a prey to misery and depression, we couldn't make a living, we had a feeling of uselessness, we were full of fear, we were unhappy, we couldn't seem to be of real help to other people— was not a basic solution of these bedevilments more important than whether we should see newsreels of lunar flight? Of course it was.

When we saw others solve their problems by a simple reliance upon the Spirit of the Universe, we had to stop doubting the power of God. Our ideas did not work. But the God idea did.

The Wright brothers' almost childish faith that they could build a machine which would fly was the mainspring of their accomplishment. Without that, nothing could have happened. We agnostics and atheists were sticking to the idea that self-sufficiency would solve our problems. When others showed us that "God-sufficiency" worked with them, we began to feel like those who had insisted the Wrights would never fly.

Logic is great stuff. We liked it. We still like it. It is not by chance we were given the power to reason, to examine the evidence of our senses, and to draw conclusions. That is one of man's magnificent attributes. We agnostically inclined would not feel satisfied with a proposal which does not lend itself to reasonable approach and interpretation. Hence we are at pains to tell why we think our present faith is reasonable, why we think it more sane and logical to believe than not to believe, why we say our former thinking was soft and mushy when we threw up our hands in doubt and said, "We don't know."

When we became alcoholics, crushed by a self-imposed crisis we could not postpone or evade, we had to fearlessly face the proposition that either God is everything or else He is nothing. God either is, or He isn't. What was our choice to be?

Arrived at this point, we were squarely confronted with the question of faith. We couldn't duck the issue. Some of us had already walked far over the Bridge of Reason toward the desired shore of faith. The outlines and the promise of the New Land had brought lustre to tired eyes and fresh courage to flagging spirits. Friendly hands had stretched out in welcome. We were grateful that Reason had brought us so far. But somehow, we couldn't quite step ashore. Perhaps we had been leaning too heavily on Reason that last mile and we did not like to lose our support.

That was natural, but let us think a little more closely. Without knowing it, had we not been brought to where we stood by a certain kind of faith? For did we not believe in our own reasoning? Did we not have confidence in our ability to think? What was that but a sort of faith? Yes, we had been faithful, abjectly faithful to the God of Reason. So, in one way or another, we discovered that faith had been involved all the time!

We found, too, that we had been worshippers. What a state of mental goose-flesh that used to bring on! Had we not variously worshipped people, sentiment, things, money, and ourselves? And then, with a better motive, had we not worshipfully beheld the sunset, the sea, or a flower? Who of us had not loved something or somebody? How much did these feelings, these loves, these worships, have to do with pure reason? Little or nothing, we saw at last. Were not these things the tissue out of which our lives were constructed? Did not these feelings, after all, determine the course of our existence? It was impossible to say we had no capacity for faith, or love, or worship. In one form or another we had been living by faith and little else.

Imagine life without faith! Were nothing left but pure reason, it wouldn't be life. But we believed in life—of course we did. We could not prove life in the sense that you can prove a straight line is the shortest distance between two points, yet, there it was. Could we still say the whole thing was nothing but a mass of electrons, created out of nothing, meaning nothing, whirling on to a destiny of nothingness? Of course we couldn't. The electrons themselves seemed more intelligent than that. At least, so the chemist said.

Hence, we saw that reason isn't everything. Neither is reason, as most of us use it, entirely dependable, though it emanate from our best minds. What about people who proved that man could never fly?

Yet we had been seeing another kind of flight, a spiritual liberation from this world, people who rose above their problems. They said God made these things possible, and we only smiled. We had seen spiritual release, but liked to tell ourselves it wasn't true.

Actually we were fooling ourselves, for deep down in every man, woman, and child, is the fundamental idea of God. It may be obscured by calamity, by pomp, by worship of other things, but in some form or other it is there. For faith in a Power greater than ourselves, and miraculous demonstrations of that power in human lives, are facts as old as man himself.

We finally saw that faith in some kind of God was a part of our make-up, just as much as the feeling we have for a friend. Sometimes we had to search fearlessly, but He was there. He was as much a fact as we were. We found the Great Reality deep down within us. In the last analysis it is only there that He may be found. It was so with us.

We can only clear the ground a bit. If our testimony helps sweep away prejudice, enables you to think honestly, encourages you to search diligently within yourself, then, if you wish, you can join us on the Broad Highway. With this attitude you cannot fail. The consciousness of your belief is sure to come to you.

In this book you will read the experience of a man who thought he was an atheist. His story is so interesting that some of it should be told now. His change of heart was dramatic, convincing, and moving.

Our friend was a minister's son. He attended church school, where he became rebellious at what he thought an overdose of religious education. For years thereafter he was dogged by trouble and frustration. Business failure, insanity, fatal illness, suicide— these calamities in his immediate family embittered and depressed him. Post-war disillusionment, ever more serious alcoholism, impending mental and physical collapse, brought him to the point of self-destruction.

One night, when confined in a hospital, he was approached by an alcoholic who had known a spiritual experience. Our friend's gorge rose as he bitterly cried out: "If there is a God, He certainly hasn't done anything for me!" But later, alone in his room, he asked himself this question: "Is it possible that all the religious people I have known are wrong?" While pondering the answer he felt as though he lived in hell. Then, like a thunderbolt, a great thought came. It crowded out all else:

"Who are you to say there is no God?"

This man recounts that he tumbled out of bed to his knees. In a few seconds he was overwhelmed by a conviction of the Presence of God. It poured over and through him with the certainty and majesty of a great tide at flood. The barriers he had built through the years were swept away. He stood in the Presence of Infinite Power and Love. He had stepped from bridge to shore. For the first time, he lived in conscious companionship with his Creator.

Thus was our friend's cornerstone fixed in place. No later vicissitude has shaken it. His alcoholic problem was taken away. That very night, years ago, it disappeared. Save for a few brief moments of temptation the thought of drink has never returned; and at such times a great revulsion has risen up in him. Seemingly he could not drink even if he would. God had restored his sanity.

What is this but a miracle of healing? Yet its elements are simple. Circumstances made him willing to believe. He humbly offered himself to his Maker— then he knew.

Even so has God restored us all to our right minds. To this man, the revelation was sudden. Some of us grow into it more slowly. But He has come to all who have honestly sought Him.

When we drew near to Him He disclosed Himself to us!

Chapter 5

HOW IT WORKS

*R*ARELY HAVE we seen a person fail who has thoroughly followed our path. Those who do not recover are people who cannot or will not completely give themselves to this simple program, usually men and women who are constitutionally incapable of being honest with themselves. There are such unfortunates. They are not at fault; they seem to have been born that way. They are naturally incapable of grasping and developing a manner of living which demands rigorous honesty. Their chances are less than average. There are those, too, who suffer from grave emotional and mental disorders, but many of them do recover if they have the capacity to be honest.

Our stories disclose in a general way what we used to be like, what happened, and what we are like now. If you have decided you want what we have and are willing to go to any length to get it—then you are ready to take certain steps.

At some of these we balked. We thought we could find an easier, softer way. But we could not. With all the earnestness at our command, we beg of you to be fearless and thorough from the very start. Some of us have tried to hold on to our old ideas and the result was nil until we let go absolutely.

Remember that we deal with alcohol—cunning, baffling, powerful! Without help it is too much for us. But there is One who has all power—that One is God. May you find Him now!

Half measures availed us nothing. We stood at the turning point. We asked His protection and care with complete abandon.

Here are the steps we took, which are suggested as a program of recovery:

1. We admitted we were powerless over alcohol—that our lives had become unmanageable.
2. Came to believe that a Power greater than ourselves could restore us to sanity.
3. Made a decision to turn our will and our lives over to the care of God *as we understood Him.*
4. Made a searching and fearless moral inventory of ourselves.
5. Admitted to God, to ourselves, and to another human being the exact nature of our wrongs.
6. Were entirely ready to have God remove all these defects of character.
7. Humbly asked Him to remove our shortcomings.
8. Made a list of all persons we had harmed, and became willing to make amends to them all.
9. Made direct amends to such people wherever possible, except when to do so would injure them or others.
10. Continued to take personal inventory and when we were wrong promptly admitted it.
11. Sought through prayer and meditation to improve our conscious contact with God *as we understood Him,* praying only for knowledge of His will for us and the power to carry that out.

12. Having had a spiritual awakening as the result of these steps, we tried to carry this message to alcoholics, and to practice these principles in all our affairs.

Many of us exclaimed, "What an order! I can't go through with it." Do not be discouraged. No one among us has been able to maintain anything like perfect adherence to these principles. We are not saints. The point is, that we are willing to grow along spiritual lines. The principles we have set down are guides to progress. We claim spiritual progress rather than spiritual perfection.

Our description of the alcoholic, the chapter to the agnostic, and our personal adventures before and after make clear three pertinent ideas:

(a) That we were alcoholic and could not manage our own lives.
(b) That probably no human power could have relieved our alcoholism.
(c) That God could and would if He were sought.

Being convinced, *we were at Step Three*, which is that we decided to turn our will and our life over to God as we understood Him. Just what do we mean by that, and just what do we do?

The first requirement is that we be convinced that any life run on self-will can hardly be a success. On that basis we are almost always in collision with something or somebody, even though our motives are good. Most people try to live by self-propulsion. Each person is like an actor who wants to run the whole show; is forever trying to arrange the lights, the ballet, the scenery and the rest of the players in his own way. If his arrangements would only stay put, if only people would do as he wished, the show would be great. Everybody, including himself, would be pleased. Life would be wonderful. In trying to make these arrangements our actor may sometimes be quite virtuous. He may be kind, considerate, patient, generous; even modest and self-sacrificing. On the other hand, he may be mean, egotistical, selfish and dishonest. But, as with most humans, he is more likely to have varied traits.

What usually happens? The show doesn't come off very well. He begins to think life doesn't treat him right. He decides to exert himself more. He becomes, on the next occasion, still more demanding or gracious, as the case may be. Still the play does not suit him. Admitting he may be somewhat at fault, he is sure that other people are more to blame. He becomes angry, indignant, self-pitying. What is his basic trouble? Is he not really a self-seeker even when trying to be kind? Is he not a victim of the delusion that he can wrest satisfaction and happiness out of this world if he only manages well? Is it not evident to all the rest of the players that these are the things he wants? And do not his actions make each of them wish to retaliate, snatching all they can get out of the show? Is he not, even in his best moments, a producer of confusion rather than harmony?

Our actor is self-centered—ego-centric, as people like to call it nowadays. He is like the retired business man who lolls in the Florida sunshine in the winter complaining of the sad state of the nation; the minister who sighs over the sins of the twentieth century; politicians and reformers who are sure all would be Utopia if the rest of the world would only behave; the outlaw safe cracker who thinks society has wronged him; and the alcoholic who has lost all and is locked up. Whatever our protestations, are not most of us concerned with ourselves, our resentments, or our self-pity?

Selfishness—self-centeredness! That, we think, is the root of our troubles. Driven by a hundred forms of fear, self-delusion, self-seeking, and self-pity, we step on the toes of our fellows and they retaliate. Sometimes they hurt us, seemingly without provocation, but we invariably find that at some time in the past we have made decisions based on self which later placed us in a position to be hurt.

So our troubles, we think, are basically of our own making. They arise out of ourselves, and the alcoholic is an extreme example of self-will run riot, though he usually doesn't think so. Above everything, we alcoholics must be rid of this selfishness. We must, or it kills us! God makes that possible. And there often seems no way of entirely getting rid of self without His aid. Many of us had moral and philosophical convictions galore, but we could not live up to them even though we would have liked to. Neither could we reduce our self-centeredness much by wishing or trying on our own power. We had to have God's help.

This is the how and why of it. First of all, we had to quit playing God. It didn't work. Next, we decided that hereafter in this drama of life, God was going to be our Director. He is the Principal; we are His agents. He is the Father, and we are His children. Most good ideas are simple, and this concept was the keystone of the new and triumphant arch through which we passed to freedom.

When we sincerely took such a position, all sorts of remarkable things followed. We had a new Employer. Being all powerful, He provided what we needed, if we kept close to Him and performed His work well. Established on such a footing we became less and less interested in ourselves, our little plans and designs. More and more we became interested in seeing what we could contribute to life. As we felt new power flow in, as we enjoyed peace of mind, as we discovered we could face life successfully, as we became conscious of His presence, we began to lose our fear of today, tomorrow or the hereafter. We were reborn.

We were now at Step Three. Many of us said to our Maker, *as we understood Him:* "God, I offer myself to Thee—to build with me and to do with me as Thou wilt. Relieve me of the bondage of self, that I may better do Thy will. Take away my difficulties, that victory over them may bear witness to those I would help of Thy Power, Thy Love, and Thy Way of life. May I do Thy will always!" We thought well before taking this step making sure we were ready; that we could at last abandon ourselves utterly to Him.

We found it very desirable to take this spiritual step with an understanding person, such as our wife, best friend, or spiritual adviser. But it is better to meet God alone than with one who might misunderstand. The wording was, of course, quite optional so long as we expressed the idea, voicing it without reservation. This was only a beginning, though if honestly and humbly made, an effect, sometimes a very great one, was felt at once.

Next we launched out on a course of vigorous action, the first step of which is a personal housecleaning, which many of us had never attempted. Though our decision was a vital and crucial step, it could have little permanent effect unless at once followed by a strenuous effort to face, and to be rid of, the things in ourselves which had been blocking us. Our liquor was but a symptom. So we had to get down to causes and conditions.

Therefore, we started upon a personal inventory. *This was Step Four.* A business which takes no regular inventory usually goes broke. Taking a commercial inventory is a fact-finding and a fact-facing process. It is an effort to discover the truth about the stock-in-trade. One object is to disclose damaged or unsalable goods, to get rid of them promptly and without regret. If the owner of the business is to be successful, he cannot fool himself about values.

We did exactly the same thing with our lives. We took stock honestly. First, we searched out the flaws in our make-up which caused our failure. Being convinced that self, manifested in various ways, was what had defeated us, we considered its common manifestations.

Resentment is the "number one" offender. It destroys more alcoholics than anything else. From it stem all forms of spiritual disease, for we have been not only mentally and physically ill, we have been spiritually sick. When the spiritual malady is overcome, we straighten out mentally and physically. In dealing with resentments, we set them on paper. We listed people, institutions or principles with whom we were angry. We asked ourselves why we were angry. In most cases it was found that our self-esteem, our pocketbooks, our ambitions, our personal relationships (including sex) were hurt or threatened. So we were sore. We were "burned up."

On our grudge list we set opposite each name our injuries. Was it our self-esteem, our security, our ambitions, our personal, or sex relations, which had been interfered with?

We were usually as definite as this example:

I'm resentful at:	The Cause	Affects my:
Mr. Brown	His attention to my wife.	Sex relations. Self-esteem (fear)
	Told my wife of my mistress.	Sex relations. Self-esteem (fear)
	Brown may get my job at the office.	Security. Self-esteem (fear)
Mrs. Jones	She's a nut—she snubbed me. She committed her husband for drinking. He's my friend. She's a gossip.	Personal relationship. Self-esteem (fear)
My employer	Unreasonable—Unjust — Overbearing — Threatens to fire me for drinking and padding my expense account.	Self-esteem (fear) Security.
My wife	Misunderstands and nags. Likes Brown. Wants house put in her name.	Pride—Personal sex relations— Security (fear)

We went back through our lives. Nothing counted but thoroughness and honesty. When we were finished we considered it carefully. The first thing apparent was that this world and its people were often quite wrong. To conclude that others were wrong was as far as most of us ever got. The usual outcome was that people continued to wrong us and we stayed sore. Sometimes it was remorse and then we were sore at ourselves. But the more we fought and tried to have our own way, the worse matters got. As in war, the victor only *seemed* to win. Our moments of triumph were short-lived.

It is plain that a life which includes deep resentment leads only to futility and unhappiness. To the precise extent that we permit these, do we squander the hours that might have been worth while. But with the alcoholic, whose hope is the maintenance and growth of a spiritual experience, this business of resentment is infinitely grave. We found that it is fatal. For when harboring such feelings we shut ourselves off from the sunlight of the Spirit. The insanity of alcohol returns and we drink again. And with us, to drink is to die.

If we were to live, we had to be free of anger. The grouch and the brainstorm were not for us. They may be the dubious luxury of normal men, but for alcoholics these things are poison.

We turned back to the list, for it held the key to the future. We were prepared to look at it from an entirely different angle. We began to see that the world and its people really dominated us. In that state, the wrong-doing of others, fancied or real, had power to actually kill. How could we escape? We saw that these resentments must be mastered, but how? We could not wish them away any more than alcohol.

This was our course: We realized that the people who wronged us were perhaps spiritually sick.

Though we did not like their symptoms and the way these disturbed us, they, like ourselves, were sick too. We asked God to help us show them the same tolerance, pity, and patience that we would cheerfully grant a sick friend. When a person offended we said to ourselves, "This is a sick man. How can I be helpful to him? God save me from being angry. Thy will be done."

We avoid retaliation or argument. We wouldn't treat sick people that way. If we do, we destroy our chance of being helpful. We cannot be helpful to all people, but at least God will show us how to take a kindly and tolerant view of each and every one.

Referring to our list again. Putting out of our minds the wrongs others had done, we resolutely looked for our own mistakes. Where had we been selfish, dishonest, self-seeking and frightened? Though a situation had not been entirely our fault, we tried to disregard the other person involved entirely. Where were we to blame? The inventory was ours, not the other man's. When we saw our faults we listed them. We placed them before us in black and white. We admitted our wrongs honestly and were willing to set these matters straight.

Notice that the word "fear" is bracketed alongside the difficulties with Mr. Brown, Mrs. Jones, the employer, and the wife. This short word somehow touches about every aspect of our lives. It was an evil and corroding thread; the fabric of our existence was shot through with it. It set in motion trains of circumstances which brought us misfortune we felt we didn't deserve. But did not we, ourselves, set the ball rolling? Sometimes we think fear ought to be classed with stealing. It seems to cause more trouble.

We reviewed our fears thoroughly. We put them on paper, even though we had no resentment in connection with them. We asked ourselves why we had them. Wasn't it because self-reliance failed us? Self-reliance was good as far as it went, but it didn't go far enough. Some of us once had great self-confidence, but it didn't fully solve the fear problem, or any other. When it made us cocky, it was worse.

Perhaps there is a better way—we think so. For we are now on a different basis; the basis of trusting and relying upon God. We trust infinite God rather than our finite selves. We are in the world to play the role He assigns. Just to the extent that we do as we think He would have us, and humbly rely on Him, does He enable us to match calamity with serenity.

We never apologize to anyone for depending upon our Creator. We can laugh at those who think spirituality the way of weakness. Paradoxically, it is the way of strength. The verdict of the ages is that faith means courage. All men of faith have courage. They trust their God. We never apologize for God. Instead we let Him demonstrate, through us, what He can do. We ask Him to remove our fear and direct our attention to what He would have us be. At once, we commence to outgrow fear.

Now about sex. Many of us needed an overhauling there. But above all, we tried to be sensible on this question. It's so easy to get way off the track. Here we find human opinions running to extremes—absurd extremes, perhaps. One set of voices cry that sex is a lust of our lower nature, a base necessity of procreation. Then we have the voices who cry for sex and more sex; who bewail the institution of marriage; who think that most of the troubles of the race are traceable to sex causes. They think we do not have enough of it, or that it isn't the right kind. They see its significance everywhere. One school would allow man no flavor for his fare and the other would have us all on a straight pepper diet. We want to stay out of this controversy. We do not want to be the arbiter of anyone's sex conduct. We all have sex problems. We'd hardly be human if we didn't. What can we do about them?

We reviewed our own conduct over the years past. Where had we been selfish, dishonest, or inconsiderate? Whom had we hurt? Did we unjustifiably arouse jealousy, suspicion or bitterness? Where were we at fault, what should we have done instead? We got this all down on paper and looked at it.

In this way we tried to shape a sane and sound ideal for our future sex life. We subjected each relation to this test—was it selfish or not? We asked God to mold our ideals and help us to live up to them. We remembered always that our sex powers were God-given and therefore good, neither to be used lightly or selfishly nor to be despised and loathed.

Whatever our ideal turns out to be, we must be willing to grow toward it. We must be willing to make amends where we have done harm, provided that we do not bring about still more harm in so doing. In other words, we treat sex as we would any other problem. In meditation, we ask God what we should do about each specific matter. The right answer will come, if we want it.

God alone can judge our sex situation. Counsel with

persons is often desirable, but we let God be the final judge. We realize that some people are as fanatical about sex as others are loose. We avoid hysterical thinking or advice.

Suppose we fall short of the chosen ideal and stumble? Does this mean we are going to get drunk? Some people tell us so. But this is only a half-truth. It depends on us and on our motives. If we are sorry for what we have done, and have the honest desire to let God take us to better things, we believe we will be forgiven and will have learned our lesson. If we are not sorry, and our conduct continues to harm others, we are quite sure to drink. We are not theorizing. These are facts out of our experience.

To sum up about sex: We earnestly pray for the right ideal, for guidance in each questionable situation, for sanity, and for the strength to do the right thing. If sex is very troublesome, we throw ourselves the harder into helping others. We think of their needs and work for them. This takes us out of ourselves. It quiets the imperious urge, when to yield would mean heartache.

If we have been thorough about our personal inventory, we have written down a lot. We have listed and analyzed our resentments. We have begun to comprehend their futility and their fatality. We have commenced to see their terrible destructiveness. We have begun to learn tolerance, patience and good will toward all men, even our enemies, for we look on them as sick people. We have listed the people we have hurt by our conduct, and are willing to straighten out the past if we can.

In this book you read again and again that faith did

for us what we could not do for ourselves. We hope you are convinced now that God can remove whatever self-will has blocked you off from Him. If you have already made a decision, and an inventory of your grosser handicaps, you have made a good beginning. That being so you have swallowed and digested some big chunks of truth about yourself.

Chapter 6

INTO ACTION

*H*AVING MADE our personal inventory, what shall we do about it? We have been trying to get a new attitude, a new relationship with our Creator, and to discover the obstacles in our path. We have admitted certain defects; we have ascertained in a rough way what the trouble is; we have put our finger on the weak items in our personal inventory. Now these are about to be cast out. This requires action on our part, which, when completed, will mean that we have admitted to God, to ourselves, and to another human being, the exact nature of our defects. This brings us to *the Fifth Step* in the program of recovery mentioned in the preceding chapter.

This is perhaps difficult—especially discussing our defects with another person. We think we have done well enough in admitting these things to ourselves. There is doubt about that. In actual practice, we usually find a solitary self-appraisal insufficient. Many of us thought it necessary to go much further. We will be more reconciled to discussing ourselves with another person when we see good reasons why we should do so. The best reason first: If we skip this vital step, we may not overcome drinking. Time after time newcomers have tried to keep to themselves certain facts about their lives. Trying to avoid this humbling experience, they have turned to easier methods. Almost invariably they got drunk. Having persevered with the rest of the program, they wondered why they fell. We think the reason is that they never completed their housecleaning. They took inventory all right, but hung on to some of the worst items in stock. They only *thought* they had lost their egoism and fear; they only *thought* they had humbled themselves. But they had not learned enough of humility, fearlessness and honesty, in the sense we find it necessary, until they told someone else *all* their life story.

More than most people, the alcoholic leads a double life. He is very much the actor. To the outer world he presents his stage character. This is the one he likes his fellows to see. He wants to enjoy a certain reputation, but knows in his heart he doesn't deserve it.

The inconsistency is made worse by the things he does on his sprees. Coming to his senses, he is revolted at certain episodes he vaguely remembers. These memories are a nightmare. He trembles to think someone might have observed him. As fast as he can, he pushes these memories far inside himself. He hopes they will never see the light of day. He is under constant fear and tension—that makes for more drinking.

Psychologists are inclined to agree with us. We have spent thousands of dollars for examinations. We know but few instances where we have given these doctors a fair break. We have seldom told them the whole truth nor have we followed their advice. Unwilling to be honest with these sympathetic men, we were honest with no one else. Small wonder many in the medical profession have a low opinion of alcoholics and their chance for recovery!

We must be entirely honest with somebody if we

expect to live long or happily in this world. Rightly and naturally, we think well before we choose the person or persons with whom to take this intimate and confidential step. Those of us belonging to a religious denomination which requires confession must, and of course, will want to go to the properly appointed authority whose duty it is to receive it. Though we have no religious connection, we may still do well to talk with someone ordained by an established religion. We often find such a person quick to see and understand our problem. Of course, we sometimes encounter people who do not understand alcoholics.

If we cannot or would rather not do this, we search our acquaintance for a close-mouthed, understanding friend. Perhaps our doctor or psychologist will be the person. It may be one of our own family, but we cannot disclose anything to our wives or our parents which will hurt them and make them unhappy. We have no right to save our own skin at another person's expense. Such parts of our story we tell to someone who will understand, yet be unaffected. The rule is we must be hard on ourself, but always considerate of others.

Notwithstanding the great necessity for discussing ourselves with someone, it may be one is so situated that there is no suitable person available. If that is so, this step may be postponed, only, however, if we hold ourselves in complete readiness to go through with it at the first opportunity. We say this because we are very anxious that we talk to the right person. It is important that he be able to keep a confidence; that he fully understand and approve what we are driving at;

that he will not try to change our plan. But we must not use this as a mere excuse to postpone.

When we decide who is to hear our story, we waste no time. We have a written inventory and we are prepared for a long talk. We explain to our partner what we are about to do and why we have to do it. He should realize that we are engaged upon a life-and-death errand. Most people approached in this way will be glad to help; they will be honored by our confidence.

We pocket our pride and go to it, illuminating every twist of character, every dark cranny of the past. Once we have taken this step, withholding nothing, we are delighted. We can look the world in the eye. We can be alone at perfect peace and ease. Our fears fall from us. We begin to feel the nearness of our Creator. We may have had certain spiritual beliefs, but now we begin to have a spiritual experience. The feeling that the drink problem has disappeared will often come strongly. We feel we are on the Broad Highway, walking hand in hand with the Spirit of the Universe.

Returning home we find a place where we can be quiet for an hour, carefully reviewing what we have done. We thank God from the bottom of our heart that we know Him better. Taking this book down from our shelf we turn to the page which contains the twelve steps. Carefully reading the first five proposals we ask if we have omitted anything, for we are building an arch through which we shall walk a free man at last. Is our work solid so far? Are the stones properly in place? Have we skimped on the cement put into the foundation? Have we tried to make mortar without sand?

If we can answer to our satisfaction, we then look at *Step Six*. We have emphasized willingness as being indispensable. Are we now ready to let God remove from us all the things which we have admitted are objectionable? Can He now take them all—every one? If we still cling to something we will not let go, we ask God to help us be willing.

When ready, we say something like this: "My Creator, I am now willing that you should have all of me, good and bad. I pray that you now remove from me every single defect of character which stands in the way of my usefulness to you and my fellows. Grant me strength, as I go out from here, to do your bidding. Amen." We have then completed *Step Seven*.

Now we need more action, without which we find that "Faith without works is dead." Let's look at *Steps Eight and Nine*. We have a list of all persons we have harmed and to whom we are willing to make amends. We made it when we took inventory. We subjected ourselves to a drastic self-appraisal. Now we go out to our fellows and repair the damage done in the past. We attempt to sweep away the debris which has accumulated out of our effort to live on self-will and run the show ourselves. If we haven't the will to do this, we ask until it comes. Remember it was agreed at the beginning *we would go to any lengths for victory over alcohol.*

Probably there are still some misgivings. As we look over the list of business acquaintances and friends we have hurt, we may feel diffident about going to some of them on a spiritual basis. Let us be reassured. To some people we need not, and probably should not emphasize the spiritual feature on our first approach.

We might prejudice them. At the moment we are trying to put our lives in order. But this is not an end in itself. Our real purpose is to fit ourselves to be of maximum service to God and the people about us. It is seldom wise to approach an individual, who still smarts from our injustice to him, and announce that we have gone religious. In the prize ring, this would be called leading with the chin. Why lay ourselves open to being branded fanatics or religious bores? We may kill a future opportunity to carry a beneficial message. But our man is sure to be impressed with a sincere desire to set right the wrong. He is going to be more interested in a demonstration of good will than in our talk of spiritual discoveries.

We don't use this as an excuse for shying away from the subject of God. When it will serve any good purpose, we are willing to announce our convictions with tact and common sense. The question of how to approach the man we hated will arise. It may be he has done us more harm than we have done him and, though we may have acquired a better attitude toward him, we are still not too keen about admitting our faults. Nevertheless, with a person we dislike, we take the bit in our teeth. It is harder to go to an enemy than to a friend, but we find it much more beneficial to us. We go to him in a helpful and forgiving spirit, confessing our former ill feeling and expressing our regret.

Under no condition do we criticize such a person or argue. Simply we tell him that we will never get over drinking until we have done our utmost to straighten out the past. We are there to sweep off our side of the street, realizing that nothing worth while can be accomplished until we do so, never trying to tell him what he should do. His faults are not discussed. We stick to our own. If our manner is calm, frank, and open, we will be gratified with the result.

In nine cases out of ten the unexpected happens. Sometimes the man we are calling upon admits his own fault, so feuds of years' standing melt away in an hour. Rarely do we fail to make satisfactory progress. Our former enemies sometimes praise what we are doing and wish us well. Occasionally, they will offer assistance. It should not matter, however, if someone does throw us out of his office. We have made our demonstration, done our part. It's water over the dam.

Most alcoholics owe money. We do not dodge our creditors. Telling them what we are trying to do, we make no bones about our drinking; they usually know it anyway, whether we think so or not. Nor are we afraid of disclosing our alcoholism on the theory it may cause financial harm. Approached in this way, the most ruthless creditor will sometimes surprise us. Arranging the best deal we can we let these people know we are sorry. Our drinking has made us slow to pay. We must lose our fear of creditors no matter how far we have to go, for we are liable to drink if we are afraid to face them.

Perhaps we have committed a criminal offense which might land us in jail if it were known to the authorities. We may be short in our accounts and unable to make good. We have already admitted this in confidence to another person, but we are sure we would be imprisoned or lose our job if it were known. Maybe it's only a petty offense such as padding the expense account. Most of us have done that sort of thing.

Maybe we are divorced, and have remarried but haven't kept up the alimony to number one. She is indignant about it, and has a warrant out for our arrest. That's a common form of trouble too.

Although these reparations take innumerable forms, there are some general principles which we find guiding. Reminding ourselves that we have decided to go to any lengths to find a spiritual experience, we ask that we be given strength and direction to do the right thing, no matter what the personal consequences may be. We may lose our position or reputation or face jail, but we are willing. We have to be. We must not shrink at anything.

Usually, however, other people are involved. Therefore, we are not to be the hasty and foolish martyr who would needlessly sacrifice others to save himself from the alcoholic pit. A man we know had remarried. Because of resentment and drinking, he had not paid alimony to his first wife. She was furious. She went to court and got an order for his arrest. He had commenced our way of life, had secured a position, and was getting his head above water. It would have been impressive heroics if he had walked up to the Judge and said, "Here I am."

We thought he ought to be willing to do that if necessary, but if he were in jail he could provide nothing for either family. We suggested he write his first wife admitting his faults and asking forgiveness. He did, and also sent a small amount of money. He told her what he would try to do in the future. He said he was perfectly willing to go to jail if she insisted. Of course she did not, and the whole situation has long since been adjusted.

Before taking drastic action which might implicate other people we secure their consent. If we have obtained permission, have consulted with others, asked God to help and the drastic step is indicated we must not shrink.

This brings to mind a story about one of our friends. While drinking, he accepted a sum of money from a bitterly-hated business rival, giving him no receipt for it. He subsequently denied having received the money and used the incident as a basis for discrediting the man. He thus used his own wrong-doing as a means of destroying the reputation of another. In fact, his rival was ruined.

He felt that he had done a wrong he could not possibly make right. If he opened that old affair, he was afraid it would destroy the reputation of his partner, disgrace his family and take away his means of livelihood. What right had he to involve those dependent upon him? How could he possibly make a public statement exonerating his rival?

After consulting with his wife and partner he came to the conclusion that it was better to take those risks than to stand before his Creator guilty of such ruinous slander. He saw that he had to place the outcome in God's hands or he would soon start drinking again, and all would be lost anyhow. He attended church for the first time in many years. After the sermon, he quietly got up and made an explanation. His action met widespread approval, and today he is one of the most trusted citizens of his town. This all happened years ago.

The chances are that we have domestic troubles. Perhaps we are mixed up with women in a fashion we wouldn't care to have advertised. We doubt if, in this respect, alcoholics are fundamentally much worse than other people. But drinking does complicate sex relations in the home. After a few years with an alcoholic, a wife gets worn out, resentful and uncommunicative. How could she be anything else? The husband begins to feel lonely, sorry for himself. He commences to look around in the night clubs, or their equivalent, for something besides liquor. Perhaps he is having a secret and exciting affair with "the girl who understands." In fairness we must say that she may understand, but what are we going to do about a thing like that? A man so involved often feels very remorseful at times, especially if he is married to a loyal and courageous girl who has literally gone through hell for him.

Whatever the situation, we usually have to do something about it. If we are sure our wife does not know, should we tell her? Not always, we think. If she knows in a general way that we have been wild, should we tell her in detail? Undoubtedly we should admit our fault. She may insist on knowing all the particulars. She will want to know who the woman is and where she is. We feel we ought to say to her that we have no right to involve another person. We are sorry for what we have done and, God willing, it shall not be repeated. More than that we cannot do; we have no right to go further. Though there may be justifiable exceptions, and though we wish to lay down no rule of any sort, we have often found this the best course to take.

Our design for living is not a one-way street. It is as good for the wife as for the husband. If we can forget, so can she. It is better, however, that one does not needlessly name a person upon whom she can vent jealousy.

Perhaps there are some cases where the utmost frankness is demanded. No outsider can appraise such an intimate situation. It may be that both will decide that the way of good sense and loving kindness is to let by-gones be by-gones. Each might pray about it, having the other one's happiness uppermost in mind. Keep it always in sight that we are dealing with that most terrible human emotion—jealousy. Good general-ship may decide that the problem be attacked on the flank rather than risk a face-to-face combat.

If we have no such complication, there is plenty we should do at home. Sometimes we hear an alcoholic say that the only thing he needs to do is to keep sober. Certainly he must keep sober, for there will be no home if he doesn't. But he is yet a long way from making good to the wife or parents whom for years he has so shockingly treated. Passing all understand-ing is the patience mothers and wives have had with alcoholics. Had this not been so, many of us would have no homes today, would perhaps be dead.

The alcoholic is like a tornado roaring his way through the lives of others. Hearts are broken. Sweet relationships are dead. Affections have been uprooted. Selfish and inconsiderate habits have kept the home in turmoil. We feel a man is unthinking when he says that sobriety is enough. He is like the farmer who came up out of his cyclone cellar to find his home ruined. To his wife, he remarked, "Don't see anything the matter here, Ma. Ain't it grand the wind stopped blowin'?"

Yes, there is a long period of reconstruction ahead. We must take the lead. A remorseful mumbling that we are sorry won't fill the bill at all. We ought to sit down with the family and frankly analyze the past as we now see it, being very careful not to criticize them. Their defects may be glaring, but the chances are that our own actions are partly responsible. So we clean house with the family, asking each morning in meditation that our Creator show us the way of patience, tolerance, kindliness and love.

The spiritual life is not a theory. *We have to live it.* Unless one's family expresses a desire to live upon spiritual principles we think we ought not to urge them. We should not talk incessantly to them about spiritual matters. They will change in time. Our behavior will convince them more than our words. We must remember that ten or twenty years of drunkenness would make a skeptic out of anyone.

There may be some wrongs we can never fully right. We don't worry about them if we can honestly say to ourselves that we would right them if we could. Some people cannot be seen—we send them an honest letter. And there may be a valid reason for postponement in some cases. But we don't delay if it can be avoided. We should be sensible, tactful, considerate and humble without being servile or scraping. As God's people we stand on our feet; we don't crawl before anyone.

If we are painstaking about this phase of our development, we will be amazed before we are half way through. We are going to know a new freedom and a new happiness. We will not regret the past nor wish to shut the door on it. We will comprehend the word serenity and we will know peace. No matter how far down the scale we have gone, we will see how our experience can benefit others. That feeling of uselessness and self-pity will disappear. We will lose interest in selfish things and gain interest in our fellows. Self-seeking will slip away. Our whole attitude and outlook upon life will change. Fear of people and of economic insecurity will leave us. We will intuitively know how to handle situations which used to baffle us. We will suddenly realize that God is doing for us what we could not do for ourselves.

Are these extravagant promises? We think not. They are being fulfilled among us—sometimes quickly, sometimes slowly. They will always materialize if we work for them.

This thought brings us to *Step Ten,* which suggests we continue to take personal inventory and continue to set right any new mistakes as we go along. We vigorously commenced this way of living as we cleaned up the past. We have entered the world of the Spirit. Our next function is to grow in understanding and effectiveness. This is not an overnight matter. It should continue for our lifetime. Continue to watch for selfishness, dishonesty, resentment, and fear. When these crop up, we ask God at once to remove them. We discuss them with someone immediately and make amends quickly if we have harmed anyone. Then we resolutely turn our thoughts to someone we can help. Love and tolerance of others is our code.

And we have ceased fighting anything or anyone— even alcohol. For by this time sanity will have returned. We will seldom be interested in liquor. If tempted, we recoil from it as from a hot flame. We react sanely and normally, and we will find that this has happened automatically. We will see that our new attitude toward liquor has been given us without any thought or effort on our part. It just comes! That is the miracle of it. We are not fighting it, neither are we avoiding temptation. We feel as though we had been placed in a position of neutrality—safe and protected. We have not even sworn off. Instead, the problem has been removed. It does not exist for us. We are neither cocky nor are we afraid. That is our experience. That is how we react so long as we keep in fit spiritual condition.

It is easy to let up on the spiritual program of action and rest on our laurels. We are headed for trouble if we do, for alcohol is a subtle foe. We are not cured of alcoholism. What we really have is a daily reprieve contingent on the maintenance of our spiritual condition. Every day is a day when we must carry the vision of God's will into all of our activities. "How can I best serve Thee—Thy will (not mine) be done." These are thoughts which must go with us constantly. We can exercise our will power along this line all we wish. It is the proper use of the will.

Much has already been said about receiving strength, inspiration, and direction from Him who has all knowledge and power. If we have carefully followed directions, we have begun to sense the flow of His Spirit into us. To some extent we have become God-conscious. We have begun to develop this vital sixth sense. But we must go further and that means more action.

Step Eleven suggests prayer and meditation. We shouldn't be shy on this matter of prayer. Better men than we are using it constantly. It works, if we have the proper attitude and work at it. It would be easy to be vague about this matter. Yet, we believe we can make some definite and valuable suggestions.

When we retire at night, we constructively review our day. Were we resentful, selfish, dishonest or afraid? Do we owe an apology? Have we kept something to ourselves which should be discussed with another person at once? Were we kind and loving toward all? What could we have done better? Were we thinking of ourselves most of the time? Or were we thinking of what we could do for others, of what we could pack into the stream of life? But we must be careful not to drift into worry, remorse or morbid reflection, for that would diminish our usefulness to others. After making our review we ask God's forgiveness and inquire what corrective measures should be taken.

On awakening let us think about the twenty-four hours ahead. We consider our plans for the day. Before we begin, we ask God to direct our thinking, especially asking that it be divorced from self-pity, dishonest or self-seeking motives. Under these conditions we can employ our mental faculties with assurance, for after all God gave us brains to use. Our thought-life will be placed on a much higher plane when our thinking is cleared of wrong motives.

In thinking about our day we may face indecision. We may not be able to determine which course to take. Here we ask God for inspiration, an intuitive thought or a decision. We relax and take it easy. We don't struggle. We are often surprised how the right answers come after we have tried this for a while.

What used to be the hunch or the occasional inspiration gradually becomes a working part of the mind. Being still inexperienced and having just made conscious contact with God, it is not probable that we are going to be inspired at all times. We might pay for this presumption in all sorts of absurd actions and ideas. Nevertheless, we find that our thinking will, as time passes, be more and more on the plane of inspiration. We come to rely upon it.

We usually conclude the period of meditation with a prayer that we be shown all through the day what our next step is to be, that we be given whatever we need to take care of such problems. We ask especially for freedom from self-will, and are careful to make no request for ourselves only. We may ask for ourselves, however, if others will be helped. We are careful never to pray for our own selfish ends. Many of us have wasted a lot of time doing that and it doesn't work. You can easily see why.

If circumstances warrant, we ask our wives or friends to join us in morning meditation. If we belong to a religious denomination which requires a definite morning devotion, we attend to that also. If not members of religious bodies, we sometimes select and memorize a few set prayers which emphasize the principles we have been discussing. There are many helpful books also. Suggestions about these may be obtained from one's priest, minister, or rabbi. Be quick to see where religious people are right. Make use of what they offer.

As we go through the day we pause, when agitated or doubtful, and ask for the right thought or action. We constantly remind ourselves we are no longer running the show, humbly saying to ourselves many times each day "Thy will be done." We are then in much less danger of excitement, fear, anger, worry, self-pity, or foolish decisions. We become much more efficient. We do not tire so easily, for we are not burning up energy foolishly as we did when we were trying to arrange life to suit ourselves.

It works—it really does.

We alcoholics are undisciplined. So we let God discipline us in the simple way we have just outlined.

But this is not all. There is action and more action. "Faith without works is dead." The next chapter is entirely devoted to *Step Twelve*.

Chapter 7

WORKING WITH OTHERS

*P*RACTICAL EXPERIENCE shows that nothing will so much insure immunity from drinking as intensive work with other alcoholics. It works when other activities fail. This is our *twelfth suggestion:* Carry this message to other alcoholics! You can help when no one else can. You can secure their confidence when others fail. Remember they are very ill.

Life will take on new meaning. To watch people recover, to see them help others, to watch loneliness vanish, to see a fellowship grow up about you, to have a host of friends—this is an experience you must not miss. We know you will not want to miss it. Frequent contact with newcomers and with each other is the bright spot of our lives.

Perhaps you are not acquainted with any drinkers who want to recover. You can easily find some by asking a few doctors, ministers, priests or hospitals. They will be only too glad to assist you. Don't start out as an evangelist or reformer. Unfortunately a lot of prejudice exists. You will be handicapped if you arouse it. Ministers and doctors are competent and you can learn much from them if you wish, but it happens that because of your own drinking experience you can be uniquely useful to other alcoholics. So cooperate; never criticize. To be helpful is our only aim.

When you discover a prospect for Alcoholics Anonymous, find out all you can about him. If he does not want to stop drinking, don't waste time trying to persuade him. You may spoil a later opportunity. This advice is given for his family also. They should be patient, realizing they are dealing with a sick person.

If there is any indication that he wants to stop, have a good talk with the person most interested in him— usually his wife. Get an idea of his behavior, his problems, his background, the seriousness of his condition, and his religious leanings. You need this information to put yourself in his place, to see how you would like him to approach you if the tables were turned.

Sometimes it is wise to wait till he goes on a binge. The family may object to this, but unless he is in a dangerous physical condition, it is better to risk it. Don't deal with him when he is very drunk, unless he is ugly and the family needs your help. Wait for the end of the spree, or at least for a lucid interval. Then let his family or a friend ask him if he wants to quit for good and if he would go to any extreme to do so. If he says yes, then his attention should be drawn to you as a person who has recovered. You should be described to him as one of a fellowship who, as part of their own recovery, try to help others and who will be glad to talk to him if he cares to see you.

If he does not want to see you, never force yourself upon him. Neither should the family hysterically plead with him to do anything, nor should they tell him much about you. They should wait for the end of his next drinking bout. You might place this book where he can see it in the interval. Here no specific rule can be given. The family must decide these things. But urge them not to be over-anxious, for that might spoil matters.

Usually the family should not try to tell your story. When possible, avoid meeting a man through his family. Approach through a doctor or an institution is a better bet. If your man needs hospitalization, he should have it, but not forcibly unless he is violent. Let the doctor, if he will, tell him he has something in the way of a solution.

When your man is better, the doctor might suggest a visit from you. Though you have talked with the family, leave them out of the first discussion. Under these conditions your prospect will see he is under no pressure. He will feel he can deal with you without being nagged by his family. Call on him while he is still jittery. He may be more receptive when depressed.

See your man alone, if possible. At first engage in general conversation. After a while, turn the talk to some phase of drinking. Tell him enough about your drinking habits, symptoms, and experiences to encourage him to speak of himself. If he wishes to talk, let him do so. You will thus get a better idea of how you ought to proceed. If he is not communicative, give him a sketch of your drinking career up to the time you quit. But say nothing, for the moment, of how that was accomplished. If he is in a serious mood dwell on the troubles liquor has caused you, being careful not to moralize or lecture. If his mood is light, tell him humorous stories of your escapades. Get him to tell some of his.

When he sees you know all about the drinking game, commence to describe yourself as an alcoholic.

Tell him how baffled you were, how you finally learned that you were sick. Give him an account of the struggles you made to stop. Show him the mental twist which leads to the first drink of a spree. We suggest you do this as we have done it in the chapter on alcoholism. If he is alcoholic, he will understand you at once. He will match your mental inconsistencies with some of his own.

If you are satisfied that he is a real alcoholic, begin to dwell on the hopeless feature of the malady. Show him, from your own experience, how the queer mental condition surrounding that first drink prevents normal functioning of the will power. Don't, at this stage, refer to this book, unless he has seen it and wishes to discuss it. And be careful not to brand him as an alcoholic. Let him draw his own conclusion. If he sticks to the idea that he can still control his drinking, tell him that possibly he can—if he is not too alcoholic. But insist that if he is severely afflicted, there may be little chance he can recover by himself.

Continue to speak of alcoholism as an illness, a fatal malady. Talk about the conditions of body and mind which accompany it. Keep his attention focussed mainly on your personal experience. Explain that many are doomed who never realize their predicament. Doctors are rightly loath to tell alcoholic patients the whole story unless it will serve some good purpose. But you may talk to him about the hopelessness of alcoholism because you offer a solution. You will soon have your friend admitting he has many, if not all, of the traits of the alcoholic. If his own doctor is willing to tell him that he is alcoholic, so much the better. Even though your protégé may not have entirely admitted his condition, he has become very curious to know how you got well. Let him ask you that question, if he will. *Tell him exactly what happened to you.* Stress the spiritual feature freely. If the man be agnostic or atheist, make it emphatic that *he does not have to agree with your conception of God.* He can choose any conception he likes, provided it makes sense to him. *The main thing is that he be willing to believe in a Power greater than himself and that he live by spiritual principles.*

When dealing with such a person, you had better use everyday language to describe spiritual principles. There is no use arousing any prejudice he may have against certain theological terms and conceptions about which he may already be confused. Don't raise such issues, no matter what your own convictions are.

Your prospect may belong to a religious denomination. His religious education and training may be far superior to yours. In that case he is going to wonder how you can add anything to what he already knows. But he will be curious to learn why his own convictions have not worked and why yours seem to work so well. He may be an example of the truth that faith alone is insufficient. To be vital, faith must be accompanied by self sacrifice and unselfish, constructive action. Let him see that you are not there to instruct him in religion. Admit that he probably knows more about it than you do, but call to his attention the fact that however deep his faith and knowledge, he could not have applied it or he would not drink. Perhaps your story will help him see where he has failed to practice the very precepts he knows so well. We represent no particular faith or denomination. We are dealing only with general principles common to most denominations.

Outline the program of action, explaining how you made a self-appraisal, how you straightened out your past and why you are now endeavoring to be helpful to him. It is important for him to realize that your attempt to pass this on to him plays a vital part in your own recovery. Actually, he may be helping you more than you are helping him. Make it plain he is under no obligation to you, that you hope only that he will try to help other alcoholics when he escapes his own difficulties. Suggest how important it is that he place the welfare of other people ahead of his own. Make it clear that he is not under pressure, that he needn't see you again if he doesn't want to. You should not be offended if he wants to call it off, for he has helped you more than you have helped him. If your talk has been sane, quiet and full of human understanding, you have perhaps made a friend. Maybe you have disturbed him about the question of alcoholism. This is all to the good. The more hopeless he feels, the better. He will be more likely to follow your suggestions.

Your candidate may give reasons why he need not follow all of the program. He may rebel at the thought of a drastic housecleaning which requires discussion with other people. Do not contradict such views. Tell him you once felt as he does, but you doubt whether you would have made much progress had you not taken action. On your first visit tell him about the Fellowship of Alcoholics Anonymous. If he shows interest, lend him your copy of this book.

Unless your friend wants to talk further about himself, do not wear out your welcome. Give him a chance to think it over. If you do stay, let him steer the conversation in any direction he likes. Sometimes a new man is anxious to proceed at once, and you may be tempted to let him do so. This is sometimes a mistake. If he has trouble later, he is likely to say you rushed him. You will be most successful with alcoholics if you do not exhibit any passion for crusade or reform. Never talk down to an alcoholic from any moral or spiritual hilltop; simply lay out the kit of spiritual tools for his inspection. Show him how they worked with you. Offer him friendship and fellowship. Tell him that if he wants to get well you will do anything to help.

If he is not interested in your solution, if he expects you to act only as a banker for his financial difficulties or a nurse for his sprees, you may have to drop him until he changes his mind. This he may do after he gets hurt some more.

If he is sincerely interested and wants to see you again, ask him to read this book in the interval. After doing that, he must decide for himself whether he wants to go on. He should not be pushed or prodded by you, his wife, or his friends. If he is to find God, the desire must come from within.

If he thinks he can do the job in some other way, or prefers some other spiritual approach, encourage him to follow his own conscience. We have no monopoly on God; we merely have an approach that worked with us. But point out that we alcoholics have much in common and that you would like, in any case, to be friendly. Let it go at that.

Do not be discouraged if your prospect does not respond at once. Search out another alcoholic and try again. You are sure to find someone desperate enough to accept with eagerness what you offer. We find it a waste of time to keep chasing a man who cannot or will not work with you. If you leave such a person alone, he may soon become convinced that he cannot recover by himself. To spend too much time on any one situation is to deny some other alcoholic an opportunity to live and be happy. One of our Fellowship failed entirely with his first half dozen prospects. He often says that if he had continued to work on them, he might have deprived many others, who have since recovered, of their chance.

Suppose now you are making your second visit to a man. He has read this volume and says he is prepared to go through with the Twelve Steps of the program of recovery. Having had the experience yourself, you can give him much practical advice. Let him know you are available if he wishes to make a decision and tell his story, but do not insist upon it if he prefers to consult someone else.

He may be broke and homeless. If he is, you might try to help him about getting a job, or give him a little financial assistance. But you should not deprive your family or creditors of money they should have. Perhaps you will want to take the man into your home for a few days. But be sure you use discretion. Be certain he will be welcomed by your family, and that he is not trying to impose upon you for money, connections, or shelter. Permit that and you only harm him. You will be making it possible for him to be insincere.

You may be aiding in his destruction rather than his recovery.

Never avoid these responsibilities, but be sure you are doing the right thing if you assume them. Helping others is the foundation stone of your recovery. A kindly act once in a while isn't enough. You have to act the Good Samaritan every day, if need be. It may mean the loss of many nights' sleep, great interference with your pleasures, interruptions to your business. It may mean sharing your money and your home, counseling frantic wives and relatives, innumerable trips to police courts, sanitariums, hospitals, jails and asylums. Your telephone may jangle at any time of the day or night. Your wife may sometimes say she is neglected. A drunk may smash the furniture in your home, or burn a mattress. You may have to fight with him if he is violent. Sometimes you will have to call a doctor and administer sedatives under his direction. Another time you may have to send for the police or an ambulance. Occasionally you will have to meet such conditions.

We seldom allow an alcoholic to live in our homes for long at a time. It is not good for him, and it sometimes creates serious complications in a family.

Though an alcoholic does not respond, there is no reason why you should neglect his family. You should continue to be friendly to them. The family should be offered your way of life. Should they accept and practice spiritual principles, there is a much better chance that the head of the family will recover. And even though he continues to drink, the family will find life more bearable.

For the type of alcoholic who is able and willing to

get well, little charity, in the ordinary sense of the word, is needed or wanted. The men who cry for money and shelter before conquering alcohol, are on the wrong track. Yet we do go to great extremes to provide each other with these very things, when such action is warranted. This may seem inconsistent, but we think it is not.

It is not the matter of giving that is in question, but when and how to give. That often makes the difference between failure and success. The minute we put our work on a service plane, the alcoholic commences to rely upon our assistance rather than upon God. He clamors for this or that, claiming he cannot master alcohol until his material needs are cared for. Nonsense. Some of us have taken very hard knocks to learn this truth: Job or no job—wife or no wife—we simply do not stop drinking so long as we place dependence upon other people ahead of dependence on God.

Burn the idea into the consciousness of every man that he can get well regardless of anyone. The only condition is that he trust in God and clean house.

Now, the domestic problem: There may be divorce, separation, or just strained relations. When your prospect has made such reparation as he can to his family, and has thoroughly explained to them the new principles by which he is living, he should proceed to put those principles into action at home. That is, if he is lucky enough to have a home. Though his family be at fault in many respects, he should not be concerned about that. He should concentrate on his own spiritual demonstration. Argument and fault-finding are to be avoided like the plague. In many homes this is a difficult thing to do, but it must be done if any results are to be expected. If persisted in for a few months, the effect on a man's family is sure to be great. The most incompatible people discover they have a basis upon which they can meet. Little by little the family may see their own defects and admit them. These can then be discussed in an atmosphere of helpfulness and friendliness.

After they have seen tangible results, the family will perhaps want to go along. These things will come to pass naturally and in good time provided, however, the alcoholic continues to demonstrate that he can be sober, considerate, and helpful, regardless of what anyone says or does. Of course, we all fall much below this standard many times. But we must try to repair the damage immediately lest we pay the penalty by a spree.

If there be divorce or separation, there should be no undue haste for the couple to get together. The man should be sure of his recovery. The wife should fully understand his new way of life. If their old relationship is to be resumed it must be on a better basis, since the former did not work. This means a new attitude and spirit all around. Sometimes it is to the best interests of all concerned that a couple remain apart. Obviously, no rule can be laid down. Let the alcoholic continue his program day by day. When the time for living together has come, it will be apparent to both parties.

Let no alcoholic say he cannot recover unless he has his family back. This just isn't so. In some cases the wife will never come back for one reason or another. Remind the prospect that his recovery is not dependent upon people. It is dependent upon his relation-ship with God. We have seen men get well whose families have not returned at all. We have seen others slip when the family came back too soon.

Both you and the new man must walk day by day in the path of spiritual progress. If you persist, remark-able things will happen. When we look back, we realize that the things which came to us when we put ourselves in God's hands were better than anything we could have planned. Follow the dictates of a Higher Power and you will presently live in a new and wonderful world, no matter what your present circumstances!

When working with a man and his family, you should take care not to participate in their quarrels. You may spoil your chance of being helpful if you do. But urge upon a man's family that he has been a very sick person and should be treated accordingly. You should warn against arousing resentment or jealousy. You should point out that his defects of character are not going to disappear over night. Show them that he has entered upon a period of growth. Ask them to remember, when they are impatient, the blessed fact of his sobriety.

If you have been successful in solving your own domestic problems, tell the newcomer's family how that was accomplished. In this way you can set them on the right track without becoming critical of them. The story of how you and your wife settled your difficulties is worth any amount of criticism.

Assuming we are spiritually fit, we can do all sorts of things alcoholics are not supposed to do. People have said we must not go where liquor is served; we must not have it in our homes; we must shun friends who drink; we must avoid moving pictures which show drinking scenes; we must not go into bars; our friends must hide their bottles if we go to their houses; we mustn't think or be reminded about alcohol at all. Our experience shows that this is not necessarily so.

We meet these conditions every day. An alcoholic who cannot meet them, still has an alcoholic mind; there is something the matter with his spiritual status. His only chance for sobriety would be some place like the Greenland Ice Cap, and even there an Eskimo might turn up with a bottle of scotch and ruin everything! Ask any woman who has sent her husband to distant places on the theory he would escape the alcohol problem.

In our belief any scheme of combating alcoholism which proposes to shield the sick man from temptation is doomed to failure. If the alcoholic tries to shield himself he may succeed for a time, but he usually winds up with a bigger explosion than ever. We have tried these methods. These attempts to do the impossible have always failed.

So our rule is not to avoid a place where there is drinking, *if we have a legitimate reason for being there.* That includes bars, nightclubs, dances, receptions, weddings, even plain ordinary whoopee parties. To a person who has had experience with an alcoholic, this may seem like tempting Providence, but it isn't.

You will note that we made an important qualification. Therefore, ask yourself on each occasion, "Have I any good social, business, or personal reason for going to this place? Or am I expecting to steal a little vicarious pleasure from the atmosphere of such places?" If you answer these questions satisfactorily, you need have no apprehension. Go or stay away, whichever seems best. But be sure you are on solid spiritual ground before you start and that your motive in going is thoroughly good. Do not think of what you will get out of the occasion. Think of what you can bring to it. But if you are shaky, you had better work with another alcoholic instead!

Why sit with a long face in places where there is drinking, sighing about the good old days. If it is a happy occasion, try to increase the pleasure of those there; if a business occasion, go and attend to your business enthusiastically. If you are with a person who wants to eat in a bar, by all means go along. Let your friends know they are not to change their habits on your account. At a proper time and place explain to all your friends why alcohol disagrees with you. If you do this thoroughly, few people will ask you to drink. While you were drinking, you were withdrawing from life little by little. Now you are getting back into the social life of this world. Don't start to withdraw again just because your friends drink liquor.

Your job now is to be at the place where you may be of maximum helpfulness to others, so never hesitate to go anywhere if you can be helpful. You should not hesitate to visit the most sordid spot on earth on such an errand. Keep on the firing line of life with these motives and God will keep you unharmed.

Many of us keep liquor in our homes. We often need it to carry green recruits through a severe hangover. Some of us still serve it to our friends provided they are not alcoholic. But some of us think we should not serve liquor to anyone. We never argue this question. We feel that each family, in the light of their own circumstances, ought to decide for themselves.

We are careful never to show intolerance or hatred of drinking as an institution. Experience shows that such an attitude is not helpful to anyone. Every new alcoholic looks for this spirit among us and is immensely relieved when he finds we are not witch-burners. A spirit of intolerance might repel alcoholics whose lives could have been saved, had it not been for such stupidity. We would not even do the cause of temperate drinking any good, for not one drinker in a thousand likes to be told anything about alcohol by one who hates it.

Some day we hope that Alcoholics Anonymous will help the public to a better realization of the gravity of the alcoholic problem, but we shall be of little use if our attitude is one of bitterness or hostility. Drinkers will not stand for it.

After all, our problems were of our own making. Bottles were only a symbol. Besides, we have stopped fighting anybody or anything. We have to!

Chapter 8

TO WIVES*

$\mathcal{W}$ITH FEW EXCEPTIONS, our book thus far has spoken of men. But what we have said applies quite as much to women. Our activities in behalf of women who drink are on the increase. There is every evidence that women regain their health as readily as men if they try our suggestions.

But for every man who drinks others are involved—the wife who trembles in fear of the next debauch; the mother and father who see their son wasting away.

Among us are wives, relatives and friends whose problem has been solved, as well as some who have not yet found a happy solution. We want the wives of Alcoholics Anonymous to address the wives of men who drink too much. What they say will apply to nearly everyone bound by ties of blood or affection to an alcoholic.

As wives of Alcoholics Anonymous, we would like you to feel that we understand as perhaps few can. We want to analyze mistakes we have made. We want to leave you with the feeling that no situation is too difficult and no unhappiness too great to be overcome.

We have traveled a rocky road, there is no mistake about that. We have had long rendezvous with hurt pride, frustration, self-pity, misunderstanding and fear. These are not pleasant companions. We have been

---

* Written in 1939, when there were few women in A.A., this chapter assumes that the alcoholic in the home is likely to be the husband. But many of the suggestions given here may be adapted to help the person who lives with a woman alcoholic—whether she is still drinking or is recovering in A.A. A further source of help is noted on page 121.

driven to maudlin sympathy, to bitter resentment. Some of us veered from extreme to extreme, ever hoping that one day our loved ones would be themselves once more.

Our loyalty and the desire that our husbands hold up their heads and be like other men have begotten all sorts of predicaments. We have been unselfish and self-sacrificing. We have told innumerable lies to protect our pride and our husbands' reputations. We have prayed, we have begged, we have been patient. We have struck out viciously. We have run away. We have been hysterical. We have been terror stricken. We have sought sympathy. We have had retaliatory love affairs with other men.

Our homes have been battle-grounds many an evening. In the morning we have kissed and made up. Our friends have counseled chucking the men and we have done so with finality, only to be back in a little while hoping, always hoping. Our men have sworn great solemn oaths that they were through drinking forever. We have believed them when no one else could or would. Then, in days, weeks, or months, a fresh outburst.

We seldom had friends at our homes, never knowing how or when the men of the house would appear. We could make few social engagements. We came to live almost alone. When we were invited out, our husbands sneaked so many drinks that they spoiled the occasion. If, on the other hand, they took nothing, their self-pity made them killjoys.

There was never financial security. Positions were always in jeopardy or gone. An armored car could not have brought the pay envelopes home. The checking account melted like snow in June.

Sometimes there were other women. How heartbreaking was this discovery; how cruel to be told they understood our men as we did not!

The bill collectors, the sheriffs, the angry taxi drivers, the policemen, the bums, the pals, and even the ladies they sometimes brought home—our husbands thought we were so inhospitable. "Joykiller, nag, wet blanket"—that's what they said. Next day they would be themselves again and we would forgive and try to forget.

We have tried to hold the love of our children for their father. We have told small tots that father was sick, which was much nearer the truth than we realized. They struck the children, kicked out door panels, smashed treasured crockery, and ripped the keys out of pianos. In the midst of such pandemonium they may have rushed out threatening to live with the other woman forever. In desperation, we have even got tight ourselves—the drunk to end all drunks. The unexpected result was that our husbands seemed to like it.

Perhaps at this point we got a divorce and took the children home to father and mother. Then we were severely criticized by our husband's parents for desertion. Usually we did not leave. We stayed on and on. We finally sought employment ourselves as destitution faced us and our families.

We began to ask medical advice as the sprees got closer together. The alarming physical and mental symptoms, the deepening pall of remorse, depression and inferiority that settled down on our loved ones—

these things terrified and distracted us. As animals on a treadmill, we have patiently and wearily climbed, falling back in exhaustion after each futile effort to reach solid ground. Most of us have entered the final stage with its commitment to health resorts, sanitariums, hospitals, and jails. Sometimes there were screaming delirium and insanity. Death was often near.

Under these conditions we naturally made mistakes. Some of them rose out of ignorance of alcoholism. Sometimes we sensed dimly that we were dealing with sick men. Had we fully understood the nature of the alcoholic illness, we might have behaved differently.

How could men who loved their wives and children be so unthinking, so callous, so cruel? There could be no love in such persons, we thought. And just as we were being convinced of their heartlessness, they would surprise us with fresh resolves and new attentions. For a while they would be their old sweet selves, only to dash the new structure of affection to pieces once more. Asked why they commenced to drink again, they would reply with some silly excuse, or none. It was so baffling, so heartbreaking. Could we have been so mistaken in the men we married? When drinking, they were strangers. Sometimes they were so inaccessible that it seemed as though a great wall had been built around them.

And even if they did not love their families, how could they be so blind about themselves? What had become of their judgment, their common sense, their will power? Why could they not see that drink meant ruin to them? Why was it, when these dangers were pointed out that they agreed, and then got drunk again immediately?

These are some of the questions which race through the mind of every woman who has an alcoholic husband. We hope this book has answered some of them. Perhaps your husband has been living in that strange world of alcoholism where everything is distorted and exaggerated. You can see that he really does love you with his better self. Of course, there is such a thing as incompatibility, but in nearly every instance the alcoholic only seems to be unloving and inconsiderate; it is usually because he is warped and sickened that he says and does these appalling things. Today most of our men are better husbands and fathers than ever before.

Try not to condemn your alcoholic husband no matter what he says or does. He is just another very sick, unreasonable person. Treat him, when you can, as though he had pneumonia. When he angers you, remember that he is very ill.

There is an important exception to the foregoing. We realize some men are thoroughly bad-intentioned, that no amount of patience will make any difference. An alcoholic of this temperament may be quick to use this chapter as a club over your head. Don't let him get away with it. If you are positive he is one of this type you may feel you had better leave. Is it right to let him ruin your life and the lives of your children? Especially when he has before him a way to stop his drinking and abuse if he really wants to pay the price.

The problem with which you struggle usually falls within one of four categories:

One: Your husband may be only a heavy drinker.

His drinking may be constant or it may be heavy only on certain occasions. Perhaps he spends too much money for liquor. It may be slowing him up mentally and physically, but he does not see it. Sometimes he is a source of embarrassment to you and his friends. He is positive he can handle his liquor, that it does him no harm, that drinking is necessary in his business. He would probably be insulted if he were called an alcoholic. This world is full of people like him. Some will moderate or stop altogether, and some will not. Of those who keep on, a good number will become true alcoholics after a while.

Two: Your husband is showing lack of control, for he is unable to stay on the water wagon even when he wants to. He often gets entirely out of hand when drinking. He admits this is true, but is positive that he will do better. He has begun to try, with or without your cooperation, various means of moderating or staying dry. Maybe he is beginning to lose his friends. His business may suffer somewhat. He is worried at times, and is becoming aware that he cannot drink like other people. He sometimes drinks in the morning and through the day also, to hold his nervousness in check. He is remorseful after serious drinking bouts and tells you he wants to stop. But when he gets over the spree, he begins to think once more how he can drink moderately next time. We think this person is in danger. These are the earmarks of a real alcoholic. Perhaps he can still tend to business fairly well. He has by no means ruined everything. As we say among ourselves, *"He wants to want to stop."*

Three: This husband has gone much further than husband number two. Though once like number two he became worse. His friends have slipped away, his home is a near-wreck and he cannot hold a position. Maybe the doctor has been called in, and the weary round of sanitariums and hospitals has begun. He admits he cannot drink like other people, but does not see why. He clings to the notion that he will yet find a way to do so. He may have come to the point where he desperately wants to stop but cannot. His case presents additional questions which we shall try to answer for you. You can be quite hopeful of a situation like this.

Four: You may have a husband of whom you completely despair. He has been placed in one institution after another. He is violent, or appears definitely insane when drunk. Sometimes he drinks on the way home from the hospital. Perhaps he has had delirium tremens. Doctors may shake their heads and advise you to have him committed. Maybe you have already been obliged to put him away. This picture may not be as dark as it looks. Many of our husbands were just as far gone. Yet they got well.

Let's now go back to husband number one. Oddly enough, he is often difficult to deal with. He enjoys drinking. It stirs his imagination. His friends feel closer over a highball. Perhaps you enjoy drinking with him yourself when he doesn't go too far. You have passed happy evenings together chatting and drinking before your fire. Perhaps you both like parties which would be dull without liquor. We have enjoyed such evenings ourselves; we had a good time. We know all about liquor as a social lubricant. Some, but not all of us, think it has its advantages when reasonably used.

The first principle of success is that you should never be angry. Even though your husband becomes unbearable and you have to leave him temporarily, you should, if you can, go without rancor. Patience and good temper are most necessary.

Our next thought is that you should never tell him what he must do about his drinking. If he gets the idea that you are a nag or a killjoy, your chance of accomplishing anything useful may be zero. He will use that as an excuse to drink more. He will tell you he is misunderstood. This may lead to lonely evenings for you. He may seek someone else to console him— not always another man.

Be determined that your husband's drinking is not going to spoil your relations with your children or your friends. They need your companionship and your help. It is possible to have a full and useful life, though your husband continues to drink. We know women who are unafraid, even happy under these conditions. Do not set your heart on reforming your husband. You may be unable to do so, no matter how hard you try.

We know these suggestions are sometimes difficult to follow, but you will save many a heartbreak if you can succeed in observing them. Your husband may come to appreciate your reasonableness and patience. This may lay the groundwork for a friendly talk about his alcoholic problem. Try to have him bring up the subject himself. Be sure you are not critical during such a discussion. Attempt instead, to put yourself in his place. Let him see that you want to be helpful rather than critical.

When a discussion does arise, you might suggest he

read this book or at least the chapter on alcoholism. Tell him you have been worried, though perhaps needlessly. You think he ought to know the subject better, as everyone should have a clear understanding of the risk he takes if he drinks too much. Show him you have confidence in his power to stop or moderate. Say you do not want to be a wet blanket; that you only want him to take care of his health. Thus you may succeed in interesting him in alcoholism.

He probably has several alcoholics among his own acquaintances. You might suggest that you both take an interest in them. Drinkers like to help other drinkers. Your husband may be willing to talk to one of them.

If this kind of approach does not catch your husband's interest, it may be best to drop the subject, but after a friendly talk your husband will usually revive the topic himself. This may take patient waiting, but it will be worth it. Meanwhile you might try to help the wife of another serious drinker. If you act upon these principles, your husband may stop or moderate.

Suppose, however, that your husband fits the description of number two. The same principles which apply to husband number one should be practiced. But after his next binge, ask him if he would really like to get over drinking for good. Do not ask that he do it for you or anyone else. Just would he *like* to?

The chances are he would. Show him your copy of this book and tell him what you have found out about alcoholism. Show him that as alcoholics, the writers of the book understand. Tell him some of the interesting stories you have read. If you think he will be shy of a spiritual remedy, ask him to look at the chapter on alcoholism. Then perhaps he will be interested enough to continue.

If he is enthusiastic your cooperation will mean a great deal. If he is lukewarm or thinks he is not an alcoholic, we suggest you leave him alone. Avoid urging him to follow our program. The seed has been planted in his mind. He knows that thousands of men, much like himself, have recovered. But don't remind him of this after he has been drinking, for he may be angry. Sooner or later, you are likely to find him reading the book once more. Wait until repeated stumbling convinces him he must act, for the more you hurry him the longer his recovery may be delayed.

If you have a number three husband, you may be in luck. Being certain he wants to stop, you can go to him with this volume as joyfully as though you had struck oil. He may not share your enthusiasm, but he is practically sure to read the book and he may go for the program at once. If he does not, you will probably not have long to wait. Again, you should not crowd him. Let him decide for himself. Cheerfully see him through more sprees. Talk about his condition or this book only when he raises the issue. In some cases it may be better to let someone outside the family present the book. They can urge action without arousing hostility. If your husband is otherwise a normal individual, your chances are good at this stage.

You would suppose that men in the fourth classification would be quite hopeless, but that is not so. Many of Alcoholics Anonymous were like that. Everybody had given them up. Defeat seemed certain. Yet often such men had spectacular and powerful recoveries.

There are exceptions. Some men have been so impaired by alcohol that they cannot stop. Sometimes there are cases where alcoholism is complicated by other disorders. A good doctor or psychiatrist can tell you whether these complications are serious. In any event, try to have your husband read this book. His reaction may be one of enthusiasm. If he is already committed to an institution, but can convince you and your doctor that he means business, give him a chance to try our method, unless the doctor thinks his mental condition too abnormal or dangerous. We make this recommendation with some confidence. For years we have been working with alcoholics committed to institutions. Since this book was first published, A.A. has released thousands of alcoholics from asylums and hospitals of every kind. The majority have never returned. The power of God goes deep!

You may have the reverse situation on your hands. Perhaps you have a husband who is at large, but who should be committed. Some men cannot or will not get over alcoholism. When they become too dangerous, we think the kind thing is to lock them up, but of course a good doctor should always be consulted. The wives and children of such men suffer horribly, but not more than the men themselves.

But sometimes you must start life anew. We know women who have done it. If such women adopt a spiritual way of life their road will be smoother.

If your husband is a drinker, you probably worry over what other people are thinking and you hate to meet your friends. You draw more and more into yourself and you think everyone is talking about conditions at your home. You avoid the subject of drinking, even with your own parents. You do not know what to tell the children. When your husband is bad, you become a trembling recluse, wishing the telephone had never been invented.

We find that most of this embarrassment is unnecessary. While you need not discuss your husband at length, you can quietly let your friends know the nature of his illness. But you must be on guard not to embarrass or harm your husband.

When you have carefully explained to such people that he is a sick person, you will have created a new atmosphere. Barriers which have sprung up between you and your friends will disappear with the growth of sympathetic understanding. You will no longer be self-conscious or feel that you must apologize as though your husband were a weak character. He may be anything but that. Your new courage, good nature and lack of self-consciousness will do wonders for you socially.

The same principle applies in dealing with the children. Unless they actually need protection from their father, it is best not to take sides in any argument he has with them while drinking. Use your energies to promote a better understanding all around. Then that terrible tension which grips the home of every problem drinker will be lessened.

Frequently, you have felt obliged to tell your husband's employer and his friends that he was sick, when as a matter of fact he was tight. Avoid answering these inquiries as much as you can. Whenever possible, let your husband explain. Your desire to protect him should not cause you to lie to people when they have a right to know where he is and what he is doing. Discuss this with him when he is sober and in good spirits. Ask him what you should do if he places you in such a position again. But be careful not to be resentful about the last time he did so.

There is another paralyzing fear. You may be afraid your husband will lose his position; you are thinking of the disgrace and hard times which will befall you and the children. This experience may come to you. Or you may already have had it several times. Should it happen again, regard it in a different light. Maybe it will prove a blessing! It may convince your husband he wants to stop drinking forever. And now you know that he can stop if he will! Time after time, this apparent calamity has been a boon to us, for it opened up a path which led to the discovery of God.

We have elsewhere remarked how much better life is when lived on a spiritual plane. If God can solve the age-old riddle of alcoholism, He can solve your problems too. We wives found that, like everybody else, we were afflicted with pride, self-pity, vanity and all the things which go to make up the self-centered person; and we were not above selfishness or dishonesty. As our husbands began to apply spiritual principles in their lives, we began to see the desirability of doing so too.

At first, some of us did not believe we needed this help. We thought, on the whole, we were pretty good women, capable of being nicer if our husbands stopped drinking. But it was a silly idea that we were too good to need God. Now we try to put spiritual principles to work in every department of our lives. When we do that, we find it solves our problems too; the ensuing lack of fear, worry and hurt feelings is a wonderful thing. We urge you to try our program, for nothing will be so helpful to your husband as the radically changed attitude toward him which God will show you how to have. Go along with your husband if you possibly can.

If you and your husband find a solution for the pressing problem of drink you are, of course, going to be very happy. But all problems will not be solved at once. Seed has started to sprout in a new soil, but growth has only begun. In spite of your new-found happiness, there will be ups and downs. Many of the old problems will still be with you. This is as it should be.

The faith and sincerity of both you and your husband will be put to the test. These work-outs should be regarded as part of your education, for thus you will be learning to live. You will make mistakes, but if you are in earnest they will not drag you down. Instead, you will capitalize them. A better way of life will emerge when they are overcome.

Some of the snags you will encounter are irritation, hurt feelings and resentments. Your husband will sometimes be unreasonable and you will want to criticize. Starting from a speck on the domestic horizon, great thunderclouds of dispute may gather. These family dissensions are very dangerous, especially to your husband. Often you must carry the burden of avoiding them or keeping them under control. Never forget that resentment is a deadly hazard to an alcoholic. We do not mean that you have to agree with your husband whenever there is an honest difference of opinion. Just be careful not to disagree in a resentful or critical spirit.

You and your husband will find that you can dispose of serious problems easier than you can the trivial ones. Next time you and he have a heated discussion, no matter what the subject, it should be the privilege of either to smile and say, "This is getting serious. I'm sorry I got disturbed. Let's talk about it later." If your husband is trying to live on a spiritual basis, he will also be doing everything in his power to avoid disagreement or contention.

Your husband knows he owes you more than sobriety. He wants to make good. Yet you must not expect too much. His ways of thinking and doing are the habits of years. Patience, tolerance, understanding and love are the watchwords. Show him these things in yourself and they will be reflected back to you from him. Live and let live is the rule. If you both show a willingness to remedy your own defects, there will be little need to criticize each other.

We women carry with us a picture of the ideal man, the sort of chap we would like our husbands to be. It is the most natural thing in the world, once his liquor problem is solved, to feel that he will now measure up to that cherished vision. The chances are he will not for, like yourself, he is just beginning his development. Be patient.

Another feeling we are very likely to entertain is one of resentment that love and loyalty could not cure our husbands of alcoholism. We do not like the thought that the contents of a book or the work of another alcoholic has accomplished in a few weeks that for which we struggled for years. At such moments we forget that alcoholism is an illness over which we could not possibly have had any power. Your husband will be the first to say it was your devotion and care which brought him to the point where he could have a spiritual experience. Without you he would have gone to pieces long ago. When resentful thoughts come, try to pause and count your blessings. After all, your family is reunited, alcohol is no longer a problem and you and your husband are working together toward an undreamed-of future.

Still another difficulty is that you may become jealous of the attention he bestows on other people, especially alcoholics. You have been starving for his companionship, yet he spends long hours helping other men and their families. You feel he should now be yours. The fact is that he should work with other people to maintain his own sobriety. Sometimes he will be so interested that he becomes really neglectful. Your house is filled with strangers. You may not like some of them. He gets stirred up about their troubles, but not at all about yours. It will do little good if you point that out and urge more attention for yourself. We find it a real mistake to dampen his enthusiasm for alcoholic work. You should join in his efforts as much as you possibly can. We suggest that you direct some of your thought to the wives of his new alcoholic friends. They need the counsel and love of a woman who has gone through what you have.

It is probably true that you and your husband have been living too much alone, for drinking many times isolates the wife of an alcoholic. Therefore, you probably need fresh interests and a great cause to live for as much as your husband. If you cooperate, rather than complain, you will find that his excess enthusiasm will tone down. Both of you will awaken to a new sense of responsibility for others. You, as well as your husband, ought to think of what you can put into life instead of how much you can take out. Inevitably your lives will be fuller for doing so. You will lose the old life to find one much better.

Perhaps your husband will make a fair start on the new basis, but just as things are going beautifully he dismays you by coming home drunk. If you are satisfied he really wants to get over drinking, you need not be alarmed. Though it is infinitely better that he have no relapse at all, as has been true with many of our men, it is by no means a bad thing in some cases. Your husband will see at once that he must redouble his spiritual activities if he expects to survive. You need not remind him of his spiritual deficiency—he will know of it. Cheer him up and ask him how you can be still more helpful.

The slightest sign of fear or intolerance may lessen your husband's chance of recovery. In a weak moment he may take your dislike of his high-stepping friends as one of those insanely trivial excuses to drink.

We never, never try to arrange a man's life so as to shield him from temptation. The slightest disposition on your part to guide his appointments or his affairs so he will not be tempted will be noticed. Make him feel absolutely free to come and go as he likes. This is important. If he gets drunk, don't blame yourself. God has either removed your husband's liquor problem or He has not. If not, it had better be found out right away. Then you and your husband can get right down to fundamentals. If a repetition is to be prevented, place the problem, along with everything else, in God's hands.

We realize that we have been giving you much direction and advice. We may have seemed to lecture. If that is so we are sorry, for we ourselves don't always care for people who lecture us. But what we have related is based upon experience, some of it painful. We had to learn these things the hard way. That is why we are anxious that you understand, and that you avoid these unnecessary difficulties.*

So to you out there who may soon be with us—we say "Good luck and God bless you!"

---

* The fellowship of Al-Anon Family Groups was formed about thirteen years after this chapter was written. Though it is entirely separate from Alcoholics Anonymous, it uses the general principles of the A.A. program as a guide for husbands, wives, relatives, friends, and others close to alcoholics. The foregoing pages (though addressed only to wives) indicate the problems such people may face. Alateen, for teen-aged children of alcoholics, is a part of Al-Anon.

If there is no Al-Anon listing in your local telephone book, you may obtain further information on Al-Anon/Alateen Family Groups by writing to its World Service Office, 1600 Corporate Landing Parkway, Virginia Beach, VA 23454-5617.

Chapter 9

THE FAMILY AFTERWARD

OUR WOMEN FOLK have suggested certain attitudes a wife may take with the husband who is recovering. Perhaps they created the impression that he is to be wrapped in cotton wool and placed on a pedestal. Successful readjustment means the opposite. All members of the family should meet upon the common ground of tolerance, understanding and love. This involves a process of deflation. The alcoholic, his wife, his children, his "in-laws," each one is likely to have fixed ideas about the family's attitude towards himself or herself. Each is interested in having his or her wishes respected. We find the more one member of the family demands that the others concede to him, the more resentful they become. This makes for discord and unhappiness.

And why? Is it not because each wants to play the lead? Is not each trying to arrange the family show to his liking? Is he not unconsciously trying to see what he can take from the family life rather than give?

Cessation of drinking is but the first step away from a highly strained, abnormal condition. A doctor said to us, "Years of living with an alcoholic is almost sure to make any wife or child neurotic. The entire family is, to some extent, ill." Let families realize, as they start their journey, that all will not be fair weather. Each in his turn may be footsore and may straggle.

There will be alluring shortcuts and by-paths down which they may wander and lose their way.

Suppose we tell you some of the obstacles a family will meet; suppose we suggest how they may be avoided—even converted to good use for others. The family of an alcoholic longs for the return of happiness and security. They remember when father was romantic, thoughtful and successful. Today's life is measured against that of other years and, when it falls short, the family may be unhappy.

Family confidence in dad is rising high. The good old days will soon be back, they think. Sometimes they demand that dad bring them back instantly! God, they believe, almost owes this recompense on a long overdue account. But the head of the house has spent years in pulling down the structures of business, romance, friendship, health—these things are now ruined or damaged. It will take time to clear away the wreck. Though old buildings will eventually be replaced by finer ones, the new structures will take years to complete.

Father knows he is to blame; it may take him many seasons of hard work to be restored financially, but he shouldn't be reproached. Perhaps he will never have much money again. But the wise family will admire him for what he is trying to be, rather than for what he is trying to get.

Now and then the family will be plagued by spectres from the past, for the drinking career of almost every alcoholic has been marked by escapades, funny, humiliating, shameful or tragic. The first impulse will be to bury these skeletons in a dark closet and padlock the door. The family may be possessed by the idea

that future happiness can be based only upon forget-
fulness of the past. We think that such a view is self-
centered and in direct conflict with the new way of
living.

Henry Ford once made a wise remark to the effect
that experience is the thing of supreme value in life.
That is true only if one is willing to turn the past to
good account. We grow by our willingness to face
and rectify errors and convert them into assets. The
alcoholic's past thus becomes the principal asset of the
family and frequently it is almost the only one!

This painful past may be of infinite value to other
families still struggling with their problem. We think
each family which has been relieved owes something
to those who have not, and when the occasion requires, each member of it should be only too willing
to bring former mistakes, no matter how grievous, out
of their hiding places. Showing others who suffer how
we were given help is the very thing which makes life
seem so worth while to us now. Cling to the thought
that, in God's hands, the dark past is the greatest possession you have—the key to life and happiness for
others. With it you can avert death and misery for
them.

It is possible to dig up past misdeeds so they become
a blight, a veritable plague. For example, we know of
situations in which the alcoholic or his wife have had
love affairs. In the first flush of spiritual experience
they forgave each other and drew closer together. The
miracle of reconciliation was at hand. Then, under
one provocation or another, the aggrieved one would
unearth the old affair and angrily cast its ashes about.
A few of us have had these growing pains and they

hurt a great deal. Husbands and wives have sometimes been obliged to separate for a time until new
perspective, new victory over hurt pride could be re-
won. In most cases, the alcoholic survived this ordeal
without relapse, but not always. So we think that
unless some good and useful purpose is to be served,
past occurrences should not be discussed.

We families of Alcoholics Anonymous keep few
skeletons in the closet. Everyone knows about the
others' alcoholic troubles. This is a condition which,
in ordinary life, would produce untold grief; there
might be scandalous gossip, laughter at the expense of
other people, and a tendency to take advantage of intimate information. Among us, these are rare occurrences. We do talk about each other a great deal, but
we almost invariably temper such talk by a spirit of
love and tolerance.

Another principle we observe carefully is that we do
not relate intimate experiences of another person unless we are sure he would approve. We find it better,
when possible, to stick to our own stories. A man may
criticize or laugh at himself and it will affect others
favorably, but criticism or ridicule coming from another often produces the contrary effect. Members of
a family should watch such matters carefully, for one
careless, inconsiderate remark has been known to raise
the very devil. We alcoholics are sensitive people. It
takes some of us a long time to outgrow that serious
handicap.

Many alcoholics are enthusiasts. They run to extremes. At the beginning of recovery a man will take,
as a rule, one of two directions. He may either plunge
into a frantic attempt to get on his feet in business, or

he may be so enthralled by his new life that he talks or thinks of little else. In either case certain family problems will arise. With these we have had experience galore.

We think it dangerous if he rushes headlong at his economic problem. The family will be affected also, pleasantly at first, as they feel their money troubles are about to be solved, then not so pleasantly as they find themselves neglected. Dad may be tired at night and preoccupied by day. He may take small interest in the children and may show irritation when reproved for his delinquencies. If not irritable, he may seem dull and boring, not gay and affectionate as the family would like him to be. Mother may complain of inattention. They are all disappointed, and often let him feel it. Beginning with such complaints, a barrier arises. He is straining every nerve to make up for lost time. He is striving to recover fortune and reputation and feels he is doing very well.

Sometimes mother and children don't think so. Having been neglected and misused in the past, they think father owes them more than they are getting. They want him to make a fuss over them. They expect him to give them the nice times they used to have before he drank so much, and to show his contrition for what they suffered. But dad doesn't give freely of himself. Resentment grows. He becomes still less communicative. Sometimes he explodes over a trifle. The family is mystified. They criticize, pointing out how he is falling down on his spiritual program.

This sort of thing can be avoided. Both father and the family are mistaken, though each side may have some justification. It is of little use to argue and only makes the impasse worse. The family must realize that dad, though marvelously improved, is still convalescing. They should be thankful he is sober and able to be of this world once more. Let them praise his progress. Let them remember that his drinking wrought all kinds of damage that may take long to repair. If they sense these things, they will not take so seriously his periods of crankiness, depression, or apathy, which will disappear when there is tolerance, love, and spiritual understanding.

The head of the house ought to remember that he is mainly to blame for what befell his home. He can scarcely square the account in his lifetime. But he must see the danger of over-concentration on financial success. Although financial recovery is on the way for many of us, we found we could not place money first. For us, material well-being always followed spiritual progress; it never preceded.

Since the home has suffered more than anything else, it is well that a man exert himself there. He is not likely to get far in any direction if he fails to show unselfishness and love under his own roof. We know there are difficult wives and families, but the man who is getting over alcoholism must remember he did much to make them so.

As each member of a resentful family begins to see his shortcomings and admits them to the others, he lays a basis for helpful discussion. These family talks will be constructive if they can be carried on without heated argument, self-pity, self-justification or resentful criticism. Little by little, mother and children will see they ask too much, and father will see he gives too little. Giving, rather than getting, will become the guiding principle.

Assume on the other hand that father has, at the outset, a stirring spiritual experience. Overnight, as it were, he is a different man. He becomes a religious enthusiast. He is unable to focus on anything else. As soon as his sobriety begins to be taken as a matter of course, the family may look at their strange new dad with apprehension, then with irritation. There is talk about spiritual matters morning, noon and night. He may demand that the family find God in a hurry, or exhibit amazing indifference to them and say he is above worldly considerations. He may tell mother, who has been religious all her life, that she doesn't know what it's all about, and that she had better get his brand of spirituality while there is yet time.

When father takes this tack, the family may react unfavorably. They may be jealous of a God who has stolen dad's affections. While grateful that he drinks no more, they may not like the idea that God has accomplished the miracle where they failed. They often forget father was beyond human aid. They may not see why their love and devotion did not straighten him out. Dad is not so spiritual after all, they say. If he means to right his past wrongs, why all this concern for everyone in the world but his family? What about his talk that God will take care of them? They suspect father is a bit balmy!

He is not so unbalanced as they might think. Many of us have experienced dad's elation. We have indulged in spiritual intoxication. Like a gaunt prospector, belt drawn in over the last ounce of food, our pick struck gold. Joy at our release from a lifetime of frustration knew no bounds. Father feels he has struck something better than gold. For a time he may try to hug the new treasure to himself. He may not see at once that he has barely scratched a limitless lode which will pay dividends only if he mines it for the rest of his life and insists on giving away the entire product.

If the family cooperates, dad will soon see that he is suffering from a distortion of values. He will perceive that his spiritual growth is lopsided, that for an average man like himself, a spiritual life which does not include his family obligations may not be so perfect after all. If the family will appreciate that dad's current behavior is but a phase of his development, all will be well. In the midst of an understanding and sympathetic family, these vagaries of dad's spiritual infancy will quickly disappear.

The opposite may happen should the family condemn and criticize. Dad may feel that for years his drinking has placed him on the wrong side of every argument, but that now he has become a superior person with God on his side. If the family persists in criticism, this fallacy may take a still greater hold on father. Instead of treating the family as he should, he may retreat further into himself and feel he has spiritual justification for so doing.

Though the family does not fully agree with dad's spiritual activities, they should let him have his head. Even if he displays a certain amount of neglect and irresponsibility towards the family, it is well to let him go as far as he likes in helping other alcoholics. During those first days of convalescence, this will do more to insure his sobriety than anything else. Though some of his manifestations are alarming and disagree-able, we think dad will be on a firmer foundation than the man who is placing business or professional suc-cess ahead of spiritual development. He will be less likely to drink again, and anything is preferable to that.

Those of us who have spent much time in the world of spiritual make-believe have eventually seen the childishness of it. This dream world has been replaced by a great sense of purpose, accompanied by a grow-ing consciousness of the power of God in our lives. We have come to believe He would like us to keep our heads in the clouds with Him, but that our feet ought to be firmly planted on earth. That is where our fel-low travelers are, and that is where our work must be done. These are the realities for us. We have found nothing incompatible between a powerful spiritual experience and a life of sane and happy usefulness.

One more suggestion: Whether the family has spiri-tual convictions or not, they may do well to examine the principles by which the alcoholic member is trying to live. They can hardly fail to approve these simple principles, though the head of the house still fails somewhat in practicing them. Nothing will help the man who is off on a spiritual tangent so much as the wife who adopts a sane spiritual program, making a better practical use of it.

There will be other profound changes in the house-hold. Liquor incapacitated father for so many years that mother became head of the house. She met these responsibilities gallantly. By force of circumstances, she was often obliged to treat father as a sick or way-ward child. Even when he wanted to assert himself he could not, for his drinking placed him constantly in the wrong. Mother made all the plans and gave the directions. When sober, father usually obeyed. Thus mother, through no fault of her own, became accustomed to wearing the family trousers. Father, coming suddenly to life again, often begins to assert himself. This means trouble, unless the family watches for these tendencies in each other and comes to a friendly agreement about them.

Drinking isolates most homes from the outside world. Father may have laid aside for years all normal activities—clubs, civic duties, sports. When he renews interest in such things, a feeling of jealousy may arise. The family may feel they hold a mortgage on dad, so big that no equity should be left for outsiders. Instead of developing new channels of activity for themselves, mother and children demand that he stay home and make up the deficiency.

At the very beginning, the couple ought to frankly face the fact that each will have to yield here and there if the family is going to play an effective part in the new life. Father will necessarily spend much time with other alcoholics, but this activity should be balanced. New acquaintances who know nothing of alcoholism might be made and thoughtful consideration given their needs. The problems of the community might engage attention. Though the family has no religious connections, they may wish to make contact with or take membership in a religious body.

Alcoholics who have derided religious people will be helped by such contacts. Being possessed of a spiritual experience, the alcoholic will find he has much in common with these people, though he may

differ with them on many matters. If he does not
argue about religion, he will make new friends and is
sure to find new avenues of usefulness and pleasure.
He and his family can be a bright spot in such con-
gregations. He may bring new hope and new courage
to many a priest, minister, or rabbi, who gives his all
to minister to our troubled world. We intend the foregoing as a helpful suggestion only. So far as we are
concerned, there is nothing obligatory about it. As
non-denominational people, we cannot make up
others' minds for them. Each individual should consult his own conscience.

We have been speaking to you of serious, sometimes
tragic things. We have been dealing with alcohol in its
worst aspect. But we aren't a glum lot. If newcomers
could see no joy or fun in our existence, they wouldn't
want it. We absolutely insist on enjoying life. We try
not to indulge in cynicism over the state of the nations,
nor do we carry the world's troubles on our shoulders.
When we see a man sinking into the mire that is alcoholism, we give him first aid and place what we have
at his disposal. For his sake, we do recount and almost
relive the horrors of our past. But those of us who have
tried to shoulder the entire burden and trouble of
others find we are soon overcome by them.

So we think cheerfulness and laughter make for usefulness. Outsiders are sometimes shocked when we
burst into merriment over a seemingly tragic experience out of the past. But why shouldn't we laugh?
We have recovered, and have been given the power
to help others.

Everybody knows that those in bad health, and
those who seldom play, do not laugh much. So let

each family play together or separately, as much as their circumstances warrant. We are sure God wants us to be happy, joyous, and free. We cannot subscribe to the belief that this life is a vale of tears, though it once was just that for many of us. But it is clear that we made our own misery. God didn't do it. Avoid then, the deliberate manufacture of misery, but if trouble comes, cheerfully capitalize it as an opportunity to demonstrate His omnipotence.

Now about health: A body badly burned by alcohol does not often recover overnight nor do twisted thinking and depression vanish in a twinkling. We are convinced that a spiritual mode of living is a most powerful health restorative. We, who have recovered from serious drinking, are miracles of mental health. But we have seen remarkable transformations in our bodies. Hardly one of our crowd now shows any mark of dissipation.

But this does not mean that we disregard human health measures. God has abundantly supplied this world with fine doctors, psychologists, and practitioners of various kinds. Do not hesitate to take your health problems to such persons. Most of them give freely of themselves, that their fellows may enjoy sound minds and bodies. Try to remember that though God has wrought miracles among us, we should never belittle a good doctor or psychiatrist. Their services are often indispensable in treating a newcomer and in following his case afterward.

One of the many doctors who had the opportunity of reading this book in manuscript form told us that the use of sweets was often helpful, of course depending upon a doctor's advice. He thought all alcoholics should constantly have chocolate available for its quick energy value at times of fatigue. He added that occasionally in the night a vague craving arose which would be satisfied by candy. Many of us have noticed a tendency to eat sweets and have found this practice beneficial.

A word about sex relations. Alcohol is so sexually stimulating to some men that they have over-indulged. Couples are occasionally dismayed to find that when drinking is stopped the man tends to be impotent. Unless the reason is understood, there may be an emotional upset. Some of us had this experience, only to enjoy, in a few months, a finer intimacy than ever. There should be no hesitancy in consulting a doctor or psychologist if the condition persists. We do not know of many cases where this difficulty lasted long.

The alcoholic may find it hard to re-establish friendly relations with his children. Their young minds were impressionable while he was drinking. Without saying so, they may cordially hate him for what he has done to them and to their mother. The children are sometimes dominated by a pathetic hardness and cynicism. They cannot seem to forgive and forget. This may hang on for months, long after their mother has accepted dad's new way of living and thinking.

In time they will see that he is a new man and in their own way they will let him know it. When this happens, they can be invited to join in morning meditation and then they can take part in the daily discussion without rancor or bias. From that point on, progress will be rapid. Marvelous results often follow such a reunion.

Whether the family goes on a spiritual basis or not, the alcoholic member has to if he would recover. The others must be convinced of his new status beyond the shadow of a doubt. Seeing is believing to most families who have lived with a drinker.

Here is a case in point: One of our friends is a heavy smoker and coffee drinker. There was no doubt he over-indulged. Seeing this, and meaning to be helpful, his wife commenced to admonish him about it. He admitted he was overdoing these things, but frankly said that he was not ready to stop. His wife is one of those persons who really feels there is something rather sinful about these commodities, so she nagged, and her intolerance finally threw him into a fit of anger. He got drunk.

Of course our friend was wrong—dead wrong. He had to painfully admit that and mend his spiritual fences. Though he is now a most effective member of Alcoholics Anonymous, he still smokes and drinks coffee, but neither his wife nor anyone else stands in judgment. She sees she was wrong to make a burning issue out of such a matter when his more serious ailments were being rapidly cured.

We have three little mottoes which are apropos. Here they are:

First Things First
Live and Let Live
Easy Does It.

Chapter 10

TO EMPLOYERS

*A*MONG MANY employers nowadays, we think of one member who has spent much of his life in the world of big business. He has hired and fired hundreds of men. He knows the alcoholic as the employer sees him. His present views ought to prove exceptionally useful to business men everywhere.

But let him tell you:

I was at one time assistant manager of a corporation department employing sixty-six hundred men. One day my secretary came in saying that Mr. B— insisted on speaking with me. I told her to say that I was not interested. I had warned him several times that he had but one more chance. Not long afterward he had called me from Hartford on two successive days, so drunk he could hardly speak. I told him he was through—finally and forever.

My secretary returned to say that it was not Mr. B— on the phone; it was Mr. B—'s brother, and he wished to give me a message. I still expected a plea for clemency, but these words came through the receiver: "I just wanted to tell you Paul jumped from a hotel window in Hartford last Saturday. He left us a note saying you were the best boss he ever had, and that you were not to blame in any way."

Another time, as I opened a letter which lay on my

desk, a newspaper clipping fell out. It was the obituary of one of the best salesmen I ever had. After two weeks of drinking, he had placed his toe on the trigger of a loaded shotgun—the barrel was in his mouth. I had discharged him for drinking six weeks before.

Still another experience: A woman's voice came faintly over long distance from Virginia. She wanted to know if her husband's company insurance was still in force. Four days before he had hanged himself in his woodshed. I had been obliged to discharge him for drinking, though he was brilliant, alert, and one of the best organizers I have ever known.

Here were three exceptional men lost to this world because I did not understand alcoholism as I do now. What irony—I became an alcoholic myself! And but for the intervention of an understanding person, I might have followed in their footsteps. My downfall cost the business community unknown thousands of dollars, for it takes real money to train a man for an executive position. This kind of waste goes on unabated. We think the business fabric is shot through with a situation which might be helped by better understanding all around.

Nearly every modern employer feels a moral responsibility for the well-being of his help, and he tries to meet these responsibilities. That he has not always done so for the alcoholic is easily understood. To him the alcoholic has often seemed a fool of the first magnitude. Because of the employee's special ability, or of his own strong personal attachment to him, the employer has sometimes kept such a man at work long beyond a reasonable period. Some employers have tried every known remedy. In only a few instances has there been a lack of patience and tolerance. And we, who have imposed on the best of employers, can scarcely blame them if they have been short with us.

Here, for instance, is a typical example: An officer of one of the largest banking institutions in America knows I no longer drink. One day he told me about an executive of the same bank who, from his description, was undoubtedly alcoholic. This seemed to me like an opportunity to be helpful, so I spent two hours talking about alcoholism, the malady, and described the symptoms and results as well as I could. His comment was, "Very interesting. But I'm sure this man is done drinking. He has just returned from a three-months leave of absence, has taken a cure, looks fine, and to clinch the matter, the board of directors told him this was his last chance."

The only answer I could make was that if the man followed the usual pattern, he would go on a bigger bust than ever. I felt this was inevitable and wondered if the bank was doing the man an injustice. Why not bring him into contact with some of our alcoholic crowd? He might have a chance. I pointed out that I had had nothing to drink whatever for three years, and this in the face of difficulties that would have made nine out of ten men drink their heads off. Why not at least afford him an opportunity to hear my story? "Oh no," said my friend, "this chap is either through with liquor, or he is minus a job. If he has your will power and guts, he will make the grade."

I wanted to throw up my hands in discouragement, for I saw that I had failed to help my banker friend understand. He simply could not believe that his brother-executive suffered from a serious illness. There was nothing to do but wait.

Presently the man did slip and was fired. Following his discharge, we contacted him. Without much ado, he accepted the principles and procedure that had helped us. He is undoubtedly on the road to recovery. To me, this incident illustrates lack of understanding as to what really ails the alcoholic, and lack of knowledge as to what part employers might profitably take in salvaging their sick employees.

If you desire to help it might be well to disregard your own drinking, or lack of it. Whether you are a hard drinker, a moderate drinker or a teetotaler, you may have some pretty strong opinions, perhaps prejudices. Those who drink moderately may be more annoyed with an alcoholic than a total abstainer would be. Drinking occasionally, and understanding your own reactions, it is possible for you to become quite sure of many things which, so far as the alcoholic is concerned, are not always so. As a moderate drinker, you can take your liquor or leave it alone. Whenever you want to, you control your drinking. Of an evening, you can go on a mild bender, get up in the morning, shake your head and go to business. To you, liquor is no real problem. You cannot see why it should be to anyone else, save the spineless and stupid.

When dealing with an alcoholic, there may be a natural annoyance that a man could be so weak, stupid and irresponsible. Even when you understand the malady better, you may feel this feeling rising.

A look at the alcoholic in your organization is many times illuminating. Is he not usually brilliant, fast-thinking, imaginative and likeable? When sober, does he not work hard and have a knack of getting things done? If he had these qualities and did not drink would he be worth retaining? Should he have the same consideration as other ailing employees? Is he worth salvaging? If your decision is yes, whether the reason be humanitarian or business or both, then the following suggestions may be helpful.

Can you discard the feeling that you are dealing only with habit, with stubbornness, or a weak will? If this presents difficulty, re-reading chapters two and three, where the alcoholic sickness is discussed at length might be worth while. You, as a business man, want to know the necessities before considering the result. If you concede that your employee is ill, can he be forgiven for what he has done in the past? Can his past absurdities be forgotten? Can it be appreciated that he has been a victim of crooked thinking, directly caused by the action of alcohol on his brain?

I well remember the shock I received when a prominent doctor in Chicago told me of cases where pressure of the spinal fluid actually ruptured the brain. No wonder an alcoholic is strangely irrational. Who wouldn't be, with such a fevered brain? Normal drinkers are not so affected, nor can they understand the aberrations of the alcoholic.

Your man has probably been trying to conceal a number of scrapes, perhaps pretty messy ones. They may be disgusting. You may be at a loss to understand how such a seemingly above-board chap could be so involved. But these scrapes can generally be charged, no matter how bad, to the abnormal action of alcohol on his mind. When drinking, or getting over a bout, an alcoholic, sometimes the model of honesty when normal, will do incredible things. Afterward, his revulsion will be terrible. Nearly always, these antics indicate nothing more than temporary conditions.

This is not to say that all alcoholics are honest and upright when not drinking. Of course that isn't so, and such people often may impose on you. Seeing your attempt to understand and help, some men will try to take advantage of your kindness. If you are sure your man does not want to stop, he may as well be discharged, the sooner the better. You are not doing him a favor by keeping him on. Firing such an individual may prove a blessing to him. It may be just the jolt he needs. I know, in my own particular case, that nothing my company could have done would have stopped me for, so long as I was able to hold my position, I could not possibly realize how serious my situation was. Had they fired me first, and had they then taken steps to see that I was presented with the solution contained in this book, I might have returned to them six months later, a well man.

But there are many men who want to stop, and with them you can go far. Your understanding treatment of their cases will pay dividends.

Perhaps you have such a man in mind. He wants to quit drinking and you want to help him, even if it be only a matter of good business. You now know more about alcoholism. You can see that he is mentally and physically sick. You are willing to overlook his past performances. Suppose an approach is made something like this:

State that you know about his drinking, and that it must stop. You might say you appreciate his abilities, would like to keep him, but cannot if he continues to drink. A firm attitude at this point has helped many of us.

Next he can be assured that you do not intend to lecture, moralize, or condemn; that if this was done formerly, it was because of misunderstanding. If possible express a lack of hard feeling toward him. At this point, it might be well to explain alcoholism, the illness. Say that you believe he is a gravely ill person, with this qualification—being perhaps fatally ill, does he want to get well? You ask, because many alcoholics, being warped and drugged, do not want to quit. But does he? Will he take every necessary step, submit to anything to get well, to stop drinking forever?

If he says yes, does he really mean it, or down inside does he think he is fooling you, and that after rest and treatment he will be able to get away with a few drinks now and then? We believe a man should be thoroughly probed on these points. Be satisfied he is not deceiving himself or you.

Whether you mention this book is a matter for your discretion. If he temporizes and still thinks he can ever drink again, even beer, he might as well be discharged after the next bender which, if an alcoholic, he is almost certain to have. He should understand that emphatically. Either you are dealing with a man who can and will get well or you are not. If not, why waste time with him? This may seem severe, but it is usually the best course.

After satisfying yourself that your man wants to recover and that he will go to any extreme to do so, you may suggest a definite course of action. For most alcoholics who are drinking, or who are just getting over a spree, a certain amount of physical treatment is desirable, even imperative. The matter of physical treatment should, of course, be referred to your own doctor. Whatever the method, its object is to thoroughly clear mind and body of the effects of alcohol. In competent hands, this seldom takes long nor is it very expensive. Your man will fare better if placed in such physical condition that he can think straight and no longer craves liquor. If you propose such a procedure to him, it may be necessary to advance the cost of treatment, but we believe it should be made plain that any expense will later be deducted from his pay. It is better for him to feel fully responsible.

If your man accepts your offer, it should be pointed out that physical treatment is but a small part of the picture. Though you are providing him with the best possible medical attention, he should understand that he must undergo a change of heart. To get over drinking will require a transformation of thought and attitude. We all had to place recovery above everything, for without recovery we would have lost both home and business.

Can you have every confidence in his ability to recover? While on the subject of confidence, can you adopt the attitude that so far as you are concerned this will be a strictly personal matter, that his alcoholic derelictions, the treatment about to be undertaken, will never be discussed without his consent? It might be well to have a long chat with him on his return.

To return to the subject matter of this book: It contains full suggestions by which the employee may solve his problem. To you, some of the ideas which it contains are novel. Perhaps you are not quite in sympathy with the approach we suggest. By no means do we offer it as the last word on this subject, but so far as we are concerned, it has worked with us. After all, are you not looking for results rather than methods? Whether your employee likes it or not, he will learn the grim truth about alcoholism. That won't hurt him a bit, even though he does not go for this remedy.

We suggest you draw the book to the attention of the doctor who is to attend your patient during treatment. If the book is read the moment the patient is able, while acutely depressed, realization of his condition may come to him.

We hope the doctor will tell the patient the truth about his condition, whatever that happens to be. When the man is presented with this volume it is best that no one tell him he must abide by its suggestions. The man must decide for himself.

You are betting, of course, that your changed attitude plus the contents of this book will turn the trick. In some cases it will, and in others it may not. But we think that if you persevere, the percentage of successes will gratify you. As our work spreads and our numbers increase, we hope your employees may be put in personal contact with some of us. Meanwhile, we are sure a great deal can be accomplished by the use of the book alone.

On your employee's return, talk with him. Ask him if he thinks he has the answer. If he feels free to discuss his problems with you, if he knows you understand and will not be upset by anything he wishes to say, he will probably be off to a fast start.

In this connection, can you remain undisturbed if the man proceeds to tell you shocking things? He may, for example, reveal that he has padded his expense account or that he has planned to take your best customers away from you. In fact, he may say almost anything if he has accepted our solution which, as you know, demands rigorous honesty. Can you charge this off as you would a bad account and start fresh with him? If he owes you money you may wish to make terms.

If he speaks of his home situation, you can undoubtedly make helpful suggestions. Can he talk frankly with you so long as he does not bear business tales or criticize his associates? With this kind of employee such an attitude will command undying loyalty.

The greatest enemies of us alcoholics are resentment, jealousy, envy, frustration, and fear. Wherever men are gathered together in business there will be rivalries and, arising out of these, a certain amount of office politics. Sometimes we alcoholics have an idea that people are trying to pull us down. Often this is not so at all. But sometimes our drinking will be used politically.

One instance comes to mind in which a malicious individual was always making friendly little jokes about an alcoholic's drinking exploits. In this way he was slyly carrying tales. In another case, an alcoholic was sent to a hospital for treatment. Only a few knew of it at first but, within a short time, it was billboarded throughout the entire company. Naturally this sort of thing decreased the man's chance of recovery. The

employer can many times protect the victim from this
kind of talk. The employer cannot play favorites, but
he can always defend a man from needless provocation and unfair criticism.

As a class, alcoholics are energetic people. They
work hard and they play hard. Your man should be
on his mettle to make good. Being somewhat weakened, and faced with physical and mental readjustment to a life which knows no alcohol, he may overdo.
You may have to curb his desire to work sixteen hours
a day. You may need to encourage him to play once
in a while. He may wish to do a lot for other alcoholics and something of the sort may come up during
business hours. A reasonable amount of latitude will
be helpful. This work is necessary to maintain his
sobriety.

After your man has gone along without drinking
for a few months, you may be able to make use of his
services with other employees who are giving you the
alcoholic run-around—provided, of course, they are
willing to have a third party in the picture. An alcoholic who has recovered, but holds a relatively unimportant job, can talk to a man with a better position.
Being on a radically different basis of life, he will never
take advantage of the situation.

Your man may be trusted. Long experience with
alcoholic excuses naturally arouses suspicion. When
his wife next calls saying he is sick, you might jump
to the conclusion he is drunk. If he is, and is still
trying to recover, he will tell you about it even if it
means the loss of his job. For he knows he must be
honest if he would live at all. He will appreciate
knowing you are not bothering your head about him,

that you are not suspicious nor are you trying to run his life so he will be shielded from temptation to drink. If he is conscientiously following the program of recovery he can go anywhere your business may call him.

In case he does stumble, even once, you will have to decide whether to let him go. If you are sure he doesn't mean business, there is no doubt you should discharge him. If, on the contrary, you are sure he is doing his utmost, you may wish to give him another chance. But you should feel under no obligation to keep him on, for your obligation has been well discharged already.

There is another thing you might wish to do. If your organization is a large one, your junior executives might be provided with this book. You might let them know you have no quarrel with the alcoholics of your organization. These juniors are often in a difficult position. Men under them are frequently their friends. So, for one reason or another, they cover these men, hoping matters will take a turn for the better. They often jeopardize their own positions by trying to help serious drinkers who should have been fired long ago, or else given an opportunity to get well.

After reading this book, a junior executive can go to such a man and say approximately this, "Look here, Ed. Do you want to stop drinking or not? You put me on the spot every time you get drunk. It isn't fair to me or the firm. I have been learning something about alcoholism. If you are an alcoholic, you are a mighty sick man. You act like one. The firm wants to help you get over it, and if you are interested, there is a way out. If you take it, your past will be forgotten

and the fact that you went away for treatment will
not be mentioned. But if you cannot or will not stop
drinking, I think you ought to resign."

Your junior executive may not agree with the contents of our book. He need not, and often should not
show it to his alcoholic prospect. But at least he will
understand the problem and will no longer be misled
by ordinary promises. He will be able to take a position with such a man which is eminently fair and
square. He will have no further reason for covering
up an alcoholic employee.

It boils right down to this: No man should be fired
just because he is alcoholic. If he wants to stop, he
should be afforded a real chance. If he cannot or does
not want to stop, he should be discharged. The exceptions are few.

We think this method of approach will accomplish
several things. It will permit the rehabilitation of good
men. At the same time you will feel no reluctance to
rid yourself of those who cannot or will not stop.
Alcoholism may be causing your organization considerable damage in its waste of time, men and reputation. We hope our suggestions will help you plug up
this sometimes serious leak. We think we are sensible
when we urge that you stop this waste and give your
worthwhile man a chance.

The other day an approach was made to the vice
president of a large industrial concern. He remarked:
"I'm mighty glad you fellows got over your drinking.
But the policy of this company is not to interfere with
the habits of our employees. If a man drinks so much
that his job suffers, we fire him. I don't see how you
can be of any help to us for, as you see, we don't have

any alcoholic problem." This same company spends millions for research every year. Their cost of production is figured to a fine decimal point. They have recreational facilities. There is company insurance. There is a real interest, both humanitarian and business, in the well-being of employees. But alcoholism —well, they just don't believe they have it.

Perhaps this is a typical attitude. We, who have collectively seen a great deal of business life, at least from the alcoholic angle, had to smile at this gentleman's sincere opinion. He might be shocked if he knew how much alcoholism is costing his organization a year. That company may harbor many actual or potential alcoholics. We believe that managers of large enterprises often have little idea how prevalent this problem is. Even if you feel your organization has no alcoholic problem, it might pay to take another look down the line. You may make some interesting discoveries.

Of course, this chapter refers to alcoholics, sick people, deranged men. What our friend, the vice president, had in mind was the habitual or whoopee drinker. As to them, his policy is undoubtedly sound, but he did not distinguish between such people and the alcoholic.

It is not to be expected that an alcoholic employee will receive a disproportionate amount of time and attention. He should not be made a favorite. The right kind of man, the kind who recovers, will not want this sort of thing. He will not impose. Far from it. He will work like the devil and thank you to his dying day.

Today I own a little company. There are two

alcoholic employees, who produce as much as five normal salesmen. But why not? They have a new attitude, and they have been saved from a living death. I have enjoyed every moment spent in getting them straightened out.*

* See Appendix VI—We shall be happy to hear from you if we can be of help.

Chapter 11

A VISION FOR YOU

FOR MOST normal folks, drinking means conviviality, companionship and colorful imagination. It means release from care, boredom and worry. It is joyous intimacy with friends and a feeling that life is good. But not so with us in those last days of heavy drinking. The old pleasures were gone. They were but memories. Never could we recapture the great moments of the past. There was an insistent yearning to enjoy life as we once did and a heartbreaking obsession that some new miracle of control would enable us to do it. There was always one more attempt—and one more failure.

The less people tolerated us, the more we withdrew from society, from life itself. As we became subjects of King Alcohol, shivering denizens of his mad realm, the chilling vapor that is loneliness settled down. It thickened, ever becoming blacker. Some of us sought out sordid places, hoping to find understanding companionship and approval. Momentarily we did—then would come oblivion and the awful awakening to face the hideous Four Horsemen—Terror, Bewilderment, Frustration, Despair. Unhappy drinkers who read this page will understand!

Now and then a serious drinker, being dry at the moment says, "I don't miss it at all. Feel better. Work better. Having a better time." As ex-problem drinkers, we smile at such a sally. We know our friend is like a boy whistling in the dark to keep up his spirits. He fools himself. Inwardly he would give anything to take half a dozen drinks and get away with them. He will presently try the old game again, for he isn't happy about his sobriety. He cannot picture life without alcohol. Some day he will be unable to imagine life either with alcohol or without it. Then he will know loneliness such as few do. He will be at the jumping-off place. He will wish for the end.

We have shown how we got out from under. You say, "Yes, I'm willing. But am I to be consigned to a life where I shall be stupid, boring and glum, like some righteous people I see? I know I must get along without liquor, but how can I? Have you a sufficient substitute?"

Yes, there is a substitute and it is vastly more than that. It is a fellowship in Alcoholics Anonymous. There you will find release from care, boredom and worry. Your imagination will be fired. Life will mean something at last. The most satisfactory years of your existence lie ahead. Thus we find the fellowship, and so will you.

"How is that to come about?" you ask. "Where am I to find these people?"

You are going to meet these new friends in your own community. Near you, alcoholics are dying helplessly like people in a sinking ship. If you live in a large place, there are hundreds. High and low, rich and poor, these are future fellows of Alcoholics Anonymous. Among them you will make lifelong friends. You will be bound to them with new and wonderful ties, for you will escape disaster together and you will commence shoulder to shoulder your common journey. Then you will know what it means to give of yourself that others may survive and rediscover life. You will learn the full meaning of "Love thy neighbor as thyself."

It may seem incredible that these men are to become happy, respected, and useful once more. How can they rise out of such misery, bad repute and hopelessness? The practical answer is that since these things have happened among us, they can happen with you. Should you wish them above all else, and be willing to make use of our experience, we are sure they will come. The age of miracles is still with us. Our own recovery proves that!

Our hope is that when this chip of a book is launched on the world tide of alcoholism, defeated drinkers will seize upon it, to follow its suggestions. Many, we are sure, will rise to their feet and march on. They will approach still other sick ones and fellowships of Alcoholics Anonymous may spring up in each city and hamlet, havens for those who must find a way out.

In the chapter "Working With Others" you gathered an idea of how we approach and aid others to health. Suppose now that through you several families have adopted this way of life. You will want to know more of how to proceed from that point. Perhaps the best way of treating you to a glimpse of your future will be to describe the growth of the fellowship among us. Here is a brief account:

Years ago, in 1935, one of our number made a journey to a certain western city. From a business standpoint, his trip came off badly. Had he been successful in his enterprise, he would have been set on his feet financially which, at the time, seemed vitally important. But his venture wound up in a law suit and bogged down completely. The proceeding was shot through with much hard feeling and controversy.

Bitterly discouraged, he found himself in a strange place, discredited and almost broke. Still physically weak, and sober but a few months, he saw that his predicament was dangerous. He wanted so much to talk with someone, but whom?

One dismal afternoon he paced a hotel lobby wondering how his bill was to be paid. At one end of the room stood a glass covered directory of local churches. Down the lobby a door opened into an attractive bar. He could see the gay crowd inside. In there he would find companionship and release. Unless he took some drinks, he might not have the courage to scrape an acquaintance and would have a lonely week-end.

Of course he couldn't drink, but why not sit hopefully at a table, a bottle of ginger ale before him? After all, had he not been sober six months now? Perhaps he could handle, say, three drinks—no more! Fear gripped him. He was on thin ice. Again it was the old, insidious insanity—that first drink. With a shiver, he turned away and walked down the lobby to the church directory. Music and gay chatter still floated to him from the bar.

But what about his responsibilities—his family and the men who would die because they would not know how to get well, ah—yes, those other alcoholics? There must be many such in this town. He would phone a clergyman. His sanity returned and he thanked

God. Selecting a church at random from the directory, he stepped into a booth and lifted the receiver.

His call to the clergyman led him presently to a certain resident of the town, who, though formerly able and respected, was then nearing the nadir of alcoholic despair. It was the usual situation: home in jeopardy, wife ill, children distracted, bills in arrears and standing damaged. He had a desperate desire to stop, but saw no way out, for he had earnestly tried many avenues of escape. Painfully aware of being somehow abnormal, the man did not fully realize what it meant to be alcoholic.*

When our friend related his experience, the man agreed that no amount of will power he might muster could stop his drinking for long. A spiritual experience, he conceded, was absolutely necessary, but the price seemed high upon the basis suggested. He told how he lived in constant worry about those who might find out about his alcoholism. He had, of course, the familiar alcoholic obsession that few knew of his drinking. Why, he argued, should he lose the remainder of his business, only to bring still more suffering to his family by foolishly admitting his plight to people from whom he made his livelihood? He would do anything, he said, but that.

Being intrigued, however, he invited our friend to his home. Some time later, and just as he thought he was getting control of his liquor situation, he went on a roaring bender. For him, this was the spree that ended all sprees. He saw that he would have to face

---

* This refers to Bill's first visit with Dr. Bob. These men later became co-founders of A.A. Bill's story opens the text of this book; Dr. Bob's heads the Story Section.

his problems squarely that God might give him mastery.

One morning he took the bull by the horns and set out to tell those he feared what his trouble had been. He found himself surprisingly well received, and learned that many knew of his drinking. Stepping into his car, he made the rounds of people he had hurt. He trembled as he went about, for this might mean ruin, particularly to a person in his line of business.

At midnight he came home exhausted, but very happy. He has not had a drink since. As we shall see, he now means a great deal to his community, and the major liabilities of thirty years of hard drinking have been repaired in four.

But life was not easy for the two friends. Plenty of difficulties presented themselves. Both saw that they must keep spiritually active. One day they called up the head nurse of a local hospital. They explained their need and inquired if she had a first class alcoholic prospect.

She replied, "Yes, we've got a corker. He's just beaten up a couple of nurses. Goes off his head completely when he's drinking. But he's a grand chap when he's sober, though he's been in here eight times in the last six months. Understand he was once a well-known lawyer in town, but just now we've got him strapped down tight."*

Here was a prospect all right but, by the description, none too promising. The use of spiritual principles in

_____

* This refers to Bill's and Dr. Bob's first visit to A.A. Number Three. See the Pioneer Section. This resulted in A.A.'s first group, at Akron, Ohio, in 1935.

such cases was not so well understood as it is now. But one of the friends said, "Put him in a private room. We'll be down."

Two days later, a future fellow of Alcoholics Anonymous stared glassily at the strangers beside his bed. "Who are you fellows, and why this private room? I was always in a ward before."

Said one of the visitors, "We're giving you a treatment for alcoholism."

Hopelessness was written large on the man's face as he replied, "Oh, but that's no use. Nothing would fix me. I'm a goner. The last three times, I got drunk on the way home from here. I'm afraid to go out the door. I can't understand it."

For an hour, the two friends told him about their drinking experiences. Over and over, he would say: "That's me. That's me. I drink like that."

The man in the bed was told of the acute poisoning from which he suffered, how it deteriorates the body of an alcoholic and warps his mind. There was much talk about the mental state preceding the first drink.

"Yes, that's me," said the sick man, "the very image. You fellows know your stuff all right, but I don't see what good it'll do. You fellows are somebody. I was once, but I'm a nobody now. From what you tell me, I know more than ever I can't stop." At this both the visitors burst into a laugh. Said the future Fellow Anonymous: "Damn little to laugh about that I can see."

The two friends spoke of their spiritual experience and told him about the course of action they carried out.

He interrupted: "I used to be strong for the church,

but that won't fix it. I've prayed to God on hangover mornings and sworn that I'd never touch another drop but by nine o'clock I'd be boiled as an owl."

Next day found the prospect more receptive. He had been thinking it over. "Maybe you're right," he said. "God ought to be able to do anything." Then he added, "He sure didn't do much for me when I was trying to fight this booze racket alone."

On the third day the lawyer gave his life to the care and direction of his Creator, and said he was perfectly willing to do anything necessary. His wife came, scarcely daring to be hopeful, though she thought she saw something different about her husband already. He had begun to have a spiritual experience.

That afternoon he put on his clothes and walked from the hospital a free man. He entered a political campaign, making speeches, frequenting men's gathering places of all sorts, often staying up all night. He lost the race by only a narrow margin. But he had found God—and in finding God had found himself.

That was in June, 1935. He never drank again. He too, has become a respected and useful member of his community. He has helped other men recover, and is a power in the church from which he was long absent.

So, you see, there were three alcoholics in that town, who now felt they had to give to others what they had found, or be sunk. After several failures to find others, a fourth turned up. He came through an acquaintance who had heard the good news. He proved to be a devil-may-care young fellow whose parents could not make out whether he wanted to stop drinking or not. They were deeply religious people, much shocked by their son's refusal to have anything to do with the church. He suffered horribly from his sprees, but it seemed as if nothing could be done for him. He consented, however, to go to the hospital, where he occupied the very room recently vacated by the lawyer.

He had three visitors. After a bit, he said, "The way you fellows put this spiritual stuff makes sense. I'm ready to do business. I guess the old folks were right after all." So one more was added to the Fellowship.

All this time our friend of the hotel lobby incident remained in that town. He was there three months. He now returned home, leaving behind his first acquaintance, the lawyer and the devil-may-care chap. These men had found something brand new in life. Though they knew they must help other alcoholics if they would remain sober, that motive became secondary. It was transcended by the happiness they found in giving themselves for others. They shared their homes, their slender resources, and gladly devoted their spare hours to fellow-sufferers. They were willing, by day or night, to place a new man in the hospital and visit him afterward. They grew in numbers. They experienced a few distressing failures, but in those cases they made an effort to bring the man's family into a spiritual way of living, thus relieving much worry and suffering.

A year and six months later these three had succeeded with seven more. Seeing much of each other, scarce an evening passed that someone's home did not shelter a little gathering of men and women, happy in their release, and constantly thinking how they might present their discovery to some newcomer. In addition to these casual get-togethers, it became customary to set apart one night a week for a meeting to be attended by anyone or everyone interested in a spiritual way of life. Aside from fellowship and sociability, the prime object was to provide a time and place where new people might bring their problems.

Outsiders became interested. One man and his wife placed their large home at the disposal of this strangely assorted crowd. This couple has since become so fascinated that they have dedicated their home to the work. Many a distracted wife has visited this house to find loving and understanding companionship among women who knew her problem, to hear from the lips of their husbands what had happened to them, to be advised how her own wayward mate might be hospitalized and approached when next he stumbled.

Many a man, yet dazed from his hospital experience, has stepped over the threshold of that home into freedom. Many an alcoholic who entered there came away with an answer. He succumbed to that gay crowd inside, who laughed at their own misfortunes and understood his. Impressed by those who visited him at the hospital, he capitulated entirely when, later, in an upper room of this house, he heard the story of some man whose experience closely tallied with his own. The expression on the faces of the women, that indefinable something in the eyes of the men, the stimulating and electric atmosphere of the place, conspired to let him know that here was haven at last.

The very practical approach to his problems, the absence of intolerance of any kind, the informality, the genuine democracy, the uncanny understanding which these people had were irresistible. He and his wife would leave elated by the thought of what they could now do for some stricken acquaintance and his family. They knew they had a host of new friends; it seemed they had known these strangers always. They had seen miracles, and one was to come to them. They had visioned the Great Reality—their loving and All Powerful Creator.

Now, this house will hardly accommodate its weekly visitors, for they number sixty or eighty as a rule. Alcoholics are being attracted from far and near. From surrounding towns, families drive long distances to be present. A community thirty miles away has fifteen fellows of Alcoholics Anonymous. Being a large place, we think that some day its Fellowship will number many hundreds.*

But life among Alcoholics Anonymous is more than attending gatherings and visiting hospitals. Cleaning up old scrapes, helping to settle family differences, explaining the disinherited son to his irate parents, lending money and securing jobs for each other, when justified—these are everyday occurrences. No one is too discredited or has sunk too low to be welcomed cordially—if he means business. Social distinctions, petty rivalries and jealousies—these are laughed out of countenance. Being wrecked in the same vessel, being restored and united under one God, with hearts and minds attuned to the welfare of others, the things which matter so much to some people no longer signify much to them. How could they?

Under only slightly different conditions, the same thing is taking place in many eastern cities. In one of

* Written in 1939.

these there is a well-known hospital for the treatment
of alcoholic and drug addiction. Six years ago one of
our number was a patient there. Many of us have felt,
for the first time, the Presence and Power of God
within its walls. We are greatly indebted to the doctor in attendance there, for he, although it might prejudice his own work, has told us of his belief in ours.

Every few days this doctor suggests our approach
to one of his patients. Understanding our work, he
can do this with an eye to selecting those who are
willing and able to recover on a spiritual basis. Many
of us, former patients, go there to help. Then, in this
eastern city, there are informal meetings such as we
have described to you, where you may now see scores
of members. There are the same fast friendships,
there is the same helpfulness to one another as you
find among our western friends. There is a good bit
of travel between East and West and we foresee a
great increase in this helpful interchange.

Some day we hope that every alcoholic who
journeys will find a Fellowship of Alcoholics Anonymous at his destination. To some extent this is already
true. Some of us are salesmen and go about. Little
clusters of twos and threes and fives of us have sprung
up in other communities, through contact with our
two larger centers. Those of us who travel drop in as
often as we can. This practice enables us to lend a
hand, at the same time avoiding certain alluring dis-
tractions of the road, about which any traveling man
can inform you.*

Thus we grow. And so can you, though you be but

* Written in 1939. In 2012, there are over 114,000 groups. There is A.A. activity in
approximately 170 countries, with an estimated membership of over two million.

one man with this book in your hand. We believe and hope it contains all you will need to begin.

We know what you are thinking. You are saying to yourself: "I'm jittery and alone. I couldn't do that." But you can. You forget that you have just now tapped a source of power much greater than yourself. To duplicate, with such backing, what we have accomplished is only a matter of willingness, patience and labor.

We know of an A.A. member who was living in a large community. He had lived there but a few weeks when he found that the place probably contained more alcoholics per square mile than any city in the country. This was only a few days ago at this writing. (1939) The authorities were much concerned. He got in touch with a prominent psychiatrist who had undertaken certain responsibilities for the mental health of the community. The doctor proved to be able and exceedingly anxious to adopt any workable method of handling the situation. So he inquired, what did our friend have on the ball?

Our friend proceeded to tell him. And with such good effect that the doctor agreed to a test among his patients and certain other alcoholics from a clinic which he attends. Arrangements were also made with the chief psychiatrist of a large public hospital to select still others from the stream of misery which flows through that institution.

So our fellow worker will soon have friends galore. Some of them may sink and perhaps never get up, but if our experience is a criterion, more than half of those approached will become fellows of Alcoholics Anonymous. When a few men in this city have found themselves, and have discovered the joy of helping others to face life again, there will be no stopping until everyone in that town has had his opportunity to recover—if he can and will.

Still you may say: "But I will not have the benefit of contact with you who write this book." We cannot be sure. God will determine that, so you must remember that your real reliance is always upon Him. He will show you how to create the fellowship you crave.*

Our book is meant to be suggestive only. We realize we know only a little. God will constantly disclose more to you and to us. Ask Him in your morning meditation what you can do each day for the man who is still sick. The answers will come, if your own house is in order. But obviously you cannot transmit something you haven't got. See to it that your relationship with Him is right, and great events will come to pass for you and countless others. This is the Great Fact for us.

Abandon yourself to God as you understand God. Admit your faults to Him and to your fellows. Clear away the wreckage of your past. Give freely of what you find and join us. We shall be with you in the Fellowship of the Spirit, and you will surely meet some of us as you trudge the Road of Happy Destiny.

May God bless you and keep you—until then.

---

* Alcoholics Anonymous will be glad to hear from you. Address P.O. Box 459, Grand Central Station, New York, NY 10163.

PERSONAL STORIES

*How Forty-Two Alcoholics
Recovered From Their Malady*

Beginning with the story of "Dr. Bob," a co-founder of A.A., there are here presented three groups of personal histories.

Part I

PIONEERS OF A.A.

This group of ten stories shows that sobriety in
A.A. can be lasting.

Part II

THEY STOPPED IN TIME

Seventeen stories may help you decide whether you
are alcoholic; also, whether A.A. is for you.

Part III

THEY LOST NEARLY ALL

Those who believe their drinking to be hopeless may
again find hope in these fifteen impressive tales.

PART I

PIONEERS OF A.A.

Dr. Bob and the nine men and women who here tell their stories were among the early members of A.A.'s first groups.

All ten have now passed away of natural causes, having maintained complete sobriety.

Today, hundreds of additional A.A. members can be found who have had no relapse for more than fifty years.

All of these, then, are the pioneers of A.A. They bear witness that release from alcoholism can really be permanent.

DOCTOR BOB'S NIGHTMARE

A co-founder of Alcoholics Anonymous. The birth of our Society dates from his first day of permanent sobriety, June 10, 1935.

To 1950, the year of his death, he carried the A.A. message to more than 5,000 alcoholic men and women, and to all these he gave his medical services without thought of charge.

In this prodigy of service, he was well assisted by Sister Ignatia at St. Thomas Hospital in Akron, Ohio, one of the greatest friends our Fellowship will ever know.

I WAS BORN in a small New England village of about seven thousand souls. The general moral standard was, as I recall it, far above the average. No beer or liquor was sold in the neighborhood, except at the State liquor agency where perhaps one might procure a pint if he could convince the agent that he really needed it. Without this proof the expectant purchaser would be forced to depart empty handed with none of what I later came to believe was the great panacea for all human ills. Men who had liquor shipped in from Boston or New York by express were looked upon with great distrust and disfavor by most of the good townspeople. The town was well supplied with churches and schools in which I pursued my early educational activities.

My father was a professional man of recognized ability and both my father and mother were most active in church affairs. Both father and mother were considerably above the average in intelligence.

Unfortunately for me, I was the only child, which perhaps engendered the selfishness which played such an important part in bringing on my alcoholism.

From childhood through high school I was more or less forced to go to church, Sunday School, and evening service, Monday night Christian Endeavor and sometimes to Wednesday evening prayer meeting. This had the effect of making me resolve that when I was free from parental domination, I would never again darken the doors of a church. This resolution I kept steadfastly for the next forty years, except when circumstances made it seem unwise to absent myself.

After high school came four years in one of the best colleges in the country where drinking seemed to be a major extra-curricular activity. Almost everyone seemed to do it. I did it more and more, and had lots of fun without much grief, either physical or financial. I seemed to be able to snap back the next morning better than most of my fellow drinkers, who were cursed (or perhaps blessed) with a great deal of morning-after nausea. Never once in my life have I had a headache, which fact leads me to believe that I was an alcoholic almost from the start. My whole life seemed to be centered around doing what I wanted to do, without regard for the rights, wishes, or privileges of anyone else; a state of mind which became more and more predominant as the years passed. I was graduated "summa cum laude" in the eyes of the drinking fraternity but not in the eyes of the Dean.

The next three years I spent in Boston, Chicago, and Montreal in the employ of a large manufacturing concern, selling railway supplies, gas engines of all sorts, and many other items of heavy hardware. During these years, I drank as much as my purse permitted, still without paying too great a penalty, although I was beginning to have morning jitters at times. I lost only a half day's work during these three years.

My next move was to take up the study of medicine, entering one of the largest universities in the country. There I took up the business of drinking with much greater earnestness than I had previously shown. On account of my enormous capacity for beer, I was elected to membership in one of the drinking societies, and soon became one of the leading spirits. Many mornings I have gone to classes, and even though fully prepared, would turn and walk back to the fraternity house because of my jitters, not daring to enter the classroom for fear of making a scene should I be called on for recitation.

This went from bad to worse until Sophomore spring when, after a prolonged period of drinking, I made up my mind that I could not complete my course, so I packed my grip and went South to spend a month on a large farm owned by a friend of mine. When I got the fog out of my brain, I decided that quitting school was very foolish and that I had better return and continue my work. When I reached school, I discovered the faculty had other ideas on the subject. After much argument they allowed me to return and take my exams, all of which I passed creditably. But they were much disgusted and told me they would attempt to struggle along without my presence. After many painful discussions, they finally gave me my credits and I migrated to another of the leading universities of the country and entered as a Junior that fall.

There my drinking became so much worse that the boys in the fraternity house where I lived felt forced to send for my father, who made a long journey in the vain endeavor to get me straightened around. This had little effect however for I kept on drinking and used a great deal more hard liquor than in former years.

Coming up to final exams I went on a particularly strenuous spree. When I went in to write the examinations, my hand trembled so I could not hold a pencil. I passed in at least three absolutely blank books. I was, of course, soon on the carpet and the upshot was that I had to go back for two more quarters and remain absolutely dry, if I wished to graduate. This I did, and proved myself satisfactory to the faculty, both in deportment and scholastically.

I conducted myself so creditably that I was able to secure a much coveted internship in a western city, where I spent two years. During these two years I was kept so busy that I hardly left the hospital at all. Consequently, I could not get into any trouble.

When those two years were up, I opened an office downtown. I had some money, all the time in the world, and considerable stomach trouble. I soon discovered that a couple of drinks would alleviate my gastric distress, at least for a few hours at a time, so it was not at all difficult for me to return to my former excessive indulgence.

By this time I was beginning to pay very dearly physically and, in hope of relief, voluntarily incarcerated myself at least a dozen times in one of the local sanitariums. I was between Scylla and Charybdis now, because if I did not drink my stomach tortured me, and if I did my nerves did the same thing. After three years of this, I wound up in the local hospital where they attempted to help me, but I would get my friends to smuggle me a quart, or I would steal the alcohol about the building, so that I got rapidly worse.

Finally, my father had to send a doctor out from my home town who managed to get me back there in some way, and I was in bed about two months before I could venture out of the house. I stayed about town a couple of months more and then returned to resume my practice. I think I must have been thoroughly scared by what had happened, or by the doctor, or probably both, so that I did not touch a drink again until the country went dry.

With the passing of the Eighteenth Amendment I felt quite safe. I knew everyone would buy a few bottles, or cases, of liquor as their exchequers permitted, and that it would soon be gone. Therefore it would make no great difference, even if I should do some drinking. At that time I was not aware of the almost unlimited supply the government made it possible for us doctors to obtain, neither had I any knowledge of the bootlegger who soon appeared on the horizon. I drank with moderation at first, but it took me only a relatively short time to drift back into the old habits, which had wound up so disastrously before.

During the next few years, I developed two distinct phobias. One was the fear of not sleeping, and the other was the fear of running out of liquor. Not being a man of means, I knew that if I did not stay sober enough to earn money, I would run out of liquor. Most of the time, therefore, I did not take the morning drink which I craved so badly, but instead would fill up on large doses of sedatives to quiet the jitters, which distressed me terribly. Occasionally, I would yield to the morning craving, but if I did, it would be only a few hours before I would be quite unfit for work. This would lessen my chances of smuggling some home that evening, which in turn would mean a night of futile tossing around in bed followed by a morning of unbearable jitters. During the subsequent fifteen years I had sense enough never to go to the hospital if I had been drinking, and very seldom did I receive patients. I would sometimes hide out in one of the clubs of which I was a member, and had the habit at times of registering at a hotel under a fictitious name. But my friends usually found me and I would go home if they promised that I should not be scolded.

If my wife was planning to go out in the afternoon, I would get a large supply of liquor and smuggle it home and hide it in the coal bin, the clothes chute, over door jambs, over beams in the cellar, and in cracks in the cellar tile. I also made use of old trunks and chests, the old can container, and even the ash container. The water tank on the toilet I never used, because that looked too easy. I found out later that my wife inspected it frequently. I used to put eight or twelve ounce bottles of alcohol in a fur lined glove and toss it onto the back airing porch when winter days got dark enough. My bootlegger had hidden alcohol at the back steps where I could get it at my convenience. Sometimes I would bring it in my pockets, but they were inspected, and that became too risky. I used also to put it up in four ounce bottles and stick several in my stocking tops. This worked nicely until my wife and I went to see Wallace Beery in "Tugboat Annie," after which the pant-leg and stocking racket were out!

I will not take space to relate all my hospital or sanitarium experiences.

During all this time we became more or less ostracized by our friends. We could not be invited out because I would surely get tight, and my wife dared not invite people in for the same reason. My phobia for sleeplessness demanded that I get drunk every night, but in order to get more liquor for the next night, I had to stay sober during the day, at least up to four o'clock. This routine went on with few interruptions for seventeen years. It was really a horrible nightmare, this earning money, getting liquor, smuggling it home, getting drunk, morning jitters, taking large doses of sedatives to make it possible for me to earn more money, and so on ad nauseam. I used to promise my wife, my friends, and my children that I would drink no more—promises which seldom kept me sober even through the day, though I was very sincere when I made them.

For the benefit of those experimentally inclined, I should mention the so-called beer experiment. When beer first came back, I thought that I was safe. I could drink all I wanted of that. It was harmless; nobody ever got drunk on beer. So I filled the cellar full, with the permission of my good wife. It was not long before I was drinking at least a case and a half a day. I put on thirty pounds of weight in about two months, looked like a pig, and was uncomfortable from shortness of breath. It then occurred to me that after one was all smelled up with beer nobody could tell what had been drunk, so I began to fortify my beer with straight alcohol. Of course, the result was very bad, and that ended the beer experiment.

About the time of the beer experiment I was thrown in with a crowd of people who attracted me because of their seeming poise, health, and happiness. They spoke with great freedom from embarrassment, which I could never do, and they seemed very much at ease on all occasions and appeared very healthy. More than these attributes, they seemed to be happy. I was self conscious and ill at ease most of the time, my health was at the breaking point, and I was thoroughly miserable. I sensed they had something I did not have, from which I might readily profit. I learned that it was something of a spiritual nature, which did not appeal to me very much, but I thought it could do no harm. I gave the matter much time and study for the next two and a half years, but I still got tight every night nevertheless. I read everything I could find, and talked to everyone who I thought knew anything about it.

My wife became deeply interested, and it was her interest that sustained mine, though I at no time sensed that it might be an answer to my liquor problem. How my wife kept her faith and courage during all those years, I'll never know, but she did. If she had not, I know I would have been dead a long time ago. For some reason, we alcoholics seem to have the gift of picking out the world's finest women. Why they should be subjected to the tortures we inflict upon them, I cannot explain.

About this time a lady called up my wife one Saturday afternoon saying she wanted me to come over that evening to meet a friend of hers who might help me. It was the day before Mother's Day and I had come home plastered, carrying a big potted plant which I set down on the table and forthwith went upstairs and passed out. The next day she called again. Wishing to be polite, though I felt very badly, I said, "Let's make the call," and extracted from my wife a promise that we would not stay over fifteen minutes.

We entered her house at exactly five o'clock and it was eleven fifteen when we left. I had a couple of shorter talks with this man afterward, and stopped drinking abruptly. This dry spell lasted for about three weeks; then I went to Atlantic City to attend several days' meeting of a national society of which I was a member. I drank all the scotch they had on the train and bought several quarts on my way to the hotel. This was on Sunday. I got tight that night, stayed sober Monday till after the dinner, and then proceeded to get tight again. I drank all I dared in the bar, and then went to my room to finish the job. Tuesday I started in the morning, getting well organized by noon. I did not want to disgrace myself so I then checked out. I bought some more liquor on the way to the depot. I had to wait some time for the train. I remember nothing from then on until I woke up at a friend's house, in a town near home. These good people notified my wife, who sent my newly made friend over to get me. He came and got me home and to bed, gave me a few drinks that night, and one bottle of beer the next morning.

That was June 10, 1935, and that was my last drink. As I write, nearly four years have passed.

The question which might naturally come into your mind would be: "What did the man do or say that was different from what others had done or said?" It must be remembered that I had read a great deal and talked to everyone who knew, or thought they knew anything about the subject of alcoholism. But this was a man who had experienced many years of frightful drinking, who had had most all the drunkard's experiences known to man, but who had been cured by the very means I had been trying to employ, that is to say the spiritual approach. He gave me information about the subject of alcoholism which was undoubtedly helpful. *Of far more importance was the fact that he was the first living human with whom I had ever talked, who knew what he was talking about in regard to alcoholism from actual experience. In other words, he talked my language.* He knew all the answers, and certainly not because he had picked them up in his reading.

It is a most wonderful blessing to be relieved of the terrible curse with which I was afflicted. My health is good and I have regained my self-respect and the respect of my colleagues. My home life is ideal and my business is as good as can be expected in these uncertain times.

I spend a great deal of time passing on what I learned to others who want and need it badly. I do it for four reasons:

1. Sense of duty.
2. It is a pleasure.
3. Because in so doing I am paying my debt to the man who took time to pass it on to me.
4. Because every time I do it I take out a little more insurance for myself against a possible slip.

Unlike most of our crowd, I did not get over my craving for liquor much during the first two and one-half years of abstinence. It was almost always with me. But at no time have I been anywhere near yielding. I used to get terribly upset when I saw my friends drink and knew I could not, but I schooled myself to believe that though I once had the same privilege, I had abused it so frightfully that it was withdrawn. So it doesn't behoove me to squawk about it for, after all, nobody ever had to throw me down and pour liquor down my throat.

If you think you are an atheist, an agnostic, a skeptic, or have any other form of intellectual pride which keeps you from accepting what is in this book, I feel sorry for you. If you still think you are strong enough to beat the game alone, that is your affair. But if you really and truly want to quit drinking liquor for good and all, and sincerely feel that you must have some help, we know that we have an answer for you. It never fails, if you go about it with one half the zeal you have been in the habit of showing when you were getting another drink.

Your Heavenly Father will never let you down!

(1)

ALCOHOLIC ANONYMOUS
NUMBER THREE

*Pioneer member of Akron's Group No. 1, the first
A.A. group in the world. He kept the faith; therefore,
he and countless others found a new life.*

ONE OF FIVE children, I was born on a Kentucky
farm in Carlyle County. My parents were well-
to-do people, and their marriage was a happy one.
My wife, a Kentucky girl, came with me to Akron
where I completed my course in law at the Akron Law
School.

My case is rather unusual in one respect. There
were no childhood episodes of unhappiness to account
for my alcoholism. I had, seemingly, just a natural
affinity for grog. My marriage was happy, and I never
had any of the reasons, conscious or unconscious,
which are often given for drinking. Yet, as my record
shows, I did become an extremely serious case.

Before my drinking had cut me down completely, I
achieved a considerable measure of success, having
been a city councilman for five years and a financial
director of a suburb later taken into the city itself.
But, of course, this all went down the drain with my
increased drinking. So, at the time Dr. Bob and Bill
came along, I had about run out my strength.

The first time that I became intoxicated I was eight
years old. This was no fault of my father or mother, as

they were both very much opposed to drinking. A couple of hired hands were cleaning out the barn on the farm, and I was riding to and fro on the sled, and while they were loading, I drank hard cider out of a barrel in the barn. On the return trip, after two or three loads, I passed out and had to be carried to the house. I remember that my father kept whiskey around the house for medical purposes and entertainment, and I would drink from this when no one was about and then water it to keep my parents from knowing I was drinking.

This continued until I enrolled in our state university, and at the end of the four years, I realized that I was a drunk. Morning after morning I awoke sick and with terrible jitters, but there was always a flask of liquor sitting on the table beside my bed. I would reach over and get this and take a shot and in a few moments get up and take another, shave, eat my breakfast, slip a half pint of liquor in my hip pocket, and go on to school. Between classes I would run down to the washroom, take enough to steady my nerves, and then go on to the next class. This was in 1917.

I left the university in the latter part of my senior year and enlisted in the army. At the time, I called it patriotism. Later I realized that I was running from alcohol. It did help to a certain extent, since I found myself in places where I could not obtain anything to drink and so broke the habitual drinking.

Then Prohibition came into effect, and the facts that the stuff obtainable was so horrible and sometimes deadly, and that I had married and had a job which I had to look after, helped me for a period of some three or four years, although I would get drunk every time I could get hold of enough to drink to get started. My wife and I belonged to some bridge clubs, and they began to make wine and serve it. However, after two or three trials, I found this was not satisfactory because they did not serve enough to satisfy me. So I would refuse to drink. This problem was soon solved, however, as I began to take my bottle along with me and hide it in the bathroom or in the shrubbery outside.

As time went on, my drinking became progressively worse. I would be away from my office two or three weeks at a time, horrible days and nights when I would lie on the floor of my home and reach over to get the bottle, take a drink, and then go back into oblivion.

During the first six months of 1935, I was hospitalized eight times for intoxication and shackled to the bed two or three days before I even knew where I was.

On June 26, 1935, I came to in the hospital, and to say I was discouraged is to put it mildly. Each of the seven times that I had left this hospital in the previous six months, I had come out fully determined in my own mind that I would not get drunk again—for at least six or eight months. It hadn't worked out that way, and I didn't know what the matter was and did not know what to do.

I was moved into another room that morning and there was my wife. I thought to myself, Well, she is going to tell me this is the end, and I certainly couldn't blame her and did not intend to try to justify myself. She told me that she had been talking to a couple of fellows about drinking. I resented this very much, until she informed me that they were a couple of drunks just as I was. That wasn't so bad, to tell it to another drunk.

She said, "You are going to quit." That was worth a lot even though I did not believe it. Then she told me that these two drunks she had been talking to had a plan whereby they thought they could quit drinking, and part of that plan was that they tell it to another drunk. This was going to help them to stay sober. All the other people who had talked to me wanted to help *me,* and my pride prevented me from listening to them and caused only resentment on my part, but I felt as if I would be a real stinker if I did not listen to a couple of fellows for a short time, if that would cure *them.* My wife also told me that I could not pay them even if I wanted to and had the money, which I did not.

They came in and began to give me instruction in the program that later became known as Alcoholics Anonymous. There was not much of it at that time.

I looked up and there were two great big fellows over six-foot tall, very likable looking. (I knew afterwards that the two who came in were Bill W. and Doctor Bob.) Before very long we began to relate some incidents of our drinking, and pretty soon I realized that both of them knew what they were talking about, because you can see things and smell things when you're drunk that you can't other times. If I had thought they didn't know what they were talking about, I wouldn't have been willing to talk to them at all.

After a while, Bill said, "Well, now, you've been talking a good long time, let me talk a minute or two." So, after hearing some more of my story, he turned around and said to Doc—I don't think he knew I heard him, but I did—he said, "Well, I believe he's worth saving and working on." They said to me, "Do you want to quit drinking? It's none of our business about your drinking. We're not up here trying to take any of your rights or privileges away from you, but we have a program whereby we think we can stay sober. Part of that program is that we take it to someone else who needs it and wants it. Now, if you don't want it, we'll not take up your time, and we'll be going and looking for someone else."

The next thing they wanted to know was if I thought I could quit of my own accord, without any help, if I could just walk out of the hospital and never take another drink. If I could, that was wonderful, that was just fine, and they would very much appreciate a person who had that kind of power, but they were looking for a man who knew he had a problem and knew he couldn't handle it himself and needed outside help. The next thing they wanted to know was if I believed in a Higher Power. I had no trouble there because I had never actually ceased to believe in God and had tried lots of times to get help but hadn't succeeded. Next they wanted to know would I be willing to go to this Higher Power and ask for help, calmly and without any reservations.

They left this with me to think over, and I lay there on that hospital bed and went back over and reviewed my life. I thought of what liquor had done to me, the opportunities that I had discarded, the abilities that had been given me and how I had wasted them, and I finally came to the conclusion that if I didn't want to quit, I certainly ought to want to, and that I was willing to do anything in the world to stop drinking.

I was willing to admit to myself that I had hit bottom, that I had gotten hold of something that I didn't know how to handle by myself. So after reviewing these things and realizing what liquor had cost me, I went to this Higher Power that, to me, was God, without any reservation, and admitted that I was completely powerless over alcohol and that I was willing to do anything in the world to get rid of the problem. In fact, I admitted that from then on I was willing to let God take over instead of me. Each day I would try to find out what His will was and try to follow that, rather than trying to get Him to always agree that the things I thought up for myself were the things best for me. So, when they came back, I told them.

One of the fellows, I think it was Doc, said, "Well, you want to quit?" I said, "Yes, Doc, I would like to quit, at least for five, six, or eight months, until I get things straightened up, and begin to get the respect of my wife and some other people back, and get my finances fixed up and so on." And they both laughed very heartily and said, "That's better than you've been doing, isn't it?" Which of course was true. They said, "We've got some bad news for you. It was bad news for us, and it will probably be bad news for you. Whether you quit six days, months, or years, if you go out and take a drink or two, you'll end up in this hospital tied down, just like you have been in these past six months. You are an alcoholic." As far as I know that was the first time I had ever paid any attention to that word. I figured I was just a drunk. And they said, "No, you have a disease, and it doesn't make any

difference how long you do without it, after a drink or
two you'll end up just like you are now." That certainly was real disheartening news, at the time.

The next question they asked was, "You can quit
twenty-four hours, can't you?" I said, "Sure, yes, anybody can do that, for twenty-four hours." They said,
"That's what we're talking about. Just twenty-four
hours at a time." That sure did take a load off of my
mind. Every time I'd start thinking about drinking, I
would think of the long, dry years ahead without having a drink; but this idea of twenty-four hours, that it
was up to me from then on, was a lot of help.

(At this point, the Editors intrude just long enough to
supplement Bill D.'s account, that of the man on the bed,
with that of Bill W., the man who sat by the side of the
bed.) Says Bill W.:

Nineteen years ago last summer, Dr. Bob and I saw him
(Bill D.) for the first time. Bill lay on his hospital bed and
looked at us in wonder.

Two days before this, Dr. Bob had said to me, "If you
and I are going to stay sober, we had better get busy."
Straightway, Bob called Akron's City Hospital and asked
for the nurse on the receiving ward. He explained that he
and a man from New York had a cure for alcoholism. Did
she have an alcoholic customer on whom it could be tried?
Knowing Bob of old, she jokingly replied, "Well, Doctor,
I suppose you've already tried it yourself?"

Yes, she did have a customer—a dandy. He had just
arrived in D.T.'s, had blacked the eyes of two nurses, and
now they had him strapped down tight. Would this one do?
After prescribing medicines, Dr. Bob ordered, "Put him in
a private room. We'll be down as soon as he clears up."

Bill didn't seem too impressed. Looking sadder than
ever, he wearily ventured, "Well, this is wonderful for you
fellows, but it can't be for me. My case is so terrible that
I'm scared to go out of this hospital at all. You don't have

to sell me religion, either. I was at one time a deacon in the church, and I still believe in God. But I guess He doesn't believe much in me."

Then Dr. Bob said, "Well, Bill, maybe you'll feel better tomorrow. Wouldn't you like to see us again?"

"Sure I would," replied Bill, "Maybe it won't do any good, but I'd like to see you both, anyhow. You certainly know what you are talking about."

Looking in later, we found Bill with his wife, Henrietta. Eagerly he pointed to us saying, "These are the fellows I told you about; they are the ones who understand."

Bill then related how he had lain awake nearly all night. Down in the pit of his depression, new hope had somehow been born. The thought flashed through his mind, "If they can do it, I can do it!" Over and over he said this to himself. Finally, out of his hope, there burst conviction. Now he was sure. Then came a great joy. At length, peace stole over him and he slept.

Before our visit was over, Bill suddenly turned to his wife and said, "Go fetch my clothes, dear. We're going to get up and get out of here." Bill D. walked out of that hospital a free man, never to drink again.

A.A.'s Number One Group dates from that very day.

(Bill D. now continues his story.)

It was in the next two or three days after I had first met Doc and Bill that I finally came to a decision to turn my will over to God and to go along with this program the best that I could. Their talk and action had instilled in me a certain amount of confidence, although I was not too absolutely certain. I wasn't afraid that the program wouldn't work, but I still was doubtful whether I would be able to hang on to the program, but I did come to the conclusion that I was willing to put everything I had into it, with God's power, and that I wanted to do just that. As soon as I had done that, I did feel a great release. I knew that

I had a helper whom I could rely upon, who wouldn't fail me. If I could stick to Him and listen, I would make it. I remember when the boys came back, I told them, "I have gone to this Higher Power, and I have told Him that I am willing to put His world first, above everything. I have already done it, and I am willing to do it again here in the presence of you, or I am willing to say it any place, anywhere in the world from now on and not be ashamed of it." And this certainly gave me a lot of confidence and seemed to take a lot of the burden off me.

I remember telling them too that it was going to be awfully tough, because I did some other things, smoked cigarettes and played penny ante poker and sometimes bet on the horse races, and they said, "Don't you think you're having more trouble with this drinking than with anything else at the present time? Don't you believe you are going to have all you can do to get rid of that?" "Yes," I said, reluctantly, "I probably will." They said, "Let's forget about those other things, that is, trying to eliminate them all at once, and concentrate on the drink." Of course, we had talked over quite a number of the failings that I had and made a sort of an inventory, which wasn't too difficult, because I had an awful lot of things wrong that were very apparent to me. Then they said, "There is one other thing. You should go out and take this program to somebody else who needs it and wants it."

Of course, by this time, my business was practically nonexistent. I didn't have any. Naturally, for quite a time, I wasn't too well physically, either. It took me a year, or a year and a half, to get to feeling physically well, and it was rather tough, but I soon found folks whose friendship I had once had, and I found, after I had been sober for quite some little time, that these people began to act like they had in previous years, before I had gotten so bad, so that I didn't pay too awful much attention to financial gains. I spent most of my time trying to get back these friendships and to make some recompense toward my wife, whom I had hurt a lot.

It would be hard to estimate how much A.A. has done for me. I really wanted the program, and I wanted to go along with it. I noticed that the others seemed to have such a release, a happiness, a something that I thought a person ought to have. I was trying to find the answer. I knew there was even more, something that I hadn't got, and I remember one day, a week or two after I had come out of the hospital, Bill was at my house talking to my wife and me. We were eating lunch, and I was listening and trying to find out why they had this release that they seemed to have. Bill looked across at my wife and said to her, "Henrietta, the Lord has been so wonderful to me, curing me of this terrible disease, that I just want to keep talking about it and telling people."

I thought, I think I have the answer. Bill was very, very grateful that he had been released from this terrible thing and he had given God the credit for having done it, and he's so grateful about it he wants to tell other people about it. That sentence, "The Lord has been so wonderful to me, curing me of this terrible disease, that I just want to keep telling people about it," has been a sort of a golden text for the A.A. program and for me.

Of course, as time went on, I began to get my health back and began to be so I didn't have to hide from people all the time—it's just been wonderful. I still go to meetings, because I like to go. I meet the people that I like to talk to. Another reason that I go is that I'm still grateful for the good years that I've had. I'm so grateful for both the program and the people in it that I still want to go. And then probably the most wonderful thing that I have learned from the program—I've seen this in the A.A. Grapevine a lot of times, and I've had people say it to me personally, and I've heard people get up in meetings and say it—is this statement: "I came into A.A. solely for the purpose of sobriety, but it has been through A.A. that I have found God."

I feel that is about the most wonderful thing that a person can do.

(2)

GRATITUDE IN ACTION

The story of Dave B., one of the founders of A.A. in Canada in 1944.

I BELIEVE IT would be good to tell the story of my life. Doing so will give me the opportunity to remember that I must be grateful to God and to those members of Alcoholics Anonymous who knew A.A. before me. Telling my story reminds me that I could go back to where I was if I forget the wonderful things that have been given to me or forget that God is the guide who keeps me on this path.

In June 1924, I was sixteen years old and had just graduated from high school in Sherbrooke, Quebec. Some of my friends suggested that we go for a beer. I had never had beer or any other form of alcohol. I don't know why, since we always had alcohol at home (I should add that no one in my family was ever considered an alcoholic). Well, I was afraid my friends wouldn't like me if I didn't do as they did. I knew firsthand that mysterious state of people who appear to be sure of themselves but are actually eaten alive with fear inside. I had a rather strong inferiority complex. I believe I lacked what my father used to call "character." So on that nice summer day in an old inn in Sherbrooke, I didn't find the courage to say no.

I became an active alcoholic from that first day, when alcohol produced a very special effect in me. I was transformed. Alcohol suddenly made me into what I had always wanted to be.

Alcohol became my everyday companion. At first, I considered it a friend; later, it became a heavy load I couldn't get rid of. It turned out to be much more powerful than I was, even if, for many years, I could stay sober for short periods. I kept telling myself that one way or another I would get rid of alcohol. I was convinced I would find a way to stop drinking. I didn't want to acknowledge that alcohol had become so important in my life. Indeed, alcohol was giving me something I didn't want to lose.

In 1934, a series of mishaps occurred because of my drinking. I had to come back from Western Canada because the bank I worked for lost confidence in me. An elevator accident cost me all of the toes of one foot and a skull fracture. I was in the hospital for months. My excessive drinking also caused a brain hemorrhage, which completely paralyzed one side of my body. I probably did my First Step the day I came by ambulance to Western Hospital. A night-shift nurse asked me, "Mr. B., why do you drink so much? You have a wonderful wife, a bright little boy. You have no reason to drink like that. Why do you?" Being honest for the first time, I said, "I don't know, Nurse. I really don't know." That was many years before I learned about the Fellowship.

You might think I'd tell myself, "If alcohol causes so much harm, I will stop drinking." But I found countless reasons to prove to myself that alcohol had nothing to do with my misfortunes. I told myself it was because of fate, because everyone was against me, because things weren't going well. I sometimes thought that God did not exist. I thought, "If this loving God exists, as they say, He would not treat me this way. God would not act like this." I felt sorry for myself a lot in those days.

My family and employers were concerned about my drinking, but I had become rather arrogant. I bought a 1931 Ford with an inheritance from my grandmother, and my wife and I made a trip to Cape Cod. On the way back, we stopped at my uncle's place in New Hampshire. This uncle had taken me under his wing at the time of my mother's death, and he worried about me. Now he said to me, "Dave, if you stop drinking for a full year, I will give you the Ford roadster I just bought." I loved that car, so I immediately promised I wouldn't drink for a whole year. And I meant it. Yet I was drinking again before we reached the Canadian border. I was powerless over alcohol. I was learning that I could do nothing to fight it off, even while I was denying the fact.

On Easter weekend 1944, I found myself in a jail cell in Montreal. By now, I was drinking to escape the horrible thoughts I had whenever I was sober enough to become aware of my situation. I was drinking to avoid seeing what I had become. The job I'd had for twenty years and the new car were long gone. I had undergone three stays in a psychiatric hospital. God knows I didn't want to drink, yet to my great despair, I always returned to the infernal merry-go-round.

I wondered how this misery would end. I was full of fear. I was afraid to tell others what I felt lest they would think I was insane. I was terribly lonely, full of self-pity, and terrified. Most of all, I was in a deep depression.

Then I recalled a book given to me by my sister Jean about drunks as desperate as I was who had found a way to stop drinking. According to this book, these drunks had found a way to live like other human beings: to get up in the morning, go to work, and return home in the evening. This book was about Alcoholics Anonymous.

I decided to get in touch with them. I had much difficulty in reaching A.A. in New York, as A.A. wasn't as well-known then. I finally spoke to a woman, Bobbie, who said words I hope I never forget: "I am an alcoholic. We have recovered. If you want, we'll help you." She told me about herself and added that many other drunks had used this method to stop drinking. What impressed me most in this conversation was the fact that these people, five hundred miles away, cared enough to try to help me. Here I was, feeling so sorry for myself, convinced that no one cared whether I was dead or alive.

I was very surprised when I got a copy of the Big Book in the mail the following day. And each day after that, for nearly a year, I got a letter or a note, something from Bobbie or from Bill or one of the other members of the central office in New York. In October 1944, Bobbie wrote: "You sound very sincere and from now on we will be counting on you to perpetuate the Fellowship of A.A. where you are. You will find enclosed some queries from alcoholics. We think you are now ready to take on this responsibility." She had enclosed some four hundred letters that I answered in the course of the following weeks. Soon, I began to get answers back.

In my new enthusiasm, and having found an answer

to my problem, I told Dorie, my wife, "You can quit your job now; I will take care of you. From now on, you will take the place you deserve in this family." However, she knew better. She said, "No, Dave, I will keep my job for a year while you go save the drunks." That is exactly what I set out to do.

As I look back on it now, I did everything wrong, but at least I was thinking of somebody else instead of myself. I had begun to get a little bit of something I am very full of now, and that is gratitude. I was becoming increasingly grateful to the people in New York and to the God they referred to but whom I found difficult to reach. (Yet I realized I had to seek the Higher Power I was told about.)

I was all alone in Quebec at that time. The Toronto Group had been in operation since the previous fall, and there was a member in Windsor who attended meetings across the river in Detroit. That was A.A. in its entirety in this country.

One day I got a letter from a man in Halifax who wrote, "One of my friends, a drunk, works in Montreal, but he is currently in Chicago, where he went on a major binge. When he returns to Montreal, I'd like you to talk to him."

I met this man at his home. His wife was cooking dinner, their young daughter at her side. The man was wearing a velvet jacket and sitting comfortably in his parlor. I hadn't met many people from high society. I immediately thought, "What's going on here? This man isn't an alcoholic!" Jack was a down-to-earth person. He was used to discussions about psychiatry, and the concept of a Higher Power didn't appeal to him very much. But from our meeting, A.A. was born here in Quebec.

The Fellowship started to grow, most particularly following the publicity we got in the *Gazette* in the spring of 1945. I will never forget the day that Mary came to see me—she was the first woman to join our Fellowship here. She was very shy and reserved, very low-key. She had heard of the Fellowship through the *Gazette*.

For the first year, all the meetings were held in my home. There were people all over the house. The wives of members used to come with their husbands, though we didn't allow them in our closed meetings. They used to sit on the bed or in the kitchen, where they would make coffee and snacks. I believe they were wondering what would happen to us. Yet they were as happy as we were.

The first two French Canadians to learn about A.A. did so in the basement of my home. All French-speaking meetings in existence today were born out of those early meetings.

At the end of my first year of sobriety, my wife agreed to leave her job after I found some work. I thought that would be easy. All I had to do was go see an employer and I'd be able to support my family in a normal fashion. However, I looked for work for many months. We didn't have much money, and I was spending the little we had going from one place to the other, answering ads and meeting people. I was getting more and more discouraged. One day, a member said, "Dave, why don't you apply at the aircraft factory? I know a fellow there who could help you." So that was where I got my first job. There really is a Higher Power looking after us.

One of the most fundamental things I have learned is to pass on our message to other alcoholics. That means I must think more about others than about myself. The most important thing is to practice these principles in all my affairs. In my opinion, that is what Alcoholics Anonymous is all about.

I never forgot a passage I first read in the copy of the Big Book that Bobbie sent me: "Abandon yourself to God as you understand God. Admit your faults to Him and to your fellows. Clear away the wreckage of your past. Give freely of what you find and join us." It is very simple—though not always easy. But it can be done.

I know the Fellowship of A.A. doesn't offer any guarantees, but I also know that in the future I do not have to drink. I want to keep this life of peace, serenity, and tranquility that I have found. Today, I have found again the home I left and the woman I married when she was still so young. We have two more children, and they think their dad is an important man. I have all these wonderful things—people who mean more to me than anything in the world. I shall keep all that, and I won't have to drink, if I remember one simple thing: to keep my hand in the hand of God.

(3)

WOMEN SUFFER TOO

Despite great opportunities, alcohol nearly ended her life. An early member, she spread the word among women in our pioneering period.

WHAT WAS I saying . . . from far away, as if in a delirium, I heard my own voice—calling someone "Dorothy," talking of dress shops, of jobs . . . the words came clearer . . . this sound of my own voice frightened me as it came closer . . . and suddenly, there I was, talking of I knew not what, to someone I'd never seen before that very moment. Abruptly I stopped speaking. Where was I?

I'd waked up in strange rooms before, fully dressed on a bed or a couch; I'd waked up in my own room, in or on my own bed, not knowing what hour or day it was, afraid to ask . . . but this was different. This time I seemed to be already awake, sitting upright in a big easy chair, in the middle of an animated conversation with a perfectly strange young woman who didn't appear to think it strange. *She* was chatting on, pleasantly and comfortably.

Terrified, I looked around. I was in a large, dark, rather poorly furnished room—the living room of a basement flat. Cold chills started chasing up and down my spine; my teeth were chattering; my hands were shaking, so I tucked them under me to keep them from flying away. My fright was real enough, but it didn't account for these violent reactions. I knew what they were, all right—a drink would fix them. It must have been a long time since I had my last drink —but I didn't dare ask this stranger for one. I must get out of here. In any case I must get out of here before I let slip my abysmal ignorance of how I came to be here and she realized that I was stark, staring mad. I was mad—I must be.

The shakes grew worse, and I looked at my watch— six o'clock. It had been one o'clock when I last remembered looking. I'd been sitting comfortably in a restaurant with Rita, drinking my sixth martini and hoping the waiter would forget about the lunch order —at least long enough for me to have a couple more. I'd only had two with her, but I'd managed four in the fifteen minutes I'd waited for her, and of course I'd had the usual uncounted swigs from the bottle as I painfully got up and did my slow spasmodic dressing. In fact, I had been in very good shape at one o'clock —feeling no pain. What *could* have happened? That had been in the center of New York, on noisy 42nd Street . . . this was obviously a quiet residential section. Why had "Dorothy" brought me here? Who was she? How had I met her? I had no answers, and I dared not ask. She gave no sign of recognizing anything wrong, but what had I been doing for those lost five hours? My brain whirled. I might have done terrible things, and I wouldn't even know it!

Somehow I got out of there and walked five blocks past brownstone houses. There wasn't a bar in sight, but I found the subway station. The name on it was unfamiliar, and I had to ask the way to Grand Central. It took three-quarters of an hour and two changes to get there—back to my starting point. I had been in the remote reaches of Brooklyn.

That night I got very drunk, which was usual, but I remembered everything, which was very unusual. I remembered going through what my sister assured me was my nightly procedure of trying to find Willie Seabrook's name in the telephone book. I remembered my loud resolution to find him and ask him to help me get into that "Asylum" he had written about. I remembered asserting that I was going to *do* something about this, that I couldn't go on . . . I remembered looking longingly at the window as an easier solution and shuddering at the memory of that other window, three years before, and the six agonizing months in a London hospital ward. I remembered filling the peroxide bottle in my medicine chest with gin, in case my sister found the bottle I hid under the mattress. And I remembered the creeping horror of the interminable night, in which I slept for short spells and woke dripping with cold sweat and shaken with utter despair, to drink hastily from my bottle and mercifully pass out again. "You're mad, you're mad, you're mad!" pounded through my brain with each returning ray of consciousness, and I drowned the refrain with drink.

That went on for two more months before I landed in a hospital and started my slow fight back to normalcy. It had been going on like that for over a year. I was thirty-two years old.

When I look back on that last horrible year of constant drinking, I wonder how I survived it, either physically or mentally. For there were, of course, periods of clear realization of what I had become, attended by memories of what I had been, what I had expected to be. And the contrast was pretty shattering. Sitting in a Second Avenue bar, accepting drinks from anyone who offered, after my small stake was gone, or sitting at home alone, with the inevitable glass in my hand, I would remember, and, remembering, I would drink faster, seeking speedy oblivion. It was hard to reconcile this ghastly present with the simple facts of the past.

My family had money—I had never known denial of any material desire. The best boarding schools and a finishing school in Europe had fitted me for the conventional role of debutante and young matron. The times in which I grew up (the Prohibition era immortalized by Scott Fitzgerald and John Held Jr.) had taught me to be gay with the gayest; my own inner urges led me to outdo them all. The year after coming out, I married. So far, so good—all according to plan, like thousands of others. But then the story became my own. My husband was an alcoholic, and since I had only contempt for those without my own amazing capacity, the outcome was inevitable. My divorce coincided with my father's bankruptcy, and I went to work, casting off all allegiances and responsibilities to anyone other than myself. For me, work was only a different means to the same end, to be able to do exactly what I wanted to do.

For the next ten years I did just that. For greater freedom and excitement I went abroad to live. I had my own business, successful enough for me to indulge most of my desires. I met all the people I wanted to meet; I saw all the places I wanted to see; I did all the things I wanted to do—I was increasingly miserable.

Headstrong and willful, I rushed from pleasure to pleasure and found the returns diminishing to the vanishing point. Hangovers began to assume monstrous proportions, and the morning drink became an urgent necessity. "Blanks" were more frequent, and I seldom knew how I'd got home. When my friends suggested that I was drinking too much, they were no longer my friends. I moved from group to group— then from place to place—and went on drinking. With a creeping insidiousness, drink had become more important than anything else. It no longer gave me pleasure—it merely dulled the pain—but I *had* to have it. I was bitterly unhappy. No doubt I had been an exile too long—I should go home to America. I did. And to my surprise, my drinking grew worse.

When I entered a sanitarium for prolonged and intensive psychiatric treatment, I was convinced that I was having a serious mental breakdown. I wanted help, and I tried to cooperate. As the treatment progressed, I began to get a picture of myself, of the temperament that had caused me so much trouble. I had been hypersensitive, shy, idealistic. My inability to accept the harsh realities of life had resulted in a disillusioned cynic, clothed in a protective armor against the world's misunderstanding. That armor had turned into prison walls, locking me in loneliness—and fear. All I had left was an iron determination to live my own life in spite of the alien world—and here I was, an inwardly frightened, outwardly defiant woman, who desperately needed a prop to keep going.

Alcohol was that prop, and I didn't see how I could live without it. When my doctor told me I should never touch a drink again, I *couldn't afford* to believe him. I had to persist in my attempts to get straightened out enough to be able to use the drinks I needed, without their turning on me. Besides, how could *he* understand? He wasn't a drinking man; he didn't know what it was to *need* a drink, nor what a drink could do for one in a pinch. I wanted to *live*, not in a desert, but in a normal world; and my idea of a normal world was being among people who drank—teetotalers were not included. And I was sure that I couldn't be with people who drank, without drinking. In that I was correct: I couldn't be comfortable with *any* kind of people without drinking. I never had been.

Naturally, in spite of my good intentions, in spite of my protected life behind sanitarium walls, I several times got drunk and was astounded . . . and badly shaken.

That was the point at which my doctor gave me the book *Alcoholics Anonymous* to read. The first chapters were a revelation to me. I wasn't the only person in the world who felt and behaved like this! I wasn't mad or vicious—I was a sick person. I was suffering from an actual disease that had a name and symptoms like diabetes or cancer or TB—and a disease was respectable, not a moral stigma! But then I hit a snag. I couldn't stomach religion, and I didn't like the mention of God or any of the other capital letters. If that was the way out, it wasn't for me. I was an intellectual and I needed an intellectual answer, not an emotional one. I told my doctor so in no uncertain terms. I wanted to learn to stand on my own feet, not to change one prop for another, and an intangible and dubious one at that. And so on and on, for several weeks, while I grudgingly plowed through some more

of the offending book and felt more and more hopeless about myself.

Then the miracle happened—to *me!* It isn't always
so sudden with everyone, but I ran into a personal crisis that filled me with a raging and righteous anger.
And as I fumed helplessly and planned to get good
and drunk and *show them,* my eye caught a sentence
in the book lying open on my bed: "We cannot live
with anger." The walls crumpled—and the light
streamed in. I wasn't trapped. I wasn't helpless. I
was *free,* and I didn't have to drink to "show them."
This wasn't "religion"—this was freedom! Freedom
from anger and fear, freedom to know happiness, and
freedom to know love.

I went to a meeting to see for myself this group of
freaks or bums who had done this thing. To go into
a gathering of people was the sort of thing that all my
life, from the time I left my private world of books
and dreams to meet the real world of people and
parties and jobs, had left me feeling an uncomfortable
outsider, needing the warming stimulus of drinks to
join in. I went trembling into a house in Brooklyn
filled with strangers . . . and I found I had come home
at last, to my own kind. There is another meaning for
the Hebrew word that in the King James version of
the Bible is translated "salvation." It is: "to come
home." I had found my salvation. I wasn't alone any
more.

That was the beginning of a new life, a fuller life,
a happier life than I had ever known or believed possible. I had found friends—understanding friends who
often knew what I was thinking and feeling better
than I knew myself—and who didn't allow me to re-

treat into my prison of loneliness and fear over a fancied slight or hurt. Talking things over with them, great floods of enlightenment showed me myself as I really was—and I was like them. We all had hundreds of character traits, fears and phobias, likes and dislikes, in common. Suddenly I could accept myself, faults and all, as I was—for weren't we all like that? And, accepting, I felt a new inner comfort and the willingness and strength to do something about the traits I couldn't live with.

It didn't stop there. They knew what to do about those black abysses that yawned, ready to swallow me, when I felt depressed or nervous. There was a concrete program, designed to secure the greatest possible inner security for us long-time escapists. The feeling of impending disaster that had haunted me for years began to dissolve as I put into practice more and more of the Twelve Steps. It worked!

An active member of A.A. since 1939, I feel myself a useful member of the human race at last. I have something to contribute to humanity, since I am peculiarly qualified, as a fellow-sufferer, to give aid and comfort to those who have stumbled and fallen over this business of meeting life. I get my greatest thrill of accomplishment from the knowledge that I have played a part in the new happiness achieved by countless others like myself. The fact that I can work again and earn my living is important but secondary. I believe that my once overweening self-will has finally found its proper place, for I can say many times daily, "Thy will be done, not mine" . . . and mean it.

(4)

OUR SOUTHERN FRIEND

Pioneer A.A., minister's son, and southern farmer,
he asked, "Who am I to say there is no God?"

ATHER IS an Episcopal minister and his work takes him over long drives on bad roads. His parishioners are limited in number, but his friends are many, for to him race, creed, or social position makes no difference. It is not long before he drives up in the buggy. Both he and old Maud are glad to get home. The drive was long and cold but he was thankful for the hot bricks that some thoughtful person had given him for his feet. Soon supper is on the table. Father says grace, which delays my attack on the buckwheat cakes and sausage.

Bedtime comes. I climb to my room in the attic. It is cold, so there is no delay. I crawl under a pile of blankets and blow out the candle. The wind is rising and howls around the house. But I am safe and warm. I fall into a dreamless sleep.

I am in church. Father is delivering his sermon. A wasp is crawling up the back of the lady in front of me. I wonder if it will reach her neck. Shucks! It has flown away. At last! The message has been delivered.

"Let your light so shine before men that they may see your good works—." I hunt for my nickel to drop in the plate so that mine will be seen.

I am in another fellow's room at college. "Freshman," said he to me, "do you ever take a drink?" I hesitated. Father had never directly spoken to me about drinking but he never drank any, so far as I knew. Mother hated liquor and feared a drunken man. Her brother had been a drinker and had died in a state hospital for the insane. But his life was unmentioned, so far as I was concerned. I had never had a drink, but I had seen enough merriment in the boys who were drinking to be interested. I would never be like the village drunkard at home.

"Well," said the older boy, "do you?"

"Once in a while," I lied. I could not let him think I was a sissy.

He poured out two drinks. "Here's looking at you," said he. I gulped it down and choked. I didn't like it, but I would not say so. A mellow glow stole over me. This wasn't so bad after all. Sure, I'd have another. The glow increased. Other boys came in. My tongue loosened. Everyone laughed loudly. I was witty. I had no inferiorities. Why, I wasn't even ashamed of my skinny legs! This was the real thing!

A haze filled the room. The electric light began to move. Then two bulbs appeared. The faces of the other boys grew dim. How sick I felt. I staggered to the bathroom. Shouldn't have drunk so much or so fast. But I knew how to handle it now. I'd drink like a gentleman after this.

And so I met John Barleycorn. The grand fellow who at my call made me a hail-fellow-well-met, who gave me such a fine voice, as we sang "Hail, hail, the gang's all here" and "Sweet Adeline," who gave me freedom from fear and feelings of inferiority. Good old John! He was my pal, all right.

Final exams of my senior year and I may somehow graduate. I would never have tried, but mother counts on it so. A case of measles saved me from being kicked out during my sophomore year.

But the end is in sight. My last exam and an easy one. I gaze at the board with its questions. Can't remember the answer to the first. I'll try the second. No soap there. I don't seem to remember anything. I concentrate on one of the questions. I don't seem to be able to keep my mind on what I am doing. I get uneasy. If I don't get started soon, I won't have time to finish. No use. I can't think.

I leave the room, which the honor system allows. I go to my room. I pour out half a tumbler of grain alcohol and fill it with ginger ale. Now back to the exam. My pen moves rapidly. I know enough of the answers to get by. Good old John Barleycorn! He can be depended on. What a wonderful power he has over the mind! He has given me my diploma!

Underweight! How I hate that word. Three attempts to enlist in the service, and three failures because of being skinny. True, I have recently recovered from pneumonia and have an alibi, but my friends are in the war or going, and I am not. I visit a friend who is awaiting orders. The atmosphere of "eat, drink, and be merry" prevails and I absorb it. I drink a lot every night. I can hold a lot now, more than the others.

I am examined for the draft and pass the physical test. I am to go to camp on November 13. The Armistice is signed on the eleventh, and the draft is called off. Never in the service! The war leaves me with a pair of blankets, a toilet kit, a sweater knit by my sister, and a still greater sense of inferiority.

It is ten o'clock of a Saturday night. I am working hard on the books of a subsidiary company of a large corporation. I have had experience in selling, in collecting, and in accounting, and I am on my way up the ladder.

Then the crack-up. Cotton struck the skids and collections went cold. A twenty-three million dollar surplus wiped out. Offices closed up and workers discharged. I, and the books of my division, have been transferred to the head office. I have no assistance and am working nights, Saturdays, and Sundays. My salary has been cut. My wife and new baby are fortunately staying with relatives. I feel exhausted. The doctor has told me that if I don't give up inside work, I'll have tuberculosis. But what am I to do? I have a family to support and have no time to be looking for another job.

I reach for the bottle that I just got from George, the elevator boy.

I am a traveling salesman. The day is over and business has been not so good. I'll go to bed. I wish I were home with the family and not in this dingy hotel.

Well—well—look who's here! Good old Charlie! It's great to see him. How's the boy? A drink? You bet your life! We buy a gallon of "corn" because it is so cheap. Yet I am fairly steady when I go to bed.

Morning comes. I feel horrible. A little drink will put me on my feet. But it takes others to keep me there.

I become a teacher in a boys' school. I am happy in my work. I like the boys and we have lots of fun, in class and out.

The doctor bills are heavy and the bank account is low. My wife's parents come to our assistance. I am filled with hurt pride and self-pity. I seem to get no sympathy for my illness and have no appreciation of the love behind the gift.

I call the bootlegger and fill up my charred keg. But I do not wait for the charred keg to work. I get drunk. My wife is extremely unhappy. Her father comes to sit with me. He never says an unkind word. He is a real friend, but I do not appreciate him.

We are staying with my wife's father. Her mother is in a critical condition at a hospital. I cannot sleep. I must get myself together. I sneak downstairs and get a bottle of whiskey from the cellaret. I pour drinks down my throat. My father-in-law appears. "Have a drink?" I ask. He makes no reply and hardly seems to see me. His wife dies that night.

Mother has been dying of cancer for a long time. She is near the end now and is in a hospital. I have been drinking a lot but never get drunk. Mother must never know. I see her about to go.

I return to the hotel where I am staying and get gin from the bellboy. I drink and go to bed; I take a few the next morning and go see my mother once more. I cannot stand it. I go back to the hotel and get more gin. I drink steadily. I come to at three in the morning. The indescribable torture has me again. I turn on the light. I must get out of the room or I shall jump out of the window. I walk miles. No use. I go to the hospital, where I have made friends with the night superintendent. She puts me to bed and gives me a hypodermic.

I am at the hospital to see my wife. We have another child. But she is not glad to see me. I have been drinking while the baby was arriving. Her father stays with her.

It is a cold, bleak day in November. I have fought hard to stop drinking. Each battle has ended in defeat. I tell my wife I cannot stop drinking. She begs me to go to a hospital for alcoholics that has been recommended. I say I will go. She makes the arrangements, but I will not go. I'll do it all myself. This time I'm off of it for good. I'll just take a few beers now and then.

It is the last day of the following October, a dark, rainy morning. I come to on a pile of hay in a barn. I look for liquor and can't find any. I wander to a table and drink five bottles of beer. I must get some liquor. Suddenly I feel hopeless, unable to go on. I go home. My wife is in the living room. She had looked for me last evening after I left the car and wandered off into the night. She had looked for me this morning. She has reached the end of her rope. There is no use trying any more, for there is nothing to try. "Don't say anything," I say to her. "I am going to do something."

I am in the hospital for alcoholics. I am an alcoholic. The insane asylum lies ahead. Could I have myself locked up at home? One more foolish idea. I might go out West on a ranch where I couldn't get anything to drink. I might do that. Another foolish idea. I wish I were dead, as I have often wished before. I am too yellow to kill myself.

Four alcoholics play bridge in a smoke-filled room. Anything to get my mind from myself. The game is over and the other three leave. I start to clean up the debris. One man comes back, closing the door behind him.

He looks at me. "You think you are hopeless, don't you?" he asks.

"I know it," I reply.

"Well, you're not," says the man. "There are men on the streets of New York today who were worse than you, and they don't drink anymore."

"What are you doing here then?" I ask.

"I went out of here nine days ago saying that I was going to be honest, but I wasn't," he answers.

A fanatic, I thought to myself, but I was polite. "What is it?" I enquire.

Then he asks me if I believe in a power greater than myself, whether I call that power God, Allah, Confucius, Prime Cause, Divine Mind, or any other name. I told him that I believe in electricity and other forces of nature, but as for a God, if there is one, He has never done anything for me. Then he asks me if I am willing to right all the wrongs I have ever done to anyone, no matter how wrong I thought the others were. Am I willing to be honest with myself about myself and tell someone about myself, and am I willing to think of other people, of their needs instead of myself, in order to get rid of the drink problem?

"I'll do anything," I reply.

"Then all of your troubles are over," says the man and leaves the room. The man is in bad mental shape certainly. I pick up a book and try to read, but I cannot concentrate. I get in bed and turn out the light. But I cannot sleep. Suddenly a thought comes. Can all the worthwhile people I have known be wrong about God? Then I find myself thinking about myself and a few things that I had wanted to forget. I begin to see I am not the person I had thought myself, that I had judged myself by comparing myself to others and always to my own advantage. It is a shock.

Then comes a thought that is like a voice. *"Who are you to say there is no God?"* It rings in my head; I can't get rid of it.

I get out of bed and go to the man's room. He is reading. "I must ask you a question," I say to the man. "How does prayer fit into this thing?"

"Well," he answers, "you've probably tried praying like I have. When you've been in a jam, you've said, 'God, please do this or that,' and if it turned out your way that was the last of it, and, if it didn't, you've said 'There isn't any God' or 'He doesn't do anything for me.' Is that right?"

"Yes," I reply.

"That isn't the way," he continued. "The thing I do is to say 'God, here I am and here are all my troubles. I've made a mess of things and can't do anything about it. You take me, and all my troubles, and do anything you want with me.' Does that answer your question?"

"Yes, it does," I answer. I return to bed. It doesn't make sense. Suddenly I feel a wave of utter hopelessness sweep over me. I am in the bottom of hell. And there, a tremendous hope is born. It might be true.

I tumble out of bed onto my knees. I know not what I say. But slowly a great peace comes to me. I feel lifted up. I believe in God. I crawl back into bed and sleep like a child.

Some men and women come to visit my friend of the night before. He invites me to meet them. They are a joyous crowd. I have never seen people that joyous before. We talk. I tell them of the peace and that I believe in God. I think of my wife. I must write her. One girl suggests that I phone her. What a wonderful idea!

My wife hears my voice and she knows that I have found the answer to life. She comes to New York. I get out of the hospital and we visit some of these new-found friends.

I am home again. I have lost the Fellowship. Those who understand me are far away. The same old problems and worries still surround me. Members of my family annoy me. Nothing seems to be working out right. I am blue and unhappy. Maybe a drink—I put on my hat and dash off in the car.

Get into the lives of other people is one thing the fellows in New York had said. I go to see a man I had been asked to visit and tell him my story. I feel much better! I have forgotten about a drink.

I am on a train, headed for a city. I have left my wife at home, sick, and I have been unkind to her in leaving. I am very unhappy. Maybe a few drinks when I get to the city will help. A great fear seizes me. I talk to the stranger in the seat beside me. The fear and the insane idea are taken away.

Things are not going so well at home. I am learning that I cannot have my own way as I used to. I blame my wife and children. Anger possesses me, anger such as I have never felt before. I will not stand for it. I pack my bag and I leave. I stay with some under-standing friends.

I see where I have been wrong in some respects. I do not feel angry any more. I return home and say I am sorry for my wrong. I am quiet again. But I have not seen yet that I should do some constructive acts of love without expecting any return. I shall learn this after some more explosions.

I am blue again. I want to sell the place and move away. I want to get where I can find some alcoholics to help and where I can have some fellowship. A man calls me on the phone. Will I take a young fellow who has been drinking for two weeks to live with me? Soon I have others who are alcoholics and some who have other problems.

I begin to play God. I feel that I can fix them all. I do not fix anyone, but I am getting part of a tremendous education and I have made some new friends.

Nothing is right. Finances are in bad shape. I must find a way to make some money. The family seems to think of nothing but spending. People annoy me. I try to read. I try to pray. Gloom surrounds me. Why has God left me? I mope around the house. I will not go out and I will not enter into anything. What is the matter? I cannot understand. I will not be that way.

I'll get drunk! It is a cold-blooded idea. It is premeditated. I fix up a little apartment over the garage with books and drinking water. I am going to town to get some liquor and food. I shall not drink until I get back to the apartment. Then I shall lock myself in and read. And as I read, I shall take little drinks at long intervals. I shall get myself "mellow" and stay that way.

I get in the car and drive off. Halfway down the driveway a thought strikes me. I'll be honest anyway. I'll tell my wife what I am going to do. I back up to the door and go into the house. I call my wife into a room where we can talk privately. I tell her quietly what I intend to do. She says nothing. She does not get excited. She maintains a perfect calm.

When I am through speaking, the whole idea has become absurd. Not a trace of fear is in me. I laugh at the insanity of it. We talk of other things. Strength has come from weakness.

I cannot see the cause of this temptation now. But I am to learn later that it began with my desire for material success becoming greater than my interest in the welfare of my fellow man. I learn more of that foundation stone of character, which is honesty. I learn that when we act upon the highest conception of honesty that is given us, our sense of honesty becomes more acute.

I learn that honesty is truth and that truth shall make us free!

(5)

THE VICIOUS CYCLE

*How it finally broke a Southerner's obstinacy and
destined this salesman to start A.A. in Philadelphia.*

ANUARY 8, 1938—that was my D-Day; the place,
Washington, D.C. This last real merry-go-round
had started the day before Christmas, and I had really
accomplished a lot in those fourteen days. First, my
new wife had walked out, bag, baggage, and furniture;
then the apartment landlord had thrown me out of the
empty apartment; and the finish was the loss of another job. After a couple of days in dollar hotels and
one night in the pokey, I finally landed on my mother's
doorstep—shaking apart, with several days' beard, and,
of course, broke as usual. Many of these same things
had happened to me many times before, but this time
they had all descended together. For me, this was It.

Here I was, thirty-nine years old and a complete
washout. Nothing had worked. Mother would take
me in only if I stayed locked in a small storeroom
and gave her my clothes and shoes. We had played
this game before. That is the way Jackie found me,
lying on a cot in my skivvies, with hot and cold sweats,
pounding heart, and that awful itchy scratchiness all
over. Somehow, I had always managed to avoid
D.T.'s.

I seriously doubt I ever would have asked for help,
but Fitz, an old school friend of mine, had persuaded

Jackie to call on me. Had he come two or three days later, I think I would have thrown him out, but he hit when I was open for anything.

Jackie arrived about seven in the evening and talked until three a.m. I don't remember much of what he said, but I did realize that here was another guy exactly like me; he had been in the same laughing academies and the same jails, known the same loss of jobs, same frustrations, same boredom, and the same loneliness. If anything, he had known all of them even better and more often than I. Yet he was happy, relaxed, confident, and laughing. That night, for the first time in my life, I really let down my hair and admitted my general loneliness. Jackie told me about a group of fellows in New York, of whom my old friend Fitz was one, who had the same problem I had, and who, by working together to help each other, were now not drinking and were happy like himself. He said something about God or a Higher Power, but I brushed that off—that was for the birds, not for me. Little more of our talk stayed in my memory, but I do know I slept the rest of that night, while before I had never known what a real night's sleep was.

This was my introduction to this "understanding Fellowship," although it was to be more than a year later before our Society was to bear the name Alcoholics Anonymous. All of us in A.A. know the tremendous happiness that is in our sobriety, but there are also tragedies. My sponsor, Jackie, was one of these. He brought in many of our original members, yet he himself could not make it and died of alcoholism. The lesson of his death still remains with me, yet I often wonder what would have happened if somebody else had made that first call on me. So I always say that as long as I remember January 8, that is how long I will remain sober.

The age-old question in A.A. is which came first, the neurosis or the alcoholism. I like to think I was fairly normal before alcohol took over. My early life was spent in Baltimore, where my father was a physician and a grain merchant. My family lived in very prosperous circumstances, and while both my parents drank, sometimes too much, neither was an alcoholic. Father was a very well-integrated person, and while mother was high-strung and a bit selfish and demanding, our home life was reasonably harmonious. There were four of us children, and although both of my brothers later became alcoholic—one died of alcoholism—my sister has never taken a drink in her life.

Until I was thirteen I attended public schools, with regular promotions and average grades. I have never shown any particular talents, nor have I had any really frustrating ambitions. At thirteen I was packed off to a very fine Protestant boarding school in Virginia, where I stayed four years, graduating without any special achievements. In sports I made the track and tennis teams; I got along well with the other boys and had a fairly large circle of acquaintances but no intimate friends. I was never homesick and was always pretty self-sufficient.

However, here I probably took my first step toward my coming alcoholism by developing a terrific aversion to all churches and established religions. At this school we had Bible readings before each meal, and church services four times on Sunday, and I became so rebellious at this that I swore I would never join or go to any church, except for weddings or for funerals.

At seventeen I entered the university, really to satisfy my father, who wanted me to study medicine there as he had. That is where I had my first drink, and I still remember it, for every "first" drink afterwards did exactly the same trick—I could feel it go right through every bit of my body and down to my very toes. But each drink after the first seemed to become less effective, and after three or four, they all seemed like water. I was never a hilarious drunk; the more I drank, the quieter I got, and the drunker I got, the harder I fought to stay sober. So it is clear that I never had any fun out of drinking—I would be the soberest-seeming one in the crowd, and, all of a sudden, I would be the drunkest. Even that first night I blacked out, which leads me to believe that I was an alcoholic from my very first drink. The first year in college I just got by in my studies. I majored in poker and drinking. I refused to join any fraternity, as I wanted to be a freelance, and that year my drinking was confined to one-night stands, once or twice a week. The second year my drinking was more or less restricted to weekends, but I was nearly kicked out for scholastic failure.

In the spring of 1917, in order to beat being fired from school, I became "patriotic" and joined the army. I am one of the lads who came out of the service with a lower rank than when I went in. I had been to OTC the previous summer, so I went into the army as a sergeant but I came out a private, and you really have to be unusual to do that. In the next two years, I washed more pans and peeled more potatoes than any other doughboy. In the army, I became a periodic alcoholic—the periods always coming whenever I could make the opportunity. However, I did manage to keep out of the guardhouse. My last bout in the army lasted from November 5 to 11, 1918. We heard by wireless on the fifth that the Armistice would be signed the next day (this was a premature report), so I had a couple of cognacs to celebrate; then I hopped a truck and went AWOL. My next conscious memory was in Bar le Duc, many miles from base. It was November 11, and bells were ringing and whistles blowing for the real Armistice. There I was, unshaven, clothes torn and dirty, with no recollection of wandering all over France but, of course, a hero to the local French. Back at camp, all was forgiven because it was the End, but in the light of what I have since learned, I know I was a confirmed alcoholic at nineteen.

With the war over and back in Baltimore with the folks, I had several small jobs for three years, and then I went to work soliciting as one of the first ten employees of a new national finance company. What an opportunity I shot to pieces there! This company now does a volume of over three billion dollars annually. Three years later, at twenty-five, I opened and operated their Philadelphia office and was earning more than I ever have since. I was the fair-haired boy all right, but two years later I was blacklisted as an irresponsible drunk. It doesn't take long.

My next job was in sales promotion for an oil company in Mississippi, where I promptly became high man and got lots of pats on the back. Then I turned two company cars over in a short time and bingo—fired again. Oddly enough, the big shot who fired me from this company was one of the first men I met when I later joined the New York A.A. Group. He had also gone all the way through the wringer and had been dry two years when I saw him again.

After the oil job blew up, I went back to Baltimore and Mother, my first wife having said a permanent goodbye. Then came a sales job with a national tire company. I reorganized their city sales policy and eighteen months later, when I was thirty, they offered me the branch managership. As part of this promotion, they sent me to their national convention in Atlantic City to tell the big wheels how I'd done it. At this time I was holding what drinking I did down to weekends, but I hadn't had a drink at all in a month. I checked into my hotel room and then noticed a placard tucked under the glass on the bureau stating "There will be positively NO drinking at this convention," signed by the president of the company. That did it! Who, me? The Big Shot? The only salesman invited to talk at the convention? The man who was going to take over one of their biggest branches come Monday? I'd show 'em who was boss! No one in that company saw me again—ten days later I wired my resignation.

As long as things were tough and the job a challenge, I could always manage to hold on pretty well, but as soon as I learned the combination, got the puzzle under control, and the boss to pat me on the back, I was gone again. Routine jobs bored me, but I would take on the toughest one I could find and work day and night until I had it under control; then it would become tedious, and I'd lose all interest in it. I could never be bothered with the follow-through and would invariably reward myself for my efforts with that "first" drink.

After the tire job came the thirties, the Depression, and the downhill road. In the eight years before A.A. found me, I had over forty jobs—selling and traveling —one thing after another, and the same old routine. I'd work like mad for three or four weeks without a single drink, save my money, pay a few bills, and then "reward" myself with alcohol. Then I'd be broke again, hiding out in cheap hotels all over the country, having one-night jail stands here and there, and always that horrible feeling "What's the use—nothing is worthwhile." Every time I blacked out, and that was every time I drank, there was always that gnawing fear, "What did I do this time?" Once I found out. Many alcoholics have learned they can bring their bottle to a cheap movie theater and drink, sleep, wake up, and drink again in the darkness. I had repaired to one of these one morning with my jug, and, when I left late in the afternoon, I picked up a newspaper on the way home. Imagine my surprise when I read in a page-one "box" that I had been taken from the theater unconscious around noon that day, removed by ambulance to a hospital and stomach-pumped, and then released. Evidently I had gone right back to the movie with a bottle, stayed there several hours, and started home with no recollection of what had happened.

The mental state of the sick alcoholic is beyond description. I had no resentments against individuals —the whole world was all wrong. My thoughts went round and round with, What's it all about anyhow? People have wars and kill each other; they struggle and cut each other's throats for success, and what does anyone get out of it? Haven't I been successful, haven't I accomplished extraordinary things in business? What do I get out of it? Everything's all wrong and the hell with it. For the last two years of my drinking, I prayed during every drunk that I wouldn't wake up again. Three months before I met Jackie, I had made my second feeble try at suicide.

This was the background that made me willing to listen on January 8. After being dry two weeks and sticking close to Jackie, all of a sudden I found I had become the sponsor of my sponsor, for he was suddenly taken drunk. I was startled to learn he had only been off the booze a month or so himself when he brought me the message! However, I made an SOS call to the New York Group, whom I hadn't met yet, and they suggested we both come there. This we did the next day, and what a trip! I really had a chance to see myself from a nondrinking point of view. We checked into the home of Hank, the man who had fired me eleven years before in Mississippi, and there I met Bill, our founder. Bill had then been dry three years and Hank, two. At the time, I thought them just a swell pair of screwballs, for they were not only going to save all the drunks in the world but also all the so-called normal people! All they talked of that first weekend was God and how they were going to straighten out Jackie's and my life. In those days we really took each other's inventories firmly and often. Despite all this, I *did* like these new friends because, again, they were like me. They had also been periodic big shots who had goofed out repeatedly at the wrong time, and they also knew how to split one paper match into three separate matches. (This is very useful knowledge in places where matches are prohibited.) They, too, had taken a train to one town and had wakened hundreds of miles in the opposite direction, never knowing how they got there. The same old routines seemed to be common to us all. During that first weekend, I decided to stay in New York and take all they gave out with, except the "God stuff." I knew they needed to straighten out *their* thinking and habits, but *I* was all right; *I* just drank too much. Just give me a good front and a couple of bucks, and I'd be right back in the big time. I'd been dry three weeks, had the wrinkles out, and had sobered up my sponsor all by myself!

Bill and Hank had just taken over a small automobile polish company, and they offered me a job—ten dollars a week and keep at Hank's house. We were all set to put DuPont out of business.

At that time the group in New York was composed of about twelve men who were working on the principle of every drunk for himself; we had no real formula and no name. We would follow one man's ideas for a while, decide he was wrong, and switch to another's method. But we *were* staying sober as long as we kept and talked together. There was one meeting a week at Bill's home in Brooklyn, and we all took turns there spouting off about how we had changed our lives overnight, how many drunks we had saved and straightened out, and last but not least, how God had touched each of us personally on the shoulder. Boy, what a circle of confused idealists! Yet we all had one really sincere purpose in our hearts, and that was not to drink. At our weekly meeting I was a menace to serenity those first few months, for I took every opportunity to lambaste that "spiritual angle," as we called it, or anything else that had any tinge of theology. Much later I discovered the elders held many prayer meetings hoping to find a way to give me the heave-ho but at the same time stay tolerant and spiritual. They did not seem to be getting an answer, for here I was staying sober and selling lots of auto polish, on which they were making one thousand percent profit. So I rocked along my merry independent way until June, when I went out selling auto polish in New England. After a very good week, two of my customers took me to lunch on Saturday. We ordered sandwiches, and one man said, "Three beers." I let mine sit. After a bit, the other man said, "Three beers." I let that sit too. Then it was my turn—I ordered, "Three beers," but this time it was different; I had a cash investment of thirty cents, and, on a ten-dollar-a-week salary, that's a big thing. So I drank all three beers, one after the other, and said, "I'll be seeing you, boys," and went around the corner for a bottle. I never saw either of them again.

I had completely forgotten the January 8 when I found the Fellowship, and I spent the next four days wandering around New England half drunk, by which I mean I couldn't get drunk and I couldn't get sober. I tried to contact the boys in New York, but telegrams bounced right back, and when I finally got Hank on the telephone he fired me right then. This was when I really took my first good look at myself. My loneliness was worse than it had ever been before, for now even my own kind had turned against me. This time it really hurt, more than any hangover ever had. My brilliant agnosticism vanished, and I saw for the first time that those who really believed, or at least honestly tried to find a Power greater than themselves, were much more composed and contented than I had ever been, and they seemed to have a degree of happiness I had never known.

Peddling off my polish samples for expenses, I crawled back to New York a few days later in a very chastened frame of mind. When the others saw my altered attitude, they took me back in, but for me they *had* to make it tough; if they hadn't, I don't think I ever would have stuck it out. Once again, there was the challenge of a tough job, but this time I was determined to follow through. For a long time the only Higher Power I could concede was the power of the group, but this was far more than I had ever recognized before, and it was at least a beginning. It was also an ending, for never since June 16, 1938, have I had to walk alone.

Around this time our big A.A. book was being written, and it all became much simpler; we had a definite formula that some sixty of us agreed was the middle course for all alcoholics who wanted sobriety, and that formula has not been changed one iota down through the years. I don't think the boys were completely convinced of my personality change, for they fought shy of including my story in the book, so my only contribution to their literary efforts was my firm conviction—since I was still a theological rebel—that the word *God* should be qualified with the phrase "as we understand Him"—for that was the only way I could accept spirituality.

After the book appeared, we all became very busy in our efforts to save all and sundry, but I was still actually on the fringes of A.A. While I went along with all that was done and attended the meetings, I never took an active job of leadership until February 1940. Then I got a very good position in Philadelphia and quickly found I would need a few fellow alcoholics around me if I was to stay sober. Thus I found myself in the middle of a brand-new group. When I started to tell the boys how we did it in New York and all about the spiritual part of the program, I found they would not believe me unless I was practicing what I preached. Then I found that as I gave in to this spiritual or personality change, I was getting a little more serenity. In telling newcomers how to change their lives and attitudes, all of a sudden I found I was doing a little changing myself. I had been too self-sufficient to write a moral inventory, but I discovered in pointing out to the new man his wrong attitudes and actions that I was really taking my own inventory, and that if I expected him to change, I would have to work on myself too. This change has been a long, slow process for me, but through these latter years the dividends have been tremendous.

In June 1945, with another member, I made my first—and only—Twelfth Step call on a female alcoholic, and a year later I married her. She has been sober all the way through, and for me that has been good. We can share in the laughter and tears of our many friends, and most important, we can share our A.A. way of life and are given a daily opportunity to help others.

In conclusion, I can only say that whatever growth or understanding has come to me, I have no wish to graduate. Very rarely do I miss the meetings of my neighborhood A.A. group, and my average has never been less than two meetings a week. I have served on only one committee in the past nine years, for I feel that I had my chance the first few years and that newer members should fill the jobs. They are far more alert and progressive than we floundering fathers were, and the future of our fellowship is in their hands. We now live in the West and are very fortunate in our area A.A.; it is good, simple, and friendly, and our one desire is to stay *in* A.A. and not *on* it. Our pet slogan is "Easy Does It."

And I still say that as long as I remember that January 8 in Washington, that is how long, by the grace of God as I understand Him, I will retain a happy sobriety.

(6)

JIM'S STORY

This physician, one of the earliest members of A.A.'s first black group, tells of how freedom came as he worked among his people.

I WAS BORN in a little town in Virginia in an average religious home. My father, a Negro, was a country physician. I remember in my early youth my mother dressed me just as she did my two sisters, and I wore curls until I was six years of age. At that time I started school, and that's how I got rid of the curls. I found that even then I had fears and inhibitions. We lived just a few doors from the First Baptist Church, and when they had funerals, I remember very often asking my mother whether the person was good or bad and whether they were going to heaven or hell. I was about six then.

My mother had been recently converted and, actually, had become a religious fanatic. That was her main neurotic manifestation. She was very possessive with us children. Mother drilled into me a very Puritanical point of view as to sex relations, as well as to motherhood and womanhood. I'm sure my ideas as to what life should be like were quite different from that of the average person with whom I associated. Later on in life that took its toll. I realize that now.

About this time an incident took place in grade school that I have never forgotten because it made me realize that I was actually a physical coward. During recess we were playing basketball, and I had accidentally tripped a fellow just a little larger than I was. He took the basketball and smashed me in the face with it. That was enough provocation to fight but I didn't fight, and I realized after recess why I didn't. It was fear. That hurt and disturbed me a great deal.

Mother was of the old school and figured that anyone I associated with should be of the proper type. Of course, in my day, times had changed; she just hadn't changed with the times. I don't know whether it was right or wrong, but at least I know that people weren't thinking the same. We weren't even permitted to play cards in our home, but Father would give us just a little toddy with whiskey and sugar and warm water now and then. We had no whiskey in the house, other than my father's private stock. I never saw him drunk in my life, although he'd take a shot in the morning and usually one in the evening, and so did I; but for the most part he kept his whiskey in his office. The only time that I ever saw my mother take anything alcoholic was around Christmas time, when she would drink some eggnog or light wine.

In my first year in high school, mother suggested that I not join the cadet unit. She got a medical certificate so that I should not have to join it. I don't know whether she was a pacifist or whether she just thought that in the event of another war it would have some bearing on my joining up.

About then I realized that my point of view on the opposite sex wasn't entirely like that of most of the boys I knew. For that reason, I believe, I married at a much younger age than I would have, had it not been for my home training. My wife and I have been married for some thirty years now. Vi was the first girl that I ever took out. I had quite a heartache about her then because she wasn't the type of girl that my mother wanted me to marry. In the first place, she had been married before; I was her second husband. My mother resented it so much that the first Christmas after our marriage, she didn't even invite us to dinner. After our first child came, my parents both became allies. Then, in later days, after I became an alcoholic, they both turned against me.

My father had come out of the South and had suffered a great deal down there. He wanted to give me the very best, and he thought that nothing but being a doctor would suffice. On the other hand, I believe that I've always been medically inclined, though I have never been able to see medicine quite as the average person sees it. I do surgery because that's something that you can see; it's more tangible. But I can remember in postgraduate days, and during internship, that very often I'd go to a patient's bed and start a process of elimination and then, very often, I'd wind up guessing. That wasn't the way it was with my father. I think with him it possibly was a gift—intuitive diagnosis. Father, through the years, had built up a very good mail-order business because, at that time, there wasn't too much money in medicine.

I don't think I suffered too much as far as the racial situation was concerned because I was born into it and knew nothing other than that. A man wasn't actually mistreated, though if he was, he could only resent it.

He could do nothing about it. On the other hand, I got quite a different picture farther south. Economic conditions had a great deal to do with it, because I've often heard my father say that his mother would take one of the old-time flour sacks and cut a hole through the bottom and two corners of it and there you'd have a gown. Of course, when Father finally came to Virginia to work his way through school, he resented the southern "cracker," as he often called them, so much that he didn't even go back to his mother's funeral. He said he never wanted to set foot in the Deep South again, and he didn't.

I went to elementary and high school in Washington, D.C., and then to Howard University. My internship was in Washington. I never had too much trouble in school. I was able to get my work out. All my troubles arose when I was thrown socially among groups of people. As far as school was concerned, I made fair grades throughout.

This was around 1935, and it was about this time that I actually started drinking. During the years 1930 to 1935, due to the Depression and its aftermath, business went from bad to worse. I then had my own medical practice in Washington, but the practice slackened and the mail-order business started to fall off. Dad, due to having spent most of his time in a small Virginia town, didn't have any too much money, and the money he had saved and the property he had acquired were in Washington. He was in his late fifties, and all that he had undertaken fell upon my shoulders at his death in 1928. For the first couple of years it wasn't too bad because the momentum kept things going. But when things became crucial, everything started going haywire and I started going haywire with them. At this point I believe I had only been intoxicated on maybe three or four occasions, and certainly whiskey was no problem to me.

My father had purchased a restaurant, which he felt would take up some of my spare time, and that's how I met Vi. She came in for her dinner. I'd known her five or six months. To get rid of me one evening, she decided to go to the movies, she and another friend. A very good friend of mine who owned a drugstore across the street from us came by only about two hours later and said that he had seen Vi downtown. I said that she told me she was going to the movies, and I became foolishly disturbed about it, and as things snowballed, I decided to go out and get drunk. That's the first time I was ever really drunk in my life. The fear of the loss of Vi and the feeling that, though she had the right to do as she pleased, she should have told me the truth about it, upset me. That was my trouble. I thought that all women should be perfect.

I don't think I actually started to drink pathologically until approximately 1935. About that time I had lost practically all my property except the place we were living in. Things had just gone from bad to worse. It meant that I had to give up a lot of the things that I had been accustomed to, and that wasn't the easiest thing in the world for me. I think that was basically the thing that started me drinking in 1935. I started drinking alone then. I'd go into my home with a bottle, and I remember clearly how I would look around to see if Vi was watching. Something should have told me then that things were haywire. I can remember her watching. There came a time when she spoke to me about it, and I would say that I had a bad cold or that I wasn't feeling well. That went on for maybe two months, and then she got after me again about drinking. At that time the repeal whiskeys were back, and I'd go to the store and buy my whiskey and take it to my office and put it under the desk, first in one place and then in another, and there soon was an accumulation of empty bottles. My brother-in-law was living with us at that time, and I said to Vi, "Maybe the bottles are Brother's. I don't know. Ask him about it. I don't know anything about the bottles." I actually *wanted* a drink, besides feeling that I had to have a drink. From that point on, it's just the average drinker's story.

I got to the place where I'd look forward to the weekend's drinking and pacify myself by saying that the weekends were mine, that it didn't interfere with my family or with my business if I drank on the weekends. But the weekends stretched on into Mondays, and the time soon came when I drank every day. My practice at that juncture was just barely getting us a living.

A peculiar thing happened in 1940. That year, on a Friday night, a man whom I had known for years came to my office. My father had treated him many years prior to this. This man's wife had been suffering for a couple of months, and when he came in he owed me a little bill. I filled a prescription for him. The following day, Saturday, he came back and said, "Jim, I owe you for that prescription last night. I didn't pay you." I thought, "I know you didn't pay me, because you didn't get a prescription." He said, "Yes. You know the prescription that you gave me for my wife last night." Fear gripped me then, because I could remember nothing about it. It was the first blackout I had to recognize as a blackout. The next morning I carried another prescription to this man's house and exchanged it for the bottle his wife had. Then I said to my wife, "Something has to be done." I took that bottle of medicine and gave it to a very good friend of mine who was a pharmacist and had it analyzed, and the bottle was perfectly all right. But I knew at that point that I couldn't stop, and I knew that I was a danger to myself and to others.

I had a long talk with a psychiatrist, but nothing came of that, and I had also, just about that time, talked with a minister for whom I had a great deal of respect. He went into the religious side and told me that I didn't attend church as regularly as I should and that he felt, more or less, that this was responsible for my trouble. I rebelled against this, because just about the time that I was getting ready to leave high school, a revelation came to me about God, and it made things very complicated for me. The thought came to me that if God, as my mother said, was a vengeful God, he couldn't be a loving God. I wasn't able to comprehend it. I rebelled, and from that time on, I don't think I attended church more than a dozen times.

After this incident in 1940, I sought some other means of livelihood. I had a very good friend who was in the government service, and I went to him about a job. He got me one. I worked for the government about a year and still maintained my evening office practice when the government agencies were decentralized. Then I went south, because they told me that the particular county I was going to in North

Carolina was a dry county. I thought that this would be a big help to me. I would meet some new faces and be in a dry county.

But I found that after I got to North Carolina, it wasn't any different. The state was different, but I wasn't. Nevertheless, I stayed sober there about six months, because I knew that Vi was to come later and bring the children. We had two girls and a boy at that time. Something happened. Vi had secured work in Washington. She was also in the government service. I started inquiring where I could get a drink, and, of course, I found that it wasn't hard. I think whiskey was cheaper there than it was in Washington. Matters got worse all the time until finally they got so bad that I was reinvestigated by the government. Being an alcoholic, slick, and having some good sense left, I survived the investigation. Then I had my first bad stomach hemorrhage. I was out of work for about four days. I got into a lot of financial difficulties too. I borrowed five hundred dollars from the bank and three hundred from the loan shop, and I drank that up pretty fast. Then I decided that I'd go back to Washington.

My wife received me graciously, although she was living in a one-room-with-kitchen affair. She'd been reduced to that. I promised that I was going to do the right thing. We were now both working in the same agency. I continued to drink. I got drunk one night in October, went to sleep in the rain, and woke up with pneumonia. We continued to work together, and I continued to drink, but I guess, deep down within our hearts, we both knew I couldn't stop drinking. Vi thought I didn't want to stop. We had several fights, and on one or two occasions I struck her with my fist. She decided that she didn't want any more of that. So she went to court and talked it over with the judge. They cooked up a plan whereby she didn't have to be molested by me if she didn't want to be.

I went back to my mother's for a few days until things cooled off, because the district attorney had put out a summons for me to come to see him in his office. A policeman came to the door and asked for James S., but there wasn't any James S. there. He came back several times. Within ten days I got locked up for being drunk, and this same policeman was in the station house as I was being booked. I had to put up a three-hundred-dollar bond because he was carrying the same summons around in his pocket for me. So I went down to talk to the district attorney, and the arrangement was made that I would go home to stay with my mother, and that meant that Vi and I were separated. I continued to work and continued to go to lunch with Vi, and none of our acquaintances on the job knew that we had separated. Very often we rode to and from work together, but being separated really galled me deep down.

The November following, I took a few days off after pay day to celebrate my birthday on the twenty-fifth of the month. As usual I got drunk and lost the money. Someone had taken it from me. That was the usual pattern. I sometimes gave it to my mother, and then I'd go back and hound her for it. I was just about broke. I guess I had five or ten dollars in my pocket. Anyhow, on the twenty-fourth, after drinking all day on the twenty-third, I must have decided I wanted to see my wife and have some kind of reconciliation or at least talk with her. I don't remember whether I went by streetcar, whether I walked or went in a taxicab. The one thing I can remember now was that Vi was on the corner of 8th and L, and I remember vividly that she had an envelope in her hand. I remember talking to her, but what happened after that I don't know. What actually happened was that I had taken a penknife and stabbed Vi three times with it. Then I left and went home to bed. Around eight or nine o'clock there came two big detectives and a policeman to arrest me for assault; and I was the most amazed person in the world when they said I had assaulted someone, and especially that I had assaulted my wife. I was taken to the station house and locked up.

The next morning I went up for arraignment. Vi was very kind and explained to the jury that I was basically a fine fellow and a good husband but that I drank too much and that she thought I had lost my mind and should be committed to an asylum. The judge said that if she felt that way, he would confine me for thirty days' examination and observation. There was no observation. There might have been some investigation. The closest I came to a psychiatrist during that time was an intern who came to take blood tests. After the trial, I got big-hearted again and felt that I should do something in payment for Vi's kindness to me; so I left Washington and went to Seattle to work. I was there about three weeks, and then I got restless and started to tramp across the country, here and there, until I finally wound up in Pennsylvania, in a steel mill.

I worked in the steel mill for possibly two months,

and then I became disgusted with myself and decided
to go back home. I think the thing that galled me was
that just after Easter I had drawn my salary for two
weeks' work and had decided that I was going to send
some money to Vi; and above all else I was going to
send my baby daughter an Easter outfit. But there
happened to be a liquor store between the post office
and the mill, and I stopped to get that one drink. Of
course the kid never got the Easter outfit. I got very
little out of the two hundred that I drew on that payday.

I knew I wasn't capable of keeping the bulk of the
money myself, so I gave it to a white fellow who
owned the bar I frequented. He kept the money
for me, but I worried him to death for it. Finally, I
broke the last one hundred dollar bill the Saturday
before I left. I got out of that bill one pair of shoes,
and the rest of that money was blown. I took the last
of it to buy my railroad ticket.

I'd been home about a week or ten days when one
of my friends asked if I could repair one of his electrical outlets. Thinking only of two or three dollars
to buy some whiskey, I did the job and that's how I
met Ella G., who was responsible for my coming into
A.A. I went to this friend's shop to repair his electrical
outlet, and I noticed this lady. She continued to watch
me, although she didn't say anything. Finally she
said, "Isn't your name Jim S.?" I said, "Yes." Then
she told me who she was. She was Ella G. When I
had known her years before, she was rather slender,
but at this time she weighed as much as she does now,
which is up around in the two hundreds or very close
to it. I had not recognized her, but as soon as she said

who she was, I remembered her right away. She didn't say anything about A.A. or getting me a sponsor at that time, but she did ask about Vi, and I told her Vi was working and how she could locate her. It was around noon, a day or two later, when the telephone rang and it was Ella. She asked me if I would let someone come up and talk to me concerning a business deal. She never mentioned anything about my whiskey drinking because if she had I would have told her no right then. I asked her just what this deal was, but she wouldn't say. She said, "He has something of interest, if you will see him." I told her that I would. She asked me one other thing. She asked me if I would try to be sober if I possibly could. So I put forth some effort that day to try to stay sober if I could, though my sobriety was just a daze.

About seven that evening my sponsor walked in, Charlie G. He didn't seem too much at ease in the beginning. I guess I felt, and he sensed it, that I wanted him to hurry up and say what he had to say and get out. Anyhow, he started talking about himself. He started telling me how much trouble he had, and I said to myself, I wonder why this guy is telling me all his troubles. I have troubles of my own. Finally, he brought in the angle of whiskey. He continued to talk and I to listen. After he'd talked half an hour, I still wanted him to hurry up and get out so I could go and get some whiskey before the liquor store closed. But as he continued to talk, I realized that this was the first time I had met a person who had the same problems I did and who, I sincerely believe, understood me as an individual. I knew my wife didn't, because I had been sincere in all my promises to her as well as to my mother and to my close friends, but the urge to take that drink was more powerful than anything else.

After Charlie had talked a while, I knew that this man had something. In that short period he built within me something that I had long since lost, which was hope. When he left, I walked with him to the streetcar line, which was just about a half a block, but there were two liquor stores, one on each corner from my home. I put Charlie on the car, and when I left him, I passed both of those liquor stores without even thinking about them.

The following Sunday we met at Ella G.'s. It was Charlie and three or four others. That was the first meeting of a colored group in A.A., so far as I know. We held some two or three meetings at Ella's home, and from there we held some two or three at her mother's home. Then Charlie or someone in the group suggested that we try to get a place in a church or hall to hold meetings. I approached several ministers and all of them thought it was a very good idea, but they never relinquished any space. So, finally, I went to the YMCA, and they graciously permitted us to use a room at two dollars a night. At that time we had our meetings on Friday nights. Of course, it wasn't very much of a meeting in the beginning; most of the time it was just Vi and myself. But, finally, we got one or two to come in and stick, and from there, of course, we started to grow.

I haven't mentioned it, but Charlie, my sponsor, was white, and when we got our group started, we got help from other white groups in Washington. They came, many of them, and stuck by us and told us how to hold meetings. They taught us a great deal about Twelfth Step work too. Indeed, without their aid we couldn't possibly have gone on. They saved us endless time and lost motion. And, not only that, but they gave us financial help. Even when we were paying that two dollars a night, they often paid it for us because our collection was so small.

At this time I wasn't working. Vi was taking care of me, and I was devoting all my time to the building of that group. I worked at that alone for six months. I just gathered up this and that alcoholic, because, in the back of my mind, I wanted to save all the world. I had found this new "something," and I wanted to give it to everyone who had a problem. We didn't save the world, but we did manage to help some individuals.

That's my story of what A.A. has done for me.

(7)

THE MAN WHO MASTERED FEAR

He spent eighteen years in running away, and then found he didn't have to run. So he started A.A. in Detroit.

FOR EIGHTEEN YEARS, from the time I was twenty-one, fear governed my life. By the time I was thirty, I had found that alcohol dissolved fear— for a little while. In the end I had two problems instead of one: fear and alcohol.

I came from a good family. I believe the sociologists would call it upper middle class. By the time I was twenty-one, I had had six years of life in foreign countries, spoke three languages fluently, and had attended college for two years. A low ebb in the family fortunes necessitated my going to work when I was twenty. I entered the business world with every confidence that success lay ahead of me. I had been brought up to believe this, and I had shown during my teens considerable enterprise and imagination about earning money. To the best of my recollection, I was completely free from any abnormal fears. Vacations from school and from work spelled "travel" to me—and I traveled with gusto. During my first year out of college, I had endless dates and went to countless dances, balls, and dinner parties.

Suddenly all this changed. I underwent a shattering nervous breakdown. Three months in bed. Three more months of being up and around the house for brief periods and in bed the rest of the time. Visits from friends that lasted over fifteen minutes exhausted me. A complete checkup at one of the best hospitals revealed nothing. I heard for the first time an expression that I was to grow to loathe: "There is nothing organically wrong." Psychiatry might have helped, but psychiatrists had not penetrated the Middle West.

Spring came. I went for my first walk. Half a block from the house, I tried to turn the corner. Fear froze me in my tracks, but the instant I turned back toward home, this paralyzing fear left me. This was the beginning of an unending series of such experiences. I told our family doctor—an understanding man who gave hours of his time trying to help me—about this experience. He told me that it was imperative that I walk around the entire block, cost me what it might in mental agony. I carried out his instructions. When I reached a point directly back of our house, where I could have cut through a friend's garden, I was almost overpowered by the desire to get home, but I made the whole journey. Probably only a few readers of this story will be able, from personal experiences of their own, to understand the exhilaration and sense of accomplishment I felt after finishing this seemingly simple assignment.

The details of the long road back to something resembling normal living—the first short streetcar ride, the purchase of a used bike, which enabled me to widen the narrow horizon of life, the first trip downtown—I will not dwell on. I got an easy, part-time job selling printing for a small neighborhood printer. This widened the scope of my activities. A year later I was able to buy a Model T roadster and take a better job with a downtown printer. From this job and the next one with yet another printer, I was courteously dismissed. I simply did not have the pep to do hard, "cold-turkey" selling. I switched to real estate brokerage and property management work. Almost simultaneously, I discovered that cocktails in the late afternoon and highballs in the evening relieved the many tensions of the day. This happy combination of pleasant work and alcohol lasted for five years. Of course, the latter ultimately killed the former, but of this, more anon.

All this changed when I was thirty years old. My parents died, both in the same year, leaving me, a sheltered and somewhat immature man, on my own. I moved into a "bachelor hall." These men all drank on Saturday nights and enjoyed themselves. My pattern of drinking became very different from theirs. I had bad, nervous headaches, particularly at the base of my neck. Liquor relieved these. At last I discovered alcohol as a cure-all. I joined their Saturday night parties and enjoyed myself too. But I also stayed up weeknights after they had retired and drank myself into bed. My thinking about drinking had undergone a great change. Liquor had become a crutch on the one hand and a means of retreat from life on the other.

The ensuing nine years were the Depression years, both nationally and personally. With the bravery born of desperation, and abetted by alcohol, I married a young and lovely girl. Our marriage lasted four years. At least three of those four years must have been a living hell for my wife, because she had to watch the man she loved disintegrate morally, mentally, and financially. The birth of a baby boy did nothing toward staying the downward spiral. When she finally took the baby and left, I locked myself in the house and stayed drunk for a month.

The next two years were simply a long, drawn-out process of less and less work and more and more whiskey. I ended up homeless, jobless, penniless, and rudderless, as the problem guest of a close friend whose family was out of town. Haunting me through each day's stupor—and there were eighteen or nineteen such days in this man's home—was the thought: Where do I go when his family comes home? When the day of their return was almost upon me, and suicide was the only answer I had been able to think of, I went into Ralph's room one evening and told him the truth. He was a man of considerable means, and he might have done what many men would have done in such a case. He might have handed me fifty dollars and said that I ought to pull myself together and make a new start. I have thanked God many times in the last sixteen years that *that* was just what he did not do!

Instead, he got dressed, took me out, bought me three or four double shots, and put me to bed. The next day he turned me over to a couple who, although neither was an alcoholic, knew Dr. Bob and were willing to drive me to Akron where they would turn me over to his care. The only stipulation they made was this: I had to make the decision myself. What decision? The choice was limited. To go north into the empty pine country and shoot myself, or to go south in the faint hope that a bunch of strangers might help me with my drinking problem. Well, suicide was a last-straw matter, and I had not drawn the last straw yet. So I was driven to Akron the very next day by these Good Samaritans and turned over to Dr. Bob and the then tiny Akron Group.

Here, while I was in a hospital bed, men with clear eyes, happy faces, and a look of assurance and purposefulness about them came to see me and told me their stories. Some of these were hard to believe, but it did not require a giant brain to perceive that they had something I could use. How could I get it? It was simple, they said, and went on to explain to me in their own language the program of recovery and daily living that we know today as the Twelve Steps of A.A. Dr. Bob dwelt at length on how prayer had given him release, time and time again, from the nearly overpowering compulsion to take a drink. It was he who convinced me, because his own conviction was so real, that a Power greater than myself could help me in the crises of life and that the means of communicating with this Power was simple prayer. Here was a tall, rugged, highly educated Yankee talking in a matter-of-course way about God and prayer. If he and these other fellows could do it, so could I.

When I got out of the hospital, I was invited to stay with Dr. Bob and his dear wife, Anne. I was suddenly and uncontrollably seized with the old, paralyzing panic. The hospital had seemed so safe. Now I was in a strange house, in a strange city, and fear gripped me. I shut myself in my room, which began to go around in circles. Panic, confusion, and chaos were supreme. Out of this maelstrom just two coherent thoughts came to the surface; one, a drink would mean homelessness and death; two, I could no longer relieve the pressure of fear by starting home, as was once my habitual solution to this problem, because I no longer had a home. Finally, and I shall never know how much later it was, one clear thought came to me: Try prayer. You can't lose, and maybe God will help you —just maybe, mind you. Having no one else to turn to, I was willing to give Him a chance, although with considerable doubt. I got down on my knees for the first time in thirty years. The prayer I said was simple. It went something like this: "God, for eighteen years I have been unable to handle this problem. Please let me turn it over to you."

Immediately a great feeling of peace descended upon me, intermingled with a feeling of being suffused with a quiet strength. I lay down on the bed and slept like a child. An hour later I awoke to a new world. *Nothing had changed and yet everything had changed.* The scales had dropped from my eyes, and I could see life in its proper perspective. I had tried to be the center of my own little world, whereas God was the center of a vast universe of which I was perhaps an essential, but a very tiny, part.

It is well over sixteen years since I came back to life. I have never had a drink since. This alone is a miracle. It is, however, only the first of a series of miracles that have followed one another as a result of my trying to apply to my daily life the principles embodied in our Twelve Steps. I would like to sketch for you the highlights of these sixteen years of a slow but steady and satisfying upward climb.

Poor health and a complete lack of money necessitated my remaining with Dr. Bob and Anne for very close to a year. It would be impossible for me to pass over this year without mentioning my love for, and my indebtedness to, these two wonderful people who are no longer with us. They made me feel as if I were a part of their family, and so did their children. The example that they and Bill W., whose visits to Akron were fairly frequent, set for me of service to their fellow men imbued me with a great desire to emulate them. Sometimes during that year I rebelled inwardly at what seemed like lost time and at having to be a burden to these good people whose means were limited. Long before I had any real opportunity to give, I had to learn the equally important lesson of receiving graciously.

During my first few months in Akron, I was quite sure that I never wanted to see my hometown again. Too many economic and social problems would beset me there. I would make a fresh start somewhere else. After six months of sobriety, I saw the picture in a different light: Detroit was the place I had to return to, not only because I must face the mess I had made there, but because it was there that I could be of the most service to A.A. In the spring of 1939, Bill stopped off in Akron on his way to Detroit on business. I jumped at the suggestion that I accompany him. We spent two days there together before he returned to New York. Friends invited me to stay on for as long as I cared to. I remained with them for three weeks, using part of the time in making many amends, which I had had no earlier opportunity of making.

The rest of my time was devoted to A.A. spadework. I wanted "ripe" prospects, and I didn't feel that I would get very far chasing individual drunks in and out of bars. So I spent much of my time calling on the people who I felt would logically come in contact with alcoholic cases—doctors, ministers, lawyers, and the personnel men in industry. I also talked A.A. to every friend who would listen, at lunch, at dinner, on street corners. A doctor tipped me off to my first prospect. I landed him and shipped him by train to Akron, with a pint of whiskey in his pocket to keep him from wanting to get off the train in Toledo! Nothing has ever to this day equaled the thrill of that first case.

Those three weeks left me completely exhausted, and I had to return to Akron for three more months of rest. While there, two or three more "cash customers" (as Dr. Bob used to call them—probably because they had so little cash) were shipped in to us from Detroit. When I finally returned to Detroit to find work and to learn to stand on my own feet, the ball was already rolling, however slowly. But it took six more months of work and disappointments before a group of three men got together in my rooming-house bedroom for their first A.A. meeting.

It sounds simple, but there were obstacles and doubts to overcome. I well remember a session I had with myself soon after I returned. It ran something like this: If I go around shouting from the rooftops about my alcoholism, it might very possibly prevent me from getting a good job. But *supposing that just one man died* because I had, for selfish reasons, kept my mouth shut? No. I was supposed to be doing God's will, not mine. His road lay clear before me, and I'd better quit rationalizing myself into any detours. I could not expect to keep what I had gained unless I gave it away.

The Depression was still on, and jobs were scarce. My health was still uncertain. So I created a job for myself selling women's hosiery and men's made-to-order shirts. This gave me the freedom to do A.A. work and to rest for periods of two or three days when I became too exhausted to carry on. There was more than one occasion when I got up in the morning with just enough money for coffee and toast and the bus fare to carry me to my first appointment. No sale—no lunch. During that first year, however, I managed to make both ends meet and to avoid ever going back to my old habit-pattern of borrowing money when I could not earn it. Here by itself was a great step forward.

During the first three months, I carried on all these activities without a car, depending entirely on buses and streetcars—I, who always had to have a car at my immediate command. I, who had never made a speech in my life and who would have been frightened sick at the prospect, stood up in front of Rotary groups in different parts of the city and talked about Alcoholics Anonymous. I, carried away with the desire to serve A.A., gave what was probably one of the first radio broadcasts about A.A., living through a case of mike fright and feeling like a million dollars when it was all over. I lived through a week of the fidgets because I had agreed to address a group of alcoholic inmates in one of our state mental hospitals. There it was the same reward—exhilaration at a mission accomplished. Do I have to tell you who gained the most out of all this?

Within a year of my return to Detroit, A.A. was a definitely established little group of about a dozen members, and I too was established in a modest but steady job handling an independent dry-cleaning route of my own. I was my own boss. It took five years of A.A. living, and a substantial improvement in my health, before I could take a full-time office job where someone else was boss.

This office job brought me face to face with a problem that I had sidestepped all my adult life, lack of training. This time I did something about it. I enrolled in a correspondence school that taught nothing but accounting. With this specialized training, and a liberal business education in the school of hard knocks, I was able to set up shop some two years later as an independent accountant. Seven years of work in this field brought an opportunity to affiliate myself actively with one of my clients, a fellow A.A. We complement each other beautifully, as he is a born salesman and my taste is for finance and management. At long last I am doing the kind of work I have always wanted to do but never had the patience and emotional stability to train myself for. The A.A. program showed me the way to come down to earth, start from the bottom, and work up. This represents another great change for me. In the long ago past I used to start at the top as president or treasurer and end up with the sheriff breathing down my neck.

So much for my business life. Obviously I have overcome fear to a sufficient degree to think in terms of success in business. With God's help I am able, for one day at a time, to carry business responsibilities that, not many years ago, I would not have dreamed of assuming. But what about my social life? What about those fears that once paralyzed me to the point of my becoming a semi-hermit? What about my fear of travel?

It would be wonderful were I able to tell you that my confidence in God and my application of the

Twelve Steps to my daily living have utterly banished fear. But this would not be the truth. The most accurate answer I *can* give you is this: Fear has never again ruled my life since that day in September 1938, when I found that a Power greater than myself could not only restore me to sanity but could keep me both sober and sane. Never in sixteen years have I dodged anything because I was afraid of it. I have faced life instead of running away from it.

Some of the things that used to stop me in my tracks from fear still make me nervous in the anticipation of their doing, but once I kick myself into doing them, nervousness disappears and I enjoy myself. In recent years I have had the happy combination of time and money to travel occasionally. I am apt to get into quite an uproar for a day or two before starting, but I *do* start, and once started, I have a swell time.

Have I ever wanted a drink during these years? Only once did I suffer from a nearly overpowering compulsion to take a drink. Oddly enough, the circumstances and surroundings were pleasant. I was at a beautifully set dinner table. I was in a perfectly happy frame of mind. I had been in A.A. a year, and the last thing in my mind was a drink. There was a glass of sherry at my place. I was seized with an almost uncontrollable desire to reach out for it. I shut my eyes and asked for help. In fifteen seconds or less, the feeling passed. There have also been numerous times when I have thought about taking a drink. Such thinking usually began with thoughts of the pleasant drinking of my youth. I learned early in my A.A. life that I could not afford to fondle such thoughts, as you might fondle a pet, because this particular pet could grow into a monster. Instead, I quickly substitute one or another vivid scene from the nightmare of my later drinking.

Twenty-odd years ago I made a mess out of my one and only marriage. It was therefore not extraordinary that I should shy away from any serious thought of marriage for a great many years after joining A.A. Here was something requiring a greater willingness to assume responsibility and a larger degree of cooperation and give and take than even business requires of one. However, I must have felt, deep down inside myself, that living the selfish life of a bachelor was only half living. By living alone you can pretty much eliminate grief from your life, but you also eliminate joy. At any rate the last great step toward a well-rounded life still lay ahead of me. So six months ago I acquired a ready-made family consisting of one charming wife, four grown children to whom I am devoted, and three grandchildren. Being an alcoholic, I couldn't dream of doing anything by halves! My wife, a sister member in A.A., had been a widow nine years and I had been single eighteen years. The adjustments in such a case are difficult and take time, but we both feel that they are certainly worth it. We are both depending upon God and our use of the Alcoholics Anonymous program to help us make a success of this joint undertaking.

It is undoubtedly too soon for me to say how much of a success I shall be as a husband in time to come. I do feel, though, that the fact that I finally *grew up* to a point where I could even tackle such a job is the apex of the story of a man who spent eighteen years running away from life.

(8)

HE SOLD HIMSELF SHORT

*But he found there was a Higher Power that had
more faith in him than he had in himself. Thus, A.A.
was born in Chicago.*

GREW UP in a small town outside Akron, Ohio,
where the life was typical of any average small
town. I was very much interested in athletics, and
because of this and parental influence, I didn't drink
or smoke in either grade or high school.

All of this changed when I went to college. I had
to adapt to new associations and associates, and it
seemed to be the smart thing to drink and smoke. I
confined drinking to weekends, and drank normally in
college and for several years thereafter.

After I left school, I went to work in Akron, living
at home with my parents. Home life was again a restraining influence. When I drank, I hid it from my
folks out of respect for their feelings. This continued
until I was twenty-seven. Then I started traveling,
with the United States and Canada as my territory
and with so much freedom and with an unlimited expense account, I was soon drinking every night and
kidding myself that it was all part of the job. I know
now that 60 percent of the time I drank alone without
benefit of customers.

In 1930, I moved to Chicago. Shortly thereafter,
aided by the Depression, I found that I had a great

deal of spare time and that a little drink in the morning helped. By 1932, I was going on two- or three-day benders. That same year, my wife became fed up with my drinking around the house and called my dad in Akron to come and pick me up. She asked him to do something about me because she couldn't. She was thoroughly disgusted.

This was the beginning of five years of bouncing back and forth between my home in Chicago and Akron to sober up. It was a period of binges coming closer and closer together and being of longer duration. Once Dad came all the way to Florida to sober me up after a hotel manager called him and said that if he wanted to see me alive he'd better get there fast. My wife could not understand why I would sober up for Dad but not for her. They went into a huddle, and Dad explained that he simply took my pants, shoes, and money away so that I could get no liquor and had to sober up.

One time my wife decided to try this too. After finding every bottle that I had hidden around the apartment, she took away my pants, my shoes, my money, and my keys, threw them under the bed in the back bedroom, and slip-locked our door. By one a.m. I was desperate. I found some wool stockings, some white flannels that had shrunk to my knees, and an old jacket. I jimmied the front door so that I could get back in, and walked out. I was hit by an icy blast. It was February with snow and ice on the ground, and I had a four-block walk to the nearest cab stand, but I made it. On my ride to the nearest bar, I sold the driver on how misunderstood I was by my wife and what an unreasonable person she was. By the time we reached the bar, he was willing to buy me a quart with his own money. Then when we got back to the apartment, he was willing to wait two or three days until I got my health back to be paid off for the liquor and fare. I was a good salesman. My wife could not understand the next morning why I was drunker than the night before, when she had taken my bottles.

After a particularly bad Christmas and New Year's holiday, Dad picked me up again early in January 1937 to go through the usual sobering up routine. This consisted of walking the floor for three or four days and nights until I could take nourishment. This time he had a suggestion to offer. He waited until I was completely sober, and on the day before I was to head back for Chicago, he told me of a small group of men in Akron who apparently had the same problem that I had but were doing something about it. He said they were sober, happy, and had their self-respect back, as well as the respect of their neighbors. He mentioned two of them whom I had known through the years and suggested that I talk with them. But I had my health back, and, besides, I reasoned, they were much worse than I would ever be. Why, even a year ago I had seen Howard, an ex-doctor, mooching a dime for a drink. I could not possibly be that bad. I would at least have asked for a quarter! So I told Dad that I would lick it on my own, that I would drink nothing for a month and after that only beer.

Several months later Dad was back in Chicago to pick me up again, but this time my attitude was entirely different. I could not wait to tell him that I wanted help, that if these men in Akron had anything,

I wanted it and would do anything to get it. I was completely licked by alcohol.

I can still remember very distinctly getting into Akron at eleven p.m. and routing this same Howard out of bed to do something about me. He spent two hours with me that night telling me his story. He said he had finally learned that drinking was a fatal illness made up of an allergy plus an obsession, and once the drinking had passed from habit to obsession, we were completely hopeless and could look forward only to spending the balance of our lives in mental institutions—or to death.

He laid great stress on the progression of his attitude toward life and people, and most of his attitudes had been very similar to mine. I thought at times that he was telling my story! I had thought that I was completely different from other people, that I was beginning to become a little balmy, even to the point of withdrawing more and more from society and wanting to be alone with my bottle.

Here was a man with essentially the same outlook on life, except that he had done something about it. He was happy, getting a kick out of life and people, and beginning to get his medical practice back again. As I look back on that first evening, I realize that I began to hope, then, for the first time; and I felt that if he could regain these things, perhaps it would be possible for me too.

The next afternoon and evening, two other men visited me, and each told me his story and the things that they were doing to try to recover from this tragic illness. They had that certain something that seemed to glow, a peace, a serenity combined with happiness.

In the next two or three days the balance of this handful of men contacted me, encouraged me, and told me how they were trying to live this program of recovery and the fun they were having doing it.

Then and then only, after a thorough indoctrination by eight or nine individuals, was I allowed to attend my first meeting. This first meeting was held in the living room of a home and was led by Bill D., the first man that Bill W. and Dr. Bob had worked with successfully.

The meeting consisted of perhaps eight or nine alcoholics and seven or eight wives. It was different from the meetings now held. The big A.A. book had not been written, and there was no literature except various religious pamphlets. The program was carried on entirely by word of mouth.

The meeting lasted an hour and closed with the Lord's Prayer. After it was closed, we all retired to the kitchen and had coffee and doughnuts and more discussion until the small hours of the morning.

I was terribly impressed by this meeting and the quality of happiness these men displayed, despite their lack of material means. In this small group, during the Depression, there was no one who was not hard up.

I stayed in Akron two or three weeks on my initial trip trying to absorb as much of the program and philosophy as possible. I spent a great deal of time with Dr. Bob, whenever he had the time to spare, and in the homes of two or three other people, trying to see how the family lived the program. Every evening we would meet at the home of one of the members and have coffee and doughnuts and spend a social evening.

The day before I was due to go back to Chicago—

it was Dr. Bob's afternoon off—he had me to the office and we spent three or four hours formally going through the Six-Step program as it was at that time. The six steps were:

1. Complete deflation.
2. Dependence and guidance from a Higher Power.
3. Moral inventory.
4. Confession.
5. Restitution.
6. Continued work with other alcoholics.

Dr. Bob led me through all of these steps. At the moral inventory, he brought up several of my bad personality traits or character defects, such as selfishness, conceit, jealousy, carelessness, intolerance, ill-temper, sarcasm, and resentments. We went over these at great length, and then he finally asked me if I wanted these defects of character removed. When I said yes, we both knelt at his desk and prayed, each of us asking to have these defects taken away.

This picture is still vivid. If I live to be a hundred, it will always stand out in my mind. It was very impressive, and I wish that every A.A. could have the benefit of this type of sponsorship today. Dr. Bob always emphasized the religious angle very strongly, and I think it helped. I know it helped me. Dr. Bob then led me through the restitution step, in which I made a list of all of the persons I had harmed and worked out the ways and the means of slowly making restitution.

I made several decisions at that time. One of them was that I would try to get a group started in Chicago; the second was that I would have to return to Akron to attend meetings at least every two months until I did get a group started in Chicago; third, I decided I must place this program above everything else, even my family, because if I did not maintain my sobriety, I would lose my family anyway. If I did not maintain my sobriety, I would not have a job. If I did not maintain my sobriety, I would have no friends left. I had few enough at that time.

The next day I went back to Chicago and started a vigorous campaign among my so-called friends or drinking companions. Their answer was always the same: If they needed it at any time, they would surely get in touch with me. I went to a minister and a doctor whom I still knew, and they, in turn, asked me how long I had been sober. When I told them six weeks, they were polite and said that they would contact me in case they had anyone with an alcoholic problem.

Needless to say, it was a year or more before they did contact me. On my trips back to Akron to get my spirits recharged and to work with other alcoholics, I would ask Dr. Bob about this delay and wonder just what was wrong with me. He would invariably reply, "When you are right and the time is right, Providence will provide. You must always be willing and continue to make contacts."

A few months after I made my original trip to Akron, I was feeling pretty cocky, and I didn't think my wife was treating me with proper respect, now that I was an outstanding citizen. So I set out to get drunk deliberately, just to teach her what she was missing. A week later I had to get an old friend from Akron to spend two days sobering me up. That was my lesson, that one could not take the moral inventory and then file it away; that the alcoholic has to continue to take inventory every day if he expects to get well and stay well. That was my only slip. It taught me a valuable lesson. In the summer of 1938, almost a year from the time I made my original contact with Akron, the man for whom I was working, and who knew about the program, approached me and asked if I could do anything about one of his salesmen who was drinking very heavily. I went to the sanitarium where this chap was incarcerated and found to my surprise that he was interested. He had been wanting to do something about his drinking for a long time but did not know how. I spent several days with him, but I did not feel adequate to pass the program on to him by myself. So I suggested that he take a trip to Akron for a couple of weeks, which he did, living with one of the A.A. families there. When he returned, we had practically daily meetings from that time on.

A few months later one of the men who had been in touch with the group in Akron came to Chicago to live, and then there were three of us who continued to have informal meetings quite regularly.

In the spring of 1939, the Big Book was printed, and we had two inquiries from the New York office because of a fifteen-minute radio talk that was made. Neither one of the two was interested for himself, one being a mother who wanted to do something for her son. I suggested to her that she should see the son's minister or doctor, and that perhaps he would recommend the A.A. program.

The doctor, a young man, immediately took fire with the idea, and while he did not convince the son, he turned over two prospects who were anxious for the program. The three of us did not feel up to the job, and after a few meetings we convinced the prospects that they, too, should go to Akron where they could see an older group in action.

In the meantime, another doctor in Evanston became convinced that the program had possibilities and turned over a woman to us to do something about. She was full of enthusiasm and also made the trip to Akron. Immediately on her return in the autumn of 1939, we began to have formal meetings once a week, and we have continued to do this and to expand ever since.

Occasionally, it is accorded to a few of us to watch something fine grow from a tiny kernel into something of gigantic goodness. Such has been my privilege, both nationally and in my home city. From a mere handful in Akron, we have spread throughout the world. From a single member in the Chicago area, commuting to Akron, we now exceed six thousand.

These last eighteen years have been the happiest of my life, trite though that statement may seem. Fifteen of those years I would not have enjoyed had I continued drinking. Doctors told me before I stopped that I had only three years at the outside to live.

This latest part of my life has had a purpose, not in great things accomplished but in daily living. Courage to face each day has replaced the fears and uncertainties of earlier years. Acceptance of things as they are has replaced the old impatient champing at the bit to conquer the world. I have stopped tilting at windmills and, instead, have tried to accomplish the little daily tasks, unimportant in themselves, but tasks that are an integral part of living fully.

Where derision, contempt, and pity were once shown me, I now enjoy the respect of many people. Where once I had casual acquaintances, all of whom were fair-weather friends, I now have a host of friends who accept me for what I am. And over my A.A. years I have made many real, honest, sincere friendships that I shall always cherish.

I'm rated as a modestly successful man. My stock of material goods isn't great. But I have a fortune in friendships, courage, self-assurance, and honest appraisal of my own abilities. Above all, I have gained the greatest thing accorded to any man, the love and understanding of a gracious God, who has lifted me from the alcoholic scrap heap to a position of trust, where I have been able to reap the rich rewards that come from showing a little love for others and from serving them as I can.

(9)

THE KEYS OF THE KINGDOM

This worldly lady helped to develop A.A. in Chicago and thus passed her keys to many.

A LITTLE MORE than fifteen years ago, through a long and calamitous series of shattering experiences, I found myself being helplessly propelled toward total destruction. I was without power to change the course my life had taken. How I had arrived at this tragic impasse, I could not have explained to anyone. I was thirty-three years old and my life was spent. I was caught in a cycle of alcohol and sedation that was proving inescapable, and consciousness had become intolerable.

I was a product of the post-war prohibition era of the Roaring '20s. That age of the flapper and the "It" girl, speakeasies and the hip flask, the boyish bob and the drugstore cowboy, John Held Jr. and F. Scott Fitzgerald, all generously sprinkled with a patent pseudo-sophistication. To be sure, this had been a dizzy and confused interval, but most everyone else I knew had emerged from it with both feet on the ground and a fair amount of adult maturity.

Nor could I blame my dilemma on my childhood environment. I couldn't have chosen more loving and conscientious parents. I was given every advantage in a well-ordered home. I had the best schools, summer camps, resort vacations, and travel. Every reasonable desire was possible of attainment for me. I was strong and healthy and quite athletic.

I experienced some of the pleasure of social drinking when I was sixteen. I definitely liked everything about alcohol—the taste, the effects; and I realize now that a drink did something for me or to me that was different from the way it affected others. It wasn't long before any party without drinks was a dud for me.

I was married at twenty, had two children, and was divorced at twenty-three. My broken home and broken heart fanned my smoldering self-pity into a fair-sized bonfire, and this kept me well supplied with reasons for having another drink, and then another.

At twenty-five I had developed an alcoholic problem. I began making the rounds of the doctors in the hope that one of them might find some cure for my accumulating ailments, preferably something that could be removed surgically.

Of course the doctors found nothing. Just an unstable woman, undisciplined, poorly adjusted, and filled with nameless fears. Most of them prescribed sedatives and advised rest and moderation.

Between the ages of twenty-five and thirty, I tried everything. I moved a thousand miles away from home to Chicago and a new environment. I studied art; I desperately endeavored to create an interest in many things, in a new place among new people. Nothing worked. My drinking habits increased in spite of my struggle for control. I tried the beer diet, the wine diet, timing, measuring, and spacing of drinks. I tried them mixed, unmixed, drinking only when happy, only when depressed. And still, by the time I was thirty years old, I was being pushed around by a compulsion to drink that was completely beyond my control. I couldn't stop drinking. I would hang on to sobriety for short intervals, but always there would come the tide of an overpowering *necessity* to drink, and, as I was engulfed in it, I felt such a sense of panic that I really believed I would die if I didn't get that drink inside.

Needless to say, this was not pleasurable drinking. I had long since given up any pretense of the social cocktail hour. This was drinking in sheer despera-tion, alone and locked behind my own door. Alone in the relative safety of my home because I knew I dare not risk the danger of blacking out in some public place or at the wheel of a car. I could no longer gauge my capacity, and it might be the second or the tenth drink that would erase my consciousness.

The next three years saw me in sanitariums, once in a ten-day coma, from which I very nearly did not re-cover, in and out of hospitals or confined at home with day and night nurses. By now I wanted to die but had lost the courage even to take my life. I was trapped, and for the life of me I did not know how or why this had happened to me. And all the while my fear fed a growing conviction that before long it would be necessary for me to be put away in some institu-tion. People didn't behave this way outside of an asy-lum. I had heartsickness, shame, and fear bordering on panic, and no complete escape any longer except in oblivion. Certainly, now, anyone would have agreed that only a miracle could prevent my final breakdown. But how does one get a prescription for a miracle?

For about one year prior to this time, there was one doctor who had continued to struggle with me. He had tried everything from having me attend daily mass at six a.m. to performing the most menial labor for his charity patients. Why he bothered with me as long as he did I shall never know, for he knew there was no answer for me in medicine, and he, like all doctors of his day, had been taught that the alcoholic was incurable and should be ignored. Doctors were advised to attend patients who could be benefited by medicine. With the alcoholic, they could only give temporary relief and in the last stages not even that. It was a waste of the doctors' time and the patients' money. Nevertheless, there were a few doctors who saw alcoholism as a disease and felt that the alcoholic was a victim of something over which he had no control. They had a hunch that there must be an answer for these apparently hopeless ones, somewhere. Fortunately for me, my doctor was one of the enlightened.

And then, in the spring of 1939, a very remarkable book was rolled off a New York press with the title *Alcoholics Anonymous*. However, due to financial difficulties, the whole printing was, for a while, held up and the book received no publicity nor, of course, was it available in the stores, even if one knew it existed. But somehow my good doctor heard of this book, and he also learned a little about the people responsible for its publication. He sent to New York for a copy, and after reading it, he tucked it under his arm and called on me. That call marked the turning point in my life.

Until now, I had never been told that I was an alcoholic. Few doctors will tell a hopeless patient that there is no answer for him or for her. But this day my doctor gave it to me straight and said, "People like you are pretty well known to the medical profession. Every doctor gets his quota of alcoholic patients. Some of us struggle with these people because we know that they are really very sick, but we also know that, short of some miracle, we are not going to help them except temporarily and that they will inevitably get worse and worse until one of two things happens. Either they die of acute alcoholism or they develop wet brains and have to be put away permanently."

He further explained that alcohol was no respecter of sex or background but that most of the alcoholics he had encountered had better-than-average minds and abilities. He said the alcoholics seemed to possess a native acuteness and usually excelled in their fields, regardless of environmental or educational advantages.

"We watch the alcoholic performing in a position of responsibility, and we know that because he is drinking heavily and daily, he has cut his capacities by 50 percent, and still he seems able to do a satisfactory job. And we wonder how much further this man could go if his alcoholic problem could be removed and he could throw 100 percent of his abilities into action.

"But, of course," he continued, "eventually the alcoholic loses all of his capacities as his disease gets progressively worse, and this is a tragedy that is painful to watch: the disintegration of a sound mind and body."

Then he told me there was a handful of people in Akron and New York who had worked out a technique for arresting their alcoholism. He asked me to read the book *Alcoholics Anonymous*, and then he wanted me to talk with a man who was experiencing success with his own arrestment. This man could tell me more. I stayed up all night reading that book. For me it was a wonderful experience. It explained so much I had not understood about myself, and, best of all, it promised recovery if I would do a few simple things and be willing to have the desire to drink removed. Here was hope. Maybe I could find my way out of this agonizing existence. Perhaps I could find freedom and peace, and be able once again to call my soul my own.

The next day I received a visit from Mr. T., a recovered alcoholic. I don't know what sort of person I was expecting, but I was very agreeably surprised to find Mr. T. a poised, intelligent, well-groomed, and mannered gentleman. I was immediately impressed with his graciousness and charm. He put me at ease with his first few words. Looking at him, I found it hard to believe he had ever been as I was then.

However, as he unfolded his story for me, I could not help but believe him. In describing his suffering, his fears, his many years of groping for some answer to that which always seemed to remain unanswerable, he could have been describing me, and nothing short of experience and knowledge could have afforded him that much insight! He had been dry for 2½ years and had been maintaining his contact with a group of recovered alcoholics in Akron. Contact with this group was extremely important to him. He told me that eventually he hoped such a group would develop in the Chicago area but that so far this had not been started. He thought it would be helpful for me to visit the Akron group and meet many like himself.

By this time, with the doctor's explanation, the revelations contained in the book, and the hope-inspiring interview with Mr. T., I was ready and willing to go to the ends of the earth, if that was what it took, for me to find what these people had.

So I went to Akron, and also to Cleveland, and I met more recovered alcoholics. I saw in these people a quality of peace and serenity that I knew I must have for myself. Not only were they at peace with themselves, but they were getting a kick out of life such as one seldom encounters, except in the very young. They seemed to have all the ingredients for successful living: philosophy, faith, a sense of humor (they could laugh at themselves), clear-cut objectives, appreciation—and most especially appreciation and sympathetic understanding for their fellow man.

Nothing in their lives took precedence over their response to a call for help from some alcoholic in need. They would travel miles and stay up all night with someone they had never laid eyes on before and think nothing of it. Far from expecting praise for their deeds, they claimed the performance a privilege and insisted that they invariably received more than they gave. Extraordinary people!

I didn't dare hope I might find for myself all that these people had found, but if I could acquire some small part of their intriguing quality of living—and sobriety—that would be enough.

Shortly after I returned to Chicago, my doctor, encouraged by the results of my contact with A.A., sent us two more of his alcoholic patients. By the latter part of September 1939, we had a nucleus of six and held our first official group meeting.

I had a tough pull back to normal good health. It had been so many years since I had not relied on some artificial crutch, either alcohol or sedatives. Letting go of everything at once was both painful and terrifying. I could never have accomplished this alone. It took the help, understanding, and wonderful companionship that was given so freely to me by my ex-alkie friends—this and the program of recovery embodied in the Twelve Steps. In learning to practice these steps in my daily living, I began to acquire faith and a philosophy to live by. Whole new vistas were opened up for me, new avenues of experience to be explored, and life began to take on color and interest. In time, I found myself looking forward to each new day with pleasurable anticipation.

A.A. is not a plan for recovery that can be finished and done with. It is a way of life, and the challenge contained in its principles is great enough to keep any human being striving for as long as he lives. We do not, cannot, outgrow this plan. As arrested alcoholics, we must have a program for living that allows for limitless expansion. Keeping one foot in front of the other is essential for maintaining our arrestment. Others may idle in a retrogressive groove without too much danger, but retrogression can spell death for us. However, this isn't as rough as it sounds, as we do become grateful for the necessity that makes us toe the line, and we find that we are compensated for a consistent effort by the countless dividends we receive.

A complete change takes place in our approach to life. Where we used to run from responsibility, we find ourselves accepting it with gratitude that we can successfully shoulder it. Instead of wanting to escape some perplexing problem, we experience the thrill of challenge in the opportunity it affords for another application of A.A. techniques, and we find ourselves tackling it with surprising vigor.

The last fifteen years of my life have been rich and meaningful. I have had my share of problems, heartaches, and disappointments because that is life, but also I have known a great deal of joy and a peace that is the handmaiden of an inner freedom. I have a wealth of friends and, with my A.A. friends, an unusual quality of fellowship. For, to these people, I am truly related. First, through mutual pain and despair, and later through mutual objectives and newfound faith and hope. And, as the years go by, working together, sharing our experiences with one another, and also sharing a mutual trust, understanding, and love—without strings, without obligation—we acquire relationships that are unique and priceless.

There is no more aloneness, with that awful ache, so deep in the heart of every alcoholic that nothing, before, could ever reach it. That ache is gone and never need return again.

Now there is a sense of belonging, of being wanted and needed and loved. In return for a bottle and a hangover, we have been given the Keys of the Kingdom.

PART II

THEY STOPPED IN TIME

Among today's incoming A.A. members, many have never reached the advanced stages of alcoholism, though given time all might have.

Most of these fortunate ones have had little or no acquaintance with delirium, with hospitals, asylums, and jails. Some were drinking heavily, and there had been occasional serious episodes. But with many, drinking had been little more than a sometimes uncontrollable nuisance. Seldom had any of these lost either health, business, family, or friends.

Why do men and women like these join A.A.?

The seventeen who now tell their experiences answer that question. They saw that they had become actual or potential alcoholics, even though no serious harm had yet been done.

They realized that repeated lack of drinking control, when they really wanted control, was the fatal symptom that spelled problem drinking. This, plus mounting emotional disturbances, convinced them that compulsive alcoholism already had them; that complete ruin would be only a question of time.

Seeing this danger, they came to A.A. They realized that in the end alcoholism could be as mortal as cancer; certainly no sane man would wait for a malignant growth to become fatal before seeking help.

Therefore, these seventeen A.A.'s, and hundreds of thousands like them, have been saved years of infinite suffering. They sum it up something like this: "We didn't wait to hit bottom because, thank God, we could see the bottom. Actually, the bottom came up and hit us. That sold us on Alcoholics Anonymous."

(1)

THE MISSING LINK

He looked at everything as the cause of his unhappiness—except alcohol.

WHEN I WAS eight or nine years old, life suddenly became very difficult. Feelings began to emerge that I did not understand. Depression crept into my life as I started to feel alone, even in crowded rooms. In fact, life didn't make much sense to me at all. It's hard to say what sparked all of this, to pinpoint one fact or event that changed everything forever. The fact of the matter was, I was miserable from early on in my life.

It was all very confusing. I remember isolating on the playground, watching all the other children laughing and playing and smiling, and not feeling like I could relate at all. I felt different. I didn't feel as if I was one of them. Somehow, I thought, I didn't fit in.

My school marks soon reflected these feelings. My behavior and attitude seemed to become troublesome to everyone around me. I soon began spending more time in the principal's office than in the classroom. My parents, perplexed by such an unhappy son, began having difficulties. My house was soon filled with the sounds of arguments and yelling about how to handle me. I found that running away from home could supply me with some sort of temporary solace. Until of course, the police would find me and bring me back to my house and my worried parents.

About that time I started seeing therapists and specialists, each with a different theory and a different solution. They conducted special tests and interviews designed to get to the root of my troubles, and came to the conclusion that I had a learning disability and was depressed. The psychiatrist started me on some medication, and the problems in school started to clear up. Even some of the depression began to ease up for a bit. However, something still seemed fundamentally wrong.

Whatever the problem, I soon found what appeared to be the solution to everything. At age fifteen, I traveled with my family to Israel. My brother was to be bar mitzvahed atop Masada. There was no legal drinking age, so I found it quite easy to walk into a bar and order a drink. New Year's Eve fell in the middle of the trip, and since the Jewish calendar celebrates a different New Year than the Gregorian calendar, the only celebration was being held in the American sector of a university. I got drunk for the first time that night. It changed everything.

A stop at a local bar began the evening. I ordered a beer from the waitress and as I took the first sip, something was immediately different. I looked around me, at the people drinking and dancing, smiling and laughing, all of whom were much older than I. Suddenly, I somehow felt I belonged. From there, I made my way to the university, where I found hundreds of other Americans celebrating New Year's Eve. Before the night was over, I had started a fight with a number of college-aged drunken fellows and returned to the hotel stinking drunk and riddled with bruises. Ah yes, what a grand evening it was! I fell in love that night—with a beverage.

Returning to the States, I was determined to continue with my newfound love affair. I found myself trying to convince my friends to join me, but I was met with resistance. Still determined, I set out to find new friends, friends who could help me maintain this fantastic solution to my most desperate problems. My escapades started as a weekend pursuit and progressed into a daily obsession. At first, it took several beers to get me drunk to my satisfaction. However, within three years, it took a fifth and a half of vodka, a bottle of wine, and several beers in an evening's time to satisfactorily black me out. I would obtain alcohol by any means necessary. That meant lying, stealing, and cheating. My motto was, if you felt like I did, you'd have to get drunk too.

As the feelings of hopelessness and depression progressed, so did my drinking. Thoughts of suicide came more and more frequently. It felt as if things were never going to change. Progress with my therapist came to almost a complete halt. The hopelessness was compounded by the fact that the one thing that was bringing me relief, the one thing I counted on to take the pain away, was ultimately destroying me. The end, I feared, was close.

My last semester in high school marked my bottom. It was everyday drinking then. Since I had already been accepted at college, I consciously decided to make that last semester one big party. But it was no fun at all. I was miserable. I graduated narrowly and took a job at a local garage. It was difficult to manage my drinking and a job since they were both full time, but I concocted all kinds of lies to ensure that nothing would interfere with my drinking. After being repeatedly reprimanded at work for being late in the mornings, I made up a story to hide the fact that I was always hung over. I told my manager that I had cancer and needed to go to the doctor for treatment every morning. I would say whatever I needed to say to protect my drinking.

More often, I was having these little moments of clarity, times I knew for sure that I was an alcoholic. Times when I was looking at the bottom of my glass asking myself, Why am I doing this? Something had to give, something had to change. I was suicidal, evaluating every part of my life for what could be wrong. It culminated in one last night of drinking and staring at the problem. It made me sick to think about it, and even sicker to continue drinking it away. I was forced to look at my drinking as the chief suspect.

The next day I went to work, late as usual, and all day long I could not stop thinking about this very real problem. I could go no further. What was happening to me? Therapy hadn't fixed my life—all those sessions; I was still miserable. I might as well just kill myself, drink my way into oblivion. In one last desperate fight for a solution, I reviewed my life, searching for the missing link. Had I left out some crucial bit of information that would lead to a breakthrough, making it possible for life to become just a little more bearable? No, there was nothing. Except of course my drinking.

The next morning I went to see my therapist. I told him I'd decided to quit therapy, because after eight years, it wasn't working. But I decided to tell him how I had been searching through my life for that missing link and had come up with only one thing I had never told him: that I drank. He began asking me questions—he asked about quantities, frequency, what I drank. Before he was even halfway through, I broke down and began sobbing. I cried, "Do you think I have a problem with drinking?" He replied, "I think that is quite obvious." I then asked, "Do you think I'm an alcoholic?" And he answered, "You are going to have to find out for yourself." He pulled a list of Alcoholics Anonymous meetings out of his desk drawer; he had already highlighted the young people's meetings.

He told me to go home and not drink at all for the rest of the day. He would call me at nine p.m. and wanted to hear that I hadn't taken a drink. It was rough, but I went home and locked myself in my room, sweating it out until he called. He asked if I had had a drink. I told him I had not and asked what I should do next. He told me to do the same thing tomorrow, except tomorrow I should also go to the first meeting on the list he had highlighted. The next day I went to my first meeting of Alcoholics Anonymous. I was eighteen years old.

In the parking lot, I sat in my car for about fifteen minutes before the meeting started, trying to work up the courage to go in and face myself. I remember finally working up the nerve to open the door and get out, only to close the door, dismissing the notion of going into the meeting as ridiculous. This dance of indecisiveness went on about fifty times before I went in. Had I not gone in, I believe I would not be alive today.

The room was very smoky and filled with apparently happy people. Finding a seat in the back, I sat down and tried to make sense of the format. When the chairperson asked if there were any newcomers present, I looked around and saw some hands go up, but I certainly wasn't ready to raise my hand and draw attention to myself. The meeting broke up into several groups, and I followed one group down the hall and took a seat. They opened a book and read a chapter titled "Step Seven." After the reading, they went around the table for comments, and for the first time in my life, I found myself surrounded by people I could really relate with. I no longer felt as if I was a total misfit, because here was a roomful of people who felt precisely as I did, and a major weight had been lifted. I happened to be in the last chair around the table to speak and, confused by the reading, all I could say was, "What the heck are shortcomings?"

A couple of members, realizing I was there for my first meeting, took me downstairs and sat down with me and outlined the program. I can recall very little of what was said. I remember telling these members that this program they outlined sounded like just what I needed, but I didn't think I could stay sober for the rest of my life. Exactly how was I supposed to not drink if my girlfriend breaks up with me, or if my best friend dies, or even through happy times like graduations, weddings, and birthdays. They suggested I could just stay sober one day at a time. They explained that it might be easier to set my sights on the twenty-four hours in front of me and to take on these other situations when and if they ever arrived. I decided to give sobriety a try, one day at a time, and I've done it that way ever since.

When I entered Alcoholics Anonymous, I had done some damage physically, had a bouquet of mental quirks, and was spiritually bankrupt. I knew I was powerless over alcohol and that I needed to be open-minded toward what people suggested for recovery. However, when it came to spirituality, I fought it nearly every step of the way. Although raised in an ethnic and religious Jewish household, I was agnostic and very resistant to anyone and anything that I perceived to be imposing religious beliefs. To my surprise, Alcoholics Anonymous suggested something different.

The idea that religion and spirituality were not one and the same was a new notion. My sponsor asked that I merely remain open-minded to the possibility that there was a Power greater than myself, one of my own understanding. He assured me that no person was going to impose a belief system on me, that it was a personal matter. Reluctantly, I opened my mind to the fact that maybe, just maybe, there was something to this spiritual lifestyle. Slowly but surely, I realized there was indeed a Power greater than myself, and I soon found myself with a full-time God in my life and following a spiritual path that didn't conflict with my personal religious convictions.

Following this spiritual path made a major difference in my life. It seemed to fill that lonely hole that I used to fill with alcohol. My self-esteem improved dramatically, and I knew happiness and serenity as I had never known it before. I started to see the beauty and usefulness in my own existence, and tried to express my gratitude through helping others in whatever ways I could. A confidence and faith entered my life and unraveled a plan for me that was bigger and better than I could have ever imagined.

It wasn't easy, and it has never been easy, but it gets so much better. Since that first meeting, my life has completely changed. Three months into the program I started college. While many of my college classmates were experimenting with alcohol for the first time, I was off at meetings and A.A. get-togethers, becoming active in service work, and developing relationships with God, family, friends, and loved ones. I rarely thought twice about this; it was what I wanted and needed to do.

Over the last seven years, nearly everything I thought I could not stay sober through has happened. Indeed, sobriety and life are full of ups and downs. Occasionally depression can creep back into my life and requires outside help. However, this program has provided me with the tools to stay sober through the death of my best friends, failed relationships, and good times like birthdays, weddings, and graduations. Life is exponentially better than it ever was before. I'm living out the life I used to fantasize about, and I have a whole lot of work still in front of me. I have hope to share and love to give, and I just keep going one day at a time, living this adventure called life.

FEAR OF FEAR

This lady was cautious. She decided she wouldn't let herself go in her drinking. And she would never, never take that morning drink!

DIDN'T THINK I was an alcoholic. I thought my problem was that I had been married to a drunk for twenty-seven years. And when my husband found A.A., I came to the second meeting with him. I thought it was wonderful, simply marvelous, for him. But not for me. Then I went to another meeting, and I still thought it was wonderful—for him, but not for me.

That was on a hot summer evening, down in the Greenwich Village Group, and there was a little porch out there in the old meeting place on Sullivan Street, and after the meeting I went out on the steps for some air. In the doorway stood a lovely young girl who said, "Are you one of us souses too?" I said, "Oh, goodness, no! My husband is. He's in there." She told me her name, and I said, "I know you from somewhere." It turned out that she had been in high school with my daughter. I said, "Eileen, are you one of those people?" And she said, "Oh, yes. I'm in this."

As we walked back through the hall, I, for the first time in my life, said to another human being, "I'm having trouble with my drinking too." She took me by the hand and introduced me to the woman that I'm very proud to call my sponsor. This woman and her husband are both in A.A., and she said to me, "Oh, but you're not the alcoholic; it's your husband." I said, "Yes." She said, "How long have you been married?" I said, "Twenty-seven years." She said, "Twenty-seven years to an alcoholic! How did you ever stand it?" I thought, now here's a nice, sympathetic soul! This is for me. I said, "Well, I stood it to keep the home together, and for the children's sake." She said, "Yes, I know. You're just a martyr, aren't you?" I walked away from that woman grinding my teeth and cursing under my breath. Fortunately, I didn't say a word to George on the way home. But that night I tried to go to sleep. And I thought, "You're some martyr, Jane! Let's look at the record." And when I looked at it, I knew I was just as much a drunk as George was, if not worse. I nudged George next morning, and I said, "I'm in," and he said, "Oh, I knew you'd make it."

I started drinking nearly thirty years ago—right after I was married. My first drinking spree was on corn liquor, and I was allergic to it, believe me. I was deathly sick every time I took a drink. But we had to do a lot of entertaining. My husband liked to have a good time; I was very young, and I wanted to have a good time too. The only way I knew to do it was to drink right along with him.

I got into terrific trouble with my drinking. I was afraid, and I had made my mind up that I would never get drunk, so I was watchful and careful. We had a small child, and I loved her dearly, so that held me back quite a bit in my drinking career. Even so, every time I drank, I seemed to get in trouble. I always wanted to drink too much, so I was watchful, always watchful, counting my drinks. If we were invited to a formal party and I knew they were only going to have one or two drinks, I wouldn't have any. I was being very cagey, because I knew that if I did take one or two, I might want to take five or six or seven or eight.

I did stay fairly good for a few years. But I wasn't happy, and I didn't ever let myself go in my drinking. After my son, our second child, came along, and as he became school age and was away at school most of the time, something happened. I really started drinking with a bang.

I never went to a hospital. I never lost a job. I was never in jail. And, unlike many others, I never took a drink in the morning. I needed a drink, but I was afraid to take a morning drink, because I didn't want to be a drunk. I became a drunk anyway, but I was scared to death to take that morning drink. I was accused of it many times when I went to play bridge in the afternoon, but I really never did take a morning drink. I was still woozy from the night before.

I should have lost my husband, and I think that only the fact that he was an alcoholic too kept us together. No one else would have stayed with me. Many women who have reached the stage that I had reached in my drinking have lost husbands, children, homes, everything they hold dear. I have been very fortunate in many ways. The important thing I lost was my own self-respect. I could feel fear coming into my life. I couldn't face people. I couldn't look them straight in the eyes, although I had always been a self-possessed, brazen person. I'd brazen anything out. I lied like a trooper to get out of many scrapes.

But I felt a fear coming into my life, and I couldn't cope with it. I got so that I hid quite a bit of the time, wouldn't answer the phone, and stayed by myself as much as I could. I noticed that I was avoiding all my social friends, except for my bridge club. I couldn't keep up with any of my other friends, and I wouldn't go to anyone's house unless I knew they drank as heavily as I did. I never knew it was the first drink that did it. I thought I was losing my mind when I realized that I couldn't stop drinking. That frightened me terribly.

George tried many times to go on the wagon. If I had been sincere in what I thought I wanted more than anything else in life—a sober husband and a happy, contented home—I would have gone on the wagon with him. I did try, for a day or two, but something would always come up that would throw me. It would be a little thing—the rugs being crooked, or any silly little thing that I'd think was wrong—and off I'd go, drinking. And sneaking my drinks. I had bottles hidden all over the apartment. I didn't think my children knew about it, but I found out they did. It's surprising, how we think we fool everybody in our drinking.

I reached a stage where I couldn't go into my apartment without a drink. It didn't bother me anymore whether George was drinking or not. I had to have liquor. Sometimes I would lie on the bathroom floor, deathly sick, praying I would die, and praying to God as I always had prayed to Him when I was drinking: "Dear God, get me out of this one and I'll never do it again." And then I'd say, "God, don't pay any attention to me. You know I'll do it tomorrow, the very same thing."

I used to make excuses to try and get George off the wagon. I'd get so fed up with drinking all alone and bearing the burden of guilt all by myself, that I'd egg him on to drink, to get started again. And then I'd fight with him because he had started! And the whole merry-go-round would be on again. And he, poor dear, didn't know what was going on. He used to wonder when he'd spot one of my bottles around the house just how he could have overlooked that particular bottle. I myself didn't know all the places I had them hidden.

We have only been in A.A. a few years, but now we're trying to make up for lost time. Twenty-seven years of confusion is what my early married life was. Now the picture has changed completely. We have faith in each other, trust in each other, and understanding. A.A. has given us that. It has taught me so many things. It has changed my thinking entirely, about everything I do. I can't afford resentments against anyone, because they are the build-up of another drunk. I must live and let live. And "think"— that one important word means so much to me. My life was always act and react. I never stopped to think. I just didn't give a whoop about myself or anyone else.

I try to live our program as it has been outlined to me, one day at a time. I try to live today so that tomorrow I won't be ashamed when I wake up in the morning. In the old days I hated to wake up and look back at what last night had been like. I never could face it the next morning. And unless I had some rosy picture of what was going to happen that day, I wouldn't even feel like getting up in the morning at all. It really wasn't living. Now I feel so very grateful not only for my sobriety, which I try to maintain day by day, but I'm grateful also for the ability to help other people. I never thought I could be useful to anyone except my husband and my children and perhaps a few friends. But A.A. has shown me that I can help other alcoholics.

Many of my neighbors devoted time to volunteer work. There was one woman especially, and I'd watch her from my window every morning, leaving faithfully to go to the hospital in the neighborhood. I said to her one day when I met her on the street, "What sort of volunteer work do you do?" She told me; it was simple; I could have done it very easily. She said, "Why don't you do it too?" I said, "I'd love to." She said, "Suppose I put your name down as a volunteer—even if you can only give one or two days?" But then I thought, well, now wait, how will I feel next Tuesday? How will I feel next Friday, if I make it a Friday? How will I feel next Saturday morning? I never knew. I was afraid to set even one day. I could never be sure I'd have a clear head and hands that were willing to do some work. So I never did any volunteer work. And I felt depleted, whipped. I had the time, I certainly had the capability, but I never did a thing.

I am trying now, each day, to make up for all those selfish, thoughtless, foolish things I did in my drinking days. I hope that I never forget to be grateful.

THE HOUSEWIFE WHO DRANK
AT HOME

She hid her bottles in clothes hampers and dresser drawers. In A.A., she discovered she had lost nothing and had found everything.

MY STORY HAPPENS to be a particular kind of woman's story: the story of the woman who drinks at home. I had to be at home—I had two babies. When alcohol took me over, my bar was my kitchen, my living room, my bedroom, the back bathroom, and the two laundry hampers.

At one time the admission that I was and am an alcoholic meant shame, defeat, and failure to me. But in the light of the new understanding that I have found in A.A., I have been able to interpret that defeat and that failure and that shame as seeds of victory. Because it was only through feeling defeat and feeling failure, the inability to cope with my life and with alcohol, that I was able to surrender and accept the fact that I had this disease and that I had to learn to live again without alcohol.

I was never a very heavy social drinker. But during a period of particular stress and strain about thirteen years ago, I resorted to using alcohol in my home, alone, as a means of temporary release and of getting a little extra sleep.

I had problems. We all have them, and I thought a little brandy or a little wine now and then could certainly hurt no one. I don't believe, when I started, that I even had in mind the thought that I was drinking. I *had* to sleep, I *had* to clear my mind and free it from worry, and I *had* to relax. But from one or two drinks of an afternoon or evening, my intake mounted, and mounted fast. It wasn't long before I was drinking all day. I had to have that wine. The only incentive that I had, toward the end, for getting dressed in the morning was to get out and get "supplies" to help me get my day started. But the only thing that got started was my drinking.

I should have realized that alcohol was getting hold of me when I started to become secretive in my drinking. I began to have to have supplies on hand for the people who "might come in." And of course a half-empty bottle wasn't worth keeping, so I finished it up and naturally had to get more in right away for the people who "might come in unexpectedly." But *I* was always the unexpected person who had to finish the bottle. I couldn't go to one wine store and look the man honestly in the face and buy a bottle, as I used to do when I had parties and entertained and did normal drinking. I had to give him a story and ask him the same question over and over again, "Well, now, how many will that bottle serve?" I wanted him to be sure that I wasn't the one who was going to drink the whole bottle.

I had to hide, as a great many people in A.A. have had to do. I did my hiding in the hampers and in my dresser drawers. When we begin to do things like that with alcohol, something's gone wrong. I needed it, and I knew I was drinking too much, but I wasn't conscious of the fact that I should stop. I kept on. My home at that time was a place to mill around in. I wandered from room to room, thinking, drinking, drinking, thinking. And the mops would come out, the vacuum would come out, everything would come out, but nothing would get done. Toward five o'clock, helter-skelter, I'd get everything put away and try to get supper on the table, and after supper I'd finish the job up and knock myself out.

I never knew which came first, the thinking or the drinking. If I could only stop thinking, I wouldn't drink. If I could only stop drinking, maybe I wouldn't think. But they were all mixed up together, and I was all mixed up inside. And yet I had to have that drink. You know the deteriorating effects, the disintegrating effects, of chronic wine-drinking. I cared nothing about my personal appearance. I didn't care what I looked like; I didn't care what I did. To me, taking a bath was just being in a place with a bottle where I could drink in privacy. I had to have it with me at night, in case I woke up and needed that drink.

How I ran my home, I don't know. I went on, realizing what I was becoming, hating myself for it, bitter, blaming life, blaming everything but the fact that I should turn about and do something about my drinking. Finally I didn't care; I was beyond caring. I just wanted to live to a certain age, carry through with what I felt was my job with the children, and after that—no matter. Half a mother was better than no mother at all.

I needed that alcohol. I couldn't live without it. I couldn't do anything without it. But there came a point when I could no longer live with it. And that came after a three-weeks' illness of my son. The doctor prescribed a teaspoon of brandy for the boy to help him through the night when he coughed. Well, of course, that was all I needed—to switch from wine to brandy for three weeks. I knew nothing about alcoholism or the D.T.'s, but when I woke up on that last morning of my son's illness, I taped the keyhole on my door because "everyone was out there." I paced back and forth in the apartment with the cold sweats. I screamed on the telephone for my mother to get up there; something was going to happen; I didn't know what, but if she didn't get there quick, I'd split wide open. I called my husband up and told him to come home.

After that I sat for a week, a body in a chair, a mind off in space. I thought the two would never get together. I knew that alcohol and I had to part. I couldn't live with it anymore. And yet, how was I going to live without it? I didn't know. I was bitter, living in hate. The very person who stood with me through it all and has been my greatest help was the person that I turned against, my husband. I also turned against my family, my mother. The people who would have come to help me were just the people I would have nothing to do with.

Nevertheless, I began to try to live without alcohol. But I only succeeded in fighting it. And believe me, an alcoholic cannot fight alcohol. I said to my husband, "I'm going to try to get interested in something outside, get myself out of this rut I'm in." I thought I was going out of my mind. If I didn't have a drink, I had to do something.

I became one of the most active women in the community, what with P.T.A., other community organizations, and drives. I'd go into an organization, and it wasn't long before I was on the committee, and then I was chairman of the committee; and if I was in a group, I'd soon be treasurer or secretary of the group. But I wasn't happy. I became a Jekyll-and-Hyde person. As long as I worked, as long as I got out, I didn't drink. But I had to get back to that first drink somehow. And when I took that first drink, I was off on the usual merry-go-round. And it was my home that suffered.

I figured I'd be all right if I could find something I liked to do. So when the children were in school from nine to three, I started up a nice little business and was fairly successful in it. But not happy. Because I found that everything I turned to became a substitute for drink. And when all of life is a substitute for drink, there's no happiness, no peace. I still had to drink; I still needed that drink. Mere cessation from drinking is not enough for an alcoholic while the need for that drink goes on. I switched to beer. I had always hated beer, but now I grew to love it. So that wasn't my answer either.

I went to my doctor again. He knew what I was doing, how I was trying. I said, "I can't find my middle road in life. I can't find it. It's either all work, or I drink." He said, "Why don't you try Alcoholics Anonymous?" I was willing to try anything. I was licked. For the second time, I was licked. The first time was when I knew I couldn't live with alcohol. But this second time, I found I couldn't live normally without it, and I was licked worse than ever.

The fellowship I found in A.A. enabled me to face my problem honestly and squarely. I couldn't do it among my relatives; I couldn't do it among my friends. No one likes to admit that they're a drunk, that they can't control this thing. But when we come into A.A., we can face our problem honestly and openly. I went to closed meetings and open meetings. And I took everything that A.A. had to give me. Easy does it, first things first, one day at a time. It was at that point that I reached surrender. I heard one very ill woman say that she didn't believe in the surrender part of the A.A. program. My heavens! Surrender to me has meant the ability to run my home, to face my responsibilities as they should be faced, to take life as it comes to me day by day and work my problems out. That's what surrender has meant to me. I surrendered once to the bottle, and I couldn't do these things. Since I gave my will over to A.A., whatever A.A. has wanted of me I've tried to do to the best of my ability. When I'm asked to go out on a call, I go. *I'm* not going; A.A. is leading me there. A.A. gives us alcoholics direction into a way of life without the need for alcohol. That life for me is lived one day at a time, letting the problems of the future rest with the future. When the time comes to solve them, God will give me strength for that day.

I had been brought up to believe in God, but I know that until I found this A.A. program, I had never found or known faith in the reality of God, the reality of His power that is now with me in everything I do.

(4)

PHYSICIAN, HEAL THYSELF!

*Psychiatrist and surgeon, he had lost his way until
he realized that God, not he, was the Great Healer.*

I AM A PHYSICIAN, licensed to practice in a western state. I am also an alcoholic. In two ways I
may be a little different from other alcoholics. First,
we all hear at A.A. meetings about those who have
lost everything, those who have been in jail, those
who have been in prison, those who have lost their
families, those who have lost their income. I never
lost any of it. I never was on skid row. I made more
money in the last year of my drinking than I made in
my whole life. My wife never hinted that she would
leave me. Everything that I touched from grammar
school on was successful. I was president of my grammar school student body. I was president of all of my
classes in high school, and in my last year I was president of that student body. I was president of each
class in the university, and president of *that* student
body. I was voted the man most likely to succeed. The
same thing occurred in medical school. I belong to
more medical societies and honor societies than men
ten to twenty years my senior.

Mine was the skid row of success. The physical
skid row in any city is miserable. The skid row of success is just as miserable.

The second way in which, perhaps, I differ from

some other alcoholics is this: Many alcoholics state that they don't particularly like the taste of alcohol but that they liked the effect. I loved alcohol! I used to like to get it on my fingers so I could lick them and get another taste. I had a lot of fun drinking. I enjoyed it immensely. And then, one ill-defined day, one day that I can't recall, I stepped across the line that alcoholics know so well, and from that day on, drinking was miserable. When a few drinks made me feel good before I went over that line, those same drinks now made me wretched. In an attempt to get over that feeling, there was a quick onslaught of a greater number of drinks, and then all was lost. Alcohol failed to serve the purpose.

On the last day I was drinking, I went up to see a friend who had had a good deal of trouble with alcohol and whose wife had left him a number of times. He had come back, however, and he was on this program. In my stupid way I went up to see him with the idea in the back of my mind that I would investigate Alcoholics Anonymous from a medical standpoint. Deep in my heart was the feeling that maybe I could get some help here. This friend gave me a pamphlet, and I took it home and had my wife read it to me. There were two sentences in it that struck me. One said, "Don't feel that you are a martyr because you stopped drinking," and this hit me between the eyes. The second one said, "Don't feel that you stop drinking for anyone other than yourself," and this hit me between the eyes. After my wife had read this to me, I said to her, as I had said many times in desperation, "I have got to do something." She's a good-natured soul and said, "I wouldn't worry about it; probably something will happen." And then we went up the side of a hill where we have a little barbecue area to make the fire for the barbecue, and on the way up I thought to myself—I'll go back down to the kitchen and refill this drink. And just then, something did happen.

The thought came to me—This is the last one! I was well into the second fifth by this time. And as that thought came to me, it was as though someone had reached down and taken a heavy overcoat off my shoulders, for that *was* the last one.

About two days later I was called by a friend of mine from Nevada City—he's a brother of my wife's closest friend. He said, "Earle?" and I said, "Yes." He said, "I'm an alcoholic; what do I do?" And I gave him some idea of what you do, and so I made my first Twelfth Step call before I ever came into the program. The satisfaction I got from giving him a little of what I had read in those pamphlets far surpassed any feeling that I had ever had before in helping patients.

So I decided that I would go to my first meeting. I was introduced as a psychiatrist. (I belong to the American Psychiatric Society, but I don't practice psychiatry as such. I am a surgeon.)

As someone in A.A. said to me once upon a time, there is nothing worse than a confused psychiatrist.

I will never forget the first meeting that I attended. There were five people present, including me. At one end of the table sat our community butcher. At the other side of the table sat one of the carpenters in our community, and at the farther end of the table sat the man who ran the bakery, while on one side sat my friend who was a mechanic. I recall, as I walked into that meeting, saying to myself, "Here I am, a Fellow of the American College of Surgeons, a Fellow of the International College of Surgeons, a diplomate of one of the great specialty boards in these United States, a member of the American Psychiatric Society, and I have to go to the butcher, the baker, and the carpenter to help make a man out of me!"

Something else happened to me. This was such a new thought that I got all sorts of books on Higher Powers, and I put a Bible by my bedside, and I put a Bible in my car. It is still there. And I put a Bible in my locker at the hospital. And I put a Bible in my desk. And I put a Big Book by my night stand, and I put a *Twelve Steps and Twelve Traditions* in my locker at the hospital, and I got books by Emmet Fox, and I got books by God-knows-who, and I got to reading all these things. And the first thing you know I was lifted right out of the A.A. group, and I floated higher and higher and even higher, until I was way up on a pink cloud, which is known as Pink Seven, and I felt miserable again. So I thought to myself, I might just as well be drunk as feel like this.

I went to Clark, the community butcher, and I said, "Clark, what is the matter with me? I don't feel right. I have been on this program for three months and I feel terrible." And he said, "Earle, why don't you come on over and let me talk to you for a minute." So he got me a cup of coffee and a piece of cake, and sat me down and said, "Why, there's nothing wrong with you. You've been sober for three months, been working hard. You've been doing all right." But then he said, "Let me say something to you. We have here in this community an organization that helps people, and this organization is known as Alcoholics Anonymous. Why don't you join it?" I said, "What do you think I've been doing?" "Well," he said, "you've been sober, but you've been floating way up on a cloud somewhere. Why don't you go home and get the Big Book and open it at page fifty-eight and see what it says?" So I did. I got the Big Book and I read it, and this is what it said: "Rarely have we seen a person fail who has thoroughly followed our path." The word "thoroughly" rang a bell. And then it went on to say: "Half measures availed us nothing. We stood at the turning point." And the last sentence was "We asked His protection and care with complete abandon."

"Complete abandon"; "Half measures availed us nothing"; "Thoroughly followed our path"; "Completely give themselves to this simple program" rang in my swelled head.

Years earlier, I had gone into psychoanalysis to get relief. I spent 5½ years in psychoanalysis and proceeded to become a drunk. I don't mean that in any sense as a derogatory statement about psychotherapy; it's a very great tool, not too potent, but a great tool. I would do it again.

I tried every gimmick that there was to get some peace of mind, but it was not until I was brought to my alcoholic knees, when I was brought to a group in my own community with the butcher, the baker, the carpenter, and the mechanic, who were able to give me the Twelve Steps, that I was finally given some semblance of an answer to the last half of the First Step. So, after taking the first half of the First Step, and very gingerly admitting myself to Alcoholics Anonymous, something happened. And then I thought to myself: Imagine an alcoholic admitting anything! But I made my admission just the same.

The Third Step said: "Made a decision to turn our will and our lives over to the care of God as we understood Him." Now they asked us to make a decision! We've got to turn the whole business over to some joker we can't even see! And this chokes the alcoholic. Here he is powerless, unmanageable, in the grip of something bigger than he is, and he's got to turn the whole business over to someone else! It fills the alcoholic with rage. We are great people. We can handle anything. And so one gets to thinking to oneself, Who is this God? Who is this fellow we are supposed to turn everything over to? What can He do for us that we can't do for ourselves? Well, I don't know who He is, but I've got my own idea.

For myself, I have an absolute proof of the existence of God. I was sitting in my office one time after I had operated on a woman. It had been a long four- or five-hour operation, a large surgical procedure, and she was on her ninth or tenth post-operative day. She was doing fine, she was up and around, and that day her husband phoned me and said, "Doctor, thanks very much for curing my wife," and I thanked him for his felicitations, and he hung up. And then I scratched my head and said to myself, What a fantastic thing for a man to say, that I cured his wife. Here I am down at my office behind my desk, and there she is out at the hospital. I am not even there, and if I was there the only thing I could do would be to give her moral support, and yet he thanks me for curing his wife. I thought to myself—What *is* curing that woman? Yes, I put in those stitches. The Great Boss has given me diagnostic and surgical talent, and He has loaned it to me to use for the rest of my life. It doesn't belong to me. He has loaned it to me and I did my job, but that ended nine days ago. What healed those tissues that I closed? I didn't. This to me is the proof of the existence of a Somethingness greater than I am. I couldn't practice medicine without the Great Physician. All I do in a very simple way is to help Him cure my patients.

Shortly after I was starting to work on the program, I realized that I was not a good father, I wasn't a good husband, but, oh, I was a good provider. I never robbed my family of anything. I gave them everything, except the greatest thing in the world, and that is peace of mind. So I went to my wife and asked her if there wasn't something that she and I could do to somehow get together, and she turned on her heel and looked me squarely in the eye, and said, "You don't care anything about my problem," and I could have smacked her, but I said to myself, "Grab on to your serenity!"

She left, and I sat down and crossed my hands and looked up and said, "For God's sake, help me." And then a silly, simple thought came to me. I didn't know anything about being a father; I didn't know how to come home and work weekends like other husbands; I didn't know how to entertain my family. But I remembered that every night after dinner my wife would get up and do the dishes. Well, I could do the dishes. So I went to her and said, "There's only one thing I want in my whole life, and I don't want any commendation; I don't want any credit; I don't want anything from you or Janey for the rest of your life except one thing, and that is the opportunity to do anything you want always, and I would like to start off by doing the dishes." And now I am doing the darn dishes every night!

Doctors have been notoriously unsuccessful in helping alcoholics. They have contributed fantastic amounts of time and work to our problem, but they aren't able, it seems, to arrest either your alcoholism or mine.

And the clergy have tried hard to help us, but we haven't been helped. And the psychiatrist has had thousands of couches and has put you and me on them many, many times, but he hasn't helped us very much, though he has tried hard; and we owe the clergy and the doctor and the psychiatrist a deep debt of gratitude, but they haven't helped our alcoholism, except in a rare few instances. But—Alcoholics Anonymous has helped.

What is this power that A.A. possesses? This curative power? I don't know what it is. I suppose the doctor might say, "This is psychosomatic medicine." I suppose the psychiatrist might say, "This is benevolent interpersonal relations." I suppose others would say, "This is group psychotherapy."

To me it is God.

(5)

MY CHANCE TO LIVE

A.A. gave this teenager the tools to climb out of her dark abyss of despair.

I CAME THROUGH the doors of Alcoholics Anonymous at age seventeen, a walking contradiction. On the outside, I was the portrait of a rebellious teenager, with miles of attitude to spare. On the inside, I was suicidal, bloodied, and beaten. My stride spoke of a confidence I didn't feel. My dress was that of a street-tough kid you didn't want to mess with. Inside I was trembling with fear that someone would see through my defenses to the real me.

If you saw who I really was, you would turn away in disgust or use my many weaknesses to destroy me. One way or the other I was convinced I'd be hurt. I couldn't allow that to happen, so I kept the real me veiled behind a force field of rough-edged attitude. How I got to this place is still a mystery to me.

I grew up in a loving middle-class home. We had our problems—what family doesn't? But there was no abuse, verbal or physical, and it certainly couldn't be said my parents didn't do the best they could by me. My grandfathers were alcoholic, and I was raised on stories of how it had ravaged their lives and the lives of those around them. Nope, I didn't want to be an alcoholic.

In my early teen years I began to be bothered by

feelings that I didn't fit in. Until this point, I had ignored the fact that I wasn't one of the "in" crowd. I thought if I tried hard enough I would fit in sooner or later. At fourteen I stopped trying. I quickly discovered the soothing effects of a drink. Telling myself I would be more careful than my unfortunate grandparents, I set out to feel better.

Drinking released me from the suffocating fear, the feelings of inadequacy, and the nagging voices at the back of my head that told me I would never measure up. All of those things melted away when I drank. The bottle was my friend, my companion, a portable vacation. Whenever life was too intense, alcohol would take the edge off or obliterate the problem altogether for a time.

Blackouts became my goal. Though it may sound strange, they never frightened me. My life was ordered by school and by home. When I blacked out, I simply went on autopilot for the remainder of the day. The thought of going through my teen years without a single memory of its passing was very appealing.

I hadn't given up on life, just childhood. Adults had it made. They made all the rules. Being a kid stunk. If I could hold out until I was eighteen, everything would turn around. I had no idea at the time how true those words would prove to be.

Diving headfirst into what remained of the subculture left over from the sixties, I took "party till you throw up" to new levels. I liked drinking. I liked the effect alcohol had on me. I didn't like throwing up at all. I soon discovered there were other substances I could take that would help me "control" my drinking.

A little bit of this or that, and I could nurse a drink all night. Then I had a good time and didn't throw up.

In no time at all I had arrived, or so I thought. I had a bunch of friends to hang around with. We did exciting things: skipping school, taking road trips, drinking were all a part of this new life. It was great for a while. Getting hauled into the principal's office or being questioned by the police, things I would have been ashamed of before, were badges of honor. My ability to come through these events without giving away information or being unnerved brought me respect and trust among my peers.

Outwardly I was a young woman who was comfortable with herself. Yet ever so slowly these actions that I knew deep down were wrong started eating holes in me. My first reaction was to drink more. The outcome wasn't what I expected. I continued to raise my intake without the desired effect. Blackouts became few and far between. It didn't seem to matter how much I drank or in what combination with other substances; I could no longer find the relief I sought.

Life at home was falling apart around me. Every time I turned around I'd done something to make my mother cry. At school they were looking for ways to be rid of me. The vice principal made it a point to explain his position to me in no uncertain terms: "Straighten up, or you are out on your ear. For good."

I started the painful spiral to my bottom a scant two years into my drinking career. Knowing I had to graduate, I made adjustments to my lifestyle to stay in school. I watched as my friends continued to have fun. A depression settled over me, encasing me in a gray haze. I couldn't skip school anymore; my boyfriend came home from boot camp with another girl; my mother was still crying, and it was all my fault.

There were several attempts at suicide. I'm grateful to say I wasn't very good at it. Then I decided since I wasn't having fun anymore, I'd quit drinking and using. I mean, why waste good booze if you're going to feel just as bad drunk as sober? I held no hope for feeling better when I stopped. I just didn't want to waste the booze.

It never occurred to me that I couldn't stop. Every day I concocted some new method of staying sober: If I wear this shirt, I won't drink. If I'm with this person, or in this place, I won't drink. It didn't work. Every morning I woke up with a new resolve to stay sober. With few exceptions, by noon I was so messed up I couldn't tell you my name.

The voices in my head became even more and more vicious. With each failed attempt, my head said: See, you failed again. You knew you wouldn't feel better. You're a loser. You're never going to beat this. Why are you even trying? Just drink until you're dead.

On the rare days I managed to make it past noon, there were few brave enough to get within a hundred yards of me. I was not a nice person sober. I was angry and frightened, and I wanted you to feel as terrible as I did. A few times I had drinks pushed on me: "Here, drink this; then maybe you won't be so difficult." I always had a nasty retort, and then took what was offered. Toward the end I prayed every night for God to take me in my sleep, and I cursed Him in the morning for allowing me to live.

It was never my intention to end up in A.A. If someone mentioned perhaps I drank too much, I laughed at them. I didn't drink any more than my friends. I never got drunk when I didn't want to— never mind that I always wanted to. I couldn't be an alcoholic. I was too young. Life was my problem. Other substances were my problem. If I could just get a handle on things, then I could drink.

I got a job as a waitress at a local pancake house. Our late hours attracted a wide variety of clientele, including some members of Alcoholics Anonymous. They were not my favorite people to wait on. They, in fact, drove me to drink. They were loud, hard to please. They table-hopped and didn't tip very well. I waited on the same bunch for six weeks in a row before finally being granted the night off.

Now, I had been thinking that my problem was insanity, and what happened on my night off clinched it: I missed this motley crew who had plagued my existence for over a month. I missed the laughter and their bright smiles. I went and had coffee with them.

Through a chain of events I choose to believe were the actions of my Higher Power, they convinced me to go to a meeting. I was told it was a special A.A. anniversary open meeting, which meant that anyone could attend. I thought to myself: What could it hurt? I wait on these people; perhaps it will help me to better understand them.

On the designated evening I arrived to find that the anniversary meeting was the following week, but they took a vote and decided I could stay. I was shocked and humbled. These people wanted me around? It was a concept I had trouble accepting. I stayed and listened, careful to let them know I didn't have a problem.

I attended the anniversary meeting the following week with no intention of ever going to another meeting. I wasn't an alcoholic. I had other problems that needed attention; then I would be okay. The next week a friend, who was admittedly an alcoholic, asked me if I was going to the meeting. My head went into hyper-speed. If this person thought I needed to go, perhaps I did. But I wasn't an alcoholic.

I attended the meeting and decided drugs were my problem. I stopped using them completely from that night forward. The result was a sharp increase in my drinking. I knew this would never do. Staggering home one night, it occurred to me that perhaps if I stopped drinking, just for a while, maybe I could get a handle on things and then I could drink again.

It took about three months for me to realize I was my problem and drinking made my problem much worse. The other substances were simply tools to control my drinking. Given a choice, I'd take a drink over the other stuff in a heartbeat. Angry doesn't begin to describe how I felt when I had to admit I was an alcoholic.

Even though I was grateful not to be nuts, as I'd first supposed, I felt cheated. All the people I saw sitting around the tables of Alcoholics Anonymous had been granted many more years of drinking than I. It just wasn't fair! Someone pointed out to me that life was rarely fair. I wasn't amused, but extending my drinking career simply wasn't an option anymore.

Ninety days sober cleared my thinking enough to make me realize I'd hit bottom. If I were to go back to drinking, it would be just a matter of time before one of two things happened: I'd succeed at suicide, or

I'd start the life of the living dead. I'd seen what the latter looked like, and real death was preferable.

At this point I surrendered. I admitted I was an alcoholic without a clue what to do about it. Many of the people around me wanted me to go to treatment, but I resisted. I didn't want the kids at school to know what was going on. If I went to treatment, they'd all know within a week. More importantly, I was afraid. I was afraid the treatment center would test me and say, "You're not an alcoholic. You're just crazy." My heart knew this wasn't true. My head took a bit more convincing. The thought of having A.A. taken away from me was terrifying. A.A. was my anchor in a sea of confusion. Anything that might pose a threat to my sense of security was quickly thrust away. I didn't have anything against treatment centers then, nor do I now. I simply didn't want to go, and I didn't.

I did stay sober. One summer with people who enjoyed life sober was all it took for me to want sobriety more than I wanted a drink. I will not tell you I did everything I was told, when I was told, how I was told, because I didn't. Like most people new to the program I set out to find an easier, softer way. As the Big Book suggests, I could not.

When I couldn't find an easier, softer way, I looked for the person with the magic wand, the one person in A.A. who could make me all better, right now. This was a frustrating task, and I finally realized that if I wanted this life, I was going to have to do what the others had done. No one made me drink, and no one was going to make me stay sober. This program is for people who want it, not people who need it.

If everyone who needed A.A. showed up, we would

be bursting at the seams. Unfortunately, most never make it to the door. I believe I was one of the lucky ones. Not just because I found this program at such a young age; I feel fortunate that I found A.A. at all. My approach to drinking brought me to the jumping-off place described in the Big Book much faster than any-one could have imagined.

I'm convinced if I had continued on my course, I wouldn't have survived much longer. I don't believe I was smarter than anyone else, as I'm often told by those who came in at a later age. It was my time, my chance to live, and I took it. If there had still been joy in my drinking or even a remote chance of the joy returning, I would not have stopped drinking when I did.

No one who drank as I did wakes up on the edge of the abyss one morning and says: Things look pretty scary; I think I'd better stop drinking before I fall in. I was convinced I could go as far as I wanted, and then climb back out when it wasn't fun anymore. What happened was, I found myself at the bottom of the canyon thinking I'd never see the sun again. A.A. didn't pull me out of that hole. It did give me the tools to construct a ladder, with Twelve Steps.

Sobriety is nothing like I thought it would be. At first it was one big emotional roller coaster, full of sharp highs and deep lows. My emotions were new, untested, and I wasn't entirely certain I wanted to deal with them. I cried when I should have been laughing. I laughed when I should have cried. Events I thought were the end of the world turned out to be gifts. It was all very confusing. Slowly things began to even out. As I began to take the steps of recovery, my role in the pitiful condition of my life became clear.

If asked what the two most important things in recovery are, I would have to say willingness and action. I was willing to believe that A.A. was telling me the truth. I wanted to believe it was true in a way I cannot relate in words. I wanted this thing to work. Then I began to take the course of action prescribed.

Following the principles laid out in the Big Book has not always been comfortable, nor will I claim perfection. I have yet to find a place in the Big Book that says, "Now you have completed the Steps; have a nice life." The program is a plan for a lifetime of daily living. There have been occasions when the temptation to slack off has won. I view each of these as learning opportunities.

When I am willing to do the right thing, I am rewarded with an inner peace no amount of liquor could ever provide. When I am unwilling to do the right thing, I become restless, irritable, and discontent. It is always my choice. Through the Twelve Steps, I have been granted the gift of choice. I am no longer at the mercy of a disease that tells me the only answer is to drink. If willingness is the key to unlock the gates of hell, it is action that opens those doors so that we may walk freely among the living.

Over the course of my sobriety I have experienced many opportunities to grow. I have had struggles and achievements. Through it all I have not had to take a drink, nor have I ever been alone. Willingness and action have seen me through it all, with the guidance of a loving Higher Power and the fellowship of the program. When I'm in doubt, I have faith that things will turn out as they should. When I'm afraid, I reach for the hand of another alcoholic to steady me.

Life has not heaped monetary riches upon my head, nor have I achieved fame in the eyes of the world. My blessings cannot be measured in those terms. No amount of money or fame could equal what has been given me. Today I can walk down any street, anywhere, without the fear of meeting someone I've harmed. Today my thoughts are not consumed with craving for the next drink or regret for the damage I did on the last drunk.

Today I reside among the living, no better, no worse than any of God's other children. Today I look in the mirror when putting on my makeup and smile, rather than shy away from looking myself in the eye. Today I fit in my skin. I am at peace with myself and the world around me.

Growing up in A.A., I have been blessed with children who have never seen their mother drunk. I have a husband who loves me simply because I am, and I have gained the respect of my family. What more could a broken-down drunk ask for? Lord knows it is more than I ever thought possible, and ever so much more than I deserved. All because I was willing to believe A.A. just might work for me too.

(6)

STUDENT OF LIFE

Living at home with her parents, she tried using willpower to beat the obsession to drink. But it wasn't until she met another alcoholic and went to an A.A. meeting that sobriety took hold.

I STARTED DRINKING at age eighteen, rather a late bloomer by today's standards. But after I started, the disease of alcoholism hit me with a vengeance and made up for lost time. After I had been drinking for several years and seriously wondering if I did indeed have a problem with alcohol, I read one of the "Are You an Alcoholic?" quiz-type checklists. Much relieved, I found that almost nothing applied to me: I had never lost a job, a spouse, children, or any material possessions through alcohol. The fact that my drinking hadn't allowed me to gain any of those things crossed my mind only after I came into A.A.

I can't blame one ounce of my drinking on my upbringing. My parents were loving and supportive and have been married thirty-five years. No one else in my family exhibits alcoholic drinking or alcoholic behavior. For some reason, despite the resources available to me growing up, I developed into an adult woman terrified of the world around me. I was extremely insecure, though I was careful to hide this fact. I was unable to handle and understand my emotions; I always felt as if everyone else knew what was going on and what they were supposed to be doing, and my life was the only one that was delivered without an instruction book.

When I discovered alcohol, everything changed. I took my first real drink my first night at college. I attended what was to be the first of many, many fraternity parties. I didn't care for the beer, so I went to the vat of innocuous-looking punch. I was told it was laced with grain alcohol. I don't remember how many drinks I had, and my recollections of the actual events of the rest of the night are fuzzy, but I do remember this much: When I was drinking, I was okay. I understood. Everything made sense. I could dance, talk, and enjoy being in my own skin. It was as if I had been an unfinished jigsaw puzzle with one piece missing; as soon as I took a drink, the last piece instantly and effortlessly snapped into place.

I don't remember getting home that night, and I woke up the next morning completely dressed and in full makeup. I was sick as a dog, but I managed to crawl into the shower and prepare for my first college class. I sat through the entire class pleading with my eyes to the professor to let us out early. He kept us to the bell, and when it rang, I flew into the women's room, crashed into the first stall, and threw everything up.

The insanity of the disease had already manifested itself. I recall thinking, as I knelt retching in the stall, that this was fantastic. Life was great; I had finally found the answer—alcohol! Yes, I overdid it the night before, but I was new to this game. I only had to learn how to drink right and I was set.

I attempted to "drink right" for the next eight years. My progression was phenomenal; there is absolutely no period in my drinking career that can be described as social drinking. I blacked out almost every time I put alcohol in my system, but I decided I could live with that; it was a small price to pay for the power and confidence alcohol gave me. After drinking for less than six months, I was almost a daily drinker.

I wound up on academic probation (I had always been on the honor roll in high school) my first semester sophomore year, and my response to that was to change my major. My life on campus revolved around parties, drinking, and men. I surrounded myself with people who drank as I did. Even though several people had already expressed their concern over my drinking, I rationalized that I was only doing what every other red-blooded college student did.

Somehow I managed to graduate, but while most of my friends were securing good jobs and abruptly stopping their boozing, I seemed to be left behind on campus. I had resolved that I, too, would now settle down and drink properly, but to my frustration I found I could not do so.

I took a pitiful sales job that paid next to nothing, so I continued to live with my parents. I kept this job for two years for one reason—it allowed me to drink with minimal interference. My pattern was to pick up a fifth of whiskey somewhere during my round of appointments and keep it under the car seat with me. When I got home in the evening, I drank at least half the fifth in front of the television set and watched reruns until I passed out. And I did this every night, by myself, for almost two years. I had become a daily, isolated drinker and was starting to get a little nervous.

My behavior at this point was textbook: I was stashing bottles all over the house; sneaking drinks from my parents' small supply when I ran out; rationing the number of bottles I threw away at the same time so the trash bags wouldn't clink; refilling my parents' vodka and gin bottles with water; and so on. I had also resorted to videotaping my favorite reruns while I was watching them because I always blacked out before the ending.

About this time the TV movie *My Name Is Bill W.,* about the co-founder of A.A., was aired. Intrigued, I sat down with my whiskey and soda bottles to watch it. When Bill whipped out a flask in the car to bolster himself before a visit with his father-in-law, I heaved a sigh of relief. "Oh, I'm not that bad," I thought to myself. I then proceeded to get drunk and to black out; I don't remember any more of the movie.

My parents were at a total loss. I was going nowhere and I was irritable and hostile. Since they had no experience with alcoholism, they had no idea what was wrong with me or what to do about it, and neither did I. I knew I drank too much and that my life was miserable, but I never made the connection between those two conditions. My parents made the only suggestion that then made sense to them—they offered to help me financially if I wanted to go back to school. Seeing no other way out, I jumped at the opportunity.

I spent two years in graduate school 750 miles from home. I can honestly say I know why they call it a geographical cure. For about nine months, I was able to cut my drinking down sharply. I still drank almost every day, but not to the point of my usual stupors, and I didn't black out very often. I was able to concentrate on my schoolwork that first year and make lots of friends. However, geographical cures are only temporary; mine lasted a little less than a year. After about ten months or so, I slowly started to slide back into my old patterns. Steadily, I worked my way back to the same quantities of whiskey I drank at home, and the blackouts returned. My grades started to drop, and my friends started to wonder. I even began watching reruns again—I had brought my homemade videotapes with me to school.

Fortunately, I managed to graduate, but I had gone nowhere. After graduation, I returned to my parents' house, as I had been unsuccessful in securing a job. I was back. I was back in my old bedroom, back to the same routine of drinking every evening until I passed out, and it was getting worse. I was starting earlier and earlier and consuming more and more liquor. I had no job, no friends; I saw no one but my parents.

I was beyond frustration at this point. Hadn't I done everything that was expected of me? Hadn't I graduated from college and gone on to earn a master's degree? I had never gone to jail, crashed any cars, or got into trouble like a real alcoholic would. When I was working, I never missed a day because of drinking. I never ran myself into debt, nor had I abused a spouse or children. Sure I drank a lot, but I didn't have a problem; how could I when I hadn't done any of the things that prove you're an alcoholic? So what was the problem? All I really wanted was a decent job so I could be independent and productive. I could not understand why life just wouldn't cut me a break.

I did odd projects around the house for my parents

to earn my keep until I took a job for a local entrepreneur. This job did not offer much opportunity for advancement, nor did it pay very well, but it got me out of the house, and it was challenging in many ways. At this point I was in a vicious battle to control my drinking. I knew that if I took only one drink, I'd lose complete control and drink until I passed out. Nevertheless, I tried day after day to beat this obsession with alcohol.

I picked up a half gallon of whiskey one day after work and drank over one-third of it in less than four hours that same night. I was so sick the next day, but I made it to work. When I got home from work, I sat on my parents' sofa and knew, *I knew,* I would start working on the half gallon again, despite the fact that I was still very ill from the night before. I also knew that I did not want to drink. Sitting on that sofa, I realized that the old "I could stop if I wanted to, I just don't want to" didn't apply here, because I did not want to drink. I watched myself get up off the sofa and pour myself a drink. When I sat back down on the sofa, I started to cry. My denial had cracked; I believe I hit bottom that night, but I didn't know it then; I just thought I was insane. I proceeded to finish the half gallon.

Six months later my boss flew me to California for a trade show. I hated working the shows, but I loved to travel, so I went. I was extremely nervous about this trip because my boss liked to party and we were flying in a guy our age from Hawaii to work the show with us. At this point I had managed to hold together thirty-one days without a drink, and I was terrified that I would give in to the temptation of being on an

all-expenses-paid trip in a fun city with two party animals. It had been very difficult for me to stay dry for
thirty-one days; the obsession spoke to me every day.

I arrived late on a Friday and managed not to drink
that night. The next morning at the show, I was offered the gift that changed my life. Our Hawaiian
sales rep seemed frustrated; I thought he was disappointed that he hadn't managed to write an order for
a couple he had just finished working with. I went
over to console him. He said, no, his mood had nothing to do with the couple; instead, he explained that
just this week he had lost his girlfriend, dropped out
of school, lost his apartment, and also lost his full-time
job. He added, "I'm an alcoholic. I've been sober for
a year and a half, except I just drank again this past
week. I'm a mess about it."

At that very instant, I heard one word in my head.
The word was "now." I knew it meant, "Say something
now!"

To my amazement I spoke the words, "Mike, I think
I'm one too." Mike's mood instantly changed. I recognize now it was hope. We started talking. Among
other things, I told him I hadn't had a drink for about
a month but didn't go to A.A. When he asked why I
had avoided A.A., I told him it was because I didn't
think I had hit bottom. Somehow he didn't laugh but
said, "You hit bottom when you stop digging." He took
me to my first three A.A. meetings.

It was the second meeting that clinched my resolve
to pursue sobriety. There were about thirty-five people in attendance, but the space was small, so the
meeting seemed very crowded. Being from out of
town, I stood up and introduced myself when asked to

by the chairperson. Later on in the meeting, the chairperson called on me to share. I got up and somehow walked over to the microphone and podium—I've never been so nervous in my life. But the words came out naturally as I described the events that led up to the meeting that night.

As I spoke, I looked around the room. More importantly, I looked at the faces of the people in the room and I saw it. I saw the understanding, the empathy, the love. Today I believe I saw my Higher Power for the first time in those faces. While still up at the podium, it hit me—this is what I had been looking for all my life. This was the answer, right here in front of me. Indescribable relief came over me; I knew the fight was over.

Later on that night, still reeling in the ecstasy of relief and hope, I remembered the afternoon in the bathroom stall at college after my first class when I was so certain I had found the answer in alcohol. I could clearly see now that had been a lie. That is the description that fits alcohol best for me; it is a lie, an evil, insidious lie. And I chased that lie for a long time—even when it was obvious that I was going nowhere and killing myself while doing it. At that A.A. meeting, when I looked out over all those faces, I finally saw the truth.

When I returned home, I threw myself into A.A. I did ninety meetings in ninety days, got a sponsor, and joined a home group. I did everything that was suggested. I made coffee, took commitments, and got involved with service. I rode the roller coaster of early sobriety; every second was worth it to get where I am today.

It is very important to my recovery to study and

work the Steps. To this day, I still make at least two Step meetings a week. I have a sponsor who guides me through the Steps gently but firmly, with a sure-handedness I hope I am able to emulate with the two women I now sponsor. The Promises have begun to materialize for me, and there's still so much work to do.

It is almost impossible to adequately describe how much the program has given me, even in just these six short years. I have been financially supporting myself in my own apartment for five years and plan to buy a house next year. I've secured a good job with a promising future—my income has increased more than 150 percent since I got sober.

But just as material losses are not necessary to indicate alcoholism, material gains are not the true indications of sobriety. The real rewards aren't material in nature. I have friends now because I know how to be a friend and I know how to nurture and encourage valuable friendships. Instead of the prolonged one-night stands I used to call my boyfriends, there is a special man in my life I've been involved with for almost five years. And, most importantly, I know who I am. I know my goals, dreams, values, and boundaries, and I know how to protect, nurture, and validate them. Those are the true rewards of sobriety, and they're what I was looking for all along. I am so grateful that my Higher Power stepped in to show me the way to the truth. I pray every day that I never turn my back on it. I came to A.A. in order to stop drinking; what I received in return was my life.

(7)

CROSSING THE RIVER OF DENIAL

She finally realized that when she enjoyed her drinking, she couldn't control it, and when she controlled it, she couldn't enjoy it.

ENIAL IS THE MOST cunning, baffling, and powerful part of my disease, the disease of alcoholism. When I look back now, it's hard to imagine I didn't see a problem with my drinking. But instead of seeing the truth when all of the "yets" (as in, that hasn't happened to me—yet) started happening, I just kept lowering my standards.

Dad was an alcoholic, and my mother drank throughout her pregnancy, but I don't blame my parents for my alcoholism. Kids with a lot worse upbringings than mine did not turn out alcoholic, while some that had it a lot better did. In fact I stopped wondering, "Why me?" a long time ago. It's like a man standing on a bridge in the middle of a river with his pants on fire wondering why his pants are on fire. It doesn't matter. Just jump in! And that is exactly what I did with A.A. once I finally crossed the river of denial!

I grew up feeling as if I was the only thing keeping my family together. This, compounded by the fear of not being good enough, was a lot of pressure for a little girl. Everything changed with my first drink at the age of sixteen. All the fear, shyness, and disease evaporated with that first burning swallow of bourbon straight from the bottle during a liquor cabinet raid at a slumber party. I got drunk, blacked out, threw up, had dry heaves, was sick to death the next day, and I knew I would do it again. For the first time, I felt part of a group without having to be perfect to get approval.

I went through college on scholarships, work study programs, and student loans. Classes and work kept me too busy to do much drinking, plus I was engaged to a boy who was not alcoholic. However, I broke off our relationship during my senior year, after discovering drugs, sex, and rock n' roll—companions to my best friend, alcohol. I proceeded to explore all that the late sixties and early seventies offered. After backpacking around Europe, I decided to settle in a large city.

Well, I made it all right, to full-blown alcoholism. A big city is a great place to be an alcoholic. Nobody notices. Three-martini lunches, drinks after work, and a nightcap at the corner bar was just a normal day. And didn't everyone have blackouts? I used to joke about how great blackouts were because you saved so much time in transit. One minute you're here, the next minute you're there! In retrospect, making jokes, just laughing it off helped solidify my unfaltering denial. Another trick was selecting companions who drank just a little bit more than I did. Then I could always point to their problem.

One such companion led to my first arrest. If the driver of the car had only pulled over when the police lights flashed, we would have been fine. If, when I had practically talked our way out of it, the driver had kept his mouth shut, we would have been fine. But no, he started babbling about how he was in rehab. I got off with a misdemeanor, and for years, I completely discounted that arrest because it was all his fault. I simply ignored that I had been drinking all day.

One morning while I was at work, a hospital called, telling me to get there quickly. My father was there, dying of alcoholism. He was sixty. I had seen him in hospitals before, but this time was different. With stomach sorely distended, swollen with fluids his nonfunctioning kidneys and liver could no longer process, he lingered for three weeks. Alcoholic death is very painful and slow. Seeing him die of alcoholism convinced me I could never become an alcoholic. I knew too much about the disease, had too much self-knowledge to ever fall prey. I shipped his body back home without attending the funeral. I could not even help my grandmother bury her only son, because by then I was inextricably involved in an affair mired in sex and alcohol.

Plummeting into the pitiful and incomprehensible demoralization that that relationship became, I had my first drunk driving arrest. It terrified me; I could have killed someone. Driving in a total blackout, I "came to" handing my driver's license to the patrolman. I swore it would never happen again. Three months later it happened again. What I didn't know then was that when I put alcohol in my body, I'm powerless over how much and with whom I drink—all good intentions drowned in denial.

I remembered joking about how most people spent their entire lives without ever seeing the inside of a jail, and here "a woman of my stature" had been arrested three times. But, I would think, I've never really done "hard time," never actually spent the night in jail. Then I met Mr. Wrong, my husband-to-be, and all that changed. I spent my wedding night in jail. Like every other time, however, it wasn't my fault. There we were, still in our wedding clothes. If he had just kept his mouth shut after the police arrived, we would have been fine. I had them convinced that he had attacked the valet because our wedding money was missing. Actually, he thought the valet had stolen the marijuana we were going to smoke. In reality, I was so drunk I had lost it.

During the interrogation of the valet in the restaurant parking lot, my husband became so violent the officer put him in the back of the patrol car. When he tried to kick out the rear windows, the policeman retaliated. I pleaded with the officer as a second policeman arrived, and both bride and groom were taken to jail. It was then that the "stolen" marijuana cigarettes were discovered, to my horror, in central booking as they catalogued my belongings. I was arrested for three felonies, including drunk and disorderly, and two misdemeanors, but it was all my husband's fault. I had practically nothing to do with it; he had a drinking problem.

I stayed in that abusive marriage for nearly seven years and continued to focus on *his* problem. Toward the end of the marriage, in my misguided attempts to set a good example for him (plus he was drinking too much of my vodka), I mandated no booze in the house. Still, why should I be denied a cocktail after returning home from a stressful day at the office just because he had a problem? So, I began hiding my vodka in the bedroom—and still did not see anything wrong with this behavior. *He* was my problem.

I accepted a transfer with a promotion (yes, my professional life was still climbing) shortly after the divorce. Now I was sure my problems were over, except that I brought me with me. Once alone in a new place, my drinking really took off. I did not have to be a good example anymore. For the first time I realized that perhaps my drinking was getting a bit out of hand, but I knew you'd drink too if you had my stress: recent divorce, new home, new job, didn't know anyone—and an unacknowledged, progressive disease that was destroying me.

Finally, I made some friends who drank just as I did. Our drinking was disguised as fishing trips and chili cook-offs, but they were really excuses for week-long binges. After a day's drinking disguised as softball, I nicked an old woman's fender driving home. Of course, it was not my fault; she pulled out in front of me. That the accident occurred at dusk and I had been drinking since 10:00 a.m. had nothing to do with it. My alcoholism had taken me to such depths of denial and heights of arrogance that I waited for the police so they'd know it was her fault too. Well, it didn't take them long to figure it out. Once again, pulled from the car, hands cuffed behind my back, I was taken to jail. But it wasn't my fault. The old broad shouldn't have even been allowed on the road, I told myself. *She* was my problem.

The judge sentenced me to six months in Alcoholics Anonymous, and was I outraged! By now I had been arrested *five* times, but all I could see was a hard partier, not an alcoholic. Didn't you people know the difference? So I started going to those stupid meetings and identified myself as an alcoholic so you'd sign my court card, even though I couldn't possibly be an alcoholic. I had a six-figure income, owned my own home. I had a car phone. I used ice cubes, for God's sake. Everyone knows an alcoholic, at least one that had to go to A.A., is a skid row bum in a dirty raincoat drinking from a brown paper bag. So each time you read that part in Chapter Five of the Big Book that says, "If you have decided you want what we have and are willing to go to any length to get it," my ears closed. You had the disease of alcoholism, and the last thing I wanted was to be an alcoholic.

Eventually, you talked about my feelings in the meetings of Alcoholics Anonymous until I could no longer close my ears. I heard women, beautiful, successful women in recovery, talk about the things they had done while drinking, and I would think, "I did that" or "I did worse than that!" Then I began to see the miracles that happen only in A.A. People who would nearly crawl in the doors, sick and broken, and who in a few weeks of meetings and not drinking one day at a time would get their health back, find a little job and friends who really cared, and then discover a God in their lives. But the most compelling part of A.A., the part that made me want to try this sober thing, was the laughter, the pure joy of the laughter that I heard only from sober alcoholics.

Still, the thought of getting sober terrified me. I hated the woman I had become, a compulsive, obsessive daily drinker, not dressing on weekends, always afraid of running out of alcohol. I'd start thinking about a drink by noon and would leave the office earlier and earlier. Or, promising myself that I wouldn't drink that night, I'd invariably find myself in front of the refrigerator with a drink in my hand, vowing,

Tomorrow. I won't drink tomorrow. I despised all of it, but at least it was familiar. I had no idea what sobriety felt like, and I could not imagine life without alcohol. I had reached that terrifying jumping-off point where I couldn't drink anymore but I just couldn't not drink. For almost twenty-three years I had done something nearly every day of my life to change reality to one degree or another, yet I had to try this sober thing.

To this day I am amazed at people who get sober before the holidays. I couldn't even attempt it until after the Super Bowl. One last blow-out party when I swore I wouldn't get drunk. When I put alcohol in my body, I'd lose the ability to choose how much I drank, and Super Bowl Sunday that year was no different. I ended up on someone's couch instead of my own bed and was sick to death all the next day at work. That week I had to go to a hockey game. It was a work event, so I tried to really watch my drinking, consuming only two large cups of beer which, for me, wasn't even enough to catch a buzz. And that was the beginning of my spiritual awakening. Sitting near the ice, frustrated, and pondering the fact that two tall beers didn't give me any relief, something in my head—and I know it wasn't me—said, "So why bother?" At that moment I knew what the Big Book meant about the great obsession of every abnormal drinker being to somehow, someday control *and* enjoy his drinking. On Super Bowl Sunday, when I enjoyed it, I couldn't control it, and at the hockey game when I controlled it, I couldn't enjoy it. There was no more denying that I was an alcoholic. What an epiphany!

I went to a meeting of Alcoholics Anonymous the next night, knowing I wanted what you had. I sat in that cold metal chair just as I had for the past five months and read Step One on the wall for the hundredth time. But this time I asked with all my heart for God to help me, and a strange thing happened. A physical sensation came over me, like a wave of pure energy, and I felt the presence of God in that dingy little room. I went home that night and for the first time in years I did not have to open the cupboard with the half-gallon jug of vodka in it—not that night or any night since. God had restored me to sanity, and I took Step Two the very moment I surrendered and accepted my powerlessness over alcohol and the unmanageability of my life.

I attended at least one meeting every day, emptied ashtrays, washed coffeepots, and on the day I took a thirty-day chip, a friend took me to an A.A. get-together. I was in absolute awe of the power of 2,000-plus sober alcoholics holding hands, saying the final prayer together, and I wanted to stay sober more than I wanted life itself. Returning home, I begged God on my knees to help me stay sober one more day. I told God to take the house, take the job, take everything if that's what was needed for me to stay sober. That day I learned two things: the real meaning of Step Three and to always be careful what I prayed for.

After five months of sobriety, I lost that six-figure job with the firm. The wreckage of my past had caught up with me, and I was out of work for a year. That job would have been lost whether I was drunk or sober, but thank goodness I was sober or I probably would have killed myself. When I was drinking, the prestige of the job was my self-worth, the only thing that made me worth loving. Now I was starting to love myself because A.A.'s had unconditionally loved me until I could. At five months I realized that the world might never build a shrine to the fact that I was sober. I understood that it was not the world's job to understand my disease; rather it was my job to work my program and not drink, no matter what.

At nine months of sobriety I lost the big house that I bought just to prove to you I couldn't possibly be an alcoholic. In between five and nine months, my house was robbed, I had a biopsy on my cervix, and I had my heart broken. And the miracle of all miracles was that I didn't have to drink over any of it. This from a woman who had had to drink over all of it. I was so unique and so arrogant when I got here, I think God knew that He had to show me early on that there was *nothing* a drink would make better. He showed me that His love and the power of the Steps and the Fellowship could keep me from picking up a drink one day at a time, sometimes one hour at a time, no matter what. A drink would not bring back the job, the house, or the man, so why bother?

I found everything I had ever looked for in Alcoholics Anonymous. I used to thank God for putting A.A. in my life; now I thank A.A. for putting God in my life. I found my tribe, the social architecture that fulfills my every need for camaraderie and conviviality. I learned how to live. When I asked how I could find self-esteem, you told me, "by doing worthwhile acts!" You explained the Big Book had no chapters titled "Into Thinking" or "Into Feeling"—only "Into Action." I found plenty of opportunity for action in A.A. I could be just as busy and helpful to others as I wanted to be as a sober woman in Alcoholics

Anonymous. I was never a "joiner," but I got deeply involved in A.A. service because you told me if I did, I would never have to drink again. You said as long as I put A.A. first in my life, everything that I put second would be first class. This has proved to be true over and over again. So I continued to put A.A. and God first, and everything I ever lost was returned many times over. The career that I lost has been restored with even greater success. The house that I lost has been replaced by a townhouse that is just the right size for me. So, here I am, sober. Successful. Serene. Just a few of the gifts of the program for surrendering, suiting up, and showing up for life every day. Good days and bad days, reality is a wild ride, and I wouldn't miss it for the world. I don't question how this program works. I trust in my God, stay involved in A.A. service, go to lots of meetings, work with others, and practice the principles of the Steps to the best of my willingness each day. I don't know which of these keeps me sober, and I'm not about to try to find out. It's worked for quite a few days now, so I think I'll try it again tomorrow.

BECAUSE I'M AN ALCOHOLIC

This drinker finally found the answer to her nag-ging question, "Why?"

I SUPPOSE I always wondered who I was. As a child, isolated in the country, I made up stories, inventing myself along with imaginary companions to play with. Later, when we moved to a large city and I was surrounded by kids, I felt separate, like an out-cast. And although I learned to go along with the cul-tural norm as I grew up, still, underneath, I felt different.

Alcohol helped. At least I thought it helped until I saw the oppressive thirty-year shadow it cast on my life. I discovered it in college, and although at first I didn't drink often (didn't have the opportunity), whenever I started, I drank as long as there was any alcohol around. It was a reflex. I don't remember lik-ing the taste, but I liked that it seemed to bring me to life and get me through a date or a party able to talk. It moved me outside of that hole I felt in myself and lowered the wall I created between me and any per-son or situation that made me uncomfortable.

For ten years, through college and graduate school interspersed with jobs, I drank periodically, so it was easy enough to think that I was a social drinker. Looking back, I see that alcohol helped me construct an image of myself as a sophisticated metropolitan woman, diminishing my feelings of being a backward country girl. I studied vintage wines and selected them with care to accompany the gourmet dishes I learned to make. I read about the correct drinks for various occasions. I learned to put just the tiniest whiff of dry vermouth into my martinis. Meanwhile, my tolerance for alcohol grew, so that while at first I got sick or passed out, as time went on I could hold larger quantities without any visible effects. Until the next morning's hangover.

Behind the façade, my real life seemed just out of reach. I wanted to consider myself grown up, but inside I felt small and helpless, hardly there at all. I would look at my friends—delightful, interesting, good people—and try to define myself through them. If they saw something in me that made them want to be with me, I must have something to offer. But their love for me was not a substitute for loving myself; it didn't fill the emptiness.

So I continued spinning fantasies, and now alcohol fueled my dreams. I would make great discoveries, win the Nobel Prize in medicine and in literature as well. Always the dream was somewhere else, further off, and I took a series of geographical cures in search of myself. I was offered a job in Paris and jumped at the chance. I packed my trunk, left my apartment to my boyfriend, and sailed off, thinking that at last I would find my real home, my real self.

I began to drink daily and rationalized that in France, of course, you have to have wine with meals. And after the dinner, after the wine, then there were liqueurs. My journals and letters bear witness in the deterioration of my handwriting as the evening wore

on, drinking as I wrote. It was there too that I first became dependent on alcohol. After work, on the way to
the Alliance Française for classes, I'd stop at a bistro
for a glass of cognac to give me courage to get me
there—my need greater than the embarrassment of
being a woman drinking alone in the 1950s. One
vacation, I went to visit friends in Scotland, traveling
slowly through the English and Welsh countryside.
The bottles of cognac and Benedictine I'd brought as
gifts for them I drank in little hotel rooms miles
before I got there. As long as it lasted, I could stay out
of the pubs.

Europe hadn't proved to be the change that would
repair my life, and I started west again. It was in
Cambridge that I pronounced my first resolutions
about cutting down—New Year's resolutions I recy-
cled for a dozen years while my drinking and my life
kept getting worse. Alcohol had enslaved me. I was in
bondage to it, although I kept assuring myself that
drinking was a pleasure and a choice.

Blackouts began, vacant places in my life when
hours would disappear, lost to memory. The first time
was after I'd given a dinner party. The next morning I
woke up without remembering that I'd told my guests
good night and gone to bed myself. I searched the
apartment for clues. The table was cluttered with
dessert dishes and coffee cups. Bottles were empty,
and the glasses too. (It was my custom to polish off
any drinks that were left.) My last memory was sometime during dinner. Did we ever finish? But there
were the plates. I was terrified that I'd done something horrendous, until my friends called to tell me
they'd enjoyed the evening.

One time we sailed from Guadelupe to a little island for a picnic, swam to shore from the ship. After lunch, and quantities of wine, I was with a French ski instructor talking to a troop of small boys on their way home from school, trying to explain to those tropical islanders what snow is like. I remember them giggling. The next thing I knew, I was back at the camp, walking to the dining room—apparently after swimming back to the ship, sailing to the port, then taking a rickety bus across the island. I had no memory of what I had done during those hours between.

The blackouts increased, and my terror increased with them. Telephone bills would inform me that I'd made late-night calls to distant places. I could tell from the numbers whom I'd called, but what had I said? Some mornings I woke up with a stranger who had brought me home from a party the night before. These things weighed heavily on me, but I couldn't stop the drinking that had caused them. That too gnawed away any remnants of self-respect I might have had. I was incapable of controlling my drinking and my life.

I needed a drink to go anyplace—to the theater, a party, a date, and, later, to work. I would leave my apartment, lock the door, and start down the stairs, and then turn around and go back in for another drink to get me where I planned to go. I needed a drink to do anything—to write, to cook, to clean the house, to paint the walls, to take a bath.

When I passed out and fell into bed early, I woke up at four or five and had Irish coffee to start the day. I discovered that beer was better than orange juice to ease my hangover. Afraid my colleagues or students would smell my breath at work, I was careful to keep my distance. When I got up late and rushed off to the lab, fortified only with coffee, my hands shook so badly it was impossible to weigh out the milligrams of compounds needed for an experiment. When I went out to lunch with another alcoholic, we might never get back to work that day.

Somehow I still managed to keep my job and most of my friends, social drinkers who were urging me to cut down on the alcohol. That counsel only made me mad, but I was concerned myself. I asked the therapist I was seeing, sometimes with beer in hand, would I have to stop? His answer was that we had to find out why I drank. I'd already tried but was never able to find out why until I learned the answer in A.A.—because I'm an alcoholic.

With my attempts to cut down, I stopped keeping alcohol around the house, drank up whatever was there, over and over deciding not to get more. Then on the way home after work or an evening out, I'd have to see if I could scrape together enough money for a bottle. There were liquor stores just about every block, and I rotated them so the salesmen wouldn't know how much I drank. On Sundays when the liquor stores were closed, I had to make do with beer or hard cider from the grocery.

The horrors grew. Inner horrors. On the surface it looked as though I was more or less keeping it together, but day by day I was dying inside, filled with fears I couldn't name but which shook me to the core. My worst fear was that I was an alcoholic. I wasn't sure what that was, except that I might end up down on the Bowery in New York, where I had seen drunks curled up on the sidewalk. I made another New Year's resolution—to stop drinking entirely until I could handle it and then, I told myself, I could go back to wine and beer.

Hands trembling, body shaky, head splitting, I survived that first day until I was fairly safe in bed in an alcohol-free apartment. Somehow I made it through a couple more days, miserable in withdrawal. In spite of managing to stay dry that time, I have no doubt that resolution would have crumbled like the others and I would have been drinking again if I hadn't found A.A.

I had left the therapist who hadn't been able to tell me why I drank, and on New Year's Eve, I went to a party at the home of my new therapist. A few days later in the group, the therapist said, "You're drinking even more than I realized. You're an alcoholic. I think you should stop drinking, see a doctor, and go to A.A."

My resolution had endured three days and I protested, "I'm not an alcoholic!" That was my very last denial.

"Say it the other way," he suggested. "I am an alcoholic." It came out in a whisper, but it sounded right. I've said it thousands of times since then, and with gratitude. What I was most afraid to admit that evening was what would set me free.

The therapist told me then and there to call someone who had been in our therapy group, a doctor on the staff of a hospital alcoholism service. "I'll call her tomorrow," I said.

"Call her now." He handed me the telephone.

When I asked her if I was an alcoholic, she said that from what she'd seen of my drinking I might be and suggested that I talk with her boss. Terrified, I made an appointment and kept it. She told me the symptoms of alcoholism, and I had them all. She gave me a list of A.A. meetings and recommended one.

I went to that meeting—a small women's group. I was scared and in withdrawal. Someone greeted me and I muttered my name aloud. Someone brought me a cup of coffee. People gave me their phone numbers and urged me to call, to pick up the telephone instead of a drink. They were warm and friendly. They said keep coming back.

And I did. For weeks I sat in the back of the rooms, silent when others shared their experience, strength, and hope. I listened to their stories and found so many areas where we overlapped—not all of the deeds, but the feelings of remorse and hopelessness. I learned that alcoholism isn't a sin, it's a disease. That lifted the guilt I had felt. I learned that I didn't have to stop drinking forever, but just not pick up that first drink one day, one hour at a time. I could manage that. There was laughter in those rooms and sometimes tears, but always love, and when I was able to let it in, that love helped me heal.

I read everything I could about this disease I have. My readings recounted the course I had lived and predicted the way I would die if I continued drinking. I had access to a good medical library, but after a while, I realized the genetics and chemistry of the disease were of no use to me as an alcoholic. All that I needed to know about it, what would help me get sober, help me recover, I could learn in A.A.

I was blessed to live in a city where there were meetings at all hours of the day and night. There I would be safe. And there, within a few blocks of my apartment, at last I would find the self I had traveled thousands of miles in search of. The slogans on the walls, which at first made me shudder, began to impress me as truths I could live by: "One Day at a Time." "Easy Does It." "Keep It Simple." "Live and Let Live." "Let Go and Let God." "The Serenity Prayer."

Commitment and service were part of recovery. I was told that to keep it we have to give it away. At first I made the coffee and later volunteered at the inter-group office answering telephones on the evening shift. I went on Twelfth Step calls, spoke at meetings, served as group officer. Ever so gradually I began to open. Just a crack at a first, with my hand on the door ready to slam it shut in a moment of fear. But my fears subsided too. I found that I could be there, open to all kinds of people from this solid base that we shared. Then I began to go back out into the world, carrying that strength with me.

I found that now I could do many things without a drink—write, answer the telephone, eat out, go to parties, make love, get through the day and the evenings. Sleep at night and get up the next morning ready to begin another day. I was amazed and proud to have gone a week without a drink, then a month. Then I lived an entire year sober, through my birth-day, Christmas, problems, successes, the mixture that makes up life.

I healed physically, felt good, my senses returned. I began to hear the delicate sound of autumn leaves rat-tling in the wind, to feel the touch of snowflakes on my face, to see the first new leaves of spring.

Then I began to heal emotionally, to experience

feelings that had long been so deeply buried they had atrophied. For a time I floated on that pink cloud. Then I cried for a year, raged for another year. My feelings returned and then began to settle down to reasonable size.

Above all, I healed spiritually. The steps took me on that path. I had admitted I was powerless over alcohol, that my life had become unmanageable. That was what got me through the door. Then I came to believe that a Power greater than myself could restore me to sanity. And eventually, I made a decision to turn my will and my life over to the care of God as I understood God. Years before, in my search, I had explored numerous religions and dropped them because they preached a patriarchal God, which I felt never included me. Alcoholics Anonymous, I was told, is a spiritual program, not a religious one. Through my years of darkness, some spark of spirit remained in me, helped me survive until I found my way into A.A. Then, nurtured by the program, that inner spirit grew, deepened, until it filled the emptiness I had so long felt inside. Step by step I moved to a spiritual awaking. Step by step I cleared up the past and got on with the present.

A.A. is my home now, and it is everywhere. I go to meetings when I travel here or in foreign countries, and the people are family I can know because of what we share. As I write this, in my twenty-eighth year of sobriety, I am amazed to look back and remember the woman—or child—I was then, to see how far I've come out of that abyss. Alcoholics Anonymous has enabled me to move from fantasies about what I might do with my life into living it, one day at a time. In my first move that was not a geographic, I left the city and moved to the country. I left research and became a gardener. I discovered that I am a lesbian and that I love women. I'm fulfilling a long-time dream of writing fiction that's being published. But these are things I do, aspects of the life I'm living in sobriety. The most precious discovery is who I really *am*—like all of us, a being far beyond any of the ego-selves, any of the fantasies I'd made up.

That sense of being different, which had long plagued me, disappeared when I saw the threads that run through all of us. Sharing our stories, our feelings, it is the areas where we are the same that impress me. The differences are but delightful flourishes on the surface, like different-colored costumes, and I enjoy them. But the basic ways we are human, the basic ways we simply are, stand out to me now. I came to see that we all are really one, and I no longer feel alone.

IT MIGHT HAVE BEEN WORSE

Alcohol was a looming cloud in this banker's bright sky. With rare foresight he realized it could become a tornado.

HOW CAN a person with a fine family, an attractive home, an excellent position, and high standing in an important city become an alcoholic?

As I later found out through Alcoholics Anonymous, alcohol is no respecter of economic status, social and business standing, or intelligence.

I was raised like the majority of American boys, coming from a family of modest circumstances, attending public schools, having the social life of a small midwestern town, with part-time work and some athletics. The ambition to succeed was instilled in me by my Scandinavian parents who came to this country where opportunities were so great. "Keep busy; always have something constructive to do." I did work of all kinds after school and during vacations, trying to find that which would appeal most as a goal for a life work. Then there was wartime service to interrupt my plans, and an education to be picked up after the war. After that came marriage, getting started in business, and a family. The story is not very different from that of thousands of other young men in my generation. It shows nothing or no one to blame for alcoholism.

The drive to get ahead, to succeed, kept me too busy for many years to have any great experience with social life. I would have begrudged the time or money for alcohol. In fact I was afraid to try it for fear that I would wind up like many examples I had seen of excessive drinking in the army. I was intolerant of people who drank, particularly those who drank to an extent that interfered with their on-the-job performance.

In time I became an officer and director of one of the largest commercial banks in the country. I achieved recognized and national standing in my profession, as well as becoming a director in many important institutions having to do with the civic life of a large city. I had a family to be proud of, actively sharing in the responsibilities of good citizenship.

My drinking did not start until after I was thirty-five and a fairly successful career had been established. But success brought increased social activities, and I realized that many of my friends enjoyed a social drink with no apparent harm to themselves or others. I disliked being different so, ultimately, I began to join them occasionally.

At first it was just that—an occasional drink. Then I looked forward to the weekend of golf and the nineteenth hole. The cocktail hour became a daily routine. Gradually, the quantity increased and the occasions for a drink came more frequently: a hard day, worries and pressure, bad news, good news—there were more and more reasons for a drink. Why did I want increasingly greater quantities of alcohol? It was frightening that drink was being substituted for more and more of the things I really enjoyed doing. Golf, hunting, and fishing were now merely excuses to drink excessively.

I made promises to myself, my family, and friends—and broke them. Short dry spells ended in heavy drinking. I tried to hide my drinking by going places where I was unlikely to see anyone I knew. Hangovers and remorse were always with me.

The next steps were bottle hiding and excuses for trips in order to drink without restraint. Cunning, baffling, powerful—the gradual creeping up of the frequency and quantity of alcohol and what it does to a person is apparent to everyone but the person involved.

When it became noticeable to the point of comment, I devised ways of sneaking drinks on the side. "Rehearsals" then became a part of the pattern, stopping at bars on the way to or from the place where drinks were to be served. Never having enough, always craving more, the obsession for alcohol gradually began to dominate all my activities, particularly while traveling. Drink planning became more important than any other plans.

I tried the wagon on numerous occasions, but I always felt unhappy and abused. I tried psychiatry, but of course I gave the psychiatrist no cooperation.

I was living in constant fear that I would get caught while driving a car, so I used taxis part of the time. Then I began to have blackouts, and that was a constant worry. To wake up at home, not knowing how I got there, and to realize I had driven my car, became torture. Not knowing where I had been or how I got home was making me desperate.

It now became necessary to have noon drinks—at

first just two, then gradually more. My hours of work were flexible, so that returning to the office was not always important. Then I became careless and returned sometimes when I shouldn't have. This worried me. The last two years of my drinking, my entire personality changed to a cynical, intolerant, and arrogant person completely different from my normal self. It was at this stage of my life that resentments came in. Resenting anyone and everyone who might interfere with my personal plans and ways of doing things —especially for any interference with my drinking—I was full of self-pity.

I will never know all the people I hurt, all the friends I abused, the humiliation of my family, the worry of my business associates, or how far reaching it was. I continue to be surprised by the people I meet who say, "You haven't had a drink for a long time, have you?" The surprise to me is the fact that I didn't know that they knew my drinking had gotten out of control. That is where we are really fooled. We think we can drink to excess without anyone's knowing it. Everyone knows it. The only one we are fooling is ourselves. We rationalize and excuse our conduct beyond all reason.

My wife and I had always encouraged our children to bring their friends home at any time, but after a few experiences with a drunken father, they eliminated home as a place to entertain friends. At the time this didn't mean much to me. I was too busy devising excuses to be out with drinking pals.

It seemed to me my wife was becoming more intolerant and narrow-minded all the time. Whenever we went out, she appeared to go out of her way to keep me from having more than one drink. What alcoholic can be satisfied with one drink? After every cocktail party or dinner party she would say she couldn't understand how I could get in such a drunken stupor on one drink. She of course didn't realize how cunning an alcoholic can be and the lengths to which he will go in finding ways to satisfy the compulsion for more and more drinks after having had the first one. Neither did I.

Finally our invitations became fewer and fewer as friends had more experience with my drinking pattern.

Two years before I joined A.A., my wife took a long trip during which she wrote me she just couldn't return unless I did something about my drinking. It was a shock of course, but I promised to stop and she returned. A year later, while we were on a vacation trip, she packed up to go home because of my excessive drinking, and I talked her out of it with the promise I would go on the wagon for at least a year. I promised, but within two months, I began again.

The following spring she left me one day without giving me any idea of where she had gone, hoping this would bring me to my senses. In a few days an attorney called on me and explained that something would have to be done, as she couldn't face returning to me as I was. Again I promised to do something about it. Broken promises, humiliation, hopelessness, worry, anxiety—but still not enough.

There comes a time when you don't want to live and are afraid to die. Some crisis brings you to a point of deciding to do something about your drinking problem—to try anything. Help you once continually rejected, suggestions once turned aside are finally accepted in desperation.

The final decision came when my daughter, following a drunk of mine that ruined my wife's birthday, said, "It's Alcoholics Anonymous—or else!" Of course, this suggestion had been made before on a number of occasions, but like all alcoholics I wanted to handle my problem my own way, which really meant I didn't want anything to interfere with my drinking. I was trying to find an easier, softer way. By now it had become difficult to visualize a life without alcohol.

However, my low had been reached. I realized I had been going down and down. I was unhappy myself, and I had brought unhappiness to all who cared for me. Physically I couldn't take it any more. Cold sweats, jumpy nerves, and lack of sleep were becoming intolerable. Mentally, the fears and tensions, the complete change in attitude and outlook bewildered me. This was no way to live. The time for decision had arrived, and it was a relief to say yes when my family said they would call Alcoholics Anonymous for me—a relief, even though I dreaded it, feeling that this was the end of everything.

Early the next morning a man whose name I knew well, a lawyer, called on me. Within thirty minutes I knew A.A. was the answer for me. We visited most of that day and attended a meeting that night. I don't know what I expected, but I most certainly didn't visualize a group of people talking about their drinking problems, making light of their personal tragedies, and at the same time enjoying themselves.

However, after I heard a few stories of jails, sanitariums, broken homes, and skid row, I wondered if I really was an alcoholic. After all, I hadn't started to drink early in life, so I had some stability and maturity to guide me for a while. My responsibilities had been a restraining influence. I had had no brushes with the law, though I should have had many. I had not yet lost my job or family, even though both were on the verge of going. My financial standing had not been impaired.

Could I be an alcoholic without some of the hair-raising experiences I had heard of in meetings? The answer came to me very simply in the first step of the Twelve Steps of A.A. "We admitted we were powerless over alcohol—that our lives had become unmanageable." This didn't say we had to be in jail, ten, fifty, or one hundred times. It didn't say I had to lose one, five, or ten jobs. It didn't say I had to lose my family. It didn't say I had to finally live on skid row and drink bay rum, canned heat, or lemon extract. It did say I admitted I was powerless over alcohol—that my life had become unmanageable.

Most certainly I was powerless over alcohol, and for me, my life had become unmanageable. It wasn't how far I had gone, but where I was headed. It was important to me to see what alcohol had done to me and would continue to do if I didn't have help.

At first it was a shock to realize I was an alcoholic, but the realization that there was hope made it easier. The baffling problem of getting drunk when I had every intention of staying sober was simplified. It was a great relief to know I didn't *have* to drink any more.

I was told that I must want sobriety for my own sake, and I am convinced this is true. There may be many reasons that bring one to A.A. for the first time, but the lasting one must be to want sobriety and the A.A. way of living for oneself.

From the start I liked everything about the A.A. program. I liked the description of the alcoholic as a person who has found that alcohol is interfering with his social or business life. The allergy idea I could understand because I am allergic to certain pollens. Some of my family are allergic to certain foods. What could be more reasonable than that some people, including myself, were allergic to alcohol?

The explanation that alcoholism was a disease of a two-fold nature, an allergy of the body and an obsession of the mind, cleared up a number of puzzling questions for me. The allergy we could do nothing about. Somehow our bodies had reached the point where we could no longer absorb alcohol in our systems. The *why* is not important; the *fact* is that one drink will set up a reaction in our system that requires more, that one drink is too much and a hundred drinks are not enough.

The obsession of the mind was a little harder to understand, and yet everyone has obsessions of various kinds. The alcoholic has them to an exaggerated degree. Over a period of time he has built up self-pity and resentments toward anyone or anything that interferes with his drinking. Dishonest thinking, prejudice, ego, antagonism toward anyone and everyone who dares to cross him, vanity, and a critical attitude are character defects that gradually creep in and become a part of his life. Living with fear and tension inevitably results in wanting to ease that tension, which alcohol seems to do temporarily. It took me some time to realize that the Twelve Steps of A.A.

were designed to help correct these defects of character and so help remove the obsession to drink. The Twelve Steps, which to me are a spiritual way of living, soon meant honest thinking, not wishful thinking, open-mindedness, a willingness to try, and a faith to accept. They meant patience, tolerance, and humility, and above all, the belief that a Power greater than myself could help. That Power I chose to call God.

A willingness to do whatever I was told to do simplified the program for me. Study the A.A. book— don't just read it. They told me to go to meetings, and I still do at every available opportunity, whether I am at home or in some other city. Attending meetings has never been a chore to me. Nor have I attended them with a feeling of just doing my duty. Meetings are both relaxing and refreshing to me after a hard day. They said, "Get active," so I helped whenever I could, and I still do.

A spiritual experience to me meant attending meetings and seeing a group of people all there for the purpose of helping each other; hearing the Twelve Steps and the Twelve Traditions read at a meeting; and hearing the Lord's Prayer, which in an A.A. meeting has such great meaning—"Thy will be done, not mine." A spiritual awakening soon came to mean trying each day to be a little more thoughtful, more considerate, a little more courteous to those with whom I came in contact.

To most of us, making amends will take the rest of our lives, but we can start immediately. Just being sober will be making amends to many we have hurt by our drunken actions. Making amends is sometimes doing what we are capable of doing but failed to do

because of alcohol—carrying out community responsibilities such as community funds, Red Cross, educational and religious activities in proportion to our
abilities and energy.

I was desperately in earnest to follow through and
understand what was expected of me as a member of
A.A. and to take each step of the twelve as rapidly
as possible. To me this meant telling my associates
that I had joined Alcoholics Anonymous; that I didn't
know what was expected of me by A.A., but that whatever it was, it was the most important thing in life for
me; that sobriety meant more to me than anything in
this world. It was so important that it must come
ahead of anything.

There are many short phrases and expressions in
A.A. that make sound sense. "First Things First."
Solve our immediate problems before we try to solve
all the others and get muddled in our thinking and
doing. "Easy Does It." Relax a little. Try for inner
contentment. No one individual can carry all the burdens of the world. Everyone has problems. Getting
drunk won't solve them. "Twenty-four hours a day."
Today is the day. Doing our best, living each day to
the fullest is the art of living. Yesterday is gone, and
we don't know whether we will be here tomorrow.
If we do a good job of living today, and if tomorrow
comes for us, then the chances are we will do a good
job when it arrives—so why worry about it?

The A.A. way of life is the way we always should
have tried to live. "Grant us the serenity to accept the
things we cannot change, courage to change the things
we can, and the wisdom to know the difference."
These thoughts become part of our daily lives. They

are not ideas of resignation but of the recognition of certain basic facts of living.

The fact that A.A. is a spiritual program didn't scare me or raise any prejudice in my mind. I couldn't afford the luxury of prejudice. I had tried my way and had failed.

When I joined A.A., I did so for the sole purpose of getting sober and staying sober. I didn't realize I would find so much more, but a new and different outlook on life started opening up almost immediately. Each day seems to be so much more productive and satisfying. I get so much more enjoyment out of living. I find an inner pleasure in simple things. Living just for today is a pleasant adventure.

Above all, I am grateful to A.A. for my sobriety, which means so much to my family, friends, and business associates, because God and A.A. were able to do for me something I was unable to do for myself.

(10)

TIGHTROPE

Trying to navigate separate worlds was a lonely charade that ended when this gay alcoholic finally landed in A.A.

DRINKING WAS ALWAYS a part of my family background. All the men in my family drank; my father—and later, my brothers—were heavy drinkers. As long as a person held down a job, didn't embarrass his family or friends too frequently, and kept out of trouble, he was entitled to get drunk on a regular basis. Drinking was an adult thing to do, a part of growing up. I don't believe it ever crossed my mind that I shouldn't drink.

I was raised in a conservative religion, and I commuted to religious schools some distance from home. Because I had a quick mind and was comfortable with academics, I became something of a teacher's pet. As a result, I was a serious, shy, somewhat bookish child and teenager who found it difficult to relate to my peers. So when I went away to college, I was an alcoholic waiting to happen. My relation to alcohol was a love affair from the very beginning. Although I wasn't too thrilled with the taste, I loved the effects. Alcohol helped me to hide my fears; the ability to converse was an almost miraculous gift to a shy and lonely individual.

It was at this time that I also began to struggle with

the question of my sexuality. For me, the idea of being homosexual—the word *gay* wasn't then in common use—was unthinkable. Drinking helped me to forget and evade. Also, it provided some cover; when you are drunk, people are not surprised at an inability or disinclination to make any serious moves toward a woman. This struggle continued throughout years of unsuccessful dating and pretending.

When I eventually decided to act on my desires, the guilt and the shame—as well as the drinking—increased. Now I had to hide not only my thoughts but also my conduct. I always tried to project the image of the conservative, masculine, deep-voiced loner with the mysterious, possibly tragic, but always heterosexual love affair in the past. I wound up living two separate and distinct lives—that of the gay man with friends and interests to match and that of the straight man with a totally separate set of friends and interests.

I had to walk this tightrope while trying to build a solid professional life as well. After college I had gone on to law school, where drinking on a daily basis became the norm. I justified myself with the thought that a few drinks helped me to relax and "focus" on my studies. Somehow, I managed to do well in law school and to land several prestigious legal positions afterward. I soon learned that I could not drink during the day; if I had even one drink at lunch, the rest of the afternoon would be lost. Instead, I postponed my drinking until immediately after work and would then make up for lost time.

Work in a law firm added a third side to my already divided life. Now I had to try to maintain social relations with clients, members, and associates of the firm, in addition to my gay and straight friends from my private lives. Needless to say, as the drinking increased, things became ever more confused. Eventually, the pressures became too great. I had formed a serious relationship and decided that I could no longer carry on the deception. Instead, I would change careers and go into teaching.

For a while things seemed to be going well. But the slide toward active alcoholism was slowly accelerating. I had had my first blackout several years before. At that time I told myself that if it ever happened again, I would stop drinking. It happened again—and again and again—but I didn't stop. I was always able to come up with some explanation, excuse, or rationalization that justified my continued drinking. In time, personality changes began to occur with regularity when I drank. I had always had a sharp tongue; when drinking, I frequently became vitriolic. At other times I could be charming and affectionate, sometimes too much so. People never knew just what I would do or say.

After a few years I was a nightly blackout drinker. My lover drank heavily as well, and I began to compare my drinking with his. I argued to myself that I could not have a problem because his drinking was worse than mine at times. In fact, I suggested that he might try A.A. When he did try this Fellowship, I did all I could to undermine his efforts to get sober—his recovery would present an obvious, if unacknowledged, threat to my drinking. Eventually, the stress became too much and we broke up, but not before I had succeeded in undermining his recovery.

The slide continued. Most of my friends were unwilling to put up with my conduct—the verbal and sometimes physical abuse, the midnight phone calls, the forgotten invitations, and the selfish disregard of anything but my own need to drink. Those few friends who did not withdraw were forced away by my resentments and increasing paranoia. I cut people out of my life, refusing to return phone calls and ignoring them when we met by chance. By the end of my drinking, only two people were willing to have anything to do with me on a social basis, and both were heavy drinkers who were not surprised by my actions.

The cases in which disaster struck when I drank outside my home increased. I made inappropriate passes at parties, or at people at work—both men and women. At other times I awakened battered or with my watch or wallet missing, or in the company of strangers whose names I did not remember and did not want to know. There were the inevitable injuries and accidents. I was ejected from bars because I would steal tips or change from bartenders or other customers to pay for the drinks I could no longer afford. At other times I would get into arguments and be forced to leave.

In consequence, I made the seemingly logical decision not to drink outside the house. Instead, most of my drinking was now solitary. When I left work, I would have a few stiff drinks at dinner and then go home. I would stop off at the kitchen to pick up a glass, some ice, and some mixer. I would go to my bedroom, where I kept half-gallon bottles of gin and vodka, and "read" while the ice melted, the mixer ran out, and sometimes the glass broke. Every night was blackout drinking. The really bad times were when I would have to struggle outside to a liquor store or bar late at night, weaving and trying not to stagger, because I had miscalculated and run out of alcohol.

I found it increasingly difficult to do anything more than work and drink. I was afraid to use public transportation or even to walk on the streets. My stomach was constantly upset and my doctor had diagnosed a number of intestinal disorders. Even though I rarely drank away from home, my body was covered with bruises because I often fell down during blackouts. I never wore short-sleeved shirts, even in summer, because people would ask me about the bruises. One morning I awoke with a numb leg and found that I had somehow ruptured two spinal discs while in a blackout at home.

For the last four years I lived alone in a small house. The ceiling of one room had collapsed, and plaster dust was everywhere, coating the garbage and newspapers that littered the floor. Empty food cartons, beer cans, bottles, and dirty clothes lay where they were tossed. I had gotten a cat because the mice were out of control. But I was not conscientious about cleaning up after the cat. It is not surprising that I had few visitors and neighbors tended to avoid me.

The last few months were filled with fear and self-pity. I began to contemplate suicide with increasing regularity, yet I was afraid of dying. I remember thinking that this life would go on and on, never getting better and slowly fading away to nothing.

Then I began to hear the whispers. I became convinced that there were people living in my house. I couldn't see them, except for occasional glimpses out of the corner of my eyes, and so I concluded that they were small and somehow living in the walls or under the stairs. I could hear them plotting to kill me. There were nights when I went to bed with a knife in hand to protect myself. Other nights I locked myself in the bathroom so they couldn't get me. One night I left a shot of vodka on the mantelpiece so they would go after that and leave me alone.

Then a miracle occurred. An evening came when I decided to have one drink outside and then go straight home. I had that drink and left for my house. The next thing I remember is waking up the next morning with a stranger I had picked up in a bar. Apparently I had gone on autopilot and, in a blackout resulting from just one drink, had gone on a tear. The look of disgust and pity on the face of that stranger was the jolt I needed. I suddenly realized that my life was totally insane, that my drinking was out of control, and that I was either an alcoholic or a candidate for committal to the local asylum. Not wanting to be locked up, I decided to try Alcoholics Anonymous.

I called my former lover, and he put me in contact with an individual who took me to my first meeting. Although I can barely recall anything about that meeting, I heard two things I have never forgotten. The first was "You don't have to drink again." This was a total revelation to me. For a long time I had believed that alcohol was one of the few positive things left in my life. I looked forward to my first drink every evening and thought that alcohol was holding my life together. I had to drink to survive, let alone to have any comfort. Yet here, people who had been in the same boat were telling me that I didn't have to drink.

I don't think I believed them that night, but it gave me enough hope to avoid drinking the rest of the day.

The second thing I heard was "You don't have to be alone anymore." This too was a revelation. For years I had rejected or been rejected by friends, lovers, family, and God. I was alone and afraid. My life had narrowed to work and the bottle, and work remained in the picture only because it was necessary to enable me to buy the bottle. The isolation and loneliness that alcoholism brought weighed heavily on me, and those words lifted an immense burden of fear. Again, I'm not sure that I completely believed, but I felt hope for the first time in years.

I did not fall in love with A.A. at first glance. The man who took me to my first meeting later became my first sponsor, and he had to put up with objections, arguments, questions, and doubts—everything a trained but very muddled legal mind could throw at him. He was gentle with me. He did not push his opinions on me. He had the sense to see that I was so afraid and so used to being alone that I could not face a "hard sell" approach. He listened to my questions, answered some, and suggested that I could best answer others myself. He refused to argue but was willing to explain and share his own experiences. I had asked him to be my sponsor before I knew what he did for a living and felt I could not back out of the relationship when I discovered he was a minister.

My alcoholism and my lifestyle had led me to reject the religion and the God of my upbringing; I had never replaced them. Instead, I was an agnostic, doubting the existence of God but afraid to say so in case I was wrong. My self-pity and sense of victimization led me to doubt that a caring God could exist; if He did, why had He given me so many problems? I was very wary of the members who talked of their spiritual lives.

My sponsor was a living damper on my intolerance. But even more, he told me that it would be all right for me to doubt God, that A.A. was not a religious program and, to belong, I did not have to adhere to any set of beliefs.

He suggested that for me a good starting point would simply be recognition of the fact that I had failed in running the world—in short, acceptance of the fact that I was not God. He also suggested that I might try occasionally to act as if I believed. Somewhere I had heard that it is easier to act yourself into a new way of thinking than to think yourself into a new way of acting, and this made sense in the context of "acting as if."

I also thought that the people in meetings some-times seemed too standoffish and overly concerned with their friends and acquaintances rather than with me, the newcomer. Well on my way toward develop-ing a resentment, I expressed this to my sponsor. He suggested that I might find people more communica-tive if I took the coffee-making commitment for the group I had joined. Although I thought I was far too special to make coffee, I did figure that as coffee maker I would have the chance to select decent cook-ies, and so I agreed. My sponsor was right again. People did start to speak with me—if only to complain about the coffee and cookies. But once a conversation starts, communication frequently continues.

I started to work on the steps, and even with my

difficulty over the Third Step and "the God concept," I began to develop a sense of trust in the A.A. group and in the ideals of the Fellowship as a manifestation of a Power greater than myself. Although for many years I did not come to an acceptance of a God who intervened personally and directly in the lives of individuals, I was able to accept the idea of a force that moved in the rooms and animated A.A. members with a sense of unconditional love. That satisfied my spiritual needs for a long time.

A later sponsor took me through Steps Eight and Nine and provided me with support during some trying times. In my third year of sobriety, I was bedridden for over a month as a result of that earlier injury to my spinal discs, my father died, a relationship ended, and the AIDS epidemic started to hit home among my friends and acquaintances. Over the course of that and the next few years, almost half of my gay friends died. I learned in that year that if I ask for help, my Higher Power will never give me anything I can't handle.

It was in this period that I started to turn to service beyond the group level. I had helped in founding the first gay A.A. group in my part of town and was elected general service representative after having served in other group offices. I knew nothing of general service at that time, and I decided to learn what it was all about so I could do a decent job and be able to pass it on to a successor as quickly as possible. After two years I went on to do a number of other service jobs for A.A.

In all these positions I never felt obligated to conceal or deny my sexuality. I have always felt that the representatives of groups in my area were concerned only with how we carried the message of recovery, not with what I might do in my personal life.

When I first came to this Fellowship, I had lost my health and sanity, my friends, much of my family, my self-respect, and my God. In the years since, all of these have been restored to me. I no longer have the sense of impending doom. I no longer wish for death or stare at myself in the mirror with loathing. I have come to terms with my Higher Power; after more than a dozen years in the A.A. Fellowship, I was able to join a religious group and have now become active in that organization. I have a full, happy life, with friends and loving family. Recently I retired and have begun to travel throughout the world. I have attended and felt welcome at A.A. meetings wherever I have gone inside and outside the United States. Even more important, I have returned to my home group and am still asked to make coffee. I now have an extended family that is international in scope, all the members of which are joined by bonds of shared pain and joy.

(11)

FLOODED WITH FEELING

When a barrier to God collapsed, this self-described agnostic was at Step Three.

HEN I FIRST came to A.A., I thought everyone had drunk more than I had, that everybody had gotten into more trouble. But I kept coming to meetings, and after a while, I began to hear the beginnings of their stories. I came to realize that I was on the same road. I just hadn't gone as far—yet.

I had my first drink in my senior year of high school. That first night, I slipped out of the window so my parents wouldn't hear me leave. There were four of us, and we only brought four bottles of home brew. I never made that mistake again!

The next week, a bunch of us went camping, and we brought cases of beer. We finished it all. The others drank a lot too, but I was the one who woke up in the middle of the night and started wandering around the countryside by the light of the moon. I was the one who walked for miles searching for something. I know now what I was looking for. Unlike the rest of them, I wanted another drink.

I had a great time that summer between high school and college. It revolved around drinking: drinking and football, drinking and hunting, drinking and playing pool, drinking and driving. Nothing really bad happened, but it could have. I nearly got arrested. A friend just missed being shot. The car I was riding in stopped just before it crashed.

I don't think most moderate, social drinkers remember so clearly the night they had their first drink. I'm sure that very few of them make that date into an annual celebration by getting as drunk as possible. It was in my second year of drinking that I started saying that if you can still feel your face, you're not drunk enough. In my third year I drank homemade peach wine, and when it was gone, I had some whiskey. That night, I vomited, in a blackout.

Soon I found that I didn't get as sick on vodka. Drinking vodka was like something out of science fiction—I could be someplace one moment and instantly transported to somewhere else the next. I could never seem to find that happy balance. I remember going to a party. I started drinking, and suddenly I could talk to anybody. I was having a lot of fun, but I kept on drinking. Soon I could barely walk. A friend drove me home that night, but I sometimes drove a car when I was too drunk to walk.

I became a teacher and didn't drink too often for a while. When I did drink, I almost always got drunk. The teachers would get together a couple times a year for a poker party. I usually didn't drink anything. One time I did, and I made a fool of myself. I decided that drinking just wasn't fun anymore. I quit.

My cure for drinking was isolation. I would get up, go to work, come home, watch TV, and go to bed. It got to the point where I couldn't remember anything good that had ever happened. I couldn't imagine anything good ever happening in the future. Life had shrunk down to an endless, awful now. The depression became so bad that only medical treatment kept me from killing myself. After seven months the doctor took me off the medication. I wasn't suicidal, but I wasn't very happy, either.

A new teacher came to my school, and I invited myself over to her place for a drink. I remember telling her, as I lifted the glass, that this might not be such a great idea but, "I believe it's worth the risk." As casually as that, I began drinking again. At the winter break she went to visit her boyfriend. I was alone again.

Two days before Christmas I went to a party. I wasn't going to drink because I had driven there and I knew that drinking and driving was a bad idea for me. I wasn't feeling particularly good or bad—just a little uncomfortable because I didn't know most of the people there. I was sitting on the couch one minute and up drinking a glass of wine the next. There was no conscious premeditation at all.

This is the point when many people say, "And I went on drinking for ten more years." Instead, an odd thing happened. A few days later a teacher came up to me at work and said that she was an alcoholic and that she was going to A.A. She had never seen me drink, so I don't know what made her do that.

The next day I asked her how often she went to meetings. "Once a week?" I asked. No. She said that she had been going nearly every day for almost six months. That seemed a little extreme, but I thought that maybe if I went to a meeting with her, it might help her out. Besides, I was lonely.

Halfway through the meeting I had the strangest idea. People were introducing themselves as alcoholics, and I had the urge to do the same. This was peculiar because I wasn't, of course. Later, my friend asked me what I thought of the meeting. I said that I didn't really know. It was only much later I realized that for the first time in years, I felt that I belonged.

The next day we went to another meeting, and this time I did say I was an alcoholic. I went to the third meeting by myself. I was nervous. I felt as if I were about to jump out of my skin. I did something that was amazing to me. Before the meeting I stuck out my hand and introduced myself as a newcomer. I had someone to talk to. I calmed down.

From time to time I would tell the truth. I said in a meeting that I was afraid to get a sponsor because I was afraid he might ask me to do something. I left that meeting with a phone number. I called it, and sure enough, my new sponsor started leading me through the steps, using the Big Book.

I called him every day. I told him that I just didn't want to be an alcoholic. He said it didn't matter what I wanted. The question I had to answer for myself was whether I was or I wasn't. He even suggested that I could try a little controlled drinking if I wasn't sure. I knew I had never been able to do that. I didn't have to do any more "research." All I really had to do was review the drinking I had already done.

I remember telling a friend years ago that I didn't have a drinking problem, I had a stopping problem. We laughed. It was true, but there was something else going on, something that never occurred to me until I came to A.A. I didn't just have a stopping problem. I had a starting problem too. No matter how often I stopped, or for how long, I always started drinking again.

After not drinking for three months, I was on the phone with the friend who had taken me to that first meeting. I was complaining to her about problems at work and how my sponsor didn't understand me. Later in the conversation I mentioned that even when I described myself as agnostic, I thought maybe something was watching out for me. She asked, "Isn't it about time you made a decision?"

I knew where to look in the Big Book, and I had been careful to avoid it until then. I turned to the Third Step Prayer and quietly read it to her over the phone. Nothing happened. I didn't expect anything to happen. Then, for some reason, I turned back to the words, "No one among us has been able to maintain anything like perfect adherence to these principles." They echoed in my mind.

Something happened. A barrier collapsed. Without moving or speaking, I was carried away on a flood of emotion, yet at the same time, I was completely aware of myself and my surroundings. I could hear my friend's voice asking what had happened to me. I couldn't answer. I still can't explain it.

I know that I took the Third Step (turning my will and my life over to a Higher Power) that night because I began writing a Fourth Step inventory the next day, and I continued to write until I did the Fifth Step with my sponsor. Soon I had a list of people I had harmed. I talked about each of the amends with my sponsor. By the time I had started setting things right with my family, I began to feel a lot better.

More than eleven years later it's hard to recapture

the feelings of that night. What do I believe as a result? I can say that doubting God's existence was no barrier at all to a spiritual experience. Also, I can say that having such an experience didn't lead me to any certainty about God. Alcoholics Anonymous gives me the freedom to believe and to doubt as much as I need to.

I do know that my life is different now. I haven't had a drink since I came to A.A. I have fewer resentments, and I don't spend much time thinking about the past. I've found that my experience can be of help to other people. I have come to believe that hard times are not just meaningless suffering and that something good might turn up at any moment. That's a big change for someone who used to come to in the morning feeling sentenced to another day of life. When I wake up today, there are lots of possibilities. I can hardly wait to see what's going to happen next.

I keep coming back because it works.

(12)

WINNER TAKES ALL

Legally blind but no longer alone, she found a way to stay sober, raise a family, and turn her life over to the care of God.

*M*Y PARENTS WERE very much in love and had been married a couple of years when they decided to start a family. They were so excited when their first son was born. They owned their own small business, and with the arrival of their son their lives seemed perfect—until tragedy struck. When their son was about two years old, my parents were eating at a local restaurant, and he was dancing to the music of the juke box and having a good time. He followed some older children outside and was hit by a car. My parents carried him in an ambulance to a hospital thirty miles away, where he was pronounced dead on arrival. My parents were stricken with grief.

One miracle that brought them some joy in the midst of all the pain was that Mom found out she was pregnant. When this little girl was born, she brought them great joy. She did not take the place of her brother, but in her own right she did bring them joy. They tried again to have another little boy, but they had me instead. Not only was I a girl, but I was also born legally blind. A year or so later they finally did get the boy they wanted, and there was a big party to celebrate his birth.

From the very beginning I felt different and un-
wanted. At a very young age, as children do, I had to
make sense out of my life, so I came to the conclusion
that I was bad and God knew I was bad, so God made
me handicapped to punish me. I thought that the un-
dertow of sadness in my family was because of me.
Later I realized that a part of it might have been due
to my handicap, but there was still a lot of grieving
going on. My father turned to alcohol and was a very
angry man. When we were growing up, he was very
critical. I was told things on a daily basis, like I was
dumb and lazy. When I started school, I truly realized
how different I was from other children. Children
were very cruel and made fun of me. I could tell you
many stories of times I was treated badly, and although the stories would be different, the feeling was
always the same. I was not good enough, and I hurt.

Special education was mostly for the mentally re-
tarded, so I did not get much support from my teachers, though there were two teachers who made a
difference in my life. One was a third-grade teacher
who got me large-print books. It felt so good that
someone understood I had a problem, but that was
overruled by the embarrassment I felt trying to carry
those big books around. The other teacher was a
freshman high school teacher who flunked me. It was
as if I heard her say, "You can do better." All the other
teachers just let me pass, whether I knew the material
or not. When I got out of high school, I felt as if I had
gotten out of some kind of prison. I graduated 150th
out of a class of 152, and I felt that I was dumb.

It was during my high school years that I discovered
alcohol, and my problems were over. Now I was pretty

and smart. For the first time I felt as if I fit in. I still could not see—oh well, no big deal, I felt good.

I got married and had two children. I married a man who was not or could not be honest. For several years after we were married, I did not drink. My sister went through a divorce and moved to the town I was living in. To be a good sister I went out with her, for she knew no one in the town. We went to a country western place that had a beer bust. You just paid a certain amount to get in, and you could drink all you wanted to drink. I thought I had arrived in heaven. We did this several times a week, and then she started meeting people and started dating. Well, I couldn't drive, so I started drinking more and more at home.

Several years later alcohol had control over my life. I had a tee shirt that I just loved; it said, "I used to hate myself in the morning. Now I sleep till noon." That described my feelings totally.

When my daughter had to go to the hospital, I stayed sober for the five days she was there and told myself that I had licked the alcohol problem. On the way home from the hospital, I got drunk again. I cannot tell you the number of times I tried to stop on my own. My son would look at me and say,"Mom, why do you have to drink so much?" He was about eleven years old at the time. So one night I got on my knees and said, "God, change me or let me die."

It was at this point in my life that I called Alcoholics Anonymous and asked for help. They sent two ladies over to my house. They sat with me, and I told them that I drank because my marriage was bad. One of the ladies held my hand and said, "That is not why you drink." I told them I drank because I was part

German. She patted my hand and said, "No, that's not why you drink." Then I told them I drank because I was legally blind. They said, "No, that's not why you drink," and they started to explain to me that alcoholism is a disease. They shared their stories with me and told me how alcohol had taken over their lives.

I started going to meetings, and my story sounded so dull next to some of the stories I heard. The most interesting thing I could think to tell was about the time my friends, who were also drunk, let me drive the car. I almost got us all killed—but what fun! Legally blind, drunk, and behind the wheel of a car. God was really taking care of me and the other people on the road that night; I just didn't know it at the time.

The truth is, most of my drinking was done at home alone. I would call people and talk, and the following mornings were awful, trying to piece together what I had said. I would say things to my husband like, "Wasn't that an interesting call last night," hoping he would volunteer information. My hands were beginning to shake without the alcohol, yet when I got to A.A., I wasn't sure I belonged because my drunkalog was not exciting.

Then one night at an A.A. meeting a friend said that even though he had been in jail and done lots and lots of stuff, he was no different from me. He felt the same things I felt. It was then that I knew I was not unique, that the people did understand the pain inside me.

I met a lady who had a handicapped child, and we learned so much from each other. One important thing that I learned was that *handicapped* is not a

four-letter word. *Handicapped* is not a dirty word. I
learned that I was not bad—that I was one of God's
special children, that God had a plan for my life. The
people of A.A. showed me how my past could and
would become an asset. I got a sponsor and started
working the steps. The promises of the Big Book
started coming true for me. The feeling of uselessness
and self-pity went away, and I could see how my experiences could help others.

When I was three years sober, I made one of the
most difficult decisions I had ever made. I left the
marriage. I did not leave because I didn't love him. I
still love him, but the marriage was not a healthy place
for me to be. I found myself with two children to
support. I was legally blind and had no job skills.
When I moved out, I first moved into public housing
for blind people. This was a shocking experience for
me, but it was full of growth. For the first time in my
life, I was learning to accept my handicap. Before this
I would plan out my day as if I could see and then
plan it out again based on the fact that my vision was
limited.

Through the commission for the blind, I got involved in a program that helps blind people become
self-employed. After three months of training, I
moved to a city a couple of hundred miles away where
I knew no one. I lived in an apartment that was about
a mile from a coffee shop that I operated. I would
walk to work at 6:30 a.m., carrying $200 in opening
cash on a dark road, and I was afraid. I had two people working for me, and on my second day one of
them did not show up. I had never run a business before, and my three months of training just didn't seem

enough. It was a hard time for me. A lady from a major food company came by to take my grocery order, and I didn't have a clue how much coffee, bacon, or hamburger meat I needed. She shared with me what the previous manager had ordered and helped me place an order.

God only knows how we got on the subject, but she was a member of A.A. and later would become my new sponsor. She picked me up and took me to meetings. At one of the meetings, I met a guy who for the next year picked me up and drove me to work. I paid him a dollar each morning. I am sure that did not cover his gas, but it helped me to feel I was paying my way. For the first time in my life, I was now supporting myself.

This is just an example of how God works in my life. No longer did I have to drink, but it was much more than that. Everything I needed was provided. I had a God of my understanding that helped me in every aspect of my life.

In working the steps, my life changed. I think differently today; I feel different today. I am new. We have a sign at the A.A. meetings I go to that says, "Expect a Miracle." My sobriety is full of miracles. When my son filled out an application for college, I filled one out too, and was accepted. Soon I will be a senior, and I have a 3.71 grade point average. Thanks to A.A. I have come a long way from being near the bottom of my high school class. It takes me a lot longer to read the material, so I have a CCTV (I put my book under this camera and it comes out in big print on a monitor). I have a talking calculator that helped me get through statistics and a telescope that can help me see the board. I accept help from the disabled student services and gladly make use of the volunteer notetakers.

I learned to accept the things I could not change (in this case my vision) and change the things I can (I could be grateful for and accept the visual aids instead of being embarrassed and rejecting them as I had when I was younger).

I have already told you about some of the miracles that have happened. However, there's more. I want to tell you how I feel inside. I am no longer spiritually bankrupt. It's as if I have a magic source in my life that has provided me with all I need. I just celebrated my twelfth year of sobriety a couple of months ago. When I first came to A.A., I didn't know who I was. My sponsor said, "Great—if you don't know who you are, you can become whomever God wants you to be."

Today I am doing things that I never dreamed possible. More importantly, it is the peace and serenity I feel inside that keeps me coming back. I have been through hard times in and out of sobriety, but before A.A. it didn't matter how good things got—I always had a feeling that something was wrong. Since A.A., it doesn't matter how bad things get—I always have a feeling that everything is going to be all right.

In working the Twelve Steps, my life and my old way of thinking have changed. I have no control over some of the things that happen in my life, but with the help of God I can now choose how I will respond. Today I choose to be happy, and when I'm not, I have the tools of this program to put me back on track.

(13)

ME AN ALCOHOLIC?

Alcohol's wringer squeezed this author—but he escaped quite whole.

WHEN I TRY to reconstruct what my life was like "before," I see a coin with two faces.

One, the side I turned to myself and the world, was respectable—even, in some ways, distinguished. I was father, husband, taxpayer, home owner. I was club-man, athlete, artist, musician, author, editor, aircraft pilot, and world traveler. I was listed in *Who's Who in America* as an American who, by distinguished achievement, had arrived.

The other side of the coin was sinister, baffling. I was inwardly unhappy most of the time. There would be times when the life of respectability and achieve-ment seemed insufferably dull—I had to break out. This I would do by going completely "bohemian" for a night, getting drunk, and rolling home with the dawn. Next day, remorse would be on me like a tiger. I'd claw my way back to respectability and stay there —until the inevitable next time.

The insidiousness of alcoholism is an appalling thing. In all the twenty-five years of my drinking, there were only a few occasions when I took a morning drink. My binges were one-night stands only. Once or twice, during my early drinking, I carried it over into the second day, and only once, that I can remember, did it continue into the third. I was never drunk on the job, never missed a day's work, was seldom rendered totally ineffective by a hangover, and kept my liquor expenses well within my adequate budget. I continued to advance in my chosen field. How could such a man possibly be called an alcoholic? Whatever the root of my unhappiness might turn out to be, I thought, it could not possibly be booze.

Of course I drank. Everybody did in the set which I regarded as the apex of civilization. My wife loved to drink, and we tied on many a hooter in the name of marital bliss. My associates, and all the wits and literary lights I so much admired, also drank. Evening cocktails were as standard as morning coffee, and I suppose my average daily consumption ran a little more or less than a pint. Even on my rare (at first) binge nights, it never ran much over a quart.

How easy it was, in the beginning, to forget that those binges ever happened! After a day or two of groveling remorse, I'd come up with an explanation. "The nervous tension had piled up and just had to spill over." Or, "My physical plant had got a little run-down and the stuff rushed right to my head." Or, "I got to talking and forgot how many I was taking and it hit me." Always we'd emerge with a new formula for avoiding future trouble. "You've got to space your drinks and take plenty of water in between," or "Coat the stomach with a little olive oil," or "Drink anything *but* those damn martinis." Weeks would go by without further trouble, and I'd be assured I'd at last hit on the right formula. The binge had been just "one of those things." After a month it seemed unlikely that it happened. Intervals between binges were eight months.

My growing inward unhappiness was a very real thing, however, and I knew that something would have to be done about it. A friend had found help in psychoanalysis. After a particularly ugly one-nighter, my wife suggested I try it, and I agreed. Educated child of the scientific age that I was, I had complete faith in the science of the mind. It would be a sure cure and also an adventure. How exciting to learn the inward mysteries that govern the behavior of people, how wonderful to know, at last, all about myself! To cut a long story short, I spent seven years and $10,000 on my psychiatric adventure, and emerged in worse condition than ever.

To be sure, I learned many fascinating things and many things that were to prove helpful later. I learned what a devastating effect it can have on a child to coddle him and build him up, and then turn and beat him savagely, as had happened to me.

Meanwhile I was getting worse, both as regards my inward misery and my drinking. My daily alcoholic consumption remained about the same through all this, with perhaps a slight increase, and my binges remained one-nighters. But they were occurring with alarming frequency. In seven years the intervals between them decreased from eight months to ten days! And they were growing uglier. One night I barely made my downtown club; if I'd had to go another fifty feet, I'd have collapsed in the gutter. On another occasion I arrived home covered with blood. I'd deliberately smashed a window. With all this it was becoming increasingly hard to maintain my front of distinction and respectability to the world. My personality was stretched almost to splitting in the effort;

schizophrenia stared me in the face, and one night I was in a suicidal despair.

My professional life looked fine on the surface. I was now head of a publishing venture in which nearly a million dollars had been invested. My opinions were quoted in *Time* and *Newsweek* along with pictures. I addressed the public by radio and TV. It was a fantastic structure, built on a crumbling foundation. It was tottering and it had to fall. It did.

After my last binge I came home and smashed my dining room furniture to splinters, kicked out six windows and two balustrades. When I woke up sober, my handiwork confronted me. It is impossible for me to reproduce my despair.

I'd had absolute faith in science, and only in science. "Knowledge is power," I'd always been taught. Now I had to face up to the fact that knowledge of this sort, applied to my individual case, was *not* power. Science could take my mind apart expertly, but it couldn't seem to put it together again. I crawled back to my analyst, not so much because I had faith in him, but because I had nowhere else to turn.

After talking with him for a time, I heard myself saying, "Doc, I think I'm an alcoholic."

"Yes," he said, surprisingly, "you are."

"Then why in God's name haven't you told me so during all these years?"

"Two reasons," he said. "First, I couldn't be sure. The line between a heavy drinker and an alcoholic is not always clear. It wasn't until just lately that, in your case, I could draw it. Second, you wouldn't have believed me even if I had told you."

I had to admit to myself that he was right. Only

through being beaten down by my own misery would I ever have accepted the term "alcoholic" as applied to myself. Now, however, I accepted it fully. I knew from my general reading that alcoholism was irreversible and fatal. And I knew that somewhere along the line I'd lost the power to stop drinking. "Well, Doc," I said, "what are we going to do?"

"There's nothing I can do," he said, "and nothing medicine can do. However, I've heard of an organization called Alcoholics Anonymous that has had some success with people like you. They make no guarantees and are not always successful. But if you want to, you're free to try them. It might work."

Many times in the intervening years I have thanked God for that man, a man who had the courage to admit failure, a man who had the humility to confess that all the hard-won learning of his profession could not turn up the answer. I looked up an A.A. meeting and went there—alone.

Here I found an ingredient that had been lacking in any other effort I had made to save myself. Here was—*power!* Here was power to live to the end of any given day, power to have the courage to face the next day, power to have friends, power to help people, power to be sane, power to stay sober. That was seven years ago—and many A.A. meetings ago—and I haven't had a drink during those seven years. Moreover, I am deeply convinced that so long as I continue to strive, in my bumbling way, toward the principles I first encountered in the earlier chapters of this book, this remarkable power will continue to flow through me. What *is* this power? With my A.A. friends, all I can say is that it's a Power greater than myself. If pressed, all I can do is follow the psalmist who said it long before me: "*Be still,* and know that I am God."

My story has a happy ending but not of the conventional kind. I had a lot more hell to go through. But what a difference there is between going through hell without a Power greater than one's self, and with it! As might have been predicted, my teetering tower of worldly success collapsed. My alcoholic associates fired me, took control, and ran the enterprise into bankruptcy. My alcoholic wife took up with someone else, divorced me, and took with her all my remaining property. The most terrible blow of my life befell me after I'd found sobriety through A.A. Perhaps the single flicker of decency that shone through the fog of my drinking days was a clumsy affection for my two children, a boy and a girl. One night my son, when he was only sixteen, was suddenly and tragically killed. The Higher Power was on deck to see me through, sober. I think He's on hand to see my son through too.

There have been some wonderful things too. My new wife and I don't own any property to speak of, and the flashy successes of another day are no longer mine. But we have a baby who, if you'll pardon a little post-alcoholic sentimentality, is right out of heaven. My work is on a much deeper and more significant level than it ever was before, and I am today a fairly creative, relatively sane human being. And should I have more bad times, I know that I'll never again have to go through them alone.

14

THE PERPETUAL QUEST

This lawyer tried psychiatrists, biofeedback, relaxation exercises, and a host of other techniques to control her drinking. She finally found a solution, uniquely tailored, in the Twelve Steps.

WHEN I WAS a newly minted lawyer starting out in the practice of criminal law, there were five of us in our law office. My favorite lawyer was the eccentric, disheveled, wild-eyed Irish law professor who was brilliant or crazy, depending on your point of view, constantly cleaning out his pipe bowl with a black fingernail and tossing back vodka martinis whenever he got the chance. Then there was the new but world-weary litigation lawyer who told endless tales of his former life of white wine and bouillabaisse under the Mediterranean sun as he conducted his exporting business on the Riviera. Why would he leave such an ideal, wine-drenched job in sunny climes to slog away at law school? I kept wondering. There was also a giant good-hearted bear of a man, who today is a judge, who spent more time listening and helping others than he did practicing criminal law. Into this office landed a pair of know-it-all, fast-acting, but not too experienced young lawyers: my husband and me.

Within a dozen years, three of these five promising lawyers were dead from alcoholism, struck down at the peak of their careers. The judge is still and always has been a sober judge. And I somehow unwittingly, and even while drinking, turned into a corporate counsel and later, thankfully, became a member of Alcoholics Anonymous. The professor's kidneys gave out from one too many martinis; the exporting lawyer kept drinking until he died, despite a liver transplant; my ex-husband died in a fire on what was to be, he had said, his last drunk before going to A.A. *again*, when I was ten years sober. I have been to too many premature funerals due to our good friend alcohol.

My husband and I met and married in law school in a romantic haze of alcohol, twinkling lights, and much promise. We stood out as the only young married couple in our class. We worked and played hard, camped and hiked and skied, threw fabulous parties for our sophisticated friends, and prided ourselves on staying away from drugs. In fact, it was fear that kept me away from drugs—fear that I might not get called to the bar (that's the other bar, the legal one) if I were convicted of possession of illegal street drugs. More importantly, my best friend was wonderful, powerful alcohol, and I loved it.

Until I was four years old, I lived upstairs from a tavern, where I saw a few drunks bounced around. My mother worked for relatives who also lived over the tavern, and whoever had time looked after me. Despite my pleas, my mother married a violent man, and we moved away to a life that made my tavern life look really holy. I kept running away back to the tavern until it was demolished. I still fondly look at pictures of that place.

By the age of fourteen I had my first drunk, which ended in a minor police visit to my home. By the age of eighteen I was a daily drinker, and by age twenty-one I had my first year-long binge in France, which I euphemistically referred to as my study year abroad. I came home very sick and drunk. A few months later I went to bed with a bottle of Scotch one night and decided I would go to law school. If you are having trouble, try something that is even more difficult, to "show them." That was my philosophy. It was enough to drive me to drink, and it did.

At law school we used to drink a lot of beer in student pubs, debating whether rocks had souls and what was the nature of the judicial process, as though it had never been considered before. As new lawyers, my husband and I eagerly beavered in the office early in the morning before running off to court to fearlessly defend the downtrodden. Lunch was the training ground for the perpetual quest for the best martini—usually two or three of them, good for taking away the knot that by this time had permanently lodged itself in my stomach. (I didn't know that it represented fear and that I was not a fearless defender after all.) Afternoons would be full of creative legal arguments in court. If court finished early, maybe we'd make it back to the office, maybe not.

Evenings we drank with the best of them: lawyers, writers, media types, everyone vying to tell the best stories, which of course got funnier and funnier the more we drank and the later it got. When I drank, the fear evaporated and I became articulate and apparently very, very funny—or so they said then. Years later I drank so much that I was no longer funny. But at the time, the drinks and the stories and the camaraderie were as wonderful as I was witty. We would get home to sleep by one or two in the morning, and the next day we would be up early to start all over again. The fortitude and resilience of youth made us invincible.

Unfortunately, by the time we thought it was time to have a "real life" and maybe start a family, the marriage disintegrated. I was then twenty-eight years old, getting divorced, drinking all the time, and seeing a psychiatrist three times a week, trying to solve my problem, whatever it was.

I thought I had found part of the answer when I stumbled into a private controlled-drinking program, which helped me, during the initial thirty-day mandatory period of abstinence, to hook a very large rug, row by row, well into many late nights. "One more row!" I kept saying, gritting my teeth against a drink. My period of abstinence also helped me get a better job in the corporate world, away from all those hard-drinking criminal lawyers, and a new three-story, four-bedroom house. Just what every single woman needs! It helped me to quit the psychiatrist. During this abstinence, I also got out of a sick relationship, which reproduced the violence of my childhood.

Incredibly, I did not connect the improved manage-ability of my life in this short period of abstinence to the absence of booze. It didn't matter in the long run, because unfortunately, I started to get drunk again. I recall being fixated on that first glass of wine I was allowed to drink the day my coach informed me that I was ready to start drinking in controlled fashion. My tongue was almost hanging out.

Many drunks later, I tried everything else I could

find: more therapy, different psychiatrists (it was always to be the next one who would solve my problem), biofeedback, relaxation exercises, Antabuse, lots of self-help books from Freud to Jung, to every current fad that was published or taught. All to no avail, of course, because I'd always end up drunk.

Came the day when I realized that I couldn't keep dragging myself off to work in the morning and spending half the energy of every day concealing the fact that I was a barely functioning drunk. I would go home to drink until I passed out, come to in the middle of the night terrified, listen to the radio, and get worldwide telephonitis, finally dozing off at dawn, just in time to be awakened by the alarm and start the process all over again. I gave up on relationships of any significance, saw my friends less, and stopped committing myself to most social occasions because I could never count on being sober. More and more, I just worked and went home to drink—and the drinking was starting to outstrip the working.

One day I was so hungover at lunchtime I called a friend and had a little cry. "I've tried everything and nothing works," I said, reciting my litany of doctors and different therapies. I did not remember that thirteen years earlier, when I was twenty-one years old, I had attended a few meetings of Alcoholics Anonymous after waking up one morning not knowing where I was. I had just started law school and was terrified most of the time, so I went on a binge to quell the fear, which only got worse. I have no idea what made me go to A.A. way back then. But there were no young people at the meetings, and people kept marveling at how young and fresh I looked. (No one at A.A. said that when I came back thirteen years later.)

My friend suggested that we contact a man she knew who was a member of Alcoholics Anonymous, and I agreed to call him. "Perhaps he could call you," she said helpfully, which was the key, because by that night I was just fine and didn't need any outside help aside from a drink or two. But he kept phoning and bothering me about going to a meeting. When he told me he went to A.A. meetings three or four times a week, I thought, Poor man, he has nothing better to do. What a boring life it must be for him, running around to A.A. meetings with nothing to drink! Boring indeed: no bouncing off walls, no falling down stairs, no regular trips to hospital emergency rooms, no lost cars, and on and on.

My first meeting back at A.A. was on an unseasonably hot June night, but there was not a cool drink in sight in that church basement. The smoke could have choked a horse (today, it is much improved), and a fanatical woman with smiling bright eyes eagerly explained to me that they had this important book I should buy. Thinking that they were doing the book promotion because they needed the money, I said firmly, "I'll give you the money, but I don't want your book!" Which about sums up my attitude and explains why, for the next few months, I continued to get drunk in spite of dragging my body to meetings every few days. I would stare at the large vodka bottle in my kitchen cupboard and say, "You won't get me!" but it did; I always lost the battle and ended up drunk.

My last hangover was on a Friday before a long summer weekend. I had struggled through the day feeling small and hopeless, hiding the trembling of my hands when I had to sign documents, and desperately working to wrap my tongue around words during meetings. Later that Friday night, after an agonizingly long workday, I was dragging myself up the deserted street thinking that the whole world, except for me, had someplace to go on that long weekend, and what's more, they all had someone to go with.

The first difference between that night and all the others was that I did not immediately go directly to a bar to get lubricated or home with my regular giant weekend supply of booze. Instead I went to my club to swim, where strangely enough I also did not drink. I was so hungover that I had to give up trying to swim and instead wrapped myself in a bathrobe and sat in a dark corner of the locker room lounge for two hours, feeling desperately sorry for myself.

I don't know what happened during those two hours, but close to eight o'clock, I leaped up, jumped into my clothes, and raced off to a meeting I'd had no intention of attending. It was a bit like getting a rap on the head with an invisible hammer and having my brain flip over, because the meeting seemed to be radically different from the last time I had been there. The people looked animatedly alive, the weirdos who had been attending before were absent that night, and the books on display actually looked interesting. I bought the book *Alcoholics Anonymous*, listened intently, and then, for the first time, I went for coffee with those people and listened some more.

Late that night at home, there was a presence in the room with me, even though I lived alone. The next morning I knew I didn't have to drink. That night I went to a Step meeting where they discussed Step

Two, "Came to believe that a Power greater than ourselves could restore us to sanity," and I actually talked about God, the one who had abandoned me when I was very little, very frightened, and very hurt. In the weeks and months that followed, I did everything that was suggested to me. I went to a meeting every day, read the books and literature, and got a sponsor who told me to have a quiet time every morning and try to pray and meditate or at least sit still for a few minutes, before racing off for the day. Since I prided myself on adhering to the intellectual principle of not having contempt for anything prior to investigation, I tried to keep an open mind no matter what anyone said and how stupid I thought it was. That probably saved my life.

I joined a downtown group that met near my office right after work at 5:15. (I would not have made it to 8:00 p.m.) Soon, I got into service. I was given bank books, notes of business meetings, and various other instructions and told to do whatever was necessary to keep the meeting going. I did that job for quite some time. I also instituted regular business meetings and found an eager newcomer to whom I eventually turned over the bank book and papers.

I had a lot of problems in those early days, but no matter what the problem, I was repeatedly told to seek more spiritual development, something that did not interest me. I was also told that my purpose here on earth was to be of maximum service to God and the people around me, and that didn't interest me too much either. However, I said nothing, listened, and kept going to meetings, mostly Step discussions, where I heard people talk about how they practiced the Steps and about the Big Book, our selfishness, and helping others. Sometimes, I thought they were nuts, those meetings; often I thought they were boring, but I kept listening and tried to relate.

Soon after a friend of mine was killed by a drunk going the wrong way on the freeway, a truck driver talked about driving long hauls drunk. I was horrified and repelled, until I paused to recall that I used to drive when I couldn't walk straight. When my friend was killed, my A.A. friends said, "Don't drink! Don't think! Go to meetings!" I went to a meeting where I sobbed and gnashed my teeth, but I didn't drink.

I became as compulsive about A.A. as I had been about drinking, which was necessary because I had been told to spend as much time at meetings as I had spent drinking. I went to every A.A. get-together possible and was saturated with A.A. I listened to tapes of A.A. talks. I read and reread the literature and books, laughing into the night over *Dr. Bob and the Good Oldtimers*. I signed up for the *Loners-Internationalist Meeting* in print *(LIM)* and shared the meetings I attended in letters to people who could not get to meetings. This helped me to remember what I had heard, and my sharing helped someone else. I once wrote to a man who received my letter the same day he had killed someone in a car accident, which would no doubt make one very, very thirsty.

Many years later, although alcohol is not part of my life and I no longer have the compulsion to drink, it can still occur to me what a good drink tastes like and what it can do for me, from my stand-at-attention alcoholic taste buds right down to my stretched out tingling toes. As my sponsor used to point out, such thoughts are like red flags, telling me that something is not right, that I am stretched beyond my sober limit. It's time to get back to basic A.A. and see what needs changing. That special relationship with alcohol will always be there, waiting to seduce me again. I can stay protected by continuing to be an active member of A.A.

The hardest thing I had to deal with in sobriety was my own anger and the violence I lived through in my childhood. I had forgiven those involved as best I could, but the mind seems never to forget. I had gratefully received years of outside help because I was told that my drinking was only the symptom of deeper troubles. Yet despite the help of many professionals, I know I would never have recovered from violence and alcoholism without A.A.'s Twelve Steps, which are uniquely tailored for people like me.

Just as importantly, I believe that I recovered through the grace of a Higher Power, despite the fact that I was very angry and wanted nothing to do with God when I arrived at Alcoholics Anonymous. In fact, I did not need to find God. I only needed an open mind, and the spirit found me.

When I was five years sober, I met a man in A.A. who was also five years sober. He said that the rocks in my head fit the holes in his. Today we have a daughter who has never seen her parents drink and who sees them try to help others in Alcoholics Anonymous. We have a nice home and sober family life in a community with lots of A.A. friends and meetings. It's a long, long way from that first A.A. meeting, and it couldn't get much better.

15

A DRUNK, LIKE YOU

The more he listened at meetings, the more he came to know about his own drinking history.

USUALLY OUR stories start out by telling what we were like, what happened, and what we are like now. For me, what it was like was nothing in particular—no problems, nothing special happened. Nothing that I realized, anyhow. Only much later, when I started listening to other people and what happened to them and when and how, did I realize that those things were in my past also.

My story starts in the middle. What happened? My family and I were attending a relative's bris, a Jewish ritual circumcision and baby-naming ceremony. After the ceremonies and brunch I fell asleep. When it was time to leave, they woke me up. The car ride home was very quiet. The wife and my two kids said nothing. Later that day I found out what the problem was.

When they came to wake me, I was very belligerent and threatening. I scared them. They were afraid I would hit them. That was it. I could see that something had to be done. My wife's sister-in-law, who is a social worker, suggested we see a counselor. I thought that might be a good idea. I was having anxiety attacks for no reason. I used to be able to demonstrate products to high-level executives of the corporation I worked for with no problem; now even minor product showcases were becoming difficult.

Also, I was having trouble getting technicians to work for me. In the past I had had my pick because I was good to work for and the projects were fun, with interesting new ideas. I always had a quick temper, but now things were getting out of hand. I would do things like beat up my desk with my desk chair.

And the most serious thing to me was that I was contemplating suicide. I had an actual plan—a plan for an accident that would raise no question in the minds of the insurance company. So in a moment of sanity, I decided it would be a good idea to seek help. If I hadn't lost my marbles, they were at the least very loose.

So my wife and I found a psychiatric social worker at the local Jewish Family Services agency. She saw us as a couple, then individually, then together, and so it went. When we were together, we worked on our interpersonal problems. When I saw her by myself, she would talk about drinking. I don't know why she kept bringing it up. I drank, but not that much. I never even mentioned my drinking except maybe to say, "Yes, I do drink," when she asked. It wasn't the problem—the other things were. One day she read me some questions from a pamphlet, which I answered honestly. She concluded that maybe I drank too much, and we talked about that for several sessions.

One day she asked if I could limit myself to five drinks in a day. I said, "Sure." Was I surprised when I found that I couldn't. That should have been my first clue that she might be right, but it didn't occur to me.

Then I hit on a clever solution. I have several academic degrees, and someone as smart as I was could solve this problem. The idea was to put off the first drink as long as possible and go to bed after the last drink. That worked out okay, and I told the counselor I was able to keep it to five a day with little or no problem. But she said if you had to control something, it was out of control.

During one session she suggested that I try not drinking at all one weekend. "Okay," I said. She also suggested that I send the kids off somewhere for the weekend because I might be irritable.

I used to watch a lot of late-night movies—it was my time to relax by having a few drinks, a habit that started in night school when I had a full-time job and was studying chemistry at night. I had seen movie versions of what happened to people who had drinking problems: *The Lost Weekend, Days of Wine and Roses*, and others. And so I was nervous about raging, losing control, and maybe being violent as my wife had said I was. So we packed up the kids and the booze (all of it) and took all to my wife's parents.

Much to my surprise the weekend went well—no problems—and in the next session I told my counselor so. She said, "What about the meeting?" I said, "What meeting?" She said, "The A.A. meeting." I said, "What A.A. meeting? We never talked about that." She said I had agreed to go to an A.A. meeting. So out came a meeting list. She explained about open and closed meetings. I decided on one I thought would be okay for me—a men's discussion group. They would be my kind of people, and the time fit into my schedule. The meeting list started on Sunday. I never started a project or anything else on a Sunday. Monday was my *M.A.S.H.* night. Tuesday was *Tuesday Night at the Movies,* and I am a big old-movie fan. So Wednesday is when I decided to try this A.A. meeting.

The meeting went okay. We talked about somebody's problem with an anonymity break at his doctor's office. The people at the meeting were telling him stuff that made no sense to me, like "Live and Let Live," "Easy Does It," "One Day at a Time," "use the Serenity Prayer," "talk to your sponsor," and as we went around the table it came my turn. Since they were all saying they were alcoholics, it wasn't too hard for me to say my name and, "Hi, I'm an alcoholic," and suggest that the man should just go to another doctor. He thanked me very much, and after the meeting he said to be sure and come back next week.

During the meeting, somebody mentioned spending too much time at discussion tables when we should have been spending more time at First Step tables for newcomers. So I went to the First Step table the following week. The discussion was very interesting. I didn't think I was "powerless over alcohol," but I knew "my life was unmanageable."

One night we were talking about when we started drinking, and I was saying that I drank all my life. Actually I was given my first drink at my bris. That is usually done when a boy is eight days old. So I said all Jewish boys start drinking early. I had to admit that after that it was just the usual milk and juice until I could sit up at the table with the family, and then there would be kiddush wine every Friday night. Not great stuff—what we got was sweet wine and seltzer, so I didn't drink very much of it. I didn't like it. Later I learned the definition of a social drinker: someone who could take it or leave it.

When I was about ten years old, we all came back from my cousin's bar mitzvah services to celebrate at my grandmother's house. There I had my first real drink. All the adults went over to the table for a schnapps. There were all these little tiny glasses in front of various liquor bottles and everybody was having one, so I had one too. It was good. It was smooth and warm and wonderful. I liked it and went back for another. This one wasn't smooth—it was hot going down, not as wonderful.

After that I drank what I could, when I could, where I could. Not much, not often, not as a ten-year-old. At that First Step table we figured out, or they did anyhow, that that was alcoholic drinking—having one and going back for a second right away. I know now I never had just one drink, ever.

One night they were talking about how much they drank, and one guy said he had so many beers, the next guy talked about shots, one about mixed drinks I never heard of, another about so many pints, and on it went around the table. When my turn came, I said I didn't know. "Wow, that much," they said. "No," I said. I meant I didn't know the amount. I drank mostly at home and poured some in a tall glass and drank that and did it several times. "Well, how many times did you refill?" "I don't know."

Somebody asked it another way. He wanted to know, how many did I buy? "Well," I said, "I stopped in the package store every day and bought one." "Oh," he said. "How many did you have left at the end of the week?" Well, he had me there. "None," I said. He said, "a bottle-a-day man." I never got to say another word—it was settled over my objections.

I saw the counselor once a week, and I went to this men's meeting once a week, and everything was getting better. Once I saw somebody get a ninety-day pin. I decided not to get one. Even though I couldn't see it from where I was sitting, I wasn't going to wear an A.A. sign. One day somebody got a ninety-day pocket piece that he could rub for luck, and I decided to get one of those. After my three months were up, I went to the literature guy and bought one. He said it would be nice if it was presented to me in front of everybody. I wasn't too keen on getting up in front of everyone. He said it would be good for the newcomers; it would show them that the program worked. So I told him okay and asked the leader of the First Step table to give it to me. They were paying him to run the meeting, or so I thought at the time. (Later I found out that they were reimbursing him for the snacks.) So the following week I got my pocket piece and thanked everybody for giving me the power over alcohol. Now I was more powerful than alcohol because for the first time in a long time I could choose not to use it.

A couple of weeks later the large company I was with, which had relocated me and my family at their expense, had a large staff cutback, and I was cut back—fired. I thought I was fire-proof. I was in a very important position, doing important work. I was the chief researcher in developing a new product; I was sitting in on strategic planning meetings. I was very upset. After all, I was better now and back to being a good employee and team player again, but to no avail.

We were able to stay on site in special offices set aside for us to conduct our job search. As part of this job search, I was allowed to go to a professional convention being held in the Southwest.

Now somehow, between the time I lost my job and my flight to the convention, I decided maybe I was not an alcoholic and I needed to test that theory. After all, I was a researcher, and things had to be tested. I decided that on the plane (it seemed like a safe place) I would put the question to the test. If I could have one drink and no more, I was not an alcoholic—alcoholics can't do that. So when the stewardess came by to ask me if I wanted a drink, I said, "Yes." She put two little bottles' worth in a glass ("No ice, thank you very much") and went up the aisle. On her way back she asked if I wanted another, and I said, "Yes." I drank for the whole flight—before dinner, during dinner, and after dinner. As we approached our destination, I searched in my pocket for a pen to fill out the in-flight magazine response card. I found this large coin. I took it out to see what it was. It was my ninety-day pocket piece, and I was reminded of what I was doing. And the thought came to me: Wow, those guys at the meeting were right—I am powerless over alcohol. I put that coin back in my pocket and from that day to this, some 15 ½ years later, I have had no urge to drink.

When I got back to my meeting, I told them what had happened. I don't know why—it was not like the old me to 'fess up to anything. They were concerned only whether I was still drinking. And I said, "No, I'm not." I was worried that they were going to take my coin back. All they wanted to know was what I was going to do now. I had no idea. They did, however. They said I needed a sponsor—so I found a sponsor. They said I needed more meetings. "How many?" I wanted to know. They said I only had to go to meetings on days I would have had a drink. They said I needed to identify, not compare. I didn't know what they meant. What was the difference? Identifying, they said, was trying to see how I was like the people I was with. Comparing, they told me, was looking for differences, usually seeing how I was better than others.

One day we were talking about spiritual awakenings. Everyone talked a little about what happened to them and when and how and all that. Then it came my turn. I said I hadn't had one yet, but I was open to it.

Well, two people were trying to talk at the same time. "What have you been telling us about the airplane flight all this time?" "Well," I said, "I was drinking and the coin reminded me of what I did. And I decided I was powerless and couldn't drink anymore and stopped." One man said, "Well, that's it. What more do you want?" I said, "What about the blinding white flash?" "What about it?" he said. "Read the Big Book. The Appendix explains the concept of a sudden change and a gradual change, and that not everybody has a blinding flash." "Oh," I said, "That was it—that was mine?" "Yes," I was told. "What more do you want?" Actually I wanted something more dramatic, and my sponsor said what he so often did: "So?" And I found myself saying, "Well, if that's it, it will have to do." "Have to do?" he replied. "It was bigger and better than most, and more importantly, it worked. You stopped and didn't start again."

Well, that worked for me. I have stayed in the

Fellowship of Alcoholics Anonymous long enough to find the program in the Big Book and to practice all its principles in all my affairs on a daily basis.

The last big hurdle was closing the meeting with the Lord's Prayer. As a Jew, I was uncomfortable with it and decided to talk to my sponsor about it. So I said, "The Lord's Prayer bothers me. I don't like closing with it." "Oh," he said, "what's the problem?" "Well, I'm Jewish and it's not a Jewish prayer." "Well then," he said "say it in Jewish." I said, "It would still be the Lord's Prayer." "Right," he said. "Then say something else that you like. Your Higher Power, whatever you call it, is helping you, and you need to say thank you."

That was a big step for me; I finally began to separate the religious aspects of my life from A.A.'s spiritual program. Now the big difference to me is that religion is the ritual, and we all differ there, and spirituality is the way we feel about what we do. It's about my personal contact with my personal Higher Power, as I understand Him.

Everything has turned around. I found a new job, which I then decided to leave. I opened my own business. I was able to put my two sons through college at large universities. My oldest son's great passion was to go on road trips to get away from home when it was time to come home on school breaks; now he comes home regularly and brings friends. The younger son comes home often and calls regularly.

My marriage is no longer on the brink and is better than ever. And the best is yet to come. All this and more I owe to the Fellowship in the rooms and the program in the book.

(16)

ACCEPTANCE WAS THE ANSWER

The physician wasn't hooked, he thought—he just prescribed drugs medically indicated for his many ailments. Acceptance was his key to liberation.

IF THERE EVER WAS anyone who came to A.A. by mistake, it was I. I just didn't belong here. Never in my wildest moments had it occurred to me that I might like to be an alcoholic. Never once had my mother even hinted at the idea that, when I grew up, I might like to be president of A.A. Not only did I not think that being an alcoholic was a good idea, I didn't even feel that I had all that much of a drinking problem! Of course, I had *problems,* all sorts of problems. "If you had my problems, you'd drink too" was my feeling.

My major problems were marital. "If you had my wife, you'd drink too." Max and I had been married for twenty-eight years when I ended up in A.A. It started out as a good marriage, but it deteriorated over the years as she progressed through the various stages of qualifying for Al-Anon. At first, she would say, "You don't love me. Why don't you admit it?" Later, she would say, "You don't like me. Why don't you admit it?" And as her disease was reaching the terminal stages, she was screaming, "You hate me! You hate me! Why don't you admit you hate me?" So I admitted it.

I remember very well saying, "There's only one person in the world whose guts I hate worse than yours, and those are my own." She cried a bit and went to bed; that was the only answer to problems that she had left. I cried a bit and then mixed myself another drink. (Today, we don't have to live like that any more.)

Max hadn't gotten that way because I didn't care. Indeed, it seemed that I cared too much. I had sent her to four consecutive psychiatrists, and not one of them had gotten me sober. I also sent my kids to psychiatrists. I remember, one time, even the dog had a psychiatric diagnosis. I yelled at Max, "What do you mean, 'The dog just needs more love'? You tell that dumb cat-and-dog doctor he's not a Beverly Hills psychiatrist. All I want to know is, why does that dog wet in my lap every time I hold him?" (That dog hasn't wet my pants once since I joined A.A., and neither have I!)

The harder I worked with Max, the sicker she got. So, when it ended up at a psycho ward, I wasn't all that surprised. But then, when that steel door slammed shut, and she was the one that went home, I truly was amazed.

I had begun to drink in the early years of pharmacy school, in order to get to sleep. After going to school all day, working in the family drugstore all evening, and then studying until one or two in the morning, I would not be able to sleep soundly, with everything I had been studying going round in my head. I would be half asleep and half awake, and in the morning I would be both tired and stupid. Then I found the solution: At the end of study time, I would drink two beers, jump in bed, sleep real fast, and wake up smart.

I drank my way through schools and always got honors. And as I went through pharmacy school, graduate school, medical school, internship, residency, and specialty training, and finally, went into practice, my drinking kept increasing. But I thought it was because my responsibilities were increasing. "If you had my responsibilities, if you needed the sleep like I do, you'd drink too."

My drinking took place after work hours. I remember finding myself in the middle of the night in the doctors' parking lot at the hospital with one foot in the car and one foot on the ground, not knowing which was the lead foot; finding myself hanging up the telephone—then realizing I had gotten out of bed, answered the phone, turned on the light, and carried on a conversation with a patient. I didn't know whether I had told him to rush to the hospital and I'd meet him there, or to take two aspirin and call me in the morning. With a problem like that, I couldn't go back to sleep. So I'd sit up, watch old Wallace Beery movies on all-night TV, and drink.

The longer the drinking continued, the shorter the time the alcohol would keep me asleep; I would have to drink myself back to sleep again and again throughout the night. But I never became a morning drinker. Instead, I had a 5:00 a.m. shutoff time. If it was one minute before five, I'd drink myself back to sleep. If it was one minute after, I'd stay up and act like a martyr all day. It became progressively harder to get up in the morning, until one day I asked myself what I would do for a patient who felt this rotten. The answer came right back: I'd give him something to pep him up.

So I immediately started taking and shooting pep pills. Eventually, I was taking forty-five milligrams of the long-acting Benzedrine and forty-five of the short-acting just to get out of bed in the morning. I took more through the day to increase the high, and more to maintain it; when I overshot the mark, I'd take tranquilizers to level off. The pep pills affected my hearing at times: I couldn't listen fast enough to hear what I was saying. I'd think, I wonder why I'm saying that again—I've already said it three times. Still, I couldn't turn my mouth off.

For the leveling-off process, I just loved intravenous Demerol, but I found it hard to practice good medicine while shooting morphine. Following an injection, I would have to keep one hand busy scratching my constantly itching nose and would also have sudden uncontrollable urges to vomit. I never got much effect out of codeine and Percodan and the tranquilizers. However, for a period of time I was injecting Pentothal intravenously to put myself to sleep. That's the stuff used when the oral surgeon puts the needle in your vein and says, "Count to ten," and before you get to two, you're asleep. Instant blackout was what it was, and it seemed delightful. I didn't feel I could lie in bed and squirt the stuff in my veins while my kids and wife stood around watching me, so I kept the drug in my bag and the bag in the car and the car in the garage. Luckily, the garage was attached to the house. In the garage I would put the needle in my vein and then try to figure out exactly how much medication to inject to overcome the pep pills while adding to the sleeping pills while ignoring the tranquilizers, in order to get just enough to be able to pull out the needle, jerk the tourniquet, throw it in the car, slam the car door shut, run down the hall, and fall in bed before I fell asleep.

It was hard to judge the right amount. One night I had to put myself back to sleep three times, and then I finally decided to give it up. But to do so, I had to get all the stuff out of the house and out of my possession. In the end I had to do the same with alcohol and *all* pills. I wasn't able to quit chemicals as long as they were in the house. If they were around, I always found a need for them—especially the pills. I never in my life took a tranquilizer, sedative, or pep pill because I was a pillhead. I always took it because I had the symptom that only that pill would relieve. Therefore, every pill was medically indicated at the time it was taken. For me, pills don't produce the desire to swallow a pill; they produce the symptoms that require that the pill be taken for relief. As a physician and pharmacist who had grown up in a drugstore-home, I had a pill for every ill, and I was sick a lot.

Today, I find I can't work my A.A. program while taking pills, nor may I even have them around for dire emergencies only. I can't say, "Thy will be done," and take a pill. I can't say, "I'm powerless over alcohol, but solid alcohol is okay." I can't say, "God could restore me to sanity, but until He does, I'll control myself —with pills." Giving up alcohol alone was not enough for me; I've had to give up all mood- and mind-affecting chemicals in order to stay sober and comfortable.

On two occasions, over weekends, I had decided I

would take absolutely nothing. On each occasion I had a convulsion on Sunday morning. Both times my reaction was that I had had nothing to drink the night before, so obviously alcohol had nothing to do with it. The neurologist in charge of my case didn't think to ask me whether I drank, and I didn't think to tell him. As a result, he couldn't figure out why I had the convulsions, and he decided to send me to the Mayo Clinic. It seemed to me I needed a consultation first. I happened to be the best diagnostician I knew at the time, and certainly I knew my case better than anyone else. So I sat down with me and went over the facts behind the convulsions: personality changes, daily headaches, sense of impending doom, sense of impending insanity. Suddenly, it was obvious to me: I had a brain tumor and would die, and everyone would be sorry for me. The Mayo Clinic seemed like a good place to have my diagnosis confirmed.

After nine days of tests at Mayo, I was put in the locked ward—of all places! That's when that steel door slammed shut, and Max was the one who went home. I didn't like being on the nut ward, and I particularly didn't like being forced to ice cookies on Christmas Eve. So I raised enough fuss that they finally agreed to let me sign out, against medical advice. Max accepted responsibility for me after I had promised never to drink again, never to take another pill, never to swear again, and never to talk to girls again. We got on the plane and immediately had a big fight over whether I'd drink the free booze. Max won; I didn't drink it. But by God, I wouldn't talk or eat either! And that was how Max and I and our two daughters spent Christmas Day, eight years ago.

When we got home, I got a bottle of Scotch and went to bed. The next day, Max called the neurologist and told him about the Mayo psychiatrist's opinion. He arranged for me to see a local psychiatrist, who quickly decided I should be in the mental-health unit of our local hospital. The people there insisted on putting me in a ward, when Max and I both knew I ought to have a private room. Finally, she asked, "Do you realize he's on the staff of this hospital?" And I got my private room.

Time went by very, very slowly on my second nut ward. I never could quite get the knack of it and kept asking myself, "What's a nice guy like me doing in a place like this?" They wanted me to make leather belts, of all things! Had I gone to school all those years just to sit and make leather belts? Besides, I couldn't understand the instructions. The girl had explained them to me four times, and I was too embarrassed to ask her again. (I am pleased to state, however, that I had gone to only a very few A.A. meetings before I was able to make a really beautiful pair of moccasins—and half of a wallet. I wore those moccasins every night for the next seven years, until they wore out. For my seventh A.A. birthday, my program-oriented, Al-Anon wife had my moccasins bronzed. Now I own perhaps the most costly pair of moccasins anyone has ever seen, and they help me remember where I've been.)

In the hospital I hung on to the idea I'd had most of my life: that if I could just control the external environment, the internal environment would then become comfortable. Much of my time was spent writing letters, notes, orders, and lists of things for Max, who was also my office nurse, to do to keep the world running while

I was locked up. One has to be pretty sick to do that, and perhaps one has to be even sicker to come back every day for a new list, as she did. (Today we don't have to live that way. Max still works with me in the office, but we have turned our wills and our lives and our work over to the care of God. Each with the other as a witness, we took the Third Step out loud—just as it says in the Big Book. And life keeps getting simpler and easier as we try to reverse my old idea, by taking care of the internal environment via the Twelve Steps, and letting the external environment take care of itself.)

One day as I sat there in the hospital, my psychiatrist walked up behind me and asked, "How'd you like to talk to the man from A.A.?" My reaction was that I'd already helped all the patients on the ward, and I still had plenty of problems of my own without trying to help some drunk from A.A. But, by the look on the psychiatrist's face, I could tell that it would really make him happy if I agreed. So, for no better reason than to make him happy, I agreed. Very shortly, I realized that had been a mistake—when this big clown came bounding into the room, almost shouting, "My name is Frank, and I'm an alcoholic, ha-ha-ha!" I really felt sorry for him; the only thing in life he had to brag about was the fact that he was an alcoholic. It wasn't until later that he told me he was an attorney.

Against my better judgment, I went to a meeting with him that night, and a strange thing began to happen. The psychiatrist, who had generally been ignoring me, now became quite interested; every day he would ask me all kinds of questions about the A.A. meetings. At first I wondered whether he was alco-

holic himself and was sending me to find out about
A.A. But it quickly became obvious that he had this
childish notion instead: If he could get me to go to
enough meetings while in the hospital, I would continue to go after he let me out. So, for no better
reason than to fool him, I asked Frank to take me to a
meeting every night. And Frank did set me up for a
meeting every night except Friday, when he thought
he might have a date with his girl friend. "That's a
devil of a way to run an organization," I thought, and
I reported Frank to the psychiatrist, who didn't seem
perturbed; he just got someone else to take me on
Fridays.

Eventually the psychiatrist discharged me from the
hospital, and Max and I began going to meetings ourselves. Right from the start, I felt that they weren't
doing anything for me, but they sure were helping
Max. We sat in the back and talked only to each other.
It was precisely a year before I spoke at an A.A. meeting. Although we enjoyed the laughter in the early
days, I heard a lot of things that I thought were stupid.
I interpreted "sober" as meaning "drinking but not
being drunk." When a big, healthy-looking young fellow stood up there and said, "I'm a success today if I
don't drink today," I thought, "Man, I've got a thousand things to do today before I can brag about not
taking a drink, for God's sake!" Of course, I was still
drinking at the time. (Today there is absolutely nothing in the world more important to me than my keeping this alcoholic sober; not taking a drink is by far the
most important thing I do each day.)

It seemed that all they talked about at meetings was
drinking, drinking, drinking. It made me thirsty. I

wanted to talk about my many *big* problems; drinking
seemed a small one. And I knew that giving up "one
drink for one day" wouldn't really do any good.
Finally, after seven months, I decided to try it. To this
day, I am amazed at how many of my problems—most
of which had nothing to do with drinking, I believed—
have become manageable or have simply disappeared
since I quit drinking.

I had already given up all the narcotics, most of the
pills, and some of the alcohol when I first came to A.A.
By early July I had tapered off alcohol completely, and
I got off all pills in the ensuing few months. When the
compulsion to drink left, it was relatively easy to stay
off alcohol. But for some time, it was difficult to keep
from taking a pill when I had an appropriate symptom, such as a cough, pain, anxiety, insomnia, a mus-
cle spasm, or an upset stomach. It has gotten
progressively easier. Today I feel I have used up my
right to chemical peace of mind.

It helped me a great deal to become convinced that
alcoholism was a disease, not a moral issue; that I had
been drinking as a result of a compulsion, even though
I had not been aware of the compulsion at the time;
and that sobriety was not a matter of willpower. The
people of A.A. had something that looked much better than what I had, but I was afraid to let go of what
I had in order to try something new; there was a
certain sense of security in the familiar.

At last, acceptance proved to be the key to my drinking problem. After I had been around A.A. for seven
months, tapering off alcohol and pills, not finding the
program working very well, I was finally able to say,
"Okay, God. It *is* true that I—of all people, strange as

it may seem, and even though I didn't give my permission—really, really am an alcoholic of sorts. And it's all right with me. Now, what am I going to do about it?" When I stopped living in the problem and began living in the answer, the problem went away. From that moment on, I have not had a single compulsion to drink.

And acceptance is the answer to *all* my problems today. When I am disturbed, it is because I find some person, place, thing, or situation—some fact of my life —unacceptable to me, and I can find no serenity until I accept that person, place, thing, or situation as being exactly the way it is supposed to be at this moment. Nothing, absolutely nothing, happens in God's world by mistake. Until I could accept my alcoholism, I could not stay sober; unless I accept life completely on life's terms, I cannot be happy. I need to concentrate not so much on what needs to be changed in the world as on what needs to be changed in me and in my attitudes.

Shakespeare said, "All the world's a stage, and all the men and women merely players." He forgot to mention that I was the chief critic. I was always able to see the flaw in every person, every situation. And I was always glad to point it out, because I knew you wanted perfection, just as I did. A.A. and acceptance have taught me that there is a bit of good in the worst of us and a bit of bad in the best of us; that we are all children of God and we each have a right to be here. When I complain about me or about you, I am complaining about God's handiwork. I am saying that I know better than God.

For years I was sure the worst thing that could

happen to a nice guy like me would be that I would turn out to be an alcoholic. Today I find it's the best thing that has ever happened to me. This proves I don't know what's good for me. And if I don't know what's good for me, then I don't know what's good or bad for you or for anyone. So I'm better off if I don't give advice, don't figure I know what's best, and just accept life on life's terms, as it is today—especially my own life, as it actually is. Before A.A. I judged myself by my intentions, while the world was judging me by my actions.

Acceptance has been the answer to my marital problems. It's as though A.A. had given me a new pair of glasses. Max and I have been married now for thirty-five years. Prior to our marriage, when she was a shy, scrawny adolescent, I was able to see things in her that others couldn't necessarily see—things like beauty, charm, gaiety, a gift for being easy to talk to, a sense of humor, and many other fine qualities. It was as if I had, rather than a Midas touch which turned everything to gold, a magnifying mind that magnified whatever it focused on. Over the years as I thought about Max, her good qualities grew and grew, and we married, and all these qualities became more and more apparent to me, and we were happier and happier.

But then as I drank more and more, the alcohol seemed to affect my vision: Instead of continuing to see what was good about my wife, I began to see her defects. And the more I focused my mind on her defects, the more they grew and multiplied. Every defect I pointed out to her became greater and greater. Each time I told her she was a nothing, she receded a little more into nowhere. The more I drank, the more she wilted.

Then, one day in A.A., I was told that I had the lenses in my glasses backwards; "the courage to change" in the Serenity Prayer meant not that I should change my marriage, but rather that I should change myself and learn to accept my spouse as she was. A.A. has given me a new pair of glasses. I can again focus on my wife's good qualities and watch them grow and grow and grow.

I can do the same thing with an A.A. meeting. The more I focus my mind on its defects—late start, long drunkalogs, cigarette smoke—the worse the meeting becomes. But when I try to see what I can add to the meeting, rather than what I can get out of it, and when I focus my mind on what's good about it, rather than what's wrong with it, the meeting keeps getting better and better. When I focus on what's good today, I have a good day, and when I focus on what's bad, I have a bad day. If I focus on a problem, the problem increases; if I focus on the answer, the answer increases.

Today Max and I try to communicate what we feel rather than what we think. We used to argue about our differing ideas, but we can't argue about our feelings. I can tell her she ought not to think a certain way, but I certainly can't take away her right to feel however she does feel. When we deal in feelings, we tend to come to know ourselves and each other much better.

It hasn't been easy to work out this relationship with Max. On the contrary, the hardest place to work this program has been in my own home, with my own children and, finally, with Max. It seems I should have learned to love my wife and family first; the newcomer to A.A., last. But it was the other way around. Eventually I had to redo each of the Twelve Steps specifically with Max in mind, from the First, saying, "I am powerless over alcohol, and my homelife is unmanageable by me," to the Twelfth, in which I tried to think of her as a sick Al-Anon and treat her with the love I would give a sick A.A. newcomer. When I do this, we get along fine.

Perhaps the best thing of all for me is to remember that my serenity is inversely proportional to my expectations. The higher my expectations of Max and other people are, the lower is my serenity. I can watch my serenity level rise when I discard my expectations. But then my "rights" try to move in, and they too can force my serenity level down. I have to discard my "rights," as well as my expectations, by asking myself, How important is it, really? How important is it compared to my serenity, my emotional sobriety? And when I place more value on my serenity and sobriety than on anything else, I can maintain them at a higher level—at least for the time being.

Acceptance is the key to my relationship with God today. I never just sit and do nothing while waiting for Him to tell me what to do. Rather, I do whatever is in front of me to be done, and I leave the results up to Him; however it turns out, that's God's will for me.

I must keep my magic magnifying mind *on* my acceptance and *off* my expectations, for my serenity is directly proportional to my level of acceptance. When I remember this, I can see I've never had it so good. Thank God for A.A.!

WINDOW OF OPPORTUNITY

This young alcoholic stepped out a second-story window and into A.A.

I GOT SOBER while I was still in college. Once, outside of a meeting, I overheard a conversation between another sober student and a woman who lived in the town where I went to school. She was explaining why so many local residents disliked the students. She described the common perception of students as arrogant and self-centered, and went on to tell the following story.

"I am a nurse and I work in the emergency room. Two years ago a student was brought in by ambulance in the middle of the night. He had gotten drunk, walked through a second-story window, and fallen twenty feet headfirst into a concrete window well. He was brought in covered with blood. His head had swollen to the size of a watermelon. He kept swearing at the nurses and doctors, telling them to keep their hands off of him, and threatening to sue them. He was, without a doubt, the single most obnoxious person I have ever met."

At that point I interrupted her. "That was me," I said. "That was my last drunk." I had walked through that window when I was nineteen years old.

How had I gotten there? I had always been a "good kid" growing up, the kind of son other mothers loved.

I was at the top of my classes academically and had been in almost no trouble for the first seventeen years of my life. I would like to say that was because of my well-developed moral fiber; in fact, much of it was a result of fear. My earliest memories included threats by my parents to throw me out onto the street for the slightest acts of disobedience. The thought of being forced to live on the street is pretty terrifying for a six-year-old. Those threats, coupled with a fair amount of physical punishment, kept me frightened and obedient.

As I grew older, however, I made a plan. I would be dutiful until I graduated from high school. Then I would escape to college, secure my economic future, and never go home again. Just after my eighteenth birthday, I left for college. I was, I thought, finally free. I was in for a rude awakening.

Like many alcoholics, I had spent much of my life feeling different, as though I just didn't quite fit in. I covered those feelings and my low self-esteem by being one of the smartest people in any group, if not the smartest. Additionally, I became a performer in crowds, always ready with a quick joke to point out the humor in any situation. I managed to bring a great deal of laughter into my life.

I went to a college filled with people who had also spent their entire lives at or near the top of their academic classes. Suddenly, I was no longer special. To make matters worse, many of them had what I only dreamed of—money. My family was strictly working class, struggling to get by on what my father earned. Money had always been a big issue, and I equated it with security, prestige, and worth. My father was fond of saying that the sole purpose of life is to make money. I had classmates whose names were household words that connoted wealth. I was ashamed, ashamed of my family and ashamed of myself. My shaky confidence crumbled. I was terrified of being found out. I knew that if others discovered who I really was, they wouldn't like me and I would be left alone, worthless and alone.

Then I discovered alcohol. I had tried it a few times in high school, but never enough to get drunk. I knew that getting drunk meant being out of control. My escape plan required that I always keep my wits about me. I was too afraid to be out of control. When I got to college, however, that fear left me. In order to fit in, I pretended, at first, that I had as extensive a drinking history as any of my classmates. It was not long before my history surpassed everyone's.

My drinking career was short and destructive, and my alcoholic progression was very fast. I got drunk for the first time in October. By November people were willing to wager money that I could not go one week without a drink. (I won and, in celebration, drank myself sick.) By January I was a daily drunk and by April a daily drug user as well. I didn't last too long.

As I look back on that period, I realize how true it is that one of the primary differences between alcoholics and nonalcoholics is that nonalcoholics change their behavior to meet their goals and alcoholics change their goals to meet their behavior. Everything that had been important to me, all of my dreams, goals, and aspirations, were swept away in a wave of booze. I realized quickly that I could not drink and function at any high level. That did not matter. I was willing to give up anything so that I could keep drinking. I went from being a solid A student to nearly flunking out of school, from being anointed a class leader to being shunned as a pariah. I almost never went to class and did little of the required reading. I never attended any of the many cultural events sponsored by the college. I forsook everything that makes college worthwhile in favor of drinking. Occasionally, some sliver of pride would work its way through the chaos, resentment, and fear and cause me to look at my life. But the shame was too great, and I would drive it back down with bottles of vodka and cases of beer.

Because my college was fairly small, it did not take long for me to come to the attention of the college deans. It was under their watchful eyes that I first agreed to enter counseling. While the administration saw this as an opportunity to help a troubled student, I saw it as a bargain. I would go to counseling to make them happy, and they would owe me one. Not surprisingly, the counseling had no effect. My daily drinking continued unabated.

About a year later I realized that I was in trouble. I had failed a class during the winter term (I had rarely attended and had not turned in the term paper on which 50 percent of our grade was based). The spring term was looking equally bleak. I was enrolled in a class that I had attended only once. I had not written any of the required papers or bothered to show up for the midterm examination. I was bound for failure and expulsion. My life had become unmanageable, and I knew it.

I went back to the dean who had guided me into

counseling and, for the first time, admitted to myself and to someone else that I had a problem with alcohol. I didn't think I was an alcoholic. I wasn't even sure what that was. But I knew my life was out of control. The dean allowed me to withdraw from that class the day before the final exam on one condition—I had to enter a treatment center. I agreed.

A few days went by. With the pressure lifted, my life did not look so unmanageable. In fact, it looked as if I was back in the saddle. So, I thanked the dean for his help but told him that I would be okay on my own. I did not go to a rehab. Two weeks later I walked through a second-story window.

After insulting the emergency room personnel, I slipped into unconsciousness, where I remained for five days. I awoke in a neck brace with complete double vision. My parents were furious. I was flown home and the future looked bleak. God's timing, however, is impeccable.

My college had a long history of drinkers, including Dr. Bob. At the time of my accident, the deans were assessing how to respond to student alcohol abuse and were waiting to try out their latest idea. Alcoholics Anonymous. I was the test case. They told me in no uncertain terms that I would never get back into this college unless I went to A.A. Under that pressure, I went to my first meeting.

Looking back, that may have been the first healthy decision I ever made with respect to alcohol. One definition of a bottom is the point when the last thing you lost or the next thing you are about to lose is more important to you than booze. That point is different for everyone, and some of us die before we get there.

For me, though, it was clear. I was willing to do anything to get back into school.

I went to my first A.A. meeting with absolutely no idea what A.A. was about. I am from a large Irish Catholic family and have had several relatives in and out of the program. A.A., like prison, was shameful, however, and was never discussed. I also had no idea what alcoholism was. I remember a girlfriend once told me that her mother had a drinking problem but that she was not an alcoholic. Curious, I asked what the difference was. "An alcoholic," she told me, "is someone who needs to drink alcohol every day, even if it is only one drink. A person with a drinking problem does not have to drink every day but once she starts, she cannot stop." By that definition, I was an alcoholic with a drinking problem.

I was surprised by my first meeting. It was in a church and, whatever I had expected, it was not this. The room was filled with well-dressed, smiling, happy people. No rancid coats or three-day beards. No bloodshot eyes, wheezing coughs, or shaky hands, but laughter. Someone was talking about God. I was sure I was in the wrong place.

Then a woman introduced herself and said that she was an alcoholic. I knew then I was in A.A. She spoke about feelings, of insecurity replaced by confidence, fear replaced by faith, resentment replaced by love, and despair replaced by joy. I knew those feelings. I had insecurity, fear, resentment, and despair. I could not believe it. Here was a person who was happy. It seemed like a long time since I had seen one of those.

After the meeting, people welcomed me with open arms and gave me their telephone numbers. The discussion meeting was followed by a speaker meeting, where I had my first awakening in A.A. The speaker said, "If you're an apple, you can be the best apple you can be, but you can never be an orange." I was an apple all right, and for the first time I understood that I had spent my life trying to be an orange. I looked around at a room filled with apples and, if I was understanding the speaker, most of them were no longer trying to be oranges.

My progress in A.A., however, was slow. I refused to go to meetings outside of my neighborhood, which meant that I went only Tuesday and Thursday nights. I always felt better after a meeting. I remember times when something upsetting would happen on a Friday and I would tell myself, "I wish it were Tuesday so I could go to the meeting." No matter how many suggestions I heard and how many rides were offered, however, I simply would not go to meetings on those other nights.

People gave me many other good suggestions as well. They suggested that I stay out of relationships. I was young and single, and I rejected this idea out of hand. For the first year I bounced from one sick relationship to another. They suggested that I get a sponsor. I had no idea what a sponsor was and was too proud to ask, but I was sure I didn't need one. After all, I was smarter than the rest of these people. They might need someone to tell them how to run their lives, but double vision, neck brace, and all, I was doing just fine on my own. People suggested that I find a Higher Power. I was not fooled. I knew when they said Higher Power they meant God. And I knew that God waited for me to step out of line just once so that he could take his revenge. I wanted no part of God.

With this resistance I plodded along for a few months. Whenever people asked me how I was doing, I would say, "Fine, just fine," no matter how hard I was crying inside. Then I reached the crossroads. I was sober about six months, and I was not getting any better. I contemplated suicide almost every day. My emotions swung between paralyzing despair and murderous rage, often in the space of a single moment. I was not happy, joyous, or free. I was miserable, and I was sick of it.

I decided I had had enough. I went to my Tuesday night meeting, fully intent on sharing honestly. I arrived at the meeting and no one else was there. This meeting, which routinely numbered twenty people, was empty. I waited for a few minutes and was preparing to leave, when a man whom I barely knew walked through the door. He suggested that he and I have a meeting. I was sure it was a bad idea. He asked me how I was doing. That was all I needed. The pain, fear, misery, anger, loss, resentment, and despair came pouring out. For the next forty-five minutes I talked at this man, who continued to nod his head, smile, and say, "Yeah, I remember feeling that way." For the first time I made completely honest contact with another human being. I showed someone who I really was, without fear of rejection. I took an action that was designed to make me feel, rather than just look, better. I was met with acceptance and love.

When I had finished talking, he told me something simple: "You don't have to drink over it." What an idea! I had thought that situations made me drink. If

I was angry, I drank. If I was happy, I drank. Bored or excited, elated or depressed, I drank. Here was a man telling me that, independent of my life situation, I did not have to drink. If I stuck with A.A., I could stay sober under any and all conditions. He gave me hope, and in many ways, he symbolized the door through which I finally walked into Alcoholics Anonymous.

I began to change. I began to pray. I became actively involved in working the steps. I had previously dismissed them as the tools of mental inferiors; now I embraced them as the rungs on the ladder to salvation. I began working with a sponsor and became active in my home group. I did not understand how making coffee or cleaning up after meetings could have anything to do with staying sober, but older members told me that service would keep me sober, so I tried it. It worked.

My life began to change. Just before my first anniversary, I was readmitted to my college. I arrived back on campus terrified. All I had known there was drinking. How was I ever going to stay sober under these conditions? The answer was simple—I threw myself into A.A. Some very loving people took me under their wings. I had the opportunity to perform a fair amount of Twelfth Step work with other students, and by the time I graduated, there was a thriving A.A. community at that school.

After graduation I attended law school. I arrived to find an A.A. that was very different from that to which I had grown accustomed. I was sure I would get drunk because "those people weren't doing it right!" My sponsor back at college, aware of my propensity for finding fault, assured me that if my new friends were not "doing it right," it was my obligation to show them how. So I did. Driven by fear and conceit, I set out to remake A.A. in my image. I am certain that if membership had depended upon being liked, I would have been expelled.

After some time I called my sponsor to report my progress. He stopped me short with a simple question: "These people who aren't doing it right, are they staying sober?" I admitted that, despite their failings, they were staying sober. "Good," he said. "You have told them what A.A. is. Now it's time for you to listen to figure out how they are staying sober." I followed that suggestion and began to listen. Slowly but surely, some wisdom and humility began to creep in. I became more teachable. I found God working all around me where previously I was sure I had been alone. When I opened my eyes enough to see the miracle, I found that it was right in front of my face. I was growing in God's love.

I was fortunate to have an opportunity to spend time abroad during law school. That was something I had dreamed of doing while drinking, but when push came to shove, I drank. Now sober, I have been in meetings in probably a dozen countries and have always been amazed at the message that transcends all linguistic and cultural differences. There is a solution. Together, we can live soberly, joyously, and freely.

My life has been one of great joy. I am now thirty-three years old, and God willing, in one month I will celebrate my fourteenth sober A.A. anniversary. I am surrounded by loving friends on whom I depend and who depend on me. I have reconciled with my parents, from whom I had been estranged. My life is filled with laughter again, something that alcohol had taken away.

I was married shortly after my ninth anniversary to a loving woman. One week before my twelfth anniversary, our son was born. Through him I learned more about unconditional love, the value of wonder, and the sheer joy of being alive. I have a wonderful job that (most days) I appreciate. I am active in A.A. service work and have both a sponsor and several sponsees with whom it is a privilege to work. All of those are gifts from God. I express my gratitude by enjoying them.

I once knew a woman who was crying before a meeting. She was approached by a five-year-old girl who told her, "You don't have to cry here. This is a good place. They took my daddy and they made him better." That is exactly what A.A. did for me; it took me and it made me better. For that I am eternally grateful.

PART III

THEY LOST NEARLY ALL

The fifteen stories in this group tell of alcoholism at its miserable worst.

Many tried everything—hospitals, special treatments, sanitariums, asylums, and jails. Nothing worked. Loneliness, great physical and mental agony—these were the common lot. Most had taken shattering losses on nearly every front of life. Some went on trying to live with alcohol. Others wanted to die.

Alcoholism had respected nobody, neither rich nor poor, learned nor unlettered. All found themselves headed for the same destruction, and it seemed they could do nothing whatever to stop it.

Now sober for years, they tell us how they got well. They prove to almost anyone's satisfaction that it's never too late to try Alcoholics Anonymous.

MY BOTTLE, MY RESENTMENTS, AND ME

From childhood trauma to skid row drunk, this hobo finally found a Higher Power, bringing sobriety and a long-lost family.

WHEN I RODE into a small mountain town in an empty freight car, my matted beard and filthy hair would have reached nearly to my belt, if I'd had a belt. I wore a lice-infested, grimy Mexican poncho over a reeking pajama top, and a ragged pair of jeans stuffed into cowboy boots with no heels. I carried a knife in one boot and a .38 revolver in the other. For six years I'd been fighting for survival on skid rows and riding across the country in freights. I hadn't eaten in a long time, so was half starved and down to 130 pounds. I was mean and I was drunk.

But, I'm ahead of myself. I believe my alcoholism really began when I was eleven years old and my mother was brutally murdered. Until then my life had been much the same as any of the other boys who lived in a small town during that period.

One night my mother failed to return home from her job at a car manufacturing plant. The next morning there was still no sign of her or any clue to why she had disappeared; with great apprehension the police were called. Since I was a mama's boy, this was especially traumatic for me. And to make matters unbelievably worse, a few days later the police came and arrested my father. They had found mom's mutilated body in a field outside of town and wanted to question him. In that instant the family life I knew was destroyed! My father was soon returned because the police had found a pair of glasses that did not belong to him at the murder scene. This clue led to the man who had so brutally killed my mother.

At school the gossip was vicious. At home there was chaos and no one would tell me what was happening, so I withdrew and began to block out the reality around me. If I could pretend it didn't exist, it might go away. I became extremely lonely and defiant. The confusion, pain, and grief had begun to subside when an article appeared in a murder mystery magazine about my family's misfortune. The children at school started the gossip and scrutiny all over again. I retreated further and became angrier and more withdrawn. It was easier that way, because people would leave me alone if I acted disturbed even before they tried to inquire.

Because my father was unable to care for all nine of us, the family had to be split up. About a year later he remarried, and my oldest brother offered to take me in. He and his new wife tried to help me, but I was just so defensive there was little they or anyone else could do. Finally, I took a job after school sorting soda bottles in a grocery store, where I found I could forget if I worked hard enough. In addition, it was a good place to steal beer and be a big guy with the other kids in school. That's the way my drinking began, as a way to make the pain go away.

After several years of semidelinquent adolescence, I

was old enough to join the marines. Leaving behind the origin of my bitterness, I thought my life would be better and the drinking not so bad. However, during boot camp, I recognized that this was not the answer. The discipline, the authority, the tight schedule went against my very nature, but it was a two-year stint, so there had to be a way to function in spite of the anger and now hatred that seethed through me. Every night found me at a bar drinking until they threw me out. That got me through the week; on weekends we went to a club nearby. This place was managed by people who drank as much as or more than I did. I became a constant customer. Arguments and fights were a regular occurrence.

I managed to complete the two years, was given an honorable discharge, and was sent on my way. Leaving the marine base behind and feeling homesick for my old environs, I hitchhiked back to my old hometown and returned to my brother's home. I soon found work as a painter for a construction company in town. By now drinking had become a constant part of my life.

Through some friends I met a woman I really cared for and soon we were married. A year later our daughter was born, and eventually two boys. Oh, how I loved my brood! This nice little family should have settled me down, but instead my drinking progressed. It finally reached the point where I was intolerable to live with, and my wife filed for divorce. I just went berserk, and the sheriff ordered me to leave town. I knew if I stayed, my anger at my wife for taking those children away from me would get me into more trouble than even I could handle, so once again I set off.

I left with my hatred, resentment, and the clothes on my back. This time for good.

In the largest city close by I could be found, dead broke, drinking myself into oblivion on skid row. At first a day-labor job provided for rent and food, but before long all the money had to go for booze. I found a mission where someone in need could sleep and eat free. But the bugs were so bad, the food so terrible, and people were such thieves, I decided that it was easier to just sleep outside and that I really didn't need to eat so often. So I found that hobo jungles, parked cars, and abandoned houses made nice places for my bottle, my resentments, and me. No one dared to bother me! I was utterly bewildered at where life had taken me.

Other hobos I met taught me the safest way to hop on a moving freight train and how to protect myself. They told me who were the easiest people to get a handout from and how to scam them. My biggest problem at that time was to find a way to get enough to drink to keep the reality of my life at bay. I was consumed by hate! For the next six years I went from skid row to skid row. One boxcar headed in any direction was as good as another. I had no place to go. One thing about it, I never got lost, because I never cared where I was! I crossed the United States three times, with no plan, no reason, not eating half the time. I hung out with other misfits like myself. Someone would say they were hiring in Florida, or New York, or Wyoming, and off we'd go. But by the time we would finally get there, they would say they were not hiring anymore. That was all right, because we didn't want to work anyway.

One scorching day, when I was in a desert town drinking, something unusual happened. I felt as though I had reached the point where I couldn't go on. To get away from everyone I managed to find some booze and started walking out into the desert, thinking, I'll just go until I die. Soon, so drunk I couldn't walk another step, I fell to the ground and moaned, "Oh, God! Please help me." I must have passed out because, hours later, I came to and found my way back to town. At the time I had no idea what made me change my mind about death. Today I know it was that my Higher Power took over my life.

By this time I was so wild-eyed and filthy, people would shy away from me. I hated the look of fear on their faces when they saw me. They looked at me as if I were not human, and maybe I wasn't. In one large city I took to sleeping on the grates with a piece of plastic over me so I wouldn't freeze. One night I found a clothing drop box I could get into; it made a nice warm place to sleep and I could get new clothes in the morning. In the middle of the night someone threw in more clothes. I opened the top, looked out, and shouted, "Thanks!" That woman threw up her hands and ran away screaming, "Lordy, Lordy!" She jumped into her car and screeched off.

I was just about as sad a figure of a man as is possible when I jumped off that freight. I found an empty refrigerator car sitting on a siding and took up residence in it. Here you could get welfare very easily, so off I went to apply. Now I could eat! It was my third time in this town, so I headed straight for my favorite bar. Here I met a barmaid who drank like a fish and was as mean a woman as I had ever seen, but she had

a place to live, so I moved in. And thus began the romance of a lifetime!

I finally had a roof over my head, sheets, and food!
All we did was drink and fight, but she worked at the
bar so it kept us going. With just enough cash for
booze, we drank continuously for several months.
Then, on my way to find a drink, I ran into one of my
old hobo buddies, an older man. I remembered him
as an excessive drinker, an "alcoholic." And here he
was walking toward me down the street in a white
shirt, tie, and suit, looking marvelous! With a big smile
on his face, he told me he'd quit drinking, and how
he'd managed to do it, and how much better he felt.
My first thought was If he can do that, I can do that
—and much better, because I'm only thirty-three.

He took me down to this club where there were
some other recovered alcoholics. I drank coffee while
they all told me how they had changed. It looked like
they might have something here! If they could do this,
maybe, just maybe, I could too. Their enthusiasm was
catching. I began to feel excitement inside but had no
idea why. I rushed off to tell my new girlfriend about
what had happened and how great it would be if we
quit drinking. "You're nuts!" she yelled at me. "You
can just drag your rear back to your refrigerator car;
I've got parties to go to!" Although I seemed unable to
transmit my excitement, I told her more.

The next day we both quit drinking. There are no
words to explain why it happened or how it happened;
it just did. It was a miracle! Every day we were able to
stay sober was another gift from a Higher Power I had
given up on many long years before.

The next year we took a job managing a camp outside of town where drunks were sent to get dried out and sobered up. It was our responsibility to see that they had food and stayed out of trouble. Both tasks were almost impossible at times, but we kept trying. With some support from oldtimers in A.A., we lasted a year. This was a volunteer job and we had little money for ourselves. When the year was up, I went over the list of drunks who had been through the place, 178 in all. I exclaimed to my partner, "Not a single one of them is sober today!" "Yeah," she replied, "but you and I are!" And so, on that happy note, we were then married.

My sponsor told me if I wanted to form a relationship with my Higher Power, it would be necessary for me to change. At a meeting one night a member said, "It's not how much you drink, it's what drinking does to you." That statement changed my whole attitude. Of course I had to surrender and accept I was an alcoholic. I had a hard time giving up the anger at my ex-wife for taking my kids, at the man who murdered my mother, and at my father for what I felt was deserting me. But these resentments eased with time as I began to comprehend my own defects of character. I became acquainted with some monks in a nearby monastery who listened to my story with some amazement and were able to help me understand myself. At the same time my sponsor and other oldtimers who had taken us under their wings loved us back to rejoin society.

Gradually the ice that was my heart melted and I changed as my relationship with my Higher Power grew. Life began to take on a whole new meaning. I made what amends were possible but knew I would have to return to my childhood home to clear up that part of my past. But we were busy with our own paint contracting company now, and as the years passed by, the opportunity to go back home just did not come.

As the months following the day we quit drinking have turned into years, I have become increasingly more devoted to this program that saved not only my life, but my wife's also. Eventually I became involved in A.A. service and helped get a central office started for our groups. We both became active in general service and began traveling all over the state going to meetings. To my surprise, both of us were given the opportunity to serve as delegates to the General Service Conference. What joy we found in this! One of my most memorable moments was when at the opening of the conference the chairman of A.A.'s General Service Board said: "We are all gathered here tonight, not as individuals, but for the betterment of Alcoholics Anonymous all over the world." The years flashed back to when I was on the grates outside that very hotel, frantically trying to keep from freezing. I was overwhelmed by God's grace just to be there!

One day a friend of mine who writes for a living asked if he could write the story of my life for a magazine. He assured me there would be no anonymity problems, so I agreed. I had been sober for almost twenty-five years at this time and had no idea what God, as I understand him, was about to do for me. My oldest brother, the one who had taken me in, just happened to subscribe to this magazine and just happened to read the article. Thus began an amazing chain of events that has altered not only our lives, but the lives of my family and many others. It is nothing short of a modern-day miracle. God has done for me what I could not do for myself!

The article gave the name of the town I live in, so after my brother and sister-in-law finished reading the story, they called directory assistance and phoned me—the first time we had spoken in more than thirty years. I burst into tears, and so did they. They told me that after my disappearance following the divorce, my family had tried repeatedly to locate me. They were concerned because someone had told them I was either dead or had left the country. I felt bad that I had worried them like that, but in my self-centeredness it had simply never occurred to me that they cared that much. One by one I talked to all my brothers and sisters in the next twenty-four hours. My brother gave me the phone number of my own daughter, whom I hadn't seen for twenty-seven years, and I called her. Next I talked to both my sons. Oh, God, what an experience! I was so overwhelmed by all the memories and the lost years that it was difficult for me even to speak. I spent several weeks crying as all the old hurts rose to the surface and were healed.

Later we had a big family reunion back in my hometown. It was a happy day for all of us to be together for the first time since we were split up. My father had passed away, but all his children were there with their families—a large and joyous crowd. Finally, after all those years of wondering about my family, my Higher Power had acted through my friend to undo the tangled circumstances and allow me to make amends to the people who had been hurt by my bitterness.

I believe that I am living proof of the A.A. saying "Don't give up until the miracle happens."

HE LIVED ONLY TO DRINK

*"I had been preached to, analyzed, cursed, and
counseled, but no one had ever said, 'I identify with
what's going on with you. It happened to me and this
is what I did about it.'"*

O N LOOKING BACK at my life, I can't see anything
that would have warned me or my family of
the devastation that alcoholism had in store for us. To
our collective memory there was no drinking on either
side of the family. We were from a long Southern
Missionary Baptist tradition. My father was a minister,
and I attended his church every Sunday with the rest
of the family and, like them, was very active in religious work. My parents were also educators; my father was principal of the school I attended, and my
mother taught there. They were both champions of
community outreach and well respected. There was
caring and togetherness among us. My maternal
grandmother, herself a deeply religious woman who
lived with us, helped raise me and was a living example of unconditional love.

Early on, the values of morality and learning were
impressed on me. I was taught that if you were well
educated and morally upstanding, there was nothing
that could stand in the way of your success in this life
or hereafter. As a child and young man, I was evan-
gelical—literally drunk with moral zeal and intellec-

tual ambition. I excelled in school and dreamed of a career in teaching and helping others.

It was not until I was an adult, away from the family and doing graduate work at a prestigious East Coast university, that I had my first real drink of alcohol. I had tasted beer and a little wine before that and long since decided that fruit juice tasted better. I had never been inside a bar until one evening some fellow students persuaded me to go with them to a local cocktail lounge. I was fascinated. I still remember the hazy, smoky atmosphere, the hushed voices, the tinkle of ice in the glasses. It was pure sophistication. But most of all I remember that first sensation of the warm whiskey radiating through my body.

I drank so much that night that nobody believed I hadn't been drinking all the time, and I didn't get drunk, although there were parts of the evening that I didn't remember the next day. But more important than anything else that night, I belonged. I was at home in the universe; I was comfortable with people. Despite my active church and school life as a child, I had never felt really comfortable; I was actually very nervous and insecure around people and most of the time forced myself to be outgoing like my parents because I thought it was my duty. But this night in the bar was like no other time in my life. Not only was I completely at ease, but I actually loved all the strangers around me and they loved me in return, I thought, all because of this magic potion, alcohol. What a discovery. What a revelation!

The following year I began my career as a teacher. My first job was at a college fifty miles from my hometown. Before the school year ended, I had been asked to resign because of my drinking. Within that short space of time, drinking had become an accepted way of life. I loved booze. I loved people who drank and the places where they drank. At that time in my life, although I had lost my first job and embarrassed my family, it never occurred to me that alcohol could be a problem. From that first night at the bar a year earlier, I had made a profound decision that was to direct my life for many years to come: Alcohol was my friend and I would follow it to the ends of the earth.

After that first job there were many more that I lost, all because of my drinking. I taught in many schools and in different states. I was no longer the moral young man who had seen his destiny in helping people live better. I was loud and arrogant, angry, abusive, always blaming and confronting others. I was getting arrested and beaten up. I had developed a foul mouth and was frequently drunk in classes and in public places. Finally my teaching career ended in total dishonor. My family could not understand what was happening to me, nor could I. In moments of clarity, I was full of shame, guilt, and remorse; I had become an embarrassment to all who had had faith in me; to others I had become a joke. I wanted to die. Now alcohol had become the only friend I had.

I wound up in an insane asylum, which probably saved my life. I do not remember how I got there; I do know that I had become suicidal. I became comfortable there, and months later I cried when I was dismissed. I knew by that time that I could not make it in the world. I was safe behind the barred hospital windows and wanted to stay there for the rest of my life. I could not drink there, but tranquilizers and other drugs abounded and I helped myself to them. The word *alcoholic* was never mentioned. I do not believe the doctors knew much more about alcoholism than I did.

When I was released from the asylum, I moved to a large city to make a new beginning. My life had become a series of new beginnings. In time I picked up the drink, got good jobs, and lost them as I had in the past. All the fear and remorse and terrible depression returned tenfold. It still did not register that the drinking might be the cause of all this misery. I sold my blood. I prostituted myself; I drank more. I became homeless and slept in the bus and train terminals. I scrounged cigarette butts off the sidewalks and drank from a common wine bottle with other drunks. I drank my way to the men's municipal shelter and made it my home. I panhandled. By this time I lived only to drink. I did not bathe or change clothes; I stank; I became thin and ill; I had begun to hear voices and accepted them as death omens. I was frightened, arrogant, enraged, and resentful of man, God, and the universe. There was nothing else to live for, but I was too frightened to die.

It was at this point that a woman who was a social worker on skid row and a sober member of Alcoholics Anonymous sat me down in her office and told me her story—how she drank, what happened, and how she got sober. No one had ever done this before. I had been preached to, analyzed, cursed, and counseled, but no one had ever said, "I identify with what's going on with you. It happened to me, and this is what I did about it." She got me to my first A.A. meeting that same evening.

The people at the meetings gathered around me in kindness in those early days, and I did not drink. But the spiritual demons of withdrawal descended on me. I was black, and these people were white. What did they know about suffering? What could they tell me? I was black and bright, and the world had consistently rejected me for it. I hated this world, its people, and its punishing God. Yet I believed the people in A.A. were sincere and whatever they believed in was working for them. I just did not believe that A.A. would work for me as a black drunk.

I genuinely believed that I was different until much later, when I had what I now know to be my first spiritual awakening: that I was an alcoholic and I didn't have to drink! I also learned that alcoholism, as an equal opportunity illness, does not discriminate—is not restricted to race, creed, or geography. At last I was released from the bondage of my uniqueness.

In early sobriety I had to continue to live in a flophouse filled with active drunks. Not drinking, I became acutely aware of my surroundings—the foul smells, the noise, the hostility and physical danger. My resentments mounted at the realization that I had flushed a career down the drain, disgraced and alienated my family, and been relegated to the meanest of institutions, a skid row shelter. But I was also able to realize that this bonfire of resentment and rage was beckoning me to pick up a drink and plunge in to my death. Then I realized that I had to separate my sobriety from everything else that was going on in my life. No matter what happened or didn't happen, I couldn't drink. In fact, none of these things that I was going through had anything to do with my sobriety;

the tides of life flow endlessly for better or worse, both good and bad, and I cannot allow my sobriety to become dependent on these ups and downs of living. Sobriety must live a life of its own.

More important, I came to believe that I cannot do this alone. From childhood, despite the love I experienced, I had never let people, even those closest to me, inside my life. All my life I had lived the deepest of lies, not sharing with anyone my true thoughts and feelings. I thought I had a direct line to God, and I built a wall of distrust around myself. In A.A. I faced the pervasive "we" of the Twelve Steps and gradually realized that I can separate and protect my sobriety from outside hazards only inasmuch as I rely on the sober experience of other A.A. members and share their journey through the steps to recovery.

The rewards of sobriety are bountiful and as progressive as the disease they counteract. Certainly among these rewards for me are release from the prison of uniqueness, and the realization that participation in the A.A. way of life is a blessing and a privilege beyond estimate—a blessing to live a life free from the pain and degradation of drinking and filled with the joy of useful, sober living, and a privilege to grow in sobriety one day at a time and bring the message of hope as it was brought to me.

(3)

SAFE HAVEN

This A.A. found that the process of discovering who he really was began with knowing who he didn't want to be.

*P*RISON. What a wonderful life it is. Here I am, sitting in a cell waiting for my hotpot to heat up so I can have a cup of instant coffee and reminisce. As I ponder my current circumstance, I reflect on the undeniable fact that I am well into my fourth year of incarceration. I still wake up some mornings wishing it were all a bad dream.

I didn't grow up in a home that used alcohol, but when I took my first drink at the age of thirteen, I knew I would drink again. Being raised in a home founded on high moral standards didn't seem to instill any fear of consequences once I took a drink of booze. Sometimes as I rode my bicycle around the neighborhood, I would spy a grown-up in his yard drinking beer. Returning later, when I knew he was not at home, I would break into his home to steal the golden beverage from the refrigerator.

I recall too well the morning when another guy and I stole my dad's credit card and pickup truck so we could run off to California to become movie stars. We had a pistol so we could rob stores when the time came to stock up on beer, cash, and cigarettes. Before the first day of travel was over, however, I told my

friend I couldn't go on any longer and needed to return home. I knew my mom and dad were climbing
the walls with worry by now. My friend refused to turn
back, so I let him out of the truck; I never saw him
again. My parents may have recognized my behavior
as some serious adolescent rebellion, but they had no
idea it was fueled by the disease of alcoholism.

At age sixteen I got a part-time job as a disc jockey
for a local radio station. Those in a position to know
observed that I had a knack for this kind of work, so I
dropped out of high school and started spinning
records full time. Drinking and partying went hand
in hand with this job. Soon, a pattern began that
lasted for many years. When the alcoholism became
obvious to my employers and began to affect my job
performance, I would simply resign and seek employment with another broadcasting company.

I recall one day when I was doing a midday show, I
realized I could not go another minute without a
drink. I put on an album and quietly walked out of
the radio station unnoticed. I drove to a liquor store
and bought a bottle of whiskey, got back in my car,
turned on the radio, and started drinking. As I sat
there listening to song after song, the album eventually came to an end, and all you could hear was the
needle scratching against the turntable. Someone at
the station finally realized I was no longer in the control room and put on another record.

During my years in the broadcast industry, I worked
from time to time as a radio storm chaser. It was my
job to use radar information to follow the storm and
spot tornados, hail, flooding, and storm-related hazards or damage. I would then use a cellular phone in

my vehicle to give live reports over the radio while chasing the storm. One night the storm was extremely turbulent. Our listening audience was larger than ever as I gave my live report, sounding as if I were on the front lines of a war zone.

The following day a newspaper honored our station with a nice article about the professional job we did on weather coverage. But what no one knew was that all of those "professional" storm reports were called in from the safety of my back patio as I ad-libbed a little better with each fresh glass of bourbon and cola.

Periodically I worked as a broadcast journalist and reported many news stories on location. I regularly drank on the job and was frequently loaded when calls came in about alcohol-related automobile accidents. There I was with microphone in one hand and flask in the other as I jumped into the news van and rushed to the scene of an accident, just as drunk or more so than the one who caused it. It was inevitable that I would one day *become* the news, rather than just report it, by causing a serious accident as a result of my drinking.

I had experienced run-ins with the law several times—for not paying fines, public intoxication, fighting, and driving while intoxicated. But nothing could compare with the time the police asked me to come downtown for questioning concerning a murder. I had been drinking the night before and had gotten involved in a dangerous incident. I knew I hadn't committed a murder, but here I was being considered a prime suspect. An hour or two into questioning it was determined that I had not committed the crime, and I was released. This was quite enough to get my full attention though.

I went home and called a friend I had seen at the local mall a week earlier. I hadn't talked to her for a couple of years, but I had noticed how different she looked and behaved. As we spoke, she said she hadn't had a drink for over a year. She told me about a group of friends who were helping her stay sober. I lied to her and claimed I hadn't had a drink myself for quite some time. I don't think she believed me, but she gave me her phone number and encouraged me to call if I would like to meet her friends. Later, when I worked up the nerve to call her, I admitted that I had a drinking problem and wanted to stop. She picked me up and took me to my first A.A. meeting.

In Alcoholics Anonymous, I knew I had found a protective haven. But during the ensuing 4½ years I fell into the category known, in A.A. parlance, as a "chronic slipper." I might get a good six months of sobriety under my belt, but then I would get a bottle to celebrate.

I did all the things that were suggested for me not to do. Within my first year around A.A., I made some major decisions, like getting married, renting the most expensive apartment I could find, not using my sponsor, avoiding the steps, hanging around old haunts with my old drinking pals, and talking more than listening during meetings. In short, I wasn't responding to the miracle of A.A. My disease progressed and I became a regular patient in detox hospitals, intensive care units, and treatment centers. Permanent insanity was drawing near, and the gates of death were in view.

There is a saying that alcoholics either get sobered

up, locked up, or covered up. Since I was not genuinely willing to do what it took to get sobered up, I
had the other options to face. I never dreamed it
would happen so quickly.

It was a beautiful September weekend just before
Labor Day. I made the decision to buy a case of beer
and a bottle of wine. Later in the evening I drank
whiskey on top of the beer and wine, blacked out,
committed a drunken crime, was arrested, and within
ten days was convicted and sentenced to twenty years
in prison. I guess an alcoholic death can come in
much the same way: I drink, I black out, I die. At least
with prison I would have another chance at life somewhere down the line.

I can't start to describe the forced humility that is
placed upon an alcoholic who comes to prison.
Although I deserved to be in prison, the trauma was
horrible. The only encouragement and hope I was
able to find was from reading the personal stories in
the back of a tattered Big Book I found in my cell.
Then one day I heard something that was music to my
ears. A correctional officer announced that an A.A.
meeting was to be held in the chapel. When I walked
into the meeting, I took a seat in the circle of chairs,
where I once again found a protective haven.

As I pen this story, 3½ years have passed since that
meeting in the chapel. I've moved to a larger prison
unit and have remained very active in the awesome
program of Alcoholics Anonymous. A.A. has accomplished so many things in my life today. It has given
me my sanity and an all-around sense of balance. Now
willing to listen and take suggestions, I have found
that the process of discovering who I really am begins

with knowing who I really don't want to be. And although the disease of alcoholism inside of me is like gravity, just waiting to pull me down, A.A. and the Twelve Steps are like the power that causes an airplane to become airborne: It only works when the pilot is doing the right things to make it work. So, as I have worked the program, I have grown emotionally and intellectually. I not only have peace *with* God, I have the peace *of* God through an active God consciousness. I have not only recovered from alcoholism, I have become whole in person—body, spirit, soul.

I've had one "God-thing" after another happen to me since submitting myself to the principles of A.A. The trial officials who convicted me and the victims of my crime have all decided to support my early release from prison. Coincidence? I think not. I've received letters from former employers who have heard of my sobriety and have offered me employment again in the radio industry. These are just samples of God doing for me what I couldn't do for myself.

One of the things I have committed to do in return for God's grace is to immediately become active in a correctional committee upon my release. Bringing the A.A. message back into jails and prisons is extremely important to me and my own sobriety today.

From experience, I've realized that I cannot go back and make a brand-new start. But through A.A., I can start from now and make a brand-new end.

LISTENING TO THE WIND

It took an "angel" to introduce this Native American woman to A.A. and recovery.

I STARTED DRINKING when I was around eleven years old. I stayed with my brother and his wife just outside of Gallup, New Mexico. We were poor. The smell of beans and fresh tortillas symbolized home to me. I slept in a bed with three other children, where we huddled close to keep warm in the freezing winter. The snow was deep around us.

I had a hard time reading and understanding school work, so I skipped school every chance I got. My dad and grandma had told me the old stories about the longhouse and the travels of our people across the deserts and mountains of this country. I met a boy and together we ditched school and stole a truck. We drank tequila and explored the red mesas together. Sometimes we sat in the shade of the trading post directly across the street from the tracks. When the train rumbled through the dusty small town near the reservation, it promised glamorous places far away.

When I was fifteen years old, I arrived alone in San Francisco with a guitar, a small suitcase, and $30. I went to several taverns and coffeehouses in search of a job singing. I believed I could pursue a career as a performer. Three days later I found myself sleeping in a doorway to stay out of the rain that had fallen all day.

I was broke and cold, and had nowhere else to go. The only thing I had left was my pride, which prevented me from trying to reach my brother by phone or finding my way back to the only people who ever really knew me.

Sometime in the middle of the long, restless night, a kindly middle-aged white man laid his hand on my shoulder. "Come on, young lady," he said. "Let's get you to someplace warm and get you something to eat." The price he asked in return seemed little, considering the cold rainy night behind me. I left his hotel with $50 in my hand. Thus began a long and somewhat profitable career in prostitution. After working all night, I would drink to forget what I had to do to pay the rent until the sunrise brought sleep. The weeks passed.

I started stealing and robbed a gas station and a liquor store. I made very few friends. I had learned to trust no one. One night, around eight o'clock, a car pulled up to the curb just as I had settled myself, half drunk, against the wall of a building. I figured I had met my companion for the evening. We made the appropriate conversation to confirm the deal, and I got into the car. Suddenly I felt a deafening blow to my temple. I was knocked senseless. In a desolate area across town, I was pulled from the car, pistol whipped, and left to die in the mud with rain falling softly upon me. I came to in a hospital room with bars on the windows. I spent seven weeks there, having repeated surgeries and barely recognizing my surroundings each time I woke up. Finally, when I was able to walk around a little, a policewoman came and I was taken to county jail. It was my third arrest in two months. Nearly two years on the streets had taken its toll.

The judge said I could not be rehabilitated, and I was charged with eighteen counts of felony. I would not see the streets again for nearly twenty-six months. I was seventeen years old. The first few months I would have done just about anything for a drink. I knew I was powerless over the drugs, but I really couldn't see what harm there was in alcohol. In the summer I was released. I wasn't sure where I was going, but a nice cold beer sure sounded like a refreshing celebration of freedom. I bought a six-pack and a bus ticket.

When I got off the bus, I got a waitressing job in a bar. By the end of my first shift, however, I had enough money to get a bottle and a sleazy motel room nearby.

A few weeks later I saw him, the only Indian I had met in a very long time. He was leaning over a pool table when I came to work. I put on my apron, grabbed a tray, and headed straight for him to see if he needed a refill.

"Who let you off the reservation?" he asked. I was furious, humiliated, and embarrassed.

That man became the father of my first-born child. My relationship with him lasted only a few months and was the first of many mutually abusive relationships that would continue over the next few years. I found myself alone, drunk, homeless, and pregnant in a matter of weeks. Afraid that I would wind up back in jail, I went to live with my brother and sister-in-law.

My brother had gotten a very good job and moved to Hawaii. My son was born there, and on the day of his birth, I found my purpose in life: I was born to be a mom. He was beautiful. Straight black hair and dark eyes. I had never felt like this in my life. I could put my past behind me once again and move forward into a new life with my child.

After a year or so I became bored with my life in the islands and the guy I had been dating. I said good-bye to my waitress job and my family, and moved to California with my one-year-old son.

I needed transportation, but cars cost too much money. Where could I get lots of money? It did not seem appropriate to go back to prostitution in the same town where I was raising my son. I could take the bus to the next town, work all night, and come home in the morning if I could get someone to watch my little boy. The night job paid well. As long as I didn't work close to home where my child would attend school, everything would be fine. Also, I could drink on the job. I kept the welfare, though, because it provided health insurance.

I did quite well financially. After one year I found a beautiful large apartment that had a view of the ocean, bought a new car and a purebred Collie dog. The social workers started getting very nosy. I could not figure out what their problem was. I led a double life. By day I was super-mom, and by night I was a drunken hooker.

I met a wonderful man at the beach, and we fell in love. Everything was like heaven on earth until he asked where I worked! Of course, I lied. I told him I worked for the government and held a top security clearance, which required complete secrecy. That's why I had to work nights, undercover, out of town, on weekends. Now, maybe he would stop asking so many questions. But instead he proposed.

We moved in together and my working arrangements became nearly impossible to live with. So did my conscience. One night on my way to work, I sat in rush-hour traffic on the freeway. I broke down in tears and felt all the lies of my life burst open inside of me. I hated myself and I wanted to die. I couldn't tell him the truth, but I couldn't continue to lie to him either. Suddenly a great light came on. It was the best idea I had ever had. I got off the freeway at the next ramp, drove home, and told him I got fired! He took it well, and we celebrated with a huge bottle of wine.

It took a lot of booze to cover the nightmares of my past, but I was sure I could get around this small problem before long. I never did. The relationship broke up over my drinking, and I packed my little car and moved myself, my son, our dog, and three cats to the mountains.

This mountain town was a place I had visited as a child with Dad and Grandma. Memories of the stories of my childhood and our Indian people flooded in. I got a job cleaning cabins for a local resort lodge and got back on welfare. Shortly after our move, my son started school. By this time I was consuming nearly a fifth of tequila each day, and blackouts were occurring on a regular basis.

One day I got up as usual. The last thing I remember was feeling so shaky I could hardly stand up. I ate a tablespoon of honey, hoping it would give me the necessary sugar rush. The next conscious memory was the emergency room. They said I was suffering from malnutrition. I was nearly thirty pounds underweight. They had the audacity to ask me how much I drank! What could that possibly have to do with anything? I promised I would never do it again.

For the first time in my life, I tried very hard to quit drinking. After a few days of shakes and nausea, I decided that a shot of tequila wouldn't hurt. I had managed to put on a little weight, but six months later I collapsed and was diagnosed with a bleeding ulcer. I was in the hospital for four days that time. They told me that if I didn't stop drinking, I would probably die.

My son called his grandparents, and they traveled to the mountains to visit us. I had not seen them for years. We got along much better than I expected. The relationship they formed with my son was incredible. My dad took his grandson hiking in the wilderness, and mom helped out with looking after him while I worked. My health continued to fail. My parents wound up moving to our town in an attempt to help their grandson and me.

My dad and I decided to go to a Native American gathering. I hadn't been to one of these pow wows since I was a child. When we heard the drums and watched the dancers, I felt some great passion well up inside me. I felt like an outsider. I wanted a drink. I wore my hair down to my waist and wore a lot of turquoise jewelry I had collected over the years. I looked like the people, but I certainly didn't feel like one of them. I felt as if they all knew something I didn't.

In an effort to prove I was getting better, I started hitting the streets again in order to make more money.

I told my parents that I was going down the mountain to visit friends. I received my third arrest for drunk driving on one of the trips back, after working all weekend. The night in jail seemed a long time to go without a drink.

Weeks and months passed, and the blackouts continued getting worse. Then I met a man in a local bar. I didn't like him very well, but he had quite a lot of money, and he sure liked me. He took me to nice restaurants and brought me expensive gifts. As long as I had a buzz on, with a few drinks, I could tolerate him.

One thing led to another, and we wound up married. The most powerful motive I had was getting out of the streets and being provided for. I had begun to think I did not have much longer to live. The faces of my doctors were looking more and more grim every time I went into the hospital to dry out.

The marriage was a farce, and it didn't take long for this man to figure that out. Someone had told him about my past, and he demanded to know the truth. I was tired, nauseated, and drunk. I just didn't care anymore, so I admitted everything. We fought every day after that, and my visits to the hospital became more frequent. One afternoon I decided I no longer wanted to live and got the gun from over the fireplace. I owe my life to the man I had married. He heard my child scream from out back and came running into the house. He grabbed the gun and wrestled it away from me. I was numb and couldn't figure out what had happened. My son was taken away from me by the authorities, and I was placed in a locked ward

for the criminally insane. I spent three days there on
legal hold.

After I was released, most of the next few weeks
was a blur. One night I caught my husband with
another woman. We fought and I followed him in my
car and tried to run him down, right in the middle of
the main street in town. The incident caused a six-car
pileup, and when the law caught up with me later, I
was sent to the locked ward again. I do not remember
arriving there, and when I woke up, I didn't know
where I was. I was tied to a table with restraints
around my wrists, both ankles, and my neck. They
shot heavy drugs into my veins and kept me like that
for a long time. I was released five days later. When I
left, there was no one there to drive me home, so I
hitchhiked. The house was dark and locked, and no
one was anywhere around to let me in. I got a bottle
and sat in the snow on the back porch and drank.

One day I decided I'd better go to the laundromat
and wash some clothes. There was a woman there
with a couple of kids. She moved around quickly,
folding clothes and stacking them neatly in a couple
of huge baskets. Where did she get her energy?
Suddenly I realized I had to put my clothes into the
dryers. I couldn't remember which washers I had put
them in. I looked into probably twenty different washers. I made up my mind how to handle the situation.
I would stay here until everyone else had left. I would
keep whatever clothes were left behind, as well as my
own. As the other woman finished her tasks, she was
writing something down on a small piece of paper. She
loaded her baskets and kids into her car, and came
back into the laundromat. She came right up to me

and handed me the small blue paper. I couldn't make out what it said. I smiled politely and slurred a friendly "Thank you." Later I made out the telephone number and the handwritten message below: "If you ever want to stop drinking, call Alcoholics Anonymous, 24 hours a day."

Why had she given me this, and what made her think I was drinking? Couldn't she see that my bottle was soda? Of all the nerve! I was mortified! I folded the paper neatly and put it in the back pocket of my jeans. As the next few weeks passed, I became sicker by the day. One morning I woke up alone as usual. I hadn't seen my husband in a long time. I needed a drink, and the bottle on the bedside table was dry. I rose on my shaky legs, but they refused to hold my weight. I fell to the floor and began crawling around the house looking for a bottle. Nothing! This meant I had to leave the house and get to a store.

I found my empty purse on the floor, but I knew I could never make it to the car. I became terrified. Who could I call? I never saw any friends anymore, and there was no way I could call family. I remembered the number in the pocket of my jeans. I hadn't even gotten dressed for several days. Where were the jeans?

I searched the house until I found them on the floor of the bedroom. The number was in the pocket. After three tries I managed to dial the number. A woman's voice answered.

"I . . . uh . . . got this number from you . . . uh . . . Is this A.A.?" I asked.

"Yes. Do you want to stop drinking?"

"Please, yes. I need help. Oh, God." I felt the fiery tears run down my face.

Five minutes later she pulled into my driveway. She must have been some kind of an angel. How had she appeared from nowhere that day in the laundromat? How had she known? How had I kept her number all that time without losing it?

The A.A. woman made sure I had no more alcohol in the house. She was very tough on me for a long time. I went to meetings every day and started taking the steps. The First Step showed me that I was powerless over alcohol and anything else that threatened my sobriety or muddled my thinking. Alcohol was only a symptom of much deeper problems of dishonesty and denial. Now it was a matter of coming to grips with a Power greater than myself. That was very hard for me. How could all these *white* people even begin to think they could understand *me*? So they brought a sober Indian woman up to work with me for a day. That was a very powerful day. That Indian woman cut me no slack at all. I will never forget her. She convinced me I was not unique. She said these *white* folks were the best thing that ever happened to me.

"Where would you be without them?" she asked. "What are the alternatives? You got any better ideas for yourself? How many *Indians* do you know who are going to help you sober up?" At the time, I couldn't think of any. I surrendered behind the tears of no answers and decided to do it their way. I found the Power greater than myself to be the magic above the heads of the people in the meetings. I chose to call that magic Great Spirit.

The Twelve Steps worked like a crowbar, prying

into my dishonesty and fear. I didn't like the things I learned about myself, but I didn't want to go back where I had come from. I found out that there was no substance on the planet that could help me get honest. I would do just about anything to avoid working on myself.

The thing that kept me sober until I got a grip on honesty was the love in the rooms of Alcoholics Anonymous. I made some friends for the first time in my life. Real friends that cared, even when I was broke and feeling desperate. At twenty-two months of sobriety, I was finally able to complete an honest inventory. The Fifth Step enabled me to see my part in my resentments and fears. In the chapter "How It Works," in the Big Book, I was shown some questions. The answers to these questions provided me with knowledge about my reactions to the conditions in my life. Every response to every resentment, real or imagined, had been sick and self-destructive. I was allowing others to control my sense of well-being and behavior. I came to understand that the behavior, opinions, and thoughts of others were none of my business. The only business I was to be concerned with was my own! I asked my Higher Power to remove from me everything that stood in the way of my usefulness to Him and others, and to help me build a new life.

I met my current husband in an A.A. meeting. Together we carry the message to Indian people on reservations all over the country. I started at the fifth-grade level in school when I had been sober nearly two years. After college I started my own business. Today I publish the books I write. Our daughter was

born during my early sobriety, and she is in high
school now. She has never seen her mother take a
drink. Our family has returned to the spirituality of
our ancestors. We attend sweat lodges and other ancient ceremonies with our people on sovereign native
land. We take panels of sober Natives into Indian
boarding schools and institutions, and share about recovery.

My life is filled with honesty today. Every action,
word, prayer, and Twelfth Step call is an investment in
my spiritual freedom and fulfillment. I am in love and
proud to be a Native American. At an A.A. meeting on
an Indian reservation, I heard the words "Sobriety is
traditional." I stand at the top of the sacred mountain,
and I listen to the wind. I have a conscious daily contact with my Creator today, and He loves me.
Everything is sacred as a result of the Twelve Steps
and the love and recovery in Alcoholics Anonymous.

(5)

TWICE GIFTED

Diagnosed with cirrhosis, this sick alcoholic got sobriety—plus a lifesaving liver transplant.

TODAY IS SUNDAY, my favorite day of the week. Things are usually peaceful, and I always get that wonderfully humbling, it's amazing to be alive, feeling. I am happy to say that very few days go by without that feeling.

Sunday used to be pretty wild in the old days. That is what I call my drinking days, the old days. It was the last day of the weekend, finishing up a few days of partying with my friends. I never went anywhere that was not a party, and if in doubt about the occasion, I'd think of a good one and bring the party with me. I cannot remember a time without booze in my life. Even when I was young and didn't drink myself, liquor was always around. I do remember a time at the beginning of my drinking, thinking to myself that I was not and would never become an alcoholic, knowing in a very personal way exactly how an alcoholic lived. I was a teenager then, and I figured I was just having fun and could control everything about my drinking. By the time I actually reached legal drinking age, I had definitely gone beyond weekend party drinking, and Sunday once again became the first day of the week, soon to become a week of daily drinking.

During my young adulthood, drinking was the way

I related to others. I did not know anyone who did not drink, and all of my interests, friendships, and more intimate relationships revolved completely around drinking. Over the years, by all appearances, I grew up and got a life, but it was only a façade. I never did mature other than in the physical way. I appeared normal on the outside. I knew I drank and so did everyone else, but I behaved pretty well and, only by chance, managed to stay out of harm's way, except for a few occasions. Looking back now, the picture of my life before I got sober looks like a long series of unfinished matters. Through the years I had quit on everything that ever mattered: college, going for promotions, relationships—at least the relationships that demanded any work.

Then a few things began to change. Some years before I finally gave up drinking, my body started to give me signals that continuing on this course might not be as carefree as it had seemed up to that point. When stomach problems began, I visited a doctor, and when queried about my drinking habits, I glossed over the idea that I overindulged. Tests were run, but no real diagnosis was ever confirmed. I was advised to maintain a healthy diet and watch alcohol intake, along with other prudent suggestions from the doctor. I was still young, and I thought to myself that just giving my body a break, by slowing down, would allow me to bounce back. Over the next few years I had quite a few episodes of feeling sick, and of course having never attended to the real problem, my drinking was still escalating. When my symptoms started to multiply, I finally had to consider the real possibility that drinking was the cause of all my health problems. For very brief moments I somehow realized that giving up the booze was probably in my future. With that realization came fear and so many questions. How will I live? What will I do with my life? Certainly a life without booze meant I would not have fun, and surely I would not be fun.

Up until the moment I realized I might have to give up drinking, I had believed I was perfectly happy. I had a fine life, a good job, a nice place to live, a car, friends, all the things I thought I needed in life. Ideas of getting help to quit drinking had surfaced but were fleeting and never grew into anything like reaching out. My health had finally taken a serious turn for the worse. I was frequently unable to get out of bed even to go to work, and strange new problems were exhibiting themselves with regularity. I resolved to divorce myself from the bottle, but trying to stop alone was disastrous. During the dry periods, I was very weak and sick. Then at times I would drink, and it was out of control. I would isolate and binge; those last drunks ended in episodes of uncontrollable shaking, dry heaves, and even hallucinations. At the end I was scared and suffering, and I felt as though I were absolutely alone in the world.

A series of circumstances brought me to a new doctor. I had to see a doctor because once again I had become fearfully ill, and I was unable to work. My stomach was distended, and my ankles were swollen nearly twice their normal size due to fluid retention. The whites of my eyes had yellowed from jaundice, I had spidery broken veins all over my body, my skin itched all over and took on an eerie greenish-gray appearance. My blood had apparently thinned, because the lightest touch would cause a terrible bruise and even a small scratch would bleed for a very long time. Dark marks appeared on my face and arms, my hair began to fall out, and because I had no appetite at all, I was very weak and extremely fatigued. The new physician took one look at my appearance and my blood test results, and asked if I drank. I said that I used to but had abstained for quite a while. This was a blatant lie.

In reality the only person who was being fooled was me. My new doctor explained that I had a disease called cirrhosis of the liver. How far it had progressed was hard to tell, but by the symptoms I was having and the results of my tests, the disease seemed fairly advanced. The picture he painted was very bleak. As the disease worsened, I would become sicker and weaker, and finally there would be a slow and painful progression, usually ending in a fatal episode of bleeding into the stomach or lapsing into a coma and death. With that, he referred me to a special clinic, not an ordinary group of doctors but a liver transplant clinic.

The initial interview with this group of doctors made it clear that if I wanted to live, I was going to have to prove that alcohol was no longer going to be part of my life. I was thirty-seven years old at the time, a relatively young woman for what was happening to my body. I was suddenly very afraid of dying, and I was desperate.

I had attended A.A. meetings prior to that time, but the words of the doctors had somehow, finally, begun to clear the way. At the meeting that first night more of what the people in A.A. were saying started to pass through my ears, and into my head, and finally into my heart. The members of Alcoholics Anonymous offered me a gift, a gift of life. I found myself willing, and after some weeks of just showing up, I began to believe that this program could work for me. The next six months were spent in A.A. meetings every single day, at least one, sometimes two or three. I found a wonderful, patient sponsor who helped me to work the steps and practice the principles.

During the six months of evaluation by the clinic, I was given a blood test at least weekly, sometimes randomly, to validate that I was not drinking. I had weekly meetings with the psychiatrist on the transplant team. My family members attended some of those meetings, and the doctor also had contact with my sponsor. Another mandate was that I enter some type of psychotherapy with a professional, either group or individual sessions. This too was not something I would have chosen for myself, but it has turned out to be a very positive force in my life. At the time of the evaluation, there had to be evidence that I was doing everything possible to assure my continued sobriety. After a six-month period I was officially listed as a candidate for a liver transplant.

By the time my name was placed on the transplant waiting list, I had become very sick. My liver had progressively continued to shut down, and the official wait had really just begun. I had no way of knowing how long it would be before a suitable organ would become available or how long it would be before I rose to the top of the list. At times I felt resentful of the selection process, the tests, the close supervision of my A.A. program, and the seemingly endless wait. Unquestionably it was only because of the program of

Alcoholics Anonymous that I was able to let go of that resentment. I actually found an abundance of peace and serenity during those months preceding the surgery. After another six months I was given a second chance and a second gift of life. The surgery itself was a wonderful success, and my recuperation was unmarked by setbacks.

Some years have passed, and as I look back from the clarity of this moment, I know that the way here for me could not have been by an easier path. I would not willingly have stopped the course my life was on. I needed harsh reality to see the damage that alcohol abuse causes, in so many ways. I needed to be forced into acceptance and humility.

My physical being has certainly undergone a transformation, but the major transformation has been spiritual. The hopelessness has been replaced by abundant hope and sincere faith. The people of Alcoholics Anonymous have provided a haven where, if I remain aware and keep my mind quiet enough, my Higher Power leads me to amazing realizations. I find joy in my daily life, in being of service, in simply being. I have found rooms full of wonderful people, and for me each and every one of the Big Book's promises have come true. The things that I have learned from my own experience, from the Big Book, and from my friends in A.A.—patience, acceptance, honesty, humility, and true faith in a Power greater than myself—are the tools I use today to live my life, this precious life.

Today my life is filled with miracles big and small, not one of which would ever have come to pass had I not found the door of Alcoholics Anonymous.

BUILDING A NEW LIFE

Hallucinating and restrained by sheriff's deputies and hospital staff, this once-happy family man received an unexpected gift from God—a firm foundation in sobriety that would hold up through good times and bad.

WE HAD BEEN in the fields all day baling hay. When the work was done, the men brought out a gallon of muscatel. I took a few drinks because I wanted to be like the men, and for a few minutes I felt like one of them. Then I fell asleep under the outdoor table where my mother fed the workers. When I was found, they carried me into bed, and the next day I got a scolding. I was six years old.

My early years were spent on my aunt and uncle's farm. They raised me after my father and mother divorced. My father kept my two brothers and two sisters; my grandmother took me, the baby, and when raising a baby was too much for her, I ended up on the farm.

Life was hard work in those days. We ate what we grew ourselves, plus the few store items we traded for. By age eight I was guiding a horse-drawn plow by myself. In the family and in our farming community, we spoke only Spanish. It wasn't until I went to school that I was forced to speak English and was told that speaking Spanish wasn't right. I never felt I was as smart as the other kids or as good as anyone else. On the farm I knew I could do anything; in school it was a different story.

At thirteen I was tall, strong, and looked older. My aunt and uncle had sent me to live with a family in a larger town to get schooling they hoped would help me. I went around with guys who were eighteen, and they took me to a Halloween party. I almost choked on the first sip of the whiskey they were passing around, but by the second sip, I thought it was pretty good stuff. It made me feel like one of the guys. It didn't matter that I was only thirteen; I felt just as old as they were. By the end of the night, I had passed out in the outhouse and had to be carried home by a friend.

By fifteen, picking produce in the summer to earn money, I was sneaking out nightly to drink beer in the fields with the other pickers. Primed with beer, I could talk to girls and go to dances. I was just like everyone else; I could enjoy the day. I was the equal of others, even if they were older.

The next summer I began working construction during school vacation. I was working with the older men, and at the end of the day, I went to the bar with them. The bartender would put the beer in front of the man next to me, but it was intended for me. I loved Fridays—payday—when we went out and got loaded. I started getting liquor on weekends so I could go to dances. I was hanging around with guys who drank like me. We'd put our money together to get enough booze for the night, and because I looked older, I bought the liquor. I could talk to the girls. I was a big shot with the guys because I had the booze and the girls.

Two days before Christmas I was on the way to basic training. On the train's next to last stop, my buddies from home and I got off and rushed to the bar to buy liquor to celebrate Christmas. Back on the train, we were warned that the M.P.'s were throwing bottles out the windows, so we drank ours hard and fast and got loaded.

After basic we were sent to different bases. I didn't drink often because I wanted to get ahead, but every time I drank, I wouldn't stop until everything was gone. I didn't know how to say, "I'm going to quit now."

At home on leave, I married a young woman from my hometown, and our first daughter was born the next year. When I came home from the air force, soon after that, the party really started. A big hero like me! I drank only on weekends at first, drinking and dancing with my old buddies and their new wives. The only car accident I was in while drunk happened that year. It was a hit-and-run on a parked car, and my buddy just pulled the car's fender off the front of my car and we kept on driving. The next morning we looked in the paper to see if the accident was mentioned. It wasn't, and we were never found out.

The same construction company I had worked for in the summers as a high school kid hired me as an apprentice carpenter. I was smart and learned fast. Then I got too smart and forgot all that company had done for me. I complained to them about money I thought they had promised, and they fired me.

Using the G.I. Bill I went to mechanic's school at night and got a job with the city. That's when I really started drinking. These guys had a ritual. As soon as they got to work, they bought a bottle of wine. At first I didn't participate. I didn't drink wine, not a tough guy like me. But then one day I decided I might as well drink. I had a couple and I liked it. For the next five years, I drank every day.

Finally I was injured on the job and sent home for a week, but I was supposed to call in every day. But I didn't, I couldn't; I was drunk every day. On the fourth day the boss came to my house to check on me. I wasn't there, but I returned, drunk, before they left. They didn't say anything, but the next day the union leader told me I was going to get fired. I went to city hall and resigned.

Three more daughters had been born to my wife and me during those years. I was filled with remorse, guilt, and fear because I didn't have a job. I knew I had screwed up. There was no unemployment then. To my mind it was bad luck, not me. I took whatever construction work I could get, even nonunion, whatever there was.

My first son was born, and my second son two years later. I had recovered my pride and wondered why I should make all this money for other people. I thought I should become a contractor and make it for myself, so I took the exam and got my license. I curtailed my drinking a little bit and business started getting good, so I started drinking more. I'd go to the bar and leave my crews working by themselves. By the third year I spent all my time in bars. I couldn't finish the jobs I had, and I had spent all the money. I was in bad shape. I was a full-blown alcoholic, blaming God and bad luck. It had me down; I just couldn't get back up, and I lost my business.

For the next three years I was working odd jobs, two days here, three days there. I was barely making it, with a big family to support. I didn't bring home enough. I drank it up. My wife was griping and cussing, and I just wanted to get away from it all.

I started taking jobs out of town. One time I was a foreman for an aluminum siding company. I don't know how we got jobs finished. Every morning I was hung-over, sick. The workers would have to wait for me to start. At noon I would go to the bar to fix myself up, and then I would party at night.

There was only fighting at home, and I finally moved out so the kids wouldn't see me drunk. Now I can really drink, I thought. My wife went on welfare, and I even stopped contributing after a while. I had to have enough to drink. I continued to work construction, but I wasn't very dependable. I'd work okay for three or four weeks, and then I wouldn't want to get up in the morning. I'll get another job, I would think, but I always got fired.

A few years later I was arrested driving while intoxicated, but it was reduced to reckless driving, with the help of a state police buddy of mine. I was told, however, that if I had one more offense, they would take my license away. That was at the same time as my first try at A.A. I couldn't get sober, and I couldn't get drunk. I was feeling scared, remorseful, guilty. I ran to a hamburger stand near my apartment, looked in the phone book for the number of a clubhouse for A.A.'s, and gave them a call. Two men came to my apartment and stayed with me, drinking coffee until after the bars closed. They kept coming, taking me to meetings for a month. I thought I was doing okay, so I didn't need it anymore. It felt like those two guys were after me, bothering me too much. So I got drunk to get back at them.

After that I moved to California. My kids were on welfare while I was touring all over. I never knew anyone could make the money I made in union construction jobs in California, so I drank it up. I didn't feel bad about the kids because I was drunk all the time. I sent them presents. When I got sober, I felt bad about them, so I'd drink again. I couldn't stand being sober because I couldn't stand thinking about how I hadn't taken care of my own kids.

I did a lot of drinking on the job. Carpenters worked in shorts and had coolers of beer. There were beer cans all around the job site. I would go to the all-night store early every morning to buy a bottle of wine for my thermos, to keep me going until lunch. Then I'd buy wine at lunch for the afternoon. And on my way home I'd buy a six-pack of beer and a bottle of wine for my evening. That was the cycle of my life.

Once, I was stopped because my truck was "weaving" while I was driving home from a friend's house, and they gave me a D.W.I. It meant a $300 fine and one year of probation, and I didn't think I would make it, so I decided to move back home.

I spent three months on unemployment, which to me meant three months of partying. When the money ran out, I looked for a job. Even though my California union card meant nothing, I got a job as a foreman back with my first employer. I look back on that now and I think, was God good to me, or what? And I was blaming God all this time for my troubles.

Since it was my first job in some three months, I

celebrated, staying drunk. I would go to the job site and get the workers set up, then take off to drink. This lasted until the day I told off the owner of a company we were working for, and I got fired. That job put me on the union hiring list, however, and I got good jobs, with good companies. I began to try to get sober. Sometimes I could last for a week or two. Then I would get drunk again. I was seeing the kids a lot then. I moved into an apartment behind my wife's house, sharing it with my father-in-law. My daughters were married by then, and my sons were in junior high school. I wasn't included in family events, but I was there.

That year I went to an alcohol treatment program twice. The first time I was in treatment, I was shaving at the mirror in the bathroom and it seemed to me that my beard was growing back in as fast as I could shave it off. Even though I was in a hospital gown, I escaped, running down the streets and jumping up and over fences. I was on the porch of a woman's house banging on the door for her to let me in when the police arrived. I tried to convince them she was my wife and my children were inside, but they saw the hospital bracelet on my wrist, and they took me back to the program.

Those were the days when they strapped you down to protect you when you went into D.T.'s. They were the worst D.T.'s I had ever experienced. I had never been so scared in my life. I thought gangsters were after me and they were going to kill me. They had me tied down, so I tried to be very quiet and hide so they wouldn't find me. The doctor told me that if I went into D.T.'s like that again I might not come out. I stayed sober three months after that experience, going to some A.A. meetings. Then I drank again. A few months later I was back in the treatment program, not as sick this time, and I stayed sober for three more months.

Then I went on a ten-day binge. I was filled with fear and I couldn't walk. I had to crawl to make it to the bathroom. I eventually cleaned myself up and managed to work. Then a Thanksgiving party on the job started me back drinking every day through Christmas. I was laid off after that; then I really got down to some serious drinking. By mid-January I was having hallucinations that would not go away.

I called a residential treatment program and said I wanted help. They told me I could be admitted in three days. I drank to maintain for those three days. Amazingly, I knew that once I got to the program my drinking would be over.

One of my daughters drove me to the program and helped me fill out the paperwork. I almost fell down going into the building. My hallucinations began again, and the staff moved me to a room with a padded floor they called the TV room. I began to think I was in prison and these guys wanted to kill me. When they opened the door to the room, I ran for a window down the hall, thinking I would escape. They grabbed me, afraid I would try to jump through it. I kept hitting my shoulder against the wall trying to break out and picked at nails with my fingertips until they were raw. The staff called the sheriff's department, and it took three deputies, two counselors, and two nurses to hold me down and give me a shot. Finally I lay there quietly, ready to die like a man.

It was three days later when I woke up, naked and stinking. They cleaned me up and I felt great. I'd never felt so good, like I'd never had a drink. I went to the treatment sessions and listened to everything that was said. They took us out to A.A. meetings. I wanted what the A.A.'s had. I don't think I ever wanted anything as much as I wanted the program. I saw men dressed in suits in those days, looking good. That's how I wanted to be. The thought of a drink has not entered my mind since. I've thought of doing some crazy things but never about taking a drink. To me sobriety is a gift from God to me. If I drank, it would be giving the gift back. If you return a gift, the person takes it back, right? If God takes it back, I'm dead.

In my first year in A.A. I was going to at least seven meetings a week. I just loved it. I dressed up in suits like the men I had seen. I went to work building a mall, and there was an A.A. member working there who had eight years of sobriety, and we would share together every day. I know now God put that guy there for me.

During that year, I was offered a job with the city and one with a construction company out of town. My sponsor counseled me to stay where I had the support of my group and my A.A. friends; I was too young in the program for an adventure. I went with the city and am now retired from there. A guy like me—with one employer for eighteen years!

Once I was sober, my wife took me back. I felt that I had to go back to take care of the kids I had once left on welfare. My third son is our A.A. baby. I also got to see all our boys play sports. There were other

A.A.'s with kids on the teams, and we would hang around together at the games. I really enjoyed myself. My sobriety baby is now in college. I have beautiful relationships with all my kids.

Pushed by my sponsor, I got into service work right away, and I really enjoyed it. Now I'm a general service representative of a Spanish-speaking group, learning how to express myself about this great gift of sobriety in my original language.

There have been some hard times too during these years of sobriety. When I was five years sober, the daughter who drove me to the treatment program and helped me get admitted disappeared. My A.A. friends helped me search for her, but she has never been found. Her mother and I raised her three daughters. I did not have to take a drink. I went to lots of meetings to relieve the pain. When I lost a second daughter to cancer a few years ago, I did the same thing.

What I've learned is that it doesn't matter what hardships and losses I've endured in sobriety, I have not had to go back to drinking. As long as I work the program, keep being of service, go to meetings, and keep my spiritual life together, I can live a decent life.

When I look back now, I think I stopped maturing at fifteen when I started to get drunk with the older guys. I wanted to feel at peace with myself and comfortable with other people. I never found it in drinking. The belonging I always wanted I have found in A.A. and in sobriety. I don't think about drinking. God is there. My sponsor is there. All the credit belongs to God. On my own I could not have quit. I know, I tried it.

(7)

ON THE MOVE

Working the A.A. program showed this alcoholic how to get from geographics to gratitude.

I THOUGHT MY LIFE had come to an end when I arrived at my first meeting of Alcoholics Anonymous at twenty-eight years old. I had been drinking since my early teens, and to my way of thinking, booze had been the answer to my problems, not the problem itself. Even I had to admit, though, that my life had gotten pretty bad and my options were quickly running out. In a moment of desperation, I agreed to go to *one* A.A. meeting.

It is easier to see now, as I look back on my drinking days, that from the very beginning alcohol had been a part of nearly every disaster in my life. As a very young boy, perhaps ten or eleven years old, I had begun to steal drinks when my parents were not looking, or my friends and I would convince someone from the local high school to buy us some beer. Slowly, but very steadily, my problems began to grow from there.

It started with simple episodes at school. My buddies and I would split a six-pack over lunch and thought nobody would notice. It never occurred to me that a thirteen-year-old could not easily hide the effects of even a single beer. By the time I was fourteen or fifteen, things were getting far more serious, and the consequences of my drinking were getting more costly in every way—socially, morally, financially.

A turning point came when I was fifteen. My mom was in the middle of an ugly divorce. Through nobody's fault but my own, I decided that I had the answer. In a drunken brawl, having planned every step of my actions, I attempted to kill my stepfather. I vaguely remember being dragged out of the house by the police and came to, yet again, trying to answer for what I had done while drunk. The results were that I was eventually given a choice by the judge: Go to juvenile hall until I was twenty-five years old, or leave the state until I was at least twenty-one. I did not want to go to juvenile hall, so I did the math and decided the better part of valor was to get as far away from there as I could.

Over the next thirteen years, until I graced the doors of A.A. for the first time, life really never got any better. I did, however, learn the fine art of geographics. From my home on the East Coast, I landed in Japan. Then I moved back to the United States and to New England, then out to California, where over the next six years I saw my alcoholism take me to new depths of disgrace, embarrassment, and despair. As one of my early A.A. sponsors used to say, I didn't hang out with lower companions—I had become one.

The specifics are pretty much the same as for most alcoholics. I went places I used to swear I would never go. I did things I could not imagine myself doing. I hung out with people that at one time I would cross the street to avoid. There came a time when, looking into the mirror, I honestly did not know just who was looking back at me. To say that I had arrived at a "jumping-off point" is an understatement. Life just could not go on like this much longer.

I began the process of speeding up the day when life would end. My doctor has six or seven suicide attempts on my medical records. Most were pitiful efforts to reach out for help, although I didn't see it at the time. My last such attempt was very public and demonstrated that I had lost touch with reality and with any sense of what my actions could do to others.

A friend took pity on me, I think, and invited me to his home for Thanksgiving. His parents were in town from the East Coast, and he was having a big party. There at the dinner table, I stood up and attempted suicide in front of everyone. The memory of that has always stuck in my mind as the definition of "pitiful, incomprehensible demoralization" that the Big Book talks about. What is sadder is that my actions had made sense to me at the time.

As a result of that episode, I ended up seeing a psychiatrist to find out what was wrong with me. At our very first session she invited me to "tell me about yourself." I proceeded to do so, only to be told to stop after I had only spoken for five minutes or so. She explained that she really only had two things to say to me: that she thought I hadn't told the truth since I walked into the office, and that I was an alcoholic. (It took me a long time to understand how a description of my life could make anyone think I was a drunk.) The doctor said that if I was going to continue to see her, I had to agree to do two things. First, she gave me a business card with a phone number on it. She said the next time I tried to kill myself, I should call that number first. Second, she was going to give me a book to read, and she wanted me to read the first few hundred pages before our next meeting. Before I left that day, she gave me a copy of the Big Book.

It took some time, but I eventually made it to my first meeting. I had gone out on New Year's Eve. When I came to, I thought it was the next morning. As I held my head steady, popped some aspirin, and tried to drink a cup of coffee, I glanced at the front page of the newspaper. It was January 9, and I had been in a blackout for over a week. After everything else that had happened, that was terrifying enough to get me to my first meeting of Alcoholics Anonymous.

When I drove up to that first meeting, though, I saw that the address I had was actually a church. As a nice Jewish boy, I was not about to wander into a church; I knew that I would not be welcome. I hid on the floorboards of the car and peeked out the window, waiting for the drunks to walk by. Everyone looked normal, so I figured I might be in the wrong place. I was about to leave, but then I saw a drinking buddy of mine go by. I jumped out of my car and greeted him. Funny thing, but it was his first meeting of Alcoholics Anonymous also. What a coincidence! In we walked— into a world that has turned everything in my life inside out.

I didn't like A.A. and the people in it for a long time. I didn't trust anyone, and I got tired of sitting at meetings listening to other newcomers as they began to talk of finding God, having their families return to them, being treated with respect by society, and finding some peace of mind. It never occurred to me that they had sponsors and were working the Twelve Steps

of recovery. I had what I now call "a sponsor of the
month." I always had a sponsor, but whenever one of
them would "lovingly suggest" I do something, I
would fire them and move on to someone else. I remained angry, bitter, and isolated, even though I was
going to five or six A.A. meetings per week and was
not drinking. At seven months sober I was getting a
little bored with A.A. and began to wonder if this was
all there was to life. The concept of not drinking again
seemed a little extreme, and I thought that perhaps it
would be different this time.

Then something happened that I now believe helped
me to stay sober and find my Higher Power. I woke up
one morning and couldn't feel my legs. I could still
walk with a little difficulty, but it got worse as time
passed. Several months and lots of medical examinations, doctors, hospital visits, and tests later, I was diagnosed with multiple sclerosis. The path since then has
been quite a journey. I now either walk with crutches
or use a wheelchair. There have been lots of times I
wanted and intended to drink again. During my second
year of sobriety, I slowly became angrier and angrier. I
was in what one of my sponsors now refers to as "the
angry years." I was one of those people we see at meetings and wonder how they stay sober.

At my home group, members didn't give up on me;
they loved me anyway. One day the group's general
service representative announced she was moving and
would have to give up her commitment, and they
elected me to her job. They explained to me that a serious, two-year service commitment was exactly what I
needed. I tried to explain that I was not eligible, but
they told me to go to the monthly general service

business meeting and tell them my problems with serving. Needless to say, they didn't allow me to quit either.

Along the way I learned, in spite of myself, that the best thing about A.A. service jobs is that, for a period of time, I got out of myself. At some point I began to shut my mouth and actually listen to what other people were saying at meetings. After white-knuckling it for almost two years in A.A., I finally broke down and saw that I could not stay sober all by myself, but I was terrified of going back to drinking. After all my suicide attempts I had no fear of dying, but I could not stand the idea that I would go back to living that way again. I was at what the oldtimers and our literature refer to as a "jumping-off point." I didn't know what to do.

One evening I did the unimaginable—at least for me. After picking up my sponsor of the month to go to a meeting, I informed him that I was ready to work the Twelve Steps of Alcoholics Anonymous. In most respects my life began again that night. That man took me through the steps in a loving, gentle way that for the remainder of my life I will be grateful for. He taught me to look inward at my soul, to welcome a Higher Power into my life, and to reach out to others. He taught me how to look into a mirror and to like, and even respect, the man who looked back at me.

When I reached the Ninth Step, I began to hesitate in my enthusiasm. One morning I woke up covered in sweat and could not get over a nightmare I had—that this was my last day of sobriety. After calling friends and my sponsor, I knew what had to be done. I spent the entire day, more than eight or nine hours, going into people's offices and making my amends. Some were thrilled to see me. One woman called the police. When they arrived, it turned out the policeman was in A.A., and he convinced the woman not to press charges. I even ran into someone who I had thought was dead, so I took a "dead guy" to lunch and made my amends to him also. For the first time I thought, and actually felt, as if I was a member of Alcoholics Anonymous, with something to share at meetings.

When I was four years sober, I took a trip back to my home city, one of the very few times since I had left so many years before under the threat of jail time. I made amends to the man I had attempted to kill when I was fifteen years old. I visited, and made amends to, several people who had sat at that Thanksgiving dinner table and had watched me attempt suicide in front of them. I came home exhausted but knew that I had somehow done the right thing. It is probably no coincidence that the following year my old friend invited me back for Thanksgiving dinner.

A.A., and the steps of recovery, have shown me how to look at events in a different way. I can now understand how some things, which once seemed like major disasters, turned out to be blessings. Certainly my alcoholism fits that category. I am truly a grateful alcoholic today. I do not regret the past nor wish to shut the door on it. Those events that once made me feel ashamed and disgraced now allow me to share with others how to become a useful member of the human race. My physical disability has not altered that attitude; if anything, it has enhanced it. Long ago I learned that no matter how uncomfortable I was physically, I felt better by getting out of myself and helping someone else. It has also helped to learn how to laugh at myself and to not take myself so seriously. I am aware that I am not the only person on this earth with problems.

Through my experiences in general service, A.A. has shown me how widespread and diverse the program is. I have traveled throughout the United States and even went to Israel for several months a few years ago. While there, I attended meetings and was the secretary to a meeting located in a bomb shelter.

Like everyone else I have good days and bad days. Unlike my attitude while I was still drinking, however, I rarely dread what is going to happen to me today. I have even had the chance to see my father come into A.A. We have been to numerous A.A. conventions together and have shared more with each other in the past few years than we ever had before. I think we are both at peace with our pasts and comfortable with the present.

In the past several years I have gone back to school and begun a new career. As I roll around in my wheelchair, I am amazed when I realize that I honestly cannot imagine life to be anything different than what it has been—and that is just fine with me. The tools of sobriety and recovery in A.A. are there for me to use in all aspects of my life, and all I ever need is the willingness to do what is in front of me. I am grateful that a drunk like me was fortunate enough to live until I arrived in Alcoholics Anonymous.

(8)

A VISION OF RECOVERY

A feeble prayer forged a lasting connection with a Higher Power for this Mic-Mac Indian.

I THOUGHT I WAS DIFFERENT because I'm an Indian." I heard that statement from many Natives at my early A.A. meetings. I would only shrug and say to myself: You think you're different, what about me? I'm a red-headed Indian.

I grew up on a reservation in Canada. As a young fellow, I was a proud Mic-Mac Indian. My family had a reputation: They were hard drinkers, violent and tough, and I was proud of this. I was told that my grandfather had been the chief of our band, but he had to step down because he went to jail for shooting a man. Jail was almost a badge of honor in my family, or so it seemed to me. As a small boy, I remember standing on top of a case of beer (there were always lots around the house), saying to myself: In a few years I will be this tall.

There were times, though, when I witnessed my father's rages and I was full of fear. I swore that I would not be like him, but I didn't see that alcohol and the rages were related.

I always thought I was different. On many occasions I wished I had black hair like my friends. Mic-Mac was the language in our home, but I would not speak it. All my family spoke Mic-Mac, but when they spoke to me, I would answer in English. I believed I couldn't speak Mic-Mac as well as my parents, so I resolved not to speak it at all.

I was ten years old when I had my first drink of alcohol. On New Year's Eve I stole two glasses of vodka from my parents. I can't say that it did what it was supposed to do, for I got deathly sick, threw up, and had diarrhea. The next day I was full of fear that my parents would find out. I learned my lesson for a while.

A few years later, in junior high school, a few friends and I got a bottle of rum from a bootlegger. I got really drunk, and it was great. I remember having a feeling of complete freedom. I drank for the next fifteen years. Drinking became a major part of my life and I thought it was normal. Then came the violence, the fighting, the illegal acts, and the image of "the tough guy." My family was proud of me, and some relatives would actually encourage me.

I spent a number of years in and out of juvenile correctional facilities, and after my eighteenth birthday, I began spending time in county jail. I actually got a high when I came home, knowing that my friends and relatives would respect me more because I had been in jail and was becoming a man.

While in a juvenile detention center about 500 miles from my home, I received word that my mother was dying of cancer. I was able to get a pass and return home to spend time with her. One evening my family asked me if I would stay home with my mother and give her the medicine she was required to take. I had already had a few drinks and was anxious to get out and party with my friends, but I reluctantly agreed to stay. Self-pity set in, and all I could think of was the good time I could have been having. I got very impatient with my mother, and when she refused to take her medicine, I almost forced it into her mouth; then I left to join my friends. The next morning I woke up in county jail, about 100 miles from home. I had attempted a break-and-enter, and was caught by the police.

That very evening, as I sat in jail, my mother died. I was allowed out for the funeral, and I still recall how alone I felt, even when I was with my family. I felt shame and remorse, and for years to come I believed I was somehow responsible for my mother's death. This incident haunted me for years. Alcohol would take it away for a while, but the remorse always returned. I tried to comfort myself by saying that my lifestyle was a part of my destiny just like many of my family members, but this did not remove the remorse.

I can remember only one good thing that happened during this time. As my mother lay dying, I talked to her in the Mic-Mac language. She seemed so happy, and she told me that it sounded beautiful to hear me speaking Mic-Mac. I cherish this memory.

I was to meet a young girl and have a son. Proud, I named him after myself, and my drinking slowed down for a little while. One day I promised my son that "tomorrow" I would take him to the movies. I really meant it from the bottom of my heart, and I was looking forward to it. That night I took a drink, and it led to many more. The next day I was hung-over, and even though I had promised to go to the movies that afternoon, I took a drink to fix myself up. That drink was followed by many more, and I justified them by telling myself: My son is so young, he will never remember the movie. The day after the promised movie I was guilty and remorseful, and felt I was just no good. I faced my son, only to hear him talking excitedly about going to a movie. I couldn't say anything, for the movie was no longer playing. I left his mother to explain.

The next few years saw me living back in the old home with my father, as my girl had left me, taking my son. My drinking escalated even more, as did the guilt, remorse, and fear. I was hospitalized for dehydration, had a mild stroke, spent a week in a psychiatric ward, and suffered a number of alcoholic seizures. I lost the trust of my family and friends. They simply could not rely on me for anything. I would stop for a while, but I always drank again.

I can certainly identify with our co-founder Bill W. when he says on page 4 of the Big Book: ". . . the old fierce determination to win came back." I would take a drink, and then I knew everything was going to be all right. I was going to clean up my act; everything was going to change—you'll see. It didn't; nothing changed. I tried so many ways of beating the game: I went to church and took a pledge; I went to a Native sweat lodge; I would do something so I would be put in jail; I vowed to stay away from hard liquor. Nothing worked. Then came the pills to stop the shakes and get off the sauce for a while.

One evening during a party at my home, an argument led to fighting, as usual. One of my brothers stabbed me in the back with a knife, and I fell to the floor unconscious. I came to in the hospital. They told me that one lung had collapsed, and they had a drain in my lung that came out the side of my body. The very next day some friends came to visit me, bringing a bottle of liquor. I still had that pride. I was still the tough guy. I lay there in bed with tubes draining my lung and smoked cigarettes and drank liquor. Later, in A.A., I had the nerve to question Step Two and wonder why I had to be "restored to sanity."

I can honestly say that nothing worked for me until I joined Alcoholics Anonymous. Eventually I ended up in a treatment center, and after a twenty-eight-day program, I began attending A.A. meetings on a regular basis. The treatment center introduced me to the Big Book of Alcoholics Anonymous, and I left there knowing that the only hope for me was the Twelve Steps.

I was told that A.A. is a spiritual program and that I had better have a Higher Power. I knew nothing of God or Higher Powers, and I began trying to find one. At first I thought that since I was a Native, maybe I should practice the Native traditional ways. Then I thought maybe I should go to the church on the reservation. Then I believed that if I went to enough A.A. meetings and just sat there, I would have a vision and achieve recovery. One day a member asked me if I believed that there actually was a Higher Power. I did believe there was a God of some sort or another. He told me that was enough. He said with that belief and attending meetings, I would find a Higher Power of my own understanding. Today I am thankful for that advice.

After three months in A.A., I returned home one evening after a meeting to hear the music and laughter of a party next door. Some of my drinking buddies were at that party, and I just knew I was going to end up there. I did not want to drink, yet the party was like a magnet. I was full of fear as I ran across the street to a pay telephone. I called my sponsor, but there was no answer. Panic set in as I ran home. In the house I went into my bedroom and sat on the side of the bed. I looked up and said these words: "Well, Buddy, I guess there's just you and me." Believe it or not, it worked; those simple words worked. Something happened: A little peace came over me, anxiety left, and then I lay down and fell asleep. I slept well that night, the first good sleep in a long time. That feeble request to God worked. I was honest and really wanted God's help. From that day on, I knew that I had found a Higher Power and that He would help me.

Over the next few months my life slowly began to change as I worked on Step One of our recovery program. I listened to speakers and began a Big Book study with an older member. In Mic-Mac folklore there are little people we call Bugalademujs. They live in the mountains, but they often sneak into our homes to play tricks on us, usually at night so we won't see them. When I noticed that Chapter 4 of the Big Book, "We Agnostics," had appeared to change, I told A.A. members that the Bugalademujs were fooling around with my Big Book. You know what—they are still at it today.

I now understand that the spiritual malady should be my main concern and that the more faith I have, the fewer problems I will have. Today I have more faith than I ever had, and as my faith grows, my fears lessen.

For a guy who has spent years in jails, hospitals, psychiatric wards, a guy who just could not stop drinking, there was only one answer—Alcoholics Anonymous and the Twelve Steps. I was very fortunate that I was steered in the right direction. A dramatic change has taken place in my life. Soon I hope to celebrate my second anniversary of continuous sobriety. In two years my whole life has changed. Today I sponsor others. I understand the word *compassion*, and I feel it. I am working on Step Eight at the present time, and I just know that more happiness is to come into my life as I "trudge the Road of Happy Destiny."

(9)

GUTTER BRAVADO

Alone and unemployable, he was given two options by the court, get help or go to jail, and his journey toward teachability began.

I WAS BORN in a major midwestern city at the tail end of the baby boom. My parents were not well-to-do, but they were employed and pursuing the American dream in the mid-1950s. Dad was an ex-policeman who had put himself through law school and worked with banks and as a real estate broker. Mom had graduated from a well-known East Coast college, majoring in journalism, and moved west to marry my father and raise a family. Both were children of hard-working European immigrants.

Growing up, my big brother and I went to church on Sundays and attended parochial schools. We had plenty to eat and more than just the basic necessities of life. I was a smart but mischievous kid, and at some point I decided it was easier to lie than to suffer the consequences of my pranks. Dad was big on law and order but especially didn't like liars. We often had conflicts. Other than this, my early childhood was a relatively happy one.

Eventually my brother went off to college, and I started venturing into the world on my own. I enjoyed my friends and our many adventures. This is where my first experiments with alcohol began. Sharing a few beers or a stolen bottle with friends on Friday nights was my approach to maturity and adulthood. In school I developed the reputation of never quite working up to my potential. I felt the world took things much too seriously. Where I saw myself as fun-loving and happy-go-lucky, others saw irresponsibility and insolence. A rebellious nature soon started to surface.

In the mid-sixties I had the opportunity to visit my brother, who had a fellowship at a university in California. These were heady times, and my experiences there left a lasting impression on me. There was music in the air and dancing in the streets. Little wonder that after returning to the Midwest I soon became a discipline problem. Disillusioned with what I saw as the mundane trivialities of school, I found it harder and harder to concentrate. I longed for the carefree life. By the fall of 1968, after leaving three different schools, I decided I'd had enough. So I quit the books, packed my guitar, left home, and headed back to the West Coast filled with the optimism of youth and intending to make a life for myself.

My tiny grubstake soon started to run out, and work was hard to find. I panhandled a little but found I was too proud for it or, more likely, not hungry enough. I began living hand-to-mouth, but my survival skills were not as sharp as I thought. In warmer weather I camped in the woods near the coastal highway. The barking of the sea lions made it hard to sleep. With winter approaching, I roamed the waterfront and the streets, sleeping in storerooms and seedy hotels or flopping with migrant farm workers in town for their off-season.

What had begun as an adventure was turning into a

nightmare. My moments of escape from this uncomfortable reality came when I persuaded someone to share their wine or vodka. With a drink in me, my confidence returned, my direction seemed clear-cut, and I reveled in lofty plans and dreams for the future. Drinking to escape became as important as eating to survive. All of the gutter bravado and determination crumbled when, in the end, I ran up against the law. The authorities sent me packing back to the Midwest with nothing more than the clothes on my back.

Arriving home, I dazzled my friends with exaggerated tales of exotic people and strange happenings, some of them true. We went straight out drinking, and I picked up right where I left off. Always the object was to go out and "get wasted." Though I sometimes had trouble holding my liquor, I was willing to try harder. I felt the key to successful drinking was the same as it is in musicianship—practice, practice, practice.

After an attempt at college, I sought employment, often with a hangover. The jobs I found I considered to be menial. I did not yet know that all work is honorable. The maintenance crews, the electroplating, the factory work, and the pharmaceutical industry (after emptying the trash, I started on the shelves) were all on my résumé. My thievery, tardiness, and absenteeism, the reasons for my dismissals, weren't on my résumé. I was becoming generally dissatisfied, but I did not know that the problem was within me. I wanted some of the finer things in life, but upon realizing they took effort, I dismissed them as trappings of the establishment. Watching out for a bag of money by the side of the road was more my idea of planning for the future.

In spite of my drinking, I managed to save a little money. With my first thousand dollars I bought a motorcycle. With this I purchased a lifestyle more than a means of transportation. For years afterward I lived the biker lifestyle. At times raw and exciting, my existence revolved around building and drag racing motorcycles. Ride hard, live fast, and die young were the new rules. Weekdays I spent bar-hopping the neighborhoods. Weekends would find me in the clubs downtown. As the years passed, my circle of friends grew smaller. Some died accidentally, some were killed, some went to jail, and some just developed the good sense to get out and grow up. These were the ones I didn't understand. I sure wasn't making any new friends, so more and more I found myself a loner.

In the mid-seventies I was hired by the steel industry, a union job at good pay. Soon I bid to a craft job and started learning the electrical trade. The work was hot, dirty, and dangerous. Everyone worked swing shift and at the end of my turn, I felt as if I had survived an ordeal. The first stop was the tavern on top of the hill. Many times there was no second stop. Liquor was not the only recreational substance available there, and I was no stranger to any of them. This was where I got my first bar tab, so no matter how broke I was, I could always stop in for drinks after work. While the guys around me were buying homes, raising families, and otherwise living responsibly, I was already having trouble keeping my utilities on and my car running. I saw to it that I paid my bar tab, however.

My life became the pursuit of intoxication. After a few drinks I felt more normal and in control. I changed from a furtive loner into a party animal. My jokes were funnier, the girls were prettier, I shot better pool, and the juke box played better tunes. I could look people in the eye and mingle with the best of them.

Every so often I took work-related college courses. Spending time with normal people, I began to see how wild I had become. My cherished individualism was turning into isolationism. I had a growing uneasiness that I was in a vicious circle. I had no friends—only acquaintances. This fact was underscored by the bullet holes in my car, courtesy of one acquaintance I had double-crossed. My only sense of relief was in the bottle, but even that was beginning to fail me. My dreams had long since faded, my direction was unclear, my confidence lost, and the drinking would not restore them as it once had. Personal hygiene became an afterthought. There were times when I would try to live without drinking, but it was difficult, often ending at the most inappropriate times. I cleaned up for special occasions such as holidays, funerals, job interviews, and court dates, only to fail in the final hour, snapping back to the bottle like a rubber band. Planned abstinence was extremely stressful.

The downward spiral of my life began making smaller circles. My driving record included many accidents and a ticket list that would raise a policeman's eyebrows. When I carried insurance, it was high risk. I grew sneakier and less outwardly defiant. Despite breaking laws routinely for years, I stayed out of big trouble for the most part. A few times they almost had me, but I managed to scam on technicalities or I got yet another break. Finally an indiscretion committed years earlier came back to haunt me. I was about to have a forced encounter with the federal judicial system. I began to feel like a clown juggling too many balls. Each ball represented a problem I was keeping up in the air. My arms were weary and I knew I couldn't keep on much longer, but I was not about to give up. My pride and ego wouldn't let me. Bosses, judges, co-workers, lawyers, car notes, bar tabs, loan sharks, utility payments, landlords, my girlfriend, people I had double-crossed—I looked to all these as the source of my problems, while overlooking the most basic problem: my drinking and myself. I'd known for a long time that I desperately wanted off this merry-go-round, but I had no idea how to do it.

The judge had no trouble coming up with a few ideas, however. I got house arrest with electronic monitoring and strictly supervised probation with random urinalysis for openers. Five years in the penitentiary waited after that. I still played the angles, until it became clear to the authorities that I could not live up to the conditions of my probation. It didn't matter what the consequences were—I couldn't not drink, and I gave up trying. When the court eventually called me in for my violations, they gave me two choices: get help or go to jail. After careful thought I chose the first. Now either they were going to send me someplace, or I could send myself. I chose the second, and they gave me a week to make arrangements. Procrastinating to the end, it took me three. This is when, once again, desperate, cornered, and at my lowest, I said the only prayer I still knew: "God help me—if you get me out of this one, I'll never do it again." My life was finally out of my control.

No longer the party animal, I was broke and my rent was overdue. I had dirty dishes piled in the sink and moldy pots on the stove. Bags of garbage and bottles were lined up by the door and the toilet had stopped. Piles of stolen junk were sitting on the floor. I had been wearing my clothes much too long and, except for a box of macaroni and cheese or a pot pie, I was not eating. When a knock came at the door, I would run into the bathroom and peep out the window to see who was coming to get me. Not drinking wasn't an option, but drinking didn't help. Such was my condition as I left the house to check myself into the hospital for my day of reckoning.

Outside of being very nervous, I don't remember much about admissions because I was so loaded at the time. After a few hours I began to feel safer. My apprehension slowly turned to relief. Maybe they could help me after all. I had no idea how sick I was to become. The first five of my seventeen days in detox were hell. I could do little more than lie in bed. It had been years since I was sober that long. After a week I felt a little better and began surveying my surroundings. I started my own counter-evaluations. I found the doctors and nurses to be knowledgeable and professional, but I sensed that while they knew much about alcoholism, they had learned it in books— they had not lived it. I did not need knowledge. I needed solutions. No one but the hopeless really knew what it felt like to exist without hope. The skeptic in me came out, searching for every loophole and excuse to pick things apart and to divert attention from my condition. My initial optimism was beginning to waver. Was this all there was?

However, there was one man on the staff who seemed different. He seemed very comfortable and at ease with a bit of a knowing sparkle in his eye. This guy was clearly not as stuffy as the rest, and when he told me his story, I was surprised to find it very similar to mine—only his was no secret. He mentioned being a member of Alcoholics Anonymous. How could it be that he obviously had the respect of the staff after having lived a life of crime? How could it be that he was a lot like me but had made it back? Here was someone who was sober, yet cool; humble, yet firm in his convictions; serious, but not without a sense of humor. This was one to whom I could relate and maybe even trust. He may have saved my life just by being there, and to this day he doesn't even know it.

Over the next few days I was still not talking much, but I was listening and watching. I learned more about how Alcoholics Anonymous works and met more of its members. I found out it was not something they left at the hospital as they went home; it was a way of life. I found out it was spirituality, not religion. I saw them enjoying themselves, and they all agreed on one thing: If I wanted to change my life as they had changed theirs, I could, as long as I became willing to do what they did. I became fascinated. Here I was, the scum of the earth, yet they came to me and invited me to join them. I started to feel that if I was ever going to try something different, I'd better do it now. It might be my last chance. After all, I still had to deal with the authorities, and I had nothing to lose by playing along. So I read their book, I started to work their steps, and (with the door closed and the lights out) I asked for a little help from a Higher Power as they suggested. Finally, they highly recommended that I attend their meetings—especially the first night out.

I walked out of there on a sunny afternoon. I intended to go to a meeting that night, but I also had ten dollars in my pocket and a reason to celebrate. I was sober for twenty-two days, and I was feeling pretty good about myself. Soon my old instincts began to take over. Sunny day. Ten bucks. Celebration. Feeling good. Before I knew it, I was walking into the back door of one of my old watering holes. The smell of alcohol hit me when I entered, and my mouth watered. I sat down at the bar. I ordered my usual ginger wash. Couldn't I make it just one day without drinking? At this last question I realized that yes, since I put it that way, I probably could make it just one day without drinking. Besides, I was going to a meeting that night and who knows, they might have breathalyzers there. I put down my dollar, got off that stool, and walked back out the door. After all, I could drink tomorrow if I wanted to—and that's just what I planned to do.

At my first meeting that night the people fulfilled their responsibility—they made me welcome. I met others like me and it felt good. Maybe this thing was for real. So I went to another meeting, and I got the same feeling. Then another meeting. The tomorrows came and went, and to this day, I still haven't found it necessary to take another drink. That was well over six years ago.

The meetings gave me what my sponsor likes to call one of the most important words in the Big Book: A.A. put a "we" in my life. "We admitted we were powerless over alcohol. . . ." I no longer had to be alone. Fellowship and activity kept me coming back long enough to work the Twelve Steps. The more I did, the better I felt. I started hanging out with my sponsor and some active people at the meetings. They showed me how gratitude is something that is demonstrated, not talked about—gratitude is action. They suggested I was lucky to still have a car, even though it was a junker; therefore, I might consider taking the less fortunate to meetings. They reminded me you can't teach anything to a know-it-all, so remain teachable. When old behaviors started to creep back in, they called me on it. When life just didn't feel right, they talked about developing faith and relying on my Higher Power. They told me lack of power was my dilemma and that there is a solution. I took to A.A. immediately and believed like a child that if I leveled my pride enough to thoroughly follow their path, I'd get what they had. And it worked. Starting out, I just wanted to keep the authorities off my back. I never bargained for this program's changing the course of my life or showing me the way to freedom and happiness.

Still very impatient, I wanted the whole deal right away. That's why I related so well to the story about a wide-eyed new person and an oldtimer. When the newcomer approached the oldtimer, envying his accomplishments and many years of sobriety, the oldtimer slapped down his hand like a gavel and said, "I'll trade you even! My thirty years for your thirty days—right now!" He knew what the newcomer had yet to find out: that true happiness is found in the journey, not the destination.

So today I'm much more comfortable with life, as Alcoholics Anonymous has promised, and I know they're right when they say it keeps getting better. My circumstances have steadily improved as my spiritual life grows and matures. Words cannot begin to describe the feelings in my heart as I sometimes ponder how much my life has changed, how far I've come, and how much there is yet to discover. And though I'm not sure where my journey may take me next, I know I'll owe it to the grace of God and to three words of the Twelve Steps: continue, improve, and practice.

Oh, and one more thing they told me: Humility is the key.

(10)

EMPTY ON THE INSIDE

*She grew up around A.A. and had all the
answers—except when it came to her own life.*

I SPENT MY LIFE "acting as if"—either acting as
if I knew (I didn't ask teachers questions in
school; they might find out I didn't know the answer)
or acting as if I didn't care. I always felt as though
everyone else had been given the directions to life
and I had been somewhere else when God was
handing them out. To me, you either knew how to do
something or you didn't. You could play the piano, or
you couldn't. You were a good ballplayer, or you
weren't.

I don't know where I learned the attitude that it
wasn't all right not to know, but it was a certainty in
my life, and it almost killed me. The concept of set a
goal, work for the goal, achieve the goal was foreign
to me. You either "had it" or you didn't, and if you
didn't, you couldn't let on—you might look bad. I
never once stopped to consider that others might
really have to work hard for what they had. Gradually
my attitude translated into contempt for those who
did know—leave it to an alcoholic to look down on
someone who is successful!

My father joined Alcoholics Anonymous when I was
seven. Many of my childhood Friday nights were
spent at open A.A. meetings because we couldn't

afford a babysitter (I was the kid sitting over in the corner with a book). What effect did it have? I knew that being alcoholic meant you couldn't drink any more and that you had to go to A.A. As my drinking career began, I was always careful not to utter the "A" word in connection with my name. At my house I would have been handed a meeting schedule. Besides, I knew that A.A. was all old guys that drank coffee, smoked, and ate donuts—I had been there. (Looking back, I'm sure most of those "old guys" were barely thirty.) So no A.A. for me. That would mean not drinking. And when I drank, life changed.

I was fifteen the first time I got drunk. I can tell you where I was, who I was with, what I was wearing. It was an important day for me. Within a year I was a poster child for adolescent treatment of alcoholism. My grades plunged, my friends changed, I wrecked a car, my appearance went downhill, I was suspended from school. (When I first got sober, I wondered why my parents never checked me into treatment. Then I remembered they didn't have adolescent treatment centers when I was a teen. As a matter of fact, I still have ceramics Dad made me in the psychiatric ward, because when *he* was drinking, they didn't have treatment centers.) I was always ready with a promise to do better, to try harder, to apply myself, to live up to my potential. Potential—now there is the curse of every budding alcoholic.

I managed to graduate somehow and went on to college, where I promptly flunked out. I couldn't make it to class. Hindsight has shown me two reasons for this. First, if someone else had a free period, I tagged along with them. I thought that I had to be with my friends all the time. I was afraid that if they spent any time without me, they might begin to wonder, Why do I hang out with her anyway? They might realize they had a better time without me. And then they might tell other people, who would tell other people, and I'd be alone.

Second, social conversation was a skill that I never acquired. When I met someone, I felt totally inadequate. To me, when I said "Hi, my name is ————," there followed a deafening silence, as if they were thinking, So? How did people have conversations anyway? How did they meet and then begin to talk as if they had known each other for years? For me it was one more thing that it wasn't all right not to know. So I kept drinking. When I drank, it didn't matter.

It's important to interject here that I loved to drink. Drinking put me into the middle of life. I was a social drinker—drinking made me extremely social. I didn't particularly like drinking with other women; I drank with the big boys. I always had a tremendous capacity for alcohol, and I learned to shoot an excellent game of pool, which made me quite popular in the local tavern scene. At one point I even had my own motorcycle. When I read "Bill's Story" in the Big Book and he said, "I had arrived," I knew what he meant.

For fourteen years my drinking took me places I never meant to go. First I moved south, since I knew the town I grew up in was my problem. (I once heard a guy remark in a meeting that there are three or four states that should just post signs on their borders: "This state doesn't work either!") I did the things women do. My first marriage was really a one-night stand that lasted five years—I certainly couldn't admit that I had made a mistake. We had two children and I wanted out, but to leave would have meant taking responsibility. I just drank until he threw me out. Then it was his fault the marriage failed.

At one point before moving home, I lost a job that meant a lot to me, as the direct result of my drinking. For the first time, I went to a meeting of Alcoholics Anonymous and said, "I am an alcoholic." When I had gone to meetings with my dad I always just said, "I'm with him." I called my father and told him I went to a meeting. Within a week he mailed me a box containing the book *Alcoholics Anonymous*, a tape of his A.A. talk, a couple of meditation books, a copy of *Twelve Steps and Twelve Traditions*, and a few other odds and ends. I think he had been saving up for the day I was willing.

So, divorced, I moved back home. Within a year I was under arrest for child endangerment. I had left my sleeping children home alone and gone to drink. They were removed from my custody and placed with my mother. Then started my rounds of the treatment centers. I could talk a good game. After all, I had grown up with A.A. I was the one the counselors asked to talk to other women who were reluctant to leave their kids long enough to go into treatment. I could give the whole speech: "We can't be good mothers if we're not sober." The problem was, inside, I was relieved that my kids had to live with my mom. It was too hard to be a parent. But I couldn't tell people that—they might think I was a bad mom.

And I *was* a bad mom. I was a terrible mom. No, I didn't beat them, and of course I told them I loved them. But the message my kids got from me was "Yes, I love you; now go away." They had to be practically invisible in their own home. I had absolutely nothing to give them emotionally. All they wanted was my love and attention, and alcoholism robbed me of the ability to give it. I was empty on the inside.

While I was in treatment, my dad died and I inherited almost enough money to kill myself. I got to drink the way I wanted to for 2½ years. I'm sure I got here faster because of it.

Near the end, I was living in an attic apartment; the money was long gone. It was November, cold and gray. When I woke up at 5:30, it was gray outside. Was it 5:30 a.m. or 5:30 p.m.? I couldn't tell. I looked out the window, watching people. Were they going to work? Or coming home? I went back to sleep. When I woke again, it would either be light or dark. Opening my eyes, after what seemed like hours, it was only 5:45. And gray. I was twenty-eight years old.

I finally got on my knees and asked God for help. I couldn't go on the way I was living. I had been in the apartment since August and hadn't bothered to unpack. I wasn't bathing. I couldn't answer my phone. I couldn't show up on weekends to visit my kids. So I prayed. Something made me go dig through a box, and I found the Big Book my father had sent me years earlier (I always tell new people to buy the hardcover version—for some reason they are harder to throw away). I read "Bill's Story" again. This time it made sense. This time I could identify. I slept, holding the book like a teddy bear. I woke up feeling rested for the first time in months. And I didn't want to drink.

I would love to tell you that I have been sober ever

since, but that is not the case. I didn't want to drink that day, but I took no action to insure against it. You see, I believe that we get more than one "moment of grace" from God—but it is up to us to seize the moment by taking action. But I heeded the voice that said, "You may as well drink. You know you're going to."

For the next few days every time I went to my favorite watering hole, I was surrounded by people talking about sobering up. My bartender wanted to quit drinking. The guy I was shooting pool with talked about going back to A.A. Someone next to me at the bar was talking about being at the local clubhouse for A.A.'s. I did stop drinking (sort of) for a few months but eventually went on the bender that would end it all.

By the end of two weeks of drinking, nobody was speaking to me, so I headed south, where I was sure they all missed me. There was no homecoming parade. People barely remembered me, and by the end of a week, I was out of money. I couldn't even book a plane ticket home. I had less than one dollar, and I had one of *those* hangovers. I knew if I tried to sit in the airport bar long enough for someone to buy me a drink, it would be obvious that was my intent, and my pride couldn't bear the thought of being asked to leave. I briefly considered mugging a little old lady and stealing her purse, but I knew I would end up picking on the one who was still in shape.

If there had been one more dollar, I might not be sober today. Once I was drinking, I always had a plan, but that day, by the grace of God, I was out of plans. I didn't have one single better idea. I called Mom, told her where I was, and asked her to fly me home. She later told me she almost didn't do it, but she was afraid they'd never see me again.

She deposited me at the local detox center, where she told me I could go in or not but that she was done with me. I was on my own. Detox gave me the same message. I thought they should send me on to a treatment center—thirty days of hot meals and rest was sounding pretty good to me—but they told me I already knew everything treatment was going to teach me, that I should go do it and save the bed for someone who needed it. I have been sober ever since. I was finally accountable for my own recovery. I was responsible for taking the action. One of my favorite games had always been making it someone else's job to see that I got my work done. That game was over.

I had never expected to live to see thirty. Suddenly I was 29½ and showing no signs of dying anytime soon. I knew in my heart that I would live whether I drank or not, and that no matter how bad it was, it could always get worse. Some people get sober because they're afraid to die. I knew I would live, and that was far more terrifying. I had surrendered.

The first night out of detox I went to a meeting, and the woman speaking commented that alcoholism had taken her to the point where she didn't want to work and didn't want to care for her daughter, she just wanted to drink. I couldn't believe it! That was me! She became my first sponsor, and I came back.

The second night I sat in what I now call the "new guy chair"—second row, against the wall (if you sit in back they know you're new, and if you sit in front you might have to talk to someone). When it came time to hold hands and pray at the end of the meeting, I had no hand to hold on one side. I remember thinking "I will never fit in here" and hanging my head. I felt my hand being taken—someone in front of me had taken the time to be sure that the circle was complete. To this day I don't know who it was, but that person is the reason I came back the next night—that person saved my life. And I kept coming back.

The local clubhouse had a noon Big Book meeting every day, and I went, every day. Not to get sober, mind you, and certainly not to learn about what was in the book. Here was my thinking: I knew you were supposed to read your Big Book every day, and they went around the room reading an entire chapter, so that should count, right? This also took up nearly thirty minutes, so it was less likely that I would get called on to talk. And the meeting was at noon, which left my nights free. I figured out all of that with my keen alcoholic mind!

Luckily, I forgot that God is in charge of results. I was finally taking action, and my motives didn't matter. I thought I'd go through the Big Book once, then "graduate" to discussion meetings, but there was a lot of laughter in that room, so I kept going. I was not one of those people who walked into meetings and said, "Thank God, I'm home." I did not particularly want what they had; I just didn't want what I had any-more—that was the humble beginning I needed.

The convenience of the noon meeting meant that I went to two meetings every day; I had nothing else to do at night. I began to notice people there with sev-eral years of sobriety—my own laziness had thrown me in with some of the most active people in

Alcoholics Anonymous. What I found out was that people who attend Big Book meetings on a regular basis tend to read the book and do what it says.

When I was two weeks sober, a man's nine-year-old daughter was killed by a drunk driver, and three days later he was at a meeting saying he had to believe it wasn't for nothing. That maybe one alcoholic would get sober because of it. As I left that day, I found myself wondering what would have happened if that had been my kids, or me? What would they remember about me? A feeling came over me (I know now it was gratitude), and I realized that I could call my children right then and tell them I loved them. That I could show up when I said I would. That my word could be worth something to them. That even though I might always just be "mom who comes over on the weekends," I could be a good weekend mom. I had a chance to move forward with them, forging a relationship built on a foundation of God and Alcoholics Anonymous, rather than always trying to make up for the past. One year later I was able to share with that man that maybe it hadn't been for nothing, because my life changed that day.

By the time a month passed, my feet were firmly planted in Alcoholics Anonymous. And I kept coming back. I cannot begin to list all the wonderful things that have happened in my years here. My kids were four and six when I got sober, and they have "grown up" in A.A. I brought them to open meetings, and the people there gave them what I couldn't in the early days—love and attention. Gradually they became part of my life again, and today I have custody of my children.

I remarried in Alcoholics Anonymous, to a man who believes in A.A. the way I do. (I knew we were off to a good start when he didn't get angry that I stood him up to go on a Twelfth Step call.) We agreed to never be higher than third on each other's list, with God always first and Alcoholics Anonymous second. He is my partner and my best friend. We both sponsor several people, and our house is filled with love and laughter. Our telephone never stops ringing. We share the joy of a common solution.

We have had some tough times. Our son is the third generation of A.A.'s in my family. After a suicide attempt at age fourteen, we found out he too was an alcoholic. After his one year in A.A., it's hard to tell what will happen, but we trust Alcoholics Anonymous, even on the days we don't trust our son. Our daughter is a beautiful, confident teenager who has found her own path to God without having to drink. She is the product of the love and faith of Alcoholics Anonymous.

I still have a sponsor and a home group today. I am a member of Alcoholics Anonymous in good standing. I learned how to be a good A.A. member by watching good A.A. members and doing what they do. I learned how to have a good marriage by watching people with good marriages and doing what they do. I learned how to be a parent by watching good parents and doing what they do. And I finally have the freedom of believing that it is all right not to know.

(11)

GROUNDED

Alcohol clipped this pilot's wings until sobriety and hard work brought him back to the sky.

I AM AN ALCOHOLIC. I am part Comanche Indian and grew up poor but in a loving home until alcoholism took both of my parents. Then the divorces came, three for each parent, and I learned the anger that is such a part of alcoholic family life. I vowed I would never be an alcoholic. Active in my Indian community, I saw what the alcohol did there also, and I was repelled and disgusted by it.

I graduated from high school at seventeen and immediately left to join the marine corps. I found a home there, relishing the tough discipline, camaraderie, and esprit de corps. I excelled and was one of three who were promoted upon graduation from boot camp. Four and a half years later I was given an opportunity to go into flight training. Success at the end of the eighteen-month period would mean pilot wings and an officer's commission. Again I excelled. Although most of my peers had college educations and fear of failure constantly plagued me, I graduated near the top of my class.

I excelled at something else also. Drinking was encouraged; the pilot persona was one of hard, gutsy flying with equally hard drinking, and attendance at happy hour was considered a duty. I did not need any encouragement and reveled in the squadron camaraderie, good-natured joking, and competition at these events.

One year into my training, I reported for the final phase and met a young beauty. I was drunk the night I met her, and she would have nothing to do with me, but I could never have approached her without the false courage the alcohol gave me. The next day I saw her again, this time sober, and we began to date. I graduated from flight training on her twentieth birthday, and she pinned my gold wings and my second lieutenant bars on me. We were married two weeks later. We have just celebrated our thirty-fifth anniversary, and she is the most wonderful person I could ever have found.

We immediately had two young sons, and I left to go to war in Vietnam. Thirteen months later I returned. I spent 11½ years total time in the marine corps before deciding to get out because of the family separation my military career required. I had seen enough family chaos to know that I could never allow that to occur in my own family, so reluctantly, even painfully, I resigned my commission and joined a major airline. I had gained a reputation in the marines I was proud of. I had many accomplishments to my credit, a good combat record with decorations, and skill as a pilot.

Slowly I worked my way up within the airline structure and finally became a captain after twenty years. It had been a strife-ridden company, and our family endured some tough times. During one of the lengthy labor strikes, we adopted a baby girl. She completed our family. Nearly half Chippewa Indian, she was a beautiful baby of seventeen days when we took her home with us.

My drinking continued to escalate, but I did not believe I was any different from my drinking comrades. I was very wrong. I had two charges of driving under the influence, years apart, which I wrote off to bad luck, and I paid handsome legal fees to get the charges reduced. This was years before the Federal Aviation Administration began cross-checking drivers' records against pilot licenses.

One night, after a hard afternoon and late evening of drinking, I and my two fellow flight crew members were arrested. We were charged with violation of a federal law that prohibits the operation of a common carrier while impaired. It had never been used against airline pilots before. I was devastated. Suddenly I was thrust into an experience beyond my worst nightmare.

I arrived home the next day, sick at heart and unable to look my wife in the face. Ashamed and destroyed, I saw two doctors that day and was diagnosed as an alcoholic. I was in treatment that night, going in with only the clothes on my back. The news media had picked up the story, and it was blared all over the world, on all the major television networks, and my shame and humiliation were beyond words. All the light in my life had gone out, and I entertained the idea of suicide. I could not envision ever smiling again or having a day with a bright horizon. I was hurting more than I ever knew a human could hurt, and I just wanted the pain to end.

I became notorious in commercial aviation, and the media had a field day with me. I lost my FAA medical certificate because of my diagnosis of alcoholism, and the FAA issued an emergency revocation of all my licenses. I thought about my parents (now both dead), my Indian people, and all those I had previously considered alcoholics, and I knew I had become exactly what I vowed I would never become.

I learned my career was over via the six o'clock news one week after entering treatment. I refused to watch TV, but my fellow patients kept me informed. I was the lead story on the news for weeks. I was joke fodder for the late-night TV comics as they ridiculed me, my profession, and my airline.

I also learned I was going to federal prison. The sentence was mandatory if convicted, and there was no doubt in my mind that I would be. With nothing left, I dedicated myself to learning about recovery. I fervently believed that the key to my sobriety, and hence my survival, lay in the power of all I was being taught, and I spent no idle moments in treatment. I worked as hard as I had worked to earn my wings, but this time my life was at stake. I struggled to regain a spiritual connection as I underwent one legal crisis after another.

I got out of treatment determined to complete ninety A.A. meetings in ninety days but was afraid my court date would interfere, so I completed my ninety meetings in sixty-seven days. I went through an intense, media-covered three-week trial. On most evenings after the day in court, I sought refuge in A.A. meetings and renewed my strength for the coming day. Recovery and all I had learned allowed me to handle things much, much differently than my two co-defendants. Many spoke of my serenity throughout this experience of horror, which surprised me. Inside I did not feel what others seemed to see.

I was found guilty and sentenced to sixteen months in federal prison. My two codefendants received twelve-month sentences and chose to remain free pending appeals, while I chose to go into prison and get it over. I had learned how to live life on life's terms and not my own. From somewhere back in my high school days, I remembered a poem that says something to the effect of, "Cowards die a thousand deaths, a brave man only once," and I wanted to do what had to be done. I was terrified of walking into prison but told my children that I could not come out the back door until I walked through the front. I remembered that courage was not the absence of fear; it was the ability to continue in the face of it.

On the day I entered prison, nine of my fellow pilots began making our family's house payments, which they did for nearly four years. After my release from prison, I made four attempts to get them to let us take over, and they refused each time. So many came to help us from places we could never have imagined.

I served 424 days in the federal prison system. I started an A.A. meeting in prison, which was opposed by the prison administration, and they hassled us weekly as we came together to meet. The weekly meeting was a quiet oasis in the desert, a few moments of serenity in a prison full of bedlam.

My prison term was followed by three years of probation, which restricted my travel and had thirteen other conditions. Upon release from prison, no longer a pilot, I returned to the same treatment center where

I had once been a patient, and worked full-time with other alcoholics. Pay was minimal, but I found I was effective at reaching others, and I wanted desperately to pay back some of what so many had given me. I did that for twenty months.

For a long time I did not consider flying again, but I could not purge the dream of doing so from my heart. One of my meditation books had said, "Before any dream can come true, there must first be a dream." I had been told if I wanted to fly again, I would have to begin at the very bottom, with a private license, even though I had previously held the highest license the FAA awarded, the air transport pilot license. I studied for and took all the lengthy FAA written examinations. I had to go back and relearn things I had learned thirty years before and had long since forgotten. I had, unexpectedly, been able to reacquire my FAA medical certificate after proving the quality of my sobriety for more than two years.

The trial judge had put sanctions on me that made it impossible for me to fly again because of my age. My lawyer had become my friend and worked for three years after my conviction without taking a cent from me. He was one more person who entered my life in a manner I could only ascribe to some kind of Divine Providence. He took a motion to the judge to lift the sanctions, and the tears came flooding down my cheeks when he called to let me know the judge had approved it. With the lifting of those sanctions, the impossible became slightly less impossible. An extraordinary amount of work was left to do, but at least the attempt could now be made.

None of my friends thought it possible to regain

licenses literally from the ground up, but I had learned how to do many things one day at a time, one small step at a time, so I went after the licenses in exactly that manner. Had I chosen to view the whole panorama of licensing requirements, I would have quit; they were simply too overwhelming. But one day and one thing at a time they were doable. So I did them.

I knew no one would ever hire me to fly passengers. I was an ex-con, a convicted felon, a drunk. I had doubts as to whether anyone would even allow me to fly cargo. It took several months for the FAA to process my licenses and mail them to me. On the exact day they arrived, another miracle occurred. I received a phone call from the head of the pilot union, who informed me that the president of the airline had decided personally to reinstate me. I had not pursued the legal grievance process I was entitled to, because I knew my actions could never be defended or excused. I had steadfastly accepted responsibility, in front of TV cameras and in the treatment center, because my recovery demanded rigorous honesty.

It was almost beyond my ability to believe that the president of the airline could ever consider having me work for them again. I marveled at the courage of such a man and such an airline. What if I relapsed? What if I flew drunk again? The media would have a field day. For days afterward, as I awoke each morning, my first thought was that it had only been a dream, that it could not possibly have occurred.

Almost four years after my arrest and the explosive devastation of my life, I signed my back-to-work agreement. Restored to full seniority, given the retirement I had lost, and once again an airline pilot! A large crowd gathered to watch me sign the document.

So much had happened in my life. I lost almost everything I had worked to acquire. My family had suffered public shame and humiliation. I had been the object of scorn, shame, and disgrace. Yet much more had also happened; every loss had been replaced with rewards. I had seen the promises of the Big Book come true in a magnitude I could never have imagined. I had gotten sober. I had regained my family, and we were once again close and loving. I had learned how to use the Twelve Steps and to live the wonderful program that was founded so many years ago by two drunks.

It took several years, but I learned to be grateful for my alcoholism and the program of recovery it forced me into, for all the things that had happened *to* me and *for* me, for a life today that transcends and far exceeds anything I had previously known. I could not have that today if I had not experienced all the yesterdays.

My back-to-work agreement said I would retire as a copilot. But the miracles in this program have never ceased for me, and last year I was notified that the president of my airline had granted permission for me to once again be a captain.

I retired at age sixty, and I checked out as a 747 captain, which means my final year at my airline concluded in the left seat. The circle, so sacred to my Indian people, will once again have been completed.

I take little credit for all that has happened. I suited up and showed up, but the process of A.A., the grace of a loving God, and the help of so many around me have been far more responsible for all the events in my life. Today one of my sons has more than 3 ½ years of sobriety after nearly losing his life to alcohol and drugs. He is truly one more miracle in my life for which I am so deeply grateful.

I have returned to my Indian people once again after a long shame-filled absence. I am dancing again and returning to the old ways I left behind. I have spoken at two Native American A.A. conventions, something I never thought I'd see when I was a youngster growing up. Adversity truly introduces us to ourselves. But we need never deal with our adversities alone as long as we can find another alcoholic in a meeting of Alcoholics Anonymous.

(12)

ANOTHER CHANCE

Poor, black, totally ruled by alcohol, she felt shut away from any life worth living. But when she began a prison sentence, a door opened.

I AM AN AFRICAN-AMERICAN alcoholic. I don't know when I became an alcoholic, but I do believe I became one because I drank too much too often.

I always blamed my drinking on being poor, or on anything other than the truth—that I liked what booze did for me, that when I had a drink I was as big and had as much as the next person. I would never admit that I was drinking too much or spending money that I should have used to buy food for my two little boys.

As time went on, I drank more. I was not able to hold a job—no one wants a drunk around. I was always able to get a boyfriend who had a drinking joint or sold whiskey, but it didn't last long. I would embarrass everyone by coming in drunk or passing out. Then it got to the place where I couldn't drink without getting in jail. On one of these trips, the judge must have thought I was worth saving, for instead of sending me to jail, he sent me to A.A. for one month.

I went to A.A. At least, my body went. I hated every minute of it. I couldn't wait until the meeting was over to get a drink. I was afraid to drink before the meeting. I thought if they smelled whiskey on my breath, they would lock me up, and I couldn't live without my bottle. I hated that judge for sending me to a place with all those drunks. I wasn't an alcoholic!

Oh, I might drink too much at times—everyone I knew drank. But I don't remember that any of them ever went to sleep in joints and woke up with no shoes on in the winter or fell out of chairs. But I did. I don't remember any of them getting put out in the winter because they didn't pay their rent. But to me, whiskey meant more than a home for my sons.

Things got so bad, I was afraid to go on the street, so I turned to Mothers' Aid. That was one of the worst things that could have happened to an alcoholic woman. I would wait for the mailman each month, like any good mother, but as soon as he handed me my check, I put on my best dress and went looking for my alcoholic friend. Once I started drinking, I didn't care that the rent wasn't paid or that there was no food in the house or that my boys needed shoes. I would stay out until my money was gone. Then I would go home full of remorse, and wonder what I was going to do until I got my next check.

In time, I began to go out and forget the way back home. I would wake to find myself in some beat-up rooming house, where roaches were crawling over everything. Then the time came when I couldn't afford whiskey, so I turned to wine. Finally I got so low-down, I was ashamed of my friends' seeing me, so I went to the worst joints I could find. If it was daylight, I would go down alleys to make sure no one saw me.

I felt that I didn't have anything to live for, so I tried suicide many times. But I would always wake up in the psychiatric ward to begin another long treatment. After a while I found that the psycho ward was a good place to hide when I had taken something stolen to the pawnshop. I thought if the cops did come to the hospital, the doctors would tell them I was crazy and didn't know what I was doing. But then one good doctor told me there was nothing wrong with me except drinking too much. He said if I came back again, they would send me to the state hospital. I didn't want that, so I stopped going to the psycho ward.

Now I had gotten to the place where I would wake up with black eyes and not know where I got them, or wake up with a lot of money and not know where I got it. Later I found out that I went into stores and stole clothes, then sold them. One morning I woke up with a thousand dollars. I was trying to remember where it came from, when two of the biggest cops I ever saw walked in and took me to jail. It came out that I had sold a woman a fur coat. The cops had picked her up, and she told them she had bought it from me. I got out on bail right away, but when I went to trial, the judge gave me thirty days. When my thirty days were up, I started back on my rounds. I didn't last long. They tell me that I killed a man during that period, but I can't remember anything. It was a total blackout for me. Because I had been drunk, the judge gave me only a twelve-year sentence in prison.

By the grace of God, I only served three years. It was there that I really found out what A.A. was. I had rejected A.A. on the outside, but now it came to me in prison. Today I thank my Higher Power for giving me another chance at life and A.A. and being able to try and help some other alcoholic. I have been home for a year and have not taken a drink in four years.

Since I have been in A.A., I have more friends than I ever had in my life—friends who care about me and my welfare, friends who don't care that I am black and that I have been in prison. All they care about is that I am a human being and that I want to stay sober. Since I've been home, I have been able to gain the respect of my two sons again.

The only thing that bothers me is that there are only about five African-Americans in A.A. in my city. Even those don't take part in A.A. functions as I would like to see them do. I don't know if it's force of habit or something else that keeps them in one place, but I do know that in A.A. there is much work to do, and none of us can do it standing still.

I do think that some of the African-Americans here—and other places too—are afraid to go to other meetings. I just want to say that you don't have to be afraid, because no one at any A.A. meeting will bite you. There are no color bars in A.A. If you give us a try, you will see that we are really human beings, and we will welcome you with open arms and hearts.

I'm writing this during an A.A. convention, where I have spent the weekend with nothing but white people. They haven't eaten me yet! I have not seen a black face but mine since I've been here, and if I didn't look in the mirror, I wouldn't know that I *was* black, because these people treat me as one of them, which I am. We all have the same sickness, and in helping one another, we are able to stay sober.

(13)

A LATE START

"It's been ten years since I retired, seven years since I joined A.A. Now I can truly say that I am a grateful alcoholic."

I AM A SEVENTY-FIVE-YEAR-OLD alcoholic. For fifty-five of those seventy-five years I led what is known as a normal middle-class life. Alcohol had as little part in it as candied yams—nice when there but unmissed when absent. The home in which I grew up included two loving parents, one older brother, a constant flow of house pets, riding horses, and friends who were welcomed. Discipline in our house was strict but not out of line with the thinking prevalent during the first quarter of the twentieth century; certainly I don't consider that I was in any way abused. I attended private school and later a midwestern college. I married, had children, worked, experienced the pain of the death of my parents and of a child. Knew, too, the pleasure of real friends and financial success. I enjoyed horseback riding, swimming, tennis, and had quiet evenings filled with children, books, and friends.

What happened to me somewhere between the ages of fifty-five and sixty-three? I've no idea! Was life too much? Did some latent gene suddenly take on a fierce life of its own? I don't know. What I do know is that at sixty-five I was a crawling, dirty maggot of a woman, willing to tarnish all I'd worked for and to desecrate every dear relationship I had. I know too that through a wonderful set of God-guided circumstances and people, I was led to the only possible course of behavior that will keep me sane, sober, constructive, and happy.

I was twenty when I had my first drink, and although I liked the taste, I didn't like the way it made me feel. I didn't drink again until I was in my early thirties and thought it made me seem cool and sophisticated. During these early years, a couple of drinks were enough, and I often nursed one Scotch on the rocks for a full evening. When I was thirty-five, my twelve-year-old son was diagnosed with an incurable cancer and within a few months my husband demanded a divorce. For the following five years while my son lived, I seldom drank and never drank alone. Agony, fear, hurt, and exhaustion did not make me a drunk. Happiness opened that door much, much later.

During my mid-forties, my interest in alcohol began to gain momentum. Although I had continued to work, I had otherwise isolated myself to care for my son and his younger sister, each of whom required a special dose of stability, love, and security. Soon after my son's death, I made a decided effort to reenter the adult world. My debut encouraged my drinking. It was not yet obsessive, but drinking became more and more a part of my daily life. I no longer entertained without serving cocktails and seldom attended gatherings where liquor wasn't provided. I always managed to find the post-activity drinking crowd whether it was after dog obedience training or an oil painting class. During my late forties, it was not unusual for me to have a drink alone in the evening, although there were still many days when I didn't drink at all. Any event was an occasion for excessive celebration, and there were increasingly frequent weekends when I drank myself to a hangover-creating high. Nevertheless, it was during this period that I received a major job promotion.

I was forty-nine when my second husband and I were married. Years before, we had dated through high school and two years of college but then were separated by World War II. Each of us had married elsewhere, divorced, and thirty years later we met by chance. We had ten years of laughter, sharing, and wonderment well laced with martinis and Scotch on the rocks. By the time I was sixty, anyone wise in the ways of alcoholism would have known I was in for big trouble. Happy plans dissolved into pouts, arguments began, and meals burned. Hurricanes of anger rushed through our once-happy cottage. We agreed we were drinking too much. We tried the switch technique, the time control schedule, the drink-only-on-weekends ploy. Nothing worked. Between us we were badly damaging our budget. My husband lost his job, and then for two harrowing years I watched him die of alcoholism. But I learned nothing from his death, and my drinking escalated as I bottle-fed my sorrow.

My early sixties saw me drunk every night and more and more frequently calling in sick or for personal leave. Life was pure and unadulterated hell! At work, I was often shaking so badly that I hesitated to give dictation because I would have to sign the letters. I made every possible excuse to meet someone for a "business luncheon" so that I could have a drink or two. As my alcoholism accelerated, my absenteeism increased and my productivity diminished. I bounced checks, pawned silver, mourned, and I continued my drinking.

Finally on one cold winter day, I called Alcoholics Anonymous, and that evening two ladies took me to a meeting. We had a twenty-five-minute ride in the car, and I remember how good it was to talk about my fear and shakes, how kind they were without encouraging my self-pity. I remember being given a cup of coffee I could hardly handle and hearing impossible promises that would materialize if I would only make the impossible commitment. I did want to stop. The ladies suggested that I go to a women's meeting the next night, and I did. I had a drink first, of course, and when it came time to identify myself, I stated that my brain told me I was an alcoholic but the rest of me didn't believe it. The next night it snowed, and I stayed home and drank. That was the end of my first try at A.A.

Some months later I invited my daughter and son-in-law for dinner to celebrate her birthday. They found me sprawled across the living room floor, passed out cold. What a mournful birthday present! It took very little persuasion to convince me to go into the detoxification program at the local hospital. I knew I was in trouble; I was ashamed and heartbroken that I had caused her such hurt. Seven days in detox and eight weeks of really good help from a psychologist, and I was dry, sober, and ready to face the world again. The doctor strongly suggested that I participate in the local A.A. program, but I would have none of it. I was cured—I needed no further help.

A year and a half later I retired. I was enjoying my

new freedom and gave myself permission to have a drink only when I was dining out. That worked so well that I made a new rule: I could have a cocktail before dinner and an after-dinner drink. Then I made a rule that said I could serve alcohol to my friends in my home. That of course is the rule that sent me spinning right back down into fearful drunkenness. I was worse than before. My self-imposed hell was in my own home. Unbathed, in the same nightclothes day after day, afraid of the phone, the doorbell, and the darkness. If the clock said six, I wouldn't know whether it was morning or evening. Days ran into each other in an agonizing blur. I crawled to bed, drank when I came to, and sat shivering in fear of some unknown tragedy that I thought was about to descend on me. I remember wailing because I couldn't make coffee, sitting curled in a corner trying to sort out how I could commit suicide without making a mess. I might have tried, but I was afraid no one would find me before I started to stink.

Once again my daughter came to my rescue, and I checked into the detox program at the hospital. This time I was there for ten days. During that time, A.A. meetings were made available at the hospital. I was genuinely touched by the fact that they were led by a young man in a leg cast and on crutches, especially when I realized that he came as a volunteer. And twice before I left, I was given a leave of absence to attend local A.A. meetings.

Others have stated that they eagerly embraced the A.A. program. Unlike them, I did not enter the rooms willingly, nor did I find myself immediately at home. However, I had no other option. There was no escape route that I had not tried, none that had not led to another failure. I was sixty-nine years old. I had neither time nor health to waste. For six months I didn't drink, attended meetings, and sometimes read the Big Book. I went to meetings exactly on time, sat quietly, and left as soon as the meeting closed. In no way was I a part of the group. I was not impressed by the sayings and didn't really believe the messages I heard. Then one day I was called on to share, and I proceeded to explode. I announced that in no way was I a "grateful alcoholic," that I hated my condition, that I did not enjoy the meetings, and that I did not leave the meetings refreshed. I found neither ease nor growth in the Fellowship.

My healing began with the arrogance of that statement. One of the women came to me after the meeting and told me I was about to "go out." She offered to help me find a sponsor and led me to exactly the person I needed. This lady had nineteen years of sobriety and, even more important, a wealth of experience in helping and guiding alcoholics through the steps of A.A. By no means do I intend to imply that I leaped with pleasure into the program. I stalled and resented and refused to accept each step as it came up. I felt challenged by each new concept and resentful toward my sponsor, who seemed intent on reducing me to abject stupidity. It was years before I realized that I resented the changes the program asked me to make, not my sponsor.

With the patience of unconditional love, she led me to acknowledge first that I was powerless over my alcoholism; then that others before me had conquered their illness. That there had to be some source of help higher than any one of us and that, together, we were a well of strength on which any one of us could draw. From that point it was not hard to venture into the realization that a Power greater than any one of us existed, and with that understanding I found direction to my own special Higher Power. On that spiritual foundation I began to build a new life.

The Third Step was the most difficult for me. But having completed it, I found that I could face or untangle the other steps if, and when, I could remember to relax, trust the program, and implement the step rather than fight it. Accepting my Higher Power did not fully change my attitude of resistance. It just made yielding to instruction a more rational and acceptable mode of behavior. For each step, I still had to go through the process of recognizing that I had no control over my drinking. I had to understand that the steps of Alcoholics Anonymous had helped others and could help me. I had to realize that if I did want sobriety, I had better do the steps whether I liked them or not. Every time I ran into trouble, I ultimately found that I was resisting change.

My mentor had to remind me that A.A. is not just a project. A.A. offers me an opportunity to improve the quality of my life. I came to recognize that there is always a deeper and wider experience awaiting me. Early in my growth I remember thanking my sponsor for the hours and hours she had given me. She said, "Don't you think that you will do the same for someone else some day?" I replied, "I will never be responsible to or for anyone else ever again." That refusal to make any kind of repayment to the program delayed my offering to be of service in any capacity and consequently delayed my maturing process. Not until two years had passed was I willing to act as group secretary. It was four years before I was willing to sponsor anyone. Today it is with real gratitude that I am allowed into the lives of a few women. My own understanding is broadened and deepened by their influence in my life. As the newcomer and I examine each step, both she and I receive new insight and find an additional facet to this jewel of sobriety. I'm proud now to be a part of the Fellowship that showed me the path up and out of hell. Now I am eager to share my experience as others have shared theirs with me.

Small miracles keep offering new opportunities just when I need change and growth. New friends have shown me hidden truths in those sayings that I once found so shallow. The lessons of tolerance and acceptance have taught me to look beyond exterior appearances to find the help and wisdom so often lurking beneath the surface. All my sobriety and growth, mentally, emotionally, and spiritually, are dependent upon my willingness to listen, understand, and change.

During my fifth year, as a part of my annual personal inventory, I realized that I had not succeeded in developing a spiritual depth in my program. I had accepted what I was taught but had not gone in search of the private growth that I saw in others. I watched for and found people who take the program with them as they live, work, and play in the real world. Through their leadership, by precept and example, I am finding the daily excitement essential to my development as a person and to my contact with my Higher Power.

I approached Alcoholics Anonymous with fear and hesitation. Then, urged by the dread of what was behind me, I took tiny delicate steps onto this new path. When I found the footing was firm, each tentative move brought me a little nearer to trust. Confidence grew, faith in my Higher Power expanded, and I came to recognize a light I had not known existed. Something within me shifted and welcomed a new source of strength, understanding, tolerance, and love. That selfish, withdrawn woman who announced that she would "never be responsible to or for anyone ever again" now finds sincere warmth in just being available. I count it a privilege to help another drunk.

It's been ten years since I retired, seven years since I joined A.A. Now I can truly say that I am a grateful alcoholic. Had I not become a drunk, I would have become another sober but sad statistic. At seventy-five I would be a lonely, unproductive old woman, watching TV, doing needlepoint, in my home without friends, and sinking further and further into an old age depression. As it is, A.A. has filled my days with friends, laughter, growth, and the feeling of worth that is rooted in constructive activity. My faith in, and contact with, my Higher Power shines more brightly than I dreamed it could. Those promises I thought were impossible are a viable force in my life. I am free to laugh all of my laughter, free to trust and be trusted, free to both give and receive help. I am free from shame and regret, free to learn and grow and work. I have left that lonely, frightening, painful express train through hell. I have accepted the gift of a safer, happier journey through life.

(14)

FREEDOM FROM BONDAGE

Young when she joined, this A.A. believes her serious drinking was the result of even deeper defects. She here tells how she was set free.

THE MENTAL TWISTS that led up to my drinking began many years before I ever took a drink, for I am one of those whose history proves conclusively that my drinking was "a symptom of a deeper trouble."

Through my efforts to get down to "causes and conditions," I stand convinced that my emotional illness has been present from my earliest recollection. I never did react normally to any emotional situation.

The medical profession would probably tell me I was conditioned for alcoholism by the things that happened to me in my childhood. And I am sure they would be right as far as they go, but A.A. has taught me I am the result of the *way I reacted* to what happened to me as a child. What is much more important to me, A.A. has taught me that through this simple program I may experience a change in this reaction pattern that will indeed allow me to "match calamity with serenity."

I am an only child, and when I was seven years old, my parents separated very abruptly. With no explanation at all, I was taken from my home in Florida to my grandparents' home in the Midwest. My mother went to a nearby city to go to work, and my father, being an alcoholic, simply went. My grandparents were strangers to me, and I remember being lonely, terrified, and hurt.

In time I concluded that the reason I was hurt was because I loved my parents, and I concluded too that if I never allowed myself to love anybody or anything, I could never be hurt again. It became second nature for me to remove myself from anything or anybody I found myself growing fond of.

I grew up believing that one had to be totally self-sufficient, for one never dared to depend on another human being. I thought that life was a pretty simple thing; you simply made a plan for your life, based upon what you wanted, and then you needed only the courage to go after it.

In my late teens I became aware of emotions I'd not counted on: restlessness, anxiety, fear, and insecurity. The only kind of security I knew anything about at that time was material security, and I decided that all these intruders would vanish immediately if I only had a lot of money. The solution seemed very simple. With cold calculation I set about to marry a fortune, and I did. The only thing this changed, however, was my surroundings, and it was soon apparent that I could have the same uncomfortable emotions with an unlimited checking account that I could on a working girl's salary. It was impossible for me to say at this point, "Maybe there is something wrong with my philosophy," and I certainly couldn't say, "Maybe there is something wrong with *me*." It was not difficult to convince myself that my unhappiness was the fault of the man I had married, and I divorced him at the end of a year.

I was married and divorced again before I was twenty-three years old, this time to a prominent band leader—a man whom many women wanted. I thought this would give me ego-strength, make me feel wanted and secure, and alleviate my fears, but again nothing changed inside me.

The only importance in all of this lies in the fact that at twenty-three I was just as sick as I was at thirty-three, when I came into A.A. But at that time I apparently had no place to go because I had no drinking problem. Had I been able to explain to a psychiatrist the feelings of futility, loneliness, and lack of purpose that had come with my deep sense of personal failure at this second divorce, I seriously doubt that the good doctor could have convinced me that my basic problem was a spiritual hunger. But A.A. has shown me this was the truth. And if I had been able to turn to the church at that time, I'm sure they could not have convinced me my sickness was within myself, nor could they have shown me that the need for self-analysis that A.A. has shown me is vital if I am to survive. So I had no place to go. Or so it seemed to me.

I wasn't afraid of anything or anybody after I learned about drinking. It seemed right from the beginning that with liquor I could always retire to my little private world where nobody could get at me to hurt me. It seems only fitting that when I did finally fall in love, it was with an alcoholic, and for the next ten years I progressed as rapidly as is humanly possible into what I believed to be hopeless alcoholism.

During this time, our country was at war. My husband was soon in uniform and among the first to go overseas. My reaction to this was identical in many respects to my reaction to my parents leaving me when I was seven. Apparently I'd grown physically at the customary rate of speed, and I had acquired an average amount of intellectual training in the intervening years, but there had been no emotional maturity at all. I realize now that this phase of my development had been arrested by my obsession with self, and my egocentricity had reached such proportions that adjustment to anything outside my personal control was impossible for me. I was immersed in self-pity and resentment, and the only people who would support this attitude or who I felt understood me at all were the people I met in bars and the ones who drank as I did. It became more and more necessary to escape from myself, for my remorse and shame and humiliation when I was sober were almost unbearable. The only way existence was possible was through rationalizing every sober moment and drinking myself into complete oblivion as often as I could.

My husband eventually returned, but it was not long until we realized we could not continue our marriage. By this time I was such a past master at kidding myself that I had convinced myself I had sat out a war and waited for this man to come home, and as my resentment and self-pity grew, so did my alcoholic problem.

The last three years of my drinking, I drank on my job. The amount of willpower exercised to control my drinking during working hours, diverted into a constructive channel, would have made me president, and the thing that made the willpower possible was the knowledge that as soon as my day was finished, I could drink myself into oblivion. Inside, though, I was

scared to death, for I knew that the time was coming
(and it couldn't be too remote) when I would be unable to hold that job. Maybe I wouldn't be able to
hold any job, or maybe (and this was my greatest fear)
I wouldn't care whether I had a job or not. I knew it
didn't make any difference where I started, the inevitable end would be skid row. The only reality I was
able to face had been forced upon me by its very repetition—*I had to drink;* and I didn't know there was
anything in the world that could be done about it.

About this time I met a man who had three mother-
less children, and it seemed that might be a solution
to my problem. I had never had a child, and this had
been a satisfactory excuse many times for my drinking.
It seemed logical to me that if I married this man and
took the responsibility for these children that they
would keep me sober. So I married again. This caused
the comment from one of my A.A. friends, when I
told my story after coming into the program, that I
had always been a cinch for the program, for I had
always been interested in mankind—I was just taking
them one man at a time.

The children kept me sober for darn near three
weeks, and then I went on (please God) my last drunk.
I've heard it said many times in A.A., "There is just
one good drunk in every alcoholic's life, and that's
the one that brings us into A.A.," and I believe it. I
was drunk for sixty days around the clock, and it was
my intention, literally, to drink myself to death. I
went to jail for the second time during this period for
being drunk in an automobile. I was the only person
I'd ever known personally who had ever been in jail,

and I guess it is most significant that the second time was less humiliating than the first had been.

Finally, in desperation, my family appealed to a doctor for advice, and he suggested A.A. The people who came knew immediately I was in no condition to absorb anything of the program. I was put in a sanitarium to be defogged so that I could make a sober decision about this for myself. It was here that I realized for the first time that as a practicing alcoholic, I had no rights. Society can do anything it chooses to do with me when I am drunk, and I can't lift a finger to stop it, for I forfeit my rights through the simple expedient of becoming a menace to myself and to the people around me. With deep shame came the knowledge too that I had lived with no sense of social obligation nor had I known the meaning of moral responsibility to my fellow men.

I attended my first A.A. meeting eight years ago, and it is with deep gratitude that I'm able to say I've not had a drink since that time and that I take no sedation or narcotics, for this program is to me one of complete sobriety. I no longer need to escape reality. One of the truly great things A.A. has taught me is that reality too has two sides; I had only known the grim side before the program, but now I had a chance to learn about the pleasant side as well.

The A.A. members who sponsored me told me in the beginning that I would not only find a way to live without having a drink, but that I would find a way to live without *wanting* to drink, if I would do these simple things. They said if you want to know *how* this program works, take the first word of your question— the "H" is for honesty, the "O" is for open-mindedness, and the "W" is for willingness; these our Big Book calls the essentials of recovery. They suggested that I study the A.A. book and try to take the Twelve Steps according to the explanation in the book, for it was their opinion that the application of these principles in our daily lives will get us sober and keep us sober. I believe this, and I believe too that it is equally impossible to practice these principles to the best of our ability, a day at a time, and still drink, for I don't think the two things are compatible.

I had no problem admitting I was powerless over alcohol, and I certainly agreed that my life had become unmanageable. I had only to reflect on the contrast between the plans I made so many years ago for my life with what really happened to know I couldn't manage my life drunk or sober. A.A. taught me that *willingness to believe* was enough for a beginning. It's been true in my case, nor could I quarrel with "restore us to sanity," for my actions drunk or sober, before A.A., were not those of a sane person. My desire to be honest with myself made it necessary for me to realize that my thinking was irrational. It had to be, or I could not have justified my erratic behavior as I did. I've been benefited from a dictionary definition I found that reads: "Rationalization is giving a socially acceptable reason for socially unacceptable behavior, and socially unacceptable behavior is a form of insanity."

A.A. has given me serenity of purpose and the opportunity to be of service to God and to the people about me, and I am serene in the infallibility of these principles that provide the fulfillment of my purpose.

A.A. has taught me that I will have peace of mind in

exact proportion to the peace of mind I bring into the lives of other people, and it has taught me the true meaning of the admonition "happy are ye who know these things *and do them*." For the only problems I have now are those I create when I break out in a rash of self-will.

I've had many spiritual experiences since I've been in the program, many that I didn't recognize right away, for I'm slow to learn and they take many guises. But one was so outstanding that I like to pass it on whenever I can in the hope that it will help someone else as it has me. As I said earlier, self-pity and resentment were my constant companions, and my inventory began to look like a thirty-three-year diary, for I seemed to have a resentment against everybody I had ever known. All but one "responded to the treatment" suggested in the steps immediately, but this one posed a problem.

This resentment was against my mother, and it was twenty-five years old. I had fed it, fanned it, and nurtured it as one might a delicate child, and it had become as much a part of me as my breathing. It had provided me with excuses for my lack of education, my marital failures, personal failures, inadequacy, and of course, my alcoholism. And though I really thought I had been willing to part with it, now I knew I was reluctant to let it go.

One morning, however, I realized I had to get rid of it, for my reprieve was running out, and if I didn't get rid of it I was going to get drunk—and I didn't want to get drunk anymore. In my prayers that morning I asked God to point out to me some way to be free of this resentment. During the day, a friend of mine brought me some magazines to take to a hospital group I was interested in. I looked through them. A banner across one featured an article by a prominent clergyman in which I caught the word *resentment*.

He said, in effect: "If you have a resentment you want to be free of, if you will pray for the person or the thing that you resent, you will be free. If you will ask in prayer for everything you want for yourself to be given to them, you will be free. Ask for their health, their prosperity, their happiness, and you will be free. Even when you don't really want it for them and your prayers are only words and you don't mean it, go ahead and do it anyway. Do it every day for two weeks, and you will find you have come to mean it and to want it for them, and you will realize that where you used to feel bitterness and resentment and hatred, you now feel compassionate understanding and love."

It worked for me then, and it has worked for me many times since, and it will work for me every time I am willing to work it. Sometimes I have to ask first for the willingness, but it too always comes. And because it works for me, it will work for all of us. As another great man says, "The only real freedom a human being can ever know is doing what you ought to do because you want to do it."

This great experience that released me from the bondage of hatred and replaced it with love is really just another affirmation of the truth I know: I get everything I need in Alcoholics Anonymous—and everything I need I get. And when I get what I need, I invariably find that it was just *what I wanted all the time.*

(15)

A.A. TAUGHT HIM TO HANDLE
SOBRIETY

"God willing, we . . . may never again have to deal with drinking, but we have to deal with sobriety every day."

WHEN I HAD been in A.A. only a short while, an oldtimer told me something that has affected my life ever since. "A.A. does not teach us how to handle our drinking," he said. "It teaches us how to handle sobriety."

I guess I always knew that the way to handle my drinking was to quit. After my very first drink—a tiny glass of sherry my father gave me to celebrate the New Year when I was thirteen—I went up to bed, dizzy with exhilaration and excitement, and I prayed I wouldn't drink anymore!

But I did, when I reached college age. Much later, when I progressed to full-blown alcoholism, people told me I should quit. Like most other alcoholics I have known, I *did* quit drinking at various times— once for ten months on my own and during other interludes when I was hospitalized. It's no great trick to stop drinking; the trick is to *stay* stopped.

To do that, I had come to A.A. to learn how to handle sobriety—which is what I could not handle in the first place. That's why I drank.

I was raised in Kansas, the only child of loving parents who just drank socially. We moved frequently.

In fact, I changed schools every year until high school. In each new place, I was the new kid—a skinny, shy kid—to be tested and beaten up. As soon as I had begun to feel accepted, we moved again.

By the time I reached high school, I was an over-achiever. An honor student in college, I became editor of the yearbook. I sold my first article to a national magazine while still an undergraduate. I also began to drink at fraternity parties and beer busts.

Upon graduation I ventured to New York to pursue my writing career. I landed a good job with a company publication and was moonlighting on other magazines. Regarded as something of a "boy wonder," I began to see myself that way. I also began visiting bars after work with my older associates. By age twenty-two, I was a daily drinker.

Then I joined the navy and was commissioned as an ensign to write speeches for admirals. Later I went to sea, serving as gunnery officer on a destroyer escort and emerging a lieutenant commander. I also got into my first disciplinary trouble caused by drinking, on two separate occasions.

In the last year of my navy service, I was married to a lovely, lively girl who enjoyed drinking. Our courtship was mainly in bars and night spots when my ship was in New York. On our honeymoon we had iced champagne by the bedside day and night.

The pattern was set. By twenty-nine I was having trouble coping with life because of my drinking. Neurotic fears plagued me, and I had occasional uncontrollable tremors. I read self-help books. I turned to religion with fervor. I swore off hard liquor and turned to wine. I got sick of the sweetness and turned to ale.

It wasn't strong enough, so I added a shot of vodka—and was right back to worse trouble than before. I began sneaking drinks when playing bartender for guests. To cure my dreadful hangovers, I discovered the morning drink.

The early promise of the "boy wonder" faded, and my career began to drift. Although my ambition still flickered, it now took the form of fantasizing. My values became distorted. To wear expensive clothes, to have bartenders know what to serve me before I ordered, to be recognized by headwaiters and shown to the best table, to play gin rummy for high stakes with the insouciance of a riverboat gambler—these were the enduring values in life, I thought.

Bewilderment, fear, and resentment moved into my life. And yet my ability to lie outwardly and to kid myself inwardly grew with every drink I took. Indeed, I *had* to drink now to live, to cope with the demands of everyday existence. When I encountered disappointments or frustrations—as I did more and more frequently—my solution was to drink. I had always been oversensitive to criticism and was acutely so now. When I was criticized or reprimanded, the bottle was my refuge and comfort.

When I was faced with a special challenge or social event—such as an important business presentation or a dinner party—I had to fortify myself with a couple of belts. Too often I would overdo it and behave badly at the very time I wanted to be at my best! For instance, the fiftieth wedding anniversary of my wife's parents was the occasion for a huge family reunion at our home. Despite my wife's entreaties to take it easy, I arrived home in bad shape. I remember being dragged, drink in hand, from under the grand piano, where I had hidden, to be locked in my room in disgrace.

Above all, I was suffering inner pain because my performance and my accomplishments in life failed to live up to my own expectations of myself. I *had* to anesthetize that pain with alcohol. Of course, the more I drank, the more unrealistic my expectations became and the poorer my performance, and the gap widened. So the need to drink grew still greater.

At age forty I developed a large lump in my pot-belly, and I feared it was a tumor. The doctor pronounced it a badly enlarged liver and said I had to quit drinking. I did. I went on the wagon, with no outside help and with no real difficulty—except that I didn't enjoy life without drinking. I had to cope with the demands of everyday living without my comforter, my anesthetic, my crutch. And I didn't like it.

So when my liver had recovered after ten months, I resumed drinking. At first, just one drink, on occasion. Then drinks came more frequently but were carefully spaced out. Soon my drinking was as bad as ever—all day long every day. But I was trying frantically to control it. And it had gone underground now, because everyone knew I shouldn't be drinking. Instead of drinking in fancy bars and clubs, I had to carry a bottle of vodka in my briefcase, duck into public toilets, and gulp from the bottle, trembling, in order to keep from falling apart.

Over the next two years I sickened rapidly. The enlargement of my liver degenerated into cirrhosis. I vomited every morning. I could not face food. I suffered frequent blackouts. I had severe nosebleeds. Bruises appeared mysteriously over my body.

I became so weak, I could barely drag myself around.

My employer gave me one warning, then another. My children avoided me. When I awoke in the middle of the night with shakes and sweats and fears, I would hear my wife weeping quietly in bed beside me. My doctor warned me that if I kept on, I might have esophageal hemorrhaging and die. But now all choice was gone. I had to drink.

What my doctor had warned me about finally happened. I was attending a convention in Chicago and carousing day and night. Suddenly I began vomiting and losing rectally great quantities of blood. Hopeless now, I felt it would be better for my wife, my children, and everyone in my life if I went ahead and died. I found myself being lifted onto a stretcher and whisked away in an ambulance to a strange hospital. I awoke next day with tubes in both arms.

Within a week I was feeling well enough to go home. The doctors told me that if I ever took another drink, it might be my last. I thought I had learned my lesson. But my thinking was still confused, and I was still unable to deal with everyday living without help. Within two months I was drinking again.

In the next half-year I experienced two more esophageal hemorrhages, miraculously surviving each one by a hair. Each time, I went back to drinking—even smuggling a bottle of vodka into the hospital as soon as the blood transfusions had ceased. My doctor finally declared he could no longer be responsible for me and sent me to a psychiatrist who practiced in the same suite of offices. He happened to be, by the grace of God, Dr. Harry Tiebout, the psychiatrist who probably knew more about alcoholism than any other in the world. At that very time he was a nonalcoholic trustee on the General Service Board of Alcoholics Anonymous.

It was the late Dr. Tiebout, then, who persuaded me to seek help through A.A. I acquired a sponsor and began attending meetings but continued to drink. Within a few days I found myself drying out on a drunk farm. While there, I read the Big Book and the Grapevine and began the slow road back to health and sanity through the recovery program of A.A.

As the sober days grew into sober months and then into sober years, a new and beautiful life began to emerge from the shambles of my former existence. The relationship between my wife and me was restored to a love and happiness that we had not known even *before* my alcoholism became acute. (She no longer weeps in the night.) As our children grew up, I was able to be a father to them when they most needed one. My company advanced me rapidly once my reliability was established again. Regaining my health, I became an avid jogger, sailor, and skier.

All these things and many, many more, A.A. gave me. But above all, it taught me how to handle sobriety. I have learned how to relate to people; before A.A., I could never do that comfortably without alcohol. I have learned to deal with disappointments and problems that once would have sent me right to the bottle. I have come to realize that the name of the game is not so much to stop drinking as to *stay sober.* Alcoholics can stop drinking in many places and many ways—but Alcoholics Anonymous offers us a way to stay sober.

God willing, we members of A.A. may never again

have to deal with drinking, but we have to deal with sobriety every day. How do we do it? By learning—through practicing the Twelve Steps and through sharing at meetings—how to cope with the problems that we looked to booze to solve, back in our drinking days.

For example, we are told in A.A. that we cannot afford resentments and self-pity, so we learn to avoid these festering mental attitudes. Similarly, we rid ourselves of guilt and remorse as we "clean out the garbage" from our minds through the Fourth and Fifth Steps of our recovery program. We learn how to level out the emotional swings that got us into trouble both when we were up and when we were down.

We are taught to differentiate between our wants (which are never satisfied) and our needs (which are always provided for). We cast off the burdens of the past and the anxieties of the future, as we begin to live in the present, one day at a time. We are granted "the serenity to accept the things we cannot change" —and thus lose our quickness to anger and our sensitivity to criticism.

Above all, we reject fantasizing and accept reality. The more I drank, the more I fantasized everything. I imagined getting even for hurts and rejections. In my mind's eye I played and replayed scenes in which I was plucked magically from the bar where I stood nursing a drink and was instantly exalted to some position of power and prestige. I lived in a dream world. A.A. led me gently from this fantasizing to embrace reality with open arms. And I found it beautiful! For, at last, I was at peace with myself. And with others. And with God.

APPENDICES

I

THE A.A. TRADITION

To those now in its fold, Alcoholics Anonymous has made the difference between misery and sobriety, and often the difference between life and death. A.A. can, of course, mean just as much to uncounted alcoholics not yet reached.

Therefore, no society of men and women ever had a more urgent *need* for continuous effectiveness and permanent unity. We alcoholics see that we must work together and hang together, else most of us will finally die alone.

The "12 Traditions" of Alcoholics Anonymous are, we A.A.'s believe, the best answers that our experience has yet given to those ever-urgent questions, "How can A.A. best function?" and, "How can A.A. best stay whole and so survive?"

On the next page, A.A.'s "12 Traditions" are seen in their so-called "short form," the form in general use today. This is a condensed version of the original "long form" A.A. Traditions as first printed in 1946. Because the "long form" is more explicit and of possible historic value, it is also reproduced.

One—Our common welfare should come first; personal recovery depends upon A.A. unity.

Two—For our group purpose there is but one ultimate authority—a loving God as He may express Himself in our group conscience. Our leaders are but trusted servants; they do not govern.

Three—The only requirement for A.A. membership is a desire to stop drinking.

Four—Each group should be autonomous except in matters affecting other groups or A.A. as a whole.

Five—Each group has but one primary purpose—to carry its message to the alcoholic who still suffers.

Six—An A.A. group ought never endorse, finance or lend the A.A. name to any related facility or outside enterprise, lest problems of money, property and prestige divert us from our primary purpose.

Seven—Every A.A. group ought to be fully self-supporting, declining outside contributions.

Eight—Alcoholics Anonymous should remain forever nonprofessional, but our service centers may employ special workers.

Nine—A.A., as such, ought never be organized; but we may create service boards or committees directly responsible to those they serve.

Ten—Alcoholics Anonymous has no opinion on outside issues; hence the A.A. name ought never be drawn into public controversy.

Eleven—Our public relations policy is based on attraction rather than promotion; we need always maintain personal anonymity at the level of press, radio and films.

Twelve—Anonymity is the spiritual foundation of all our Traditions, ever reminding us to place principles before personalities.

THE TWELVE TRADITIONS
(The Long Form)

Our A.A. experience has taught us that:

1.—Each member of Alcoholics Anonymous is but a small part of a great whole. A.A. must continue to live or most of us will surely die. Hence our common welfare comes first. But individual welfare follows close afterward.

2.—For our group purpose there is but one ultimate authority—a loving God as He may express Himself in our group conscience.

3.—Our membership ought to include all who suffer from alcoholism. Hence we may refuse none who wish to recover. Nor ought A.A. membership ever depend upon money or conformity. Any two or three alcoholics gathered together for sobriety may call themselves an A.A. group, provided that, as a group, they have no other affiliation.

4.—With respect to its own affairs, each A.A. group should be responsible to no other authority than its own conscience. But when its plans concern the welfare of neighboring groups also, those groups ought to be consulted. And no group, regional committee, or individual should ever take any action that might greatly affect A.A. as a whole without conferring with the trustees of the General Service Board. On such issues our common welfare is paramount.

5.—Each Alcoholics Anonymous group ought to be a spiritual entity *having but one primary purpose*—that of carrying its message to the alcoholic who still suffers.

6.—Problems of money, property, and authority may easily divert us from our primary spiritual aim. We think, therefore, that any considerable property of genuine use to A.A. should be separately incorporated and managed, thus dividing the material from the spiritual. An A.A. group, as such, should never go into business. Secondary aids to A.A., such as clubs or hospitals which require much property or administration, ought to be incorporated and so set apart that, if necessary, they can be freely discarded by the groups. Hence such facilities ought not to use the A.A. name. Their management should be the sole responsibility of those people who financially support them. For clubs, A.A. managers are usually preferred. But hospitals, as well as other places of recuperation, ought to be well outside A.A.—and medically supervised. While an A.A. group may cooperate with anyone, such cooperation ought never go so far as affiliation or endorsement, actual or implied. An A.A. group can bind itself to no one.

7.—The A.A. groups themselves ought to be fully supported by the voluntary contributions of their own members. We think that each group should soon achieve this ideal; that any public solicitation of funds using the name of Alcoholics Anonymous is highly dangerous, whether by groups, clubs, hospitals, or other outside agencies; that acceptance of large gifts from any source, or of contributions carrying any obligation whatever, is unwise. Then too, we view with much concern those A.A. treasuries which continue, beyond prudent reserves, to accumulate funds for no stated A.A. purpose. Experience has often warned us that nothing can so surely destroy our spiritual heritage as futile disputes over property, money, and authority.

8.—Alcoholics Anonymous should remain forever nonprofessional. We define professionalism as the occupation of counseling alcoholics for fees or hire. But we may employ alcoholics where they are going to perform those services for which we might otherwise have to engage nonalcoholics. Such special services may be well recompensed. But our usual A.A. "12 Step" work is never to be paid for.

9.—Each A.A. group needs the least possible organization. Rotating leadership is the best. The small group may elect its secretary, the large group its rotating committee, and the groups of a large metropolitan area their central or intergroup committee, which often employs a full-time secretary. The trustees of the General Service Board are, in effect, our A.A. General Service Committee. They are the custodians of our A.A. Tradition and the receivers of voluntary A.A. contributions by which we maintain our A.A. General Service Office at New York. They are authorized by the groups to handle our over-all public relations and they guarantee the integrity of our principal newspaper, the A.A. Grapevine. All such representatives are to be guided in the spirit of service, for true leaders in A.A. are but trusted and experienced servants of the whole. They derive no real authority from their titles; they do not govern. Universal respect is the key to their usefulness.

10.—No A.A. group or member should ever, in such a way as to implicate A.A., express any opinion on outside controversial issues—particularly those of politics, alcohol reform, or sectarian religion. The Alcoholics Anonymous groups oppose no one. Concerning such matters they can express no views whatever.

11.—Our relations with the general public should be characterized by personal anonymity. We think A.A. ought to avoid sensational advertising. Our names and pictures as A.A. members ought not be broadcast, filmed, or publicly printed. Our public relations should be guided by the principle of attraction rather than promotion. There is never need to praise ourselves. We feel it better to let our friends recommend us.

12.—And finally, we of Alcoholics Anonymous believe

that the principle of anonymity has an immense spiritual significance. It reminds us that we are to place principles before personalities; that we are actually to practice a genuine humility. This to the end that our great blessings may never spoil us; that we shall forever live in thankful contemplation of Him who presides over us all.

II

SPIRITUAL EXPERIENCE

The terms "spiritual experience" and "spiritual awakening" are used many times in this book which, upon careful reading, shows that the personality change sufficient to bring about recovery from alcoholism has manifested itself among us in many different forms.

Yet it is true that our first printing gave many readers the impression that these personality changes, or religious experiences, must be in the nature of sudden and spectacular upheavals. Happily for everyone, this conclusion is erroneous.

In the first few chapters a number of sudden revolutionary changes are described. Though it was not our intention to create such an impression, many alcoholics have nevertheless concluded that in order to recover they must acquire an immediate and overwhelming "God-consciousness" followed at once by a vast change in feeling and outlook.

Among our rapidly growing membership of thousands of alcoholics such transformations, though frequent, are by no means the rule. Most of our experiences are what the psychologist William James calls the "educational variety" because they develop slowly over a period of time. Quite often friends of the newcomer are aware of the difference long before he is himself. He finally realizes that he has undergone a profound alteration in his reaction to life; that such a change could hardly have been brought about by himself alone. What often takes place in a few months could seldom have been accomplished by years of self-discipline. With few exceptions our members find that they have tapped an unsuspected inner resource which they presently identify with their own conception of a Power greater than themselves.

Most of us think this awareness of a Power greater than ourselves is the essence of spiritual experience. Our more religious members call it "God-consciousness."

Most emphatically we wish to say that any alcoholic capable of honestly facing his problems in the light of our experience can recover, provided he does not close his mind to all spiritual concepts. He can only be defeated by an attitude of intolerance or belligerent denial.

We find that no one need have difficulty with the spirituality of the program. *Willingness, honesty and open mindedness are the essentials of recovery. But these are indispensable.*

"There is a principle which is a bar against all information, which is proof against all arguments and which cannot fail to keep a man in everlasting ignorance— that principle is contempt prior to investigation."

—HERBERT SPENCER

III

THE MEDICAL VIEW ON A.A.

Since Dr. Silkworth's first endorsement of Alcoholics Anonymous, medical societies and physicians throughout the world have set their approval upon us. Following are excerpts from the comments of doctors present at the annual meeting* of the Medical Society of the State of New York where a paper on A.A. was read:

Dr. Foster Kennedy, neurologist: "This organization of Alcoholics Anonymous calls on two of the greatest reservoirs of power known to man, religion and that instinct for association with one's fellows . . . the 'herd instinct.' I think our profession must take appreciative cognizance of this great therapeutic weapon. If we do not do so, we shall stand convicted of emotional sterility and of having lost the faith that moves mountains, without which medicine can do little."

Dr. G. Kirby Collier, psychiatrist: "I have felt that A.A. is a group unto themselves and their best results can be had under their own guidance, as a result of their philosophy. Any therapeutic or philosophic procedure which can prove a recovery rate of 50% to 60% must merit our consideration."

Dr. Harry M. Tiebout, psychiatrist: "As a psychiatrist, I have thought a great deal about the relationship of my specialty to A.A. and I have come to the conclusion that our particular function can very often lie in preparing the way for the patient to accept any sort of treatment or outside help. I now conceive the psychiatrist's job to be the task of breaking down the patient's inner resistance so that which is inside him will flower, as under the activity of the A.A. program."

* 1944.

Dr. W. W. Bauer, broadcasting under the auspices of The American Medical Association in 1946, over the NBC network, said, in part: "Alcoholics Anonymous are no crusaders; not a temperance society. They know that they must never drink. They help others with similar problems ... In this atmosphere the alcoholic often overcomes his excessive concentration upon himself. Learning to depend upon a higher power and absorb himself in his work with other alcoholics, he remains sober day by day. The days add up into weeks, the weeks into months and years."

Dr. John F. Stouffer, Chief Psychiatrist, Philadelphia General Hospital, citing his experience with A.A., said: "The alcoholics we get here at Philadelphia General are mostly those who cannot afford private treatment, and A.A. is by far the greatest thing we have been able to offer them. Even among those who occasionally land back in here again, we observe a profound change in personality. You would hardly recognize them."

The American Psychiatric Association requested, in 1949, that a paper be prepared by one of the older members of Alcoholics Anonymous to be read at the Association's annual meeting of that year. This was done, and the paper was printed in the *American Journal of Psychiatry* for November 1949.

(This address is now available in pamphlet form at nominal cost through most A.A. groups or from Box 459, Grand Central Station, New York, NY 10163, under the title "Three Talks to Medical Societies by Bill W."— formerly called "Bill on Alcoholism" and earlier "Alcoholism the Illness.")

IV

THE LASKER AWARD

In 1951 the Lasker Award was given Alcoholics Anonymous. The citation reads in part as follows:

"The American Public Health Association presents a Lasker Group Award for 1951 to Alcoholics Anonymous in recognition of its unique and highly successful approach to that age-old public health and social problem, alcoholism . . . In emphasizing alcoholism as an illness, the social stigma associated with this condition is being blotted out . . . Historians may one day recognize Alcoholics Anonymous to have been a great venture in social pioneering which forged a new instrument for social action; a new therapy based on the kinship of common suffering; one having a vast potential for the myriad other ills of mankind."

V

THE RELIGIOUS VIEW ON A.A.

Clergymen of practically every denomination have given A.A. their blessing.

Edward Dowling, S.J.,* of the Queen's Work staff, says, "Alcoholics Anonymous is natural; it is natural at the point where nature comes closest to the supernatural, namely in humiliations and in consequent humility. There is something spiritual about an art museum or a symphony, and the Catholic Church approves of our use of them. There is something spiritual about A.A. too, and Catholic participation in it almost invariably results in poor Catholics becoming better Catholics."

The Episcopal magazine, *The Living Church*, observes editorially: "The basis of the technique of Alcoholics Anonymous is the truly Christian principle that a man cannot help himself except by helping others. The A.A. plan is described by the members themselves as 'self-insurance.' This self-insurance has resulted in the restoration of physical, mental and spiritual health and self-respect to hundreds of men and women who would be hopelessly down and out without its unique but effective therapy."

Speaking at a dinner given by John D. Rockefeller Jr. to introduce Alcoholics Anonymous to some of his friends, Dr. Harry Emerson Fosdick remarked:

"I think that psychologically speaking there is a point of advantage in the approach that is being made in this movement that cannot be duplicated. I suspect that if it is wisely handled—and it seems to be in wise and prudent hands—there are doors of opportunity ahead of this project that may surpass our capacities to imagine."

* Father Ed, an early and wonderful friend of A.A., died in the spring of 1960.

VI

HOW TO GET IN TOUCH WITH A.A.

In the United States and Canada, most towns and cities have A.A. groups. In such places, A.A. can be located through the local telephone directory, newspaper office, or police station, or by contacting local priests or ministers. In large cities, groups often maintain local offices where alcoholics or their families may arrange for interviews or hospitalization. These so-called intergroup associations are found under the listing "A.A." or "Alcoholics Anonymous" in telephone directories.

At New York, USA, Alcoholics Anonymous maintains its international service center. The General Service Board of A.A. (the trustees) administers A.A.'s General Service Office, A.A. World Services, Inc., and our monthly magazine, the A.A. Grapevine.

If you cannot find A.A. in your locality, visit our Web site: www.aa.org; or a letter addressed to Alcoholics Anonymous, Box 459, Grand Central Station, New York, NY 10163, USA, will receive a prompt reply from this world center, referring you to the nearest A.A. group. If there is none nearby, you will be invited to carry on a correspondence which will do much to insure your sobriety no matter how isolated you are.

Should you be the relative or friend of an alcoholic who shows no immediate interest in A.A., it is suggested that you write the Al-Anon Family Groups, Inc., 1600 Corporate Landing Parkway, Virginia Beach, VA 23454-5617, USA.

This is a world clearing house for the Al-Anon Family Groups, composed largely of the wives, husbands and friends of A.A. members. This headquarters will give the location of the nearest family group and will, if you wish, correspond with you about your special problems.

VII

THE TWELVE CONCEPTS (SHORT FORM)

A.A.'s Twelve Steps are principles for personal *recovery*. The Twelve Traditions ensure the *unity* of the Fellowship. Written by co-founder Bill W. in 1962, the *Twelve Concepts for World Service* provide a group of related principles to help ensure that various elements of A.A.'s service structure remain responsive and responsible to those they serve.

The "short form" of the Concepts, which follows, was approved by the 1971 General Service Conference.

   I.   Final responsibility and ultimate authority for A.A. world services should always reside in the collective conscience of our whole Fellowship.

  II.   The General Service Conference of A.A. has become, for nearly every practical purpose, the active voice and the effective conscience of our whole Society in its world affairs.

 III.   To insure effective leadership, we should endow each element of A.A.—the Conference, the General Service Board and its service corporations, staffs, committees, and executives—with a traditional "Right of Decision."

  IV.   At all responsible levels, we ought to maintain a traditional "Right of Participation," allowing a voting representation in reasonable proportion to the responsibility that each must discharge.

   V.   Throughout our structure, a traditional "Right of Appeal" ought to prevail, so that minority opinion will be heard and personal grievances receive careful consideration.

  VI.   The Conference recognizes that the chief initiative and active responsibility in most world service matters should be exercised by the trustee members of the Conference acting as the General Service Board.

VII. The Charter and Bylaws of the General Service Board are legal instruments, empowering the trustees to manage and conduct world service affairs. The Conference Charter is not a legal document; it relies upon tradition and the A.A. purse for final effectiveness.

VIII. The trustees are the principal planners and administrators of overall policy and finance. They have custodial oversight of the separately incorporated and constantly active services, exercising this through their ability to elect all the directors of these entities.

IX. Good service leadership at all levels is indispensable for our future functioning and safety. Primary world service leadership, once exercised by the founders, must necessarily be assumed by the trustees.

X. Every service responsibility should be matched by an equal service authority, with the scope of such authority well defined.

XI. The trustees should always have the best possible committees, corporate service directors, executives, staffs, and consultants. Composition, qualifications, induction procedures, and rights and duties will always be matters of serious concern.

XII. The Conference shall observe the spirit of A.A. tradition, taking care that it never becomes the seat of perilous wealth or power; that sufficient operating funds and reserve be its prudent financial principle; that it place none of its members in a position of unqualified authority over others; that it reach all important decisions by discussion, vote, and, whenever possible, by substantial unanimity; that its actions never be personally punitive nor an incitement to public controversy; that it never perform acts of government, and that, like the Society it serves, it will always remain democratic in thought and action.

A.A. Literature

A.A. Publications Complete order forms available from General Service Office of Alcoholics Anonymous, Box 459, Grand Central Station, New York, NY 10163

Books

Alcoholics Anonymous
  (Regular, Portable, Large-Print And Abridged Pocket Editions)
Alcoholics Anonymous Comes Of Age
Twelve Steps and Twelve Traditions *(Regular, Soft-Cover, Large-Print, Pocket and Gift Editions)*
Experience, Strength And Hope
As Bill Sees It *(Regular & Soft Cover Editions)*
Dr. Bob and The Good Oldtimers
"Pass It On"
Daily Reflections

Booklets

Came To Believe
Living Sober
A.A. In Prison: Inmate To Inmate

Pamphlets

Frequently Asked Questions About A.A.
A.A. Tradition—How It Developed
Members of the Clergy Ask About A.A.
Three Talks to Medical Societies by Bill W.
Alcoholics Anonymous as a Resource
  for the Health Care Professional
A.A. in Your Community
Is A.A. for You?
Is A.A. for Me?
This Is A.A.
A Newcomer Asks
Is There An Alcoholic in the Workplace?
Do You Think You're Different?
A.A. for the Black and African
  American Alcoholic
Questions and Answers on Sponsorship
A.A. for the Woman
A.A. for the Native North American
A.A. and the Gay/Lesbian Alcoholic
A.A. for the Older Alcoholic—
  Never Too Late
The Jack Alexander Article
Young People and A.A.
A.A. and the Armed Services
The A.A. Member—Medications
  and Other Drugs
Is There an Alcoholic in Your Life?
Inside A.A.
The A.A. Group

G.S.R.
Memo to an Inmate
The Twelve Steps Illustrated
The Twelve Concepts Illustrated
The Twelve Traditions Illustrated
Let's Be Friendly With Our Friends
How A.A. Members Cooperate
A.A. in Correctional Facilities
A Message to Corrections Professionals
A.A. in Treatment Settings
Bridging the Gap
If You Are a Professional
A.A. Membership Survey
A Member's-Eye View of
  Alcoholics Anonymous
Problems Other Than Alcohol
Understanding Anonymity
The Co-Founders of Alcoholics Anonymous
Speaking at Non-A.A. Meetings
A Brief Guide to A.A.
A Newcomer Asks
What Happened to Joe;
  It Happened to Alice
  *(Two Full-Color, Comic-Book
  Style Pamphlets)*
Too Young? *(A Cartoon Pamphlet
  for Teenagers)*
It Sure Beats Sitting in a Cell
  (An Illustrated Pamphlets for Inmates)

Periodicals

The A.A. Grapevine (Monthly)

La Viña (Bimonthly)

Newsletter

Box 4-5-9